NECESSITY, CAUSE, AND BLAME

Perspectives on Aristotle's Theory

Aristotle's example of a coincidence: digging in the garden where treasure happens to be buried (from a 1492 *ms* of Boethius' *Consolation of Philosophy*, Paris B.N., Néerlandais 1, fol. 318 v°).

NECESSITY, CAUSE, AND BLAME

Perspectives on Aristotle's Theory

by

RICHARD SORABJI

Cornell University Press
Ithaca, New York

To my mother
Mary K. Sorabji

First published 1980 by Cornell University Press
First published Cornell Paperbacks 1983

Library of Congress Cataloging in Publication Data

Sorabji, Richard.
  Necessity, cause, and blame.

  Bibliography: p.
  Includes index.
  1. Aristotle's—Ethics.   2. Ethics.   3. Free will and determinism   4. Necessity (Philosophy).   5. Causation.   I. Title.
B491.E7S67   185   79-2449
ISBN 0-8014-1162-9 (cloth)
ISBN 0-8014-9244-0 (paper)

The paper in this book is acid-free and meets the guidelines for permanence and durability of the Committee on Production Guidelines for Book Longevity of the Council on Library Resources.

Printed in the United States of America

Contents

Contents

Acknowledgments

The earliest part of this book arose from a seminar I gave at King's College, London, with William Fortenbaugh on the *Nicomachean Ethics* in Spring 1973; and I continued thereafter to have the benefit of his comments on the ethics. Early drafts of many chapters were criticised by Myles Burnyeat, Jim Dybikowski and Malcolm Schofield. Julia Annas and Jim Hopkins discussed Donald Davidson with me and also my treatment of Aristotle's 'mixed' actions, while A. A. Long drew my attention to various matters in Sophocles, Empedocles and the Stoics. I am indebted to the series of instructive papers given by Robert Sharples at the Institute of Classical Studies, all now in print, on the treatment of determinism by Aristotle's successors; I learned both from these and from a number of comments he sent me privately. Jonathan Barnes helped me by criticising the chapters concerned with the *Posterior Analytics* and, indirectly, by the publication of his excellent commentary on that work. I also benefited from discussions with King's College students: with David Bradley and Marcus Cohen on coincidences, and with Nigel Carden on whether effects are necessitated. On relativity theory and quantum theory, I have had the advice of Clive Kilmister, and on modern logic of David Wiggins, Bill Hart, Christopher Kirwan, Jonathan Barnes, Jonathan Lear, Hans Kamp and Ron Ashby. I learnt also from the members of the Eighth Symposium Aristotelicum and of the Oxford Conference on Hellenistic Epistemology, both held in 1978, and from the comments of an anonymous referee. Further acknowledgments will be made in the footnotes. I count myself lucky to have had so much friendly advice and criticism from so many excellent sources. Above all, I should like to thank Myles Burnyeat, with whom I have done so much of my teaching in London over the last eight years, to my own great pleasure and profit.

I am grateful to the British Academy for an award to cover the final typing from the Small Grants Research Fund in the Humanities, and to Mrs D. Woods for so sympathetically undertaking the work.

My colleagues in King's kindly took over a large part of my teaching duties for a term when I was beginning the book, and again for a term when I was finishing it. Throughout the period of writing I have been helped, entertained and educated by my wife and three children (Kate,

Dick, Cornelia and Tahmina), who have discussed ideas with me, endured my preoccupations and supported my work. Finally, I have great pleasure in dedicating the book to my mother, who first taught me the Greek irregular verbs, by her own ingenious phonetic devices.

King's College London, 1978   R.R.K.S.

Introduction

This book centres on Aristotle's treatment of determinism and culpability. One of the advantages of studying Aristotle's treatment of determinism is that we get a sense of what a multiform thesis it is. Arguments from causation are by no means the only ones that have been used to support it, and Aristotle is the grandfather, even if not the father, of many of these arguments. I am not myself convinced by any of the arguments for determinism, nor by the arguments that it would be compatible with moral responsibility. But in order to discuss the question, I shall have to consider some very diverse topics: cause, explanation, time, necessity, essence and purpose in nature.

These are all subjects of intense controversy today, and time and again Aristotle's discussions are intimately bound up with modern ones. Often, I believe and shall argue, we can benefit from going back to the views of another period, views which are sometimes refreshingly different from our own. I shall try to explain, when necessary, where those differences lie. The discussion will not be confined to Aristotle. I shall try to supply a historical perspective and a sense of continuity, by seeing how the views of his successors and predecessors fit on to his own. But at the same time it will remain a central aim to build up a picture of Aristotle's own position on determinism and culpability, by tracing it through the many areas of his thought.

By *determinism* I shall mean the view that whatever happens has all along been necessary, that is, fixed or inevitable. I say 'whatever happens', intending to cover not merely every event, but every aspect of every event – every state of affairs, one might say. I shall make no further attempt to define necessity, although various kinds of necessity will come to be distinguished as we go along, and these will be recapitulated at the end of Chapter Thirteen. I have deliberately defined determinism by reference, not to causation, but to necessity. This will leave me free in the first eight chapters to consider the many arguments which do not appeal to causation. I have not defined determinism as a view which denies us moral responsibility. The latter idea, often known as 'hard' determinism, is comparatively rare, and was rarer still in antiquity. Many determinists have tried to argue that it is not a consequence of their position. I believe that it is a consequence, but not usually an intended one. I have spoken of things as having 'all along' been necessary, because there would be little moral interest in a view which declared that things became necessary at the last moment, or irrevocable once they had happened. Indeed, Aristotle admits the point about irrevocability; what he denies is that everything has been necessary all along.

I shall be representing Aristotle as an *indeterminist*; but opinions on this issue have been diverse since the earliest times.[1] Loening provides a list of nineteen modern commentators who have offered an indeterministic interpretation.[2] But some of the most eloquent interpretations are deterministic, notably those of Loening himself and of Gomperz, and the latest contribution to the debate, Hintikka's, is deterministic in tendency.[3] Loening adds that Aristotle did not *consciously* consider the clash between determinism and indeterminism, nor the implications of determinism for moral responsibility, and this view has become something of an orthodoxy.[4] Clearly there is room for discussion. In a way, it is misleading to tot up lists of commentators, because people mean such different things by ascribing determinism or indeterminism to Aristotle, or qualify their ascription in such different ways.[5] What is very much commoner than a straightforward deterministic interpretation is the ascription of a deterministic slant to a particular area of Aristotle's work, for example, to his treatment of coincidences,[6] of possibility,[7] or of action.[8] As to which areas are deterministically treated, disagreement is as strong as ever: Gauthier, Allan and others say the area of human action,[9] while A. Mansion says everything except that area.[10]

[1] Cicero in the first century B.C. made him a determinist (*De Fato* 39), Alexander of Aphrodisias in the third century A.D. an indeterminist (*De Fato*).

[2] Richard Loening (1.2), Jena 1903. ch. 18, notes 2, 3 and 4. M. Wittmann, talking of free will rather than indeterminism provides a somewhat different list of twenty-four (*Aristoteles und die Willensfreiheit*, Fulda 1921, 5–6). In Chapter Nine I shall consider a rather extreme indeterminist interpretation endorsed by D. M. Balme, W. D. Ross, A. Preus, H. Weiss, W. Wieland, S. Sambursky and I. Düring, all writing since Loening and Wittmann. Others who can be added to the list are: H. Maier (*Die Syllogistik des Aristoteles* II 2, Tübingen 1900, 208–9); A. Rivaud (*Le Problème du Devenir*, Paris 1906, 417); W. Kullmann ((16.2) 1974, 292–3).

[3] Richard Loening, (loc. cit.); Theodor Gomperz (1.1) vol. 4, chapters 10 and 16, translated 1912 from the German of 1896; Jaakko Hintikka (1.3) 1973, esp chs. 5, 8, 9; and (1.4) 1977. To these may be added H. Hildebrand (*Aristoteles' Stellung zum Determinismus und Indeterminismus*, Diss., Leipzig 1885).

[4] See Chapter Fifteen.

[5] Thus Hintikka claims only that there were many pressures driving Aristotle in the direction of determinism, Gomperz that he was 'nine tenths a determinist', and Loening that he was unwittingly so.

[6] Chapter One, esp. note 2.

[7] Chapter Eight, esp. note 1.

[8] Chapter Fifteen, esp. note 1.

[9] Chapter Fifteen, note 1.

[10] A. Mansion (*Introduction à la Physique Aristotélicienne*, Louvain, 2nd ed. 1946, 325–6; 1st ed. 1913).

Necessity and cause

I turn now to a more detailed account of the contents. It is not always recognised that Aristotle gave any consideration to *causal* determinism, that is, to determinism based on *causal* considerations. But I shall argue that in a little-understood passage he maintains that coincidences lack causes. To understand why he thinks so, we must recall his view that a cause is one of four kinds of *explanation*. On both counts, I think he is right. His account of cause, I believe, is more promising than any of those current today, and also justifies the denial that coincidences have causes.

There is another strut in the causal determinist's case. Besides the view that everything has a cause, he holds that whatever is caused or explicable is necessitated. If this idea is once accepted, he has a powerful argument, already wielded by the Stoics, against the indeterminist: any action that is not necessitated becomes causeless, inexplicable and hence a thing for which no one can be held responsible. On this issue, regrettably, Aristotle is less firm; he wavers on whether what is caused is necessitated. But insofar as he sometimes implies that it is not, we will be better placed, later in the book, to understand the argument of *Nicomachean Ethics* III 5. In denying that voluntary actions have been necessary all along, Aristotle need not be implying that something is uncaused.

A preoccupation of the opening two chapters is to drive a wedge between necessity and causation. Actions may be caused yet not necessitated, coincidences necessitated yet not caused. Modern theories have tended to connect cause and explanation on the one hand with laws and necessity on the other, and again to connect necessity and laws with *each other*. In the third and fourth chapters, I argue that these connexions did not at first seem self-evident to the Greeks, and that it was the Stoics who (wisely or unwisely) took the decisive step in the direction of modern views.

Necessity and time

The best-known arguments in Aristotle on determinism have to do with *time* rather than cause. In *Int.* 9, he tries to reply to the deterministic 'sea battle' argument, which is based on considerations of time and truth. Hintikka has also brought into prominence the question whether Aristotle was driven towards a deterministic account of possibility, which defines possibility in terms of time. In Chapters Five to Eight, I shall distinguish certain *further* deterministic arguments based on the necessity of the past, or on divine foreknowledge. The only one of these arguments articulated by Aristotle (and opposed by him) is the sea battle argument. But he is a more or less remote ancestor of many of the others, and of some of the answers to them.

These chapters between them will have surveyed many of the main arguments for determinism. They extend from the so-called Master Argument of Diodorus Cronus to modern interpretations, or misinterpretations, of Relativity Theory. To assess them, we shall need to get clear a number of issues about time and possibility.

Necessity and purpose in nature

I shall have shown by the end of Chapter Eight why I think Aristotle an *indeterminist*. I do not believe that he came close to the determinism of Diodorus Cronus, or of the author of the sea battle, nor that he treated coincidences as necessary. In a later chapter (Fourteen), I shall further deny that he treated all human action as necessary. But it will be time in Chapter Nine to guard against the ascription to him of too extreme an indeterminism. His occasional denials that natural events can ever occur of necessity seem to be contradicted elsewhere. Certainly, his belief that there is purpose in nature does not require, and is not thought by him to require, the denial of causal necessitation. To show why such a denial is not required, I shall have to try to show how Aristotle's purposive explanations in biology work. It will be argued that they work in several different ways, and that most of these ways leave Aristotle immune to modern criticisms of purposive explanation in biology. Criticism of Aristotle here has been widespread and vitriolic; I hope to show that it is largely mistaken.

Modern evolutionary explanations in biology are in a certain sense purposive. Yet Empedocles' appeal to natural selection in his account of animals is regarded by Aristotle as the antithesis of a purposive explanation. Does this suggest that after all Aristotle requires much more of a purposive explanation than I have allowed? Or is it rather that Empedocles' appeal to natural selection falls far short of any modern evolutionary theory? This will be the subject of Chapter Eleven.

Necessity and the essences of kinds

It will be clear by the beginning of Chapter Twelve that Aristotle recognises many kinds of necessity, far more than modern philosophers acknowledge, and it will be useful to draw up a list. But first, it will be a good thing to take into account his treatment of the necessity which attaches to statements giving the essences of kinds. This sort of necessity does not bear directly on determinism, but it is of great topical interest. On the one hand, there is a question whether Aristotle's necessity here is analytic or *de re*. I shall side with the *de re* interpretation; he is not open to the charge of misguidedly trying to base science solely on analytic truths. But if his necessity is often *de re*, is he to be castigated for that, or congratulated? This is a subject of immediate current concern; for some say that there is no *de re* necessity, and some that no necessity of any kind should be postulated in these contexts. Kripke, on the other hand, has maintained that the postulation of *de re* necessity here is justified. What is Kripke's justification and what is Aristotle's? I shall argue that in spite of the similarity of their conclusions, they have in the end very different reasons, and that neither has a justification which will apply to every example.

Necessity and blame

With Chapter Fourteen, I shall turn to necessity and blame. I have already indicated that the account of voluntary action in *NE* III 5 may be intended to deny necessity *without* denying causation. In Chapter Fifteen, I shall consider the widespread view that Aristotle was unaware of any clash between determinism and our ordinary ways of thinking about conduct and morality, particularly between determinism and the ascription of blame. I shall argue that on the contrary he was almost *too* ready to see a clash, but his dialectical method encouraged him to think that any clash would be so much the worse for *determinism*, not for morality. Moreover, his successors agreed. The Stoics and Epicureans were *not* the first to detect a clash. What made the subject of determinism take centre stage among his successors is the fact that Diodorus and the Stoics persisted in endorsing determinism in a context where many people, Aristotle included, had become aware of the clash. It then became the Stoics' task to try to show that the clash was after all illusory; for most of them agreed that, if it was real, it would count against *determinism*.

The Stoics' attempts to get out of the resulting difficulty seem to me unsuccessful. Many of them will have been reviewed earlier in Chapter Four. What I do think striking is that once again the Stoics appear as very modern (which is not to say right) in their ways of thinking. They anticipated many present-day attempts to reconcile determinism with morality.

In the last three chapters, Sixteen to Eighteen, I shall consider Aristotle's treatment of blame, independently of deterministic questions. He has been praised by Austin and others because, in defining voluntariness, he does not appeal to a mental act, like the Stoics' 'assent'. Instead, he lists various negative conditions that must be satisfied, before an action can be treated as voluntary. The falsity of determinism is only one negative condition; the conditions which interest Austin are that certain special excusing factors must be absent. At this point, however, if *NE* III is taken as the canonical account, Aristotle's discussion may cause disappointment, because he recognises so few excusing factors. To correct this impression, we must, for one thing, notice the sharp distinction that was drawn in Athens between the prescriptions of the written law and the area of discretion left to judges. What Aristotle classes as involuntary he would like to see automatically excused by the *written* law. But some of what he classes as voluntary he would *also* expect to see excused at the discretion of the *judges*. Witness his great interest in what he calls 'equity', the ability to exercise discretion. He would think it wrong to try and cover all excusable cases under a *written* formula. Some cases require perceptive treatment from the man on the spot.

Another corrective to our first impression is this: *NE* III constitutes only one of four or five attempts by Aristotle to make up his mind on voluntariness. He is feeling his way, and in some places he includes more under the heading of involuntary than in others. In Chapter Seventeen, I shall try to trace these attempts and to see whether any philosophical progress can be detected, and whether any of the scholarly issues can be settled about the order of composition. It is not only voluntariness but also, for example, temptation on which Aristotle seems to have tried out a series of treatments. In *NE* V, I shall argue, he allows what in *NE* VII notoriously he denies, that one can give in to temptation with full knowledge of all relevant facts. A further topic on which Aristotle's thought developed is negligence, and the treatment in *NE* V has been thought to have some bearing on his account of the ideal tragic hero in the *Poetics*. His downfall must be due to *hamartia*: does that mean moral flaw? negligence? simple error?

In the final chapter, I shall ask what was Aristotle's main contribution to legal theory. Plato's was a brilliant but barmy theory of punishment as a tool of reform, set out in *Laws* IX, a work often assigned by those who have not read it to his senility. Aristotle's was the very antithesis: a painstaking classification of offences designed to promote fairness. When we take into account earlier and later legal history, we see that he made a great advance on his predecessors, and had a real impact on Roman law.

There will be more modern philosophy in this book than is perhaps customary for a book on ancient philosophy. This is partly because I shall be proceeding topic by topic rather than text by text, and partly because I hope to show that there is some philosophical value in going back to ancient views. But I recognise that the intertwining of ancient and modern may create difficulties for the reader, who may have more interest in, or familiarity with, one side than the other. Some of the philosophical literature is highly technical and specialised, and I have tried as far as possible to remove technical terms, jargon and symbols, and present things in a simple form. At the same time, I have avoided the use of Greek, offering transliterations and explanations of Greek terms, where it seemed desirable. Still, readers may welcome advice on skipping, so I should say that those whose interest is more in modern philosophy will find the following chapters most relevant: One, Two, Five to Seven, Ten, Twelve, Thirteen and Fifteen. It is harder to advise those whose interest is chiefly historical. The first part of Chapter Two, for example, will seem almost exclusively concerned with modern philosophy, but it will after all prove relevant to an assessment of Aristotle's meaning in *NE* III 5, and the correctness of the Stoics' views on determinism.

Abbreviations

An. Post.	*Analytica Posteriora*
An. Pr.	*Analytica Priora*
Ath. Resp.	*Atheniensium Respublica*
Cael.	*De Caelo*
Cat.	*Categoriae*
DA	*De Anima*
EE	*Ethica Eudemia*
GA	*De Generatione Animalium*
GC	*De Generatione et Corruptione*
HA	*Historia Animalium*
Int.	*De Interpretatione*
Long.	*De Longitudine et Brevitate Vitae*
Mem.	*De Memoria et Reminiscentia*
Metaph.	*Metaphysica*
Meteor.	*Meteorologica*
Mot.	*De Motu Animalium*
NE	*Ethica Nicomachea*
PA	*De Partibus Animalium*
Phys.	*Physica*
Poet.	*Poetica*
Pol.	*Politica*
Resp.	*De Respiratione*
Rhet.	*Rhetorica*
SE	*De Sophisticis Elenchis*
Sens.	*De Sensu et Sensibili*
Top.	*Topica*
CIAG	*Commentaria in Aristotelem Graeca*, published by the Prussian Academy, Berlin 1882–1909.

PART I

NECESSITY AND CAUSE

CHAPTER ONE

Do Coincidences have Causes?
(*Metaph.* VI 3)

There is a chapter in Aristotle's *Metaphysics* that has baffled commentators. W. D. Ross remarks, 'the argument is at this point very obscure', and the latest interpreter declares that the chapter 'has not yet received a satisfactory interpretation'.[1] I believe it contains an argument that coincidences do not have causes, and that when we reflect on the connexion Aristotle makes between cause and explanation we can both understand why he says it and come to agree that he is right.

If so, there are both historical and philosophical implications. There are historical ones, because many of the most distinguished interpreters of Aristotle (T. Gomperz, H. H. Joachim, G. E. L. Owen, W. D. Ross, J. Hintikka and others) have taken it that Aristotle's conception of coincidences does not involve any denial of necessity or causation.[2] Certainly, the other main chapters on the subject, while perfectly consistent with the denial, do not make it explicitly. The most eloquent account is that of Gomperz who is moved by Aristotle's treatment of coincidences to call him 'nine tenths a determinist',[3] (the one tenth represents Aristotle's treatment of other, distinct issues).

Another ground for historical interest is that, as we shall see in Chapter Fifteen, it is often thought that Aristotle was unaware of the thesis of determinism. Or else it is thought that he was aware only of the deterministic arguments cited in *Int.* 9, which are based on considerations of time and truth, not of cause. Yet in this chapter of the *Metaphysics*, as it will be interpreted here, we can see him meeting causal determinism head on.

[1] W. D. Ross, *Aristotle's Metaphysics* vol. 1, Oxford 1924, 363; Christopher Kirwan, *Aristotle's Metaphysics, Books Γ, Δ, and E*, Oxford 1971, 198.
[2] Theodor Gomperz (1.1) 98–9, 192. W. D. Ross, *Aristotle's Metaphysics,* Oxford 1924, lxxxi and note *ad* 1027a25, *Aristotle's Physics*, Oxford 1936, *ad* 196b10–17, and *Aristotle*, Oxford 1923, Meridian edition 1959, ch. 3, 80, ch. 6, 162, and ch. 7, 196–7. H. H. Joachim, *Aristotle on Coming-to-be and Passing-away*, Oxford 1922, xxvii-xxviii. G. E. L. Owen, 'Aristotle', in *Dictionary of Scientific Biography*, ed. C. C. Gillispie, vol. 1, New York 1970, 251. Jaakko Hintikka (1.4) 1977, 111–13. A. A. Long endorses the view in (31.11) 252, n. 15. James Bogen argues for it in, 'Moravcsik on explanation', *Synthese* 28, 1974, 24. Sanford Etheridge supports it in 'Aristotle's practical syllogism and necessity', *Philologus* 112, 1968.
[3] Theodor Gomperz, op. cit.

There are philosophical implications, because if, as I believe, Aristotle is right, the causal determinist loses one of his favourite premises, that whatever happens has a cause. I say 'whatever happens', rather than 'every event', because I hesitate to count a coincidence as an event. For our purposes, it will make no important difference whether we do or not.

I am not so ready, however, to follow Aristotle in his further conclusion that coincidences cannot be necessitated. On the contrary, I think the examples of coincidence show us something which he himself was more willing to allow for elsewhere, that the notions of cause and explanation on the one hand come apart from those of necessitation, predictability and law on the other. In coincidences I think we have an instance of something which *may* be necessitated by antecedents and which yet lacks a cause.

Before we can enjoy these results, we must look closely at the text in question. And for a start, I shall drop the word 'coincidences'. For although that is what Aristotle is talking about, his phrase *to kata sumbebēkos* will not quite match the English expression in all contexts, as we shall see. So to preserve a sense of unfamiliarity with his expression, I shall render it in a more usual way as 'accident' or 'accidental conjunction'. (Others talk of the 'incidental'.)

Examples of accidents are finding buried treasure when you were only digging a hole for a plant, catching your debtor and getting your money back when you went to market on other business, getting blown to the island of Aegina when caught in a storm, the combination of being a builder or pastrycook and curing someone, or of being artistic and being literate, there being cold at midsummer or an eclipse tomorrow, or a man's being pale (*Phys.* ii 4–6; *Metaph.* v 30, vi 2, xi 8). In the more complicated situations, there are several different combinations which can be described as accidental, and several different ways of describing each: getting to market at the same time as your debtor, or going to where your debtor is. Each accident involves a relation between two items which have come together (etymologically, the expression *sumbebēkota* meant having come together), when things of this kind do not come together always or for the most part. Thus being a pastrycook is not usually conjoined with curing anyone. But whether something can be called an accident sometimes depends on how it is described, for the pastrycook may have produced something wholesome, and it is no accident if the producer of something wholesome cures someone. This account of accidents is given in *Metaph.* v 30, vi 2 and xi 8, and a further point is added. The two items are not associated with each other *because* they are of the kind specified in the description (not *dihoti* v 30, 1025a23; similarly *An. Post.* i 4, 73b10–16). The pastrycook does not effect his cure *because* he is a pastrycook (not *kata tēn opsopoiētikēn* vi 2, 1027a4). We might sum up this account, in Christopher Kirwan's words,[4] by saying that accidents are unusual conjunctions of items whose association is not self-explanatory.

It will now be clear that not all accidents are coincidences: a man's being pale is not, nor, to take an example that will be important later, is a man's dying by violence rather than disease. The interesting remarks that Aristotle goes on to make, however, are best taken as applying not to *all* accidents, but to those (the majority of his examples) which can naturally be thought of as coincidences.

Aristotle makes some important claims about accidents, the first of which is that they have only accidental causes. This is most clearly stated at *Metaph*. vi 2, 1027a7–8 (cf. xi 8, 1065a6–8): 'For the cause of things that are or come to be accidentally is itself accidental'.[5]

But if accidents have only accidental causes, are we to think of them as having genuine causes or not? To answer this question, we must distinguish two ways in which a cause can be accidental. For Aristotle, the cause *par excellence* of a statue is a sculptor. If in a given case, the sculptor happens to be the man Polyclitus, Polyclitus is merely an *accidental* cause of the statue (*Phys*. ii 3). To this it might be objected that 'sculptors' will only be a good answer to somebody who wants to know the causes of statues *in general*. Such a person may not even know that statues are artifacts. But someone who wants to know the cause of a *particular* statue is likely to know that the cause is some sculptor or other, and will want to know which sculptor in particular. Certainly, this objection represents one way of seeing things, but Aristotle also has a point. Polyclitus is a merely accidental cause, because he is not linked for the most part, nor in a self-explanatory way, to statues. Because of this, if someone wants to know why a certain statue has come into being, it will only be explanatory to cite Polyclitus, if the enquirer knows or can assume, the further fact that Polyclitus is a sculptor. We might put this by saying that citing Polyclitus is only indirectly explanatory.

In this first example, the accidental cause is a cause all right, because, at least indirectly, it is explanatory. But not all examples of accidental cause are obtained in the same way as this one. We obtained this example by citing something (Polyclitus) that was accidentally associated with the cause (sculptor). But one can also obtain an accidental cause by citing something accidentally associated with an *effect*. A wish to go to the theatre can be the cause of going to the market place, and getting to where one's debtor is (*Phys*. ii 5). In that case, the wish to go to the theatre will be a merely accidental cause of going to where one's debtor is. It is merely accidental, because it is not associated for the most part, nor in a self-explanatory way, with encountering one's debtor. Is it,

---

[4] I have benefited from his excellent account, op. cit. 180–2.

[5] The argument requires that there be *only* accidental causes; otherwise there could be arts dealing with accidents.

however, a cause? We must wait and see, bearing in mind that Aristotle will not necessarily wish to treat the two cases of accidental cause in the same way. Most of Aristotle's examples in his discussion of coincidences are of the *second* type: that is, he considers cases in which the *effect*, rather than the cause, has an accidental concomitant.[6]

A second claim about accidents is closely linked to the first one. Accidental conjunctions begin to exist without going through a process of coming into existence (*Metaph.* vi 2, 1026b22–4). The two claims are linked because it emerges in *Metaph.* vi 3 (1027a31–2) that going through a process of coming into being implies having a non-accidental cause (cf. *Phys.* ii 5, 197a12–14; *Metaph.* v 30, 1025a28–30). The reason why accidents are said not to go through a process of coming into being may be precisely that they have only accidental causes.

As I have indicated, Aristotle does not treat all his examples of accidents in the same way. It is not clear why there should be only an accidental cause for pale man, and I shall later argue that the accident of a man's death being violent is assigned a non-accidental cause (namely, a meeting with ruffians at a well). But I believe he is none the less consistent in treating *some* accidents, the ones we can think of as coincidences, as possessing only accidental causes.[7] Thus when the lucky accident[8] of catching one's debtor in the market place is said to have many possible causes – wanting to see someone, going to litigate, or going to the theatre (*Phys.* ii 5, 197a12–21), Aristotle makes clear that he thinks of these causes as accidental, because he describes them as 'indefinite', which he had just before (196b24–9) made a mark of accidental causes. And he says at the same time that, though lucky accidents can be said to be due to luck, this is only to ascribe them an accidental cause. *Metaph.* v 30 is similar: accidents have only 'indefinite' causes (1025a24–5). A storm may be the cause of your getting to the wrong destination, but in the case where that wrong destination happens to be Aegina, Aristotle pointedly omits to say that there is a cause of getting to Aegina. Indeed, he denies that getting to Aegina can have gone through a process of coming about (something he later connects with having a non-accidental cause), so long as we take it for what it is (*hēi auto*). It is only insofar as we take it as something else (*hēi heteron*),

[6] Further examples of the second type are that getting to the wrong destination (the *effect* of a storm) is accidentally associated with getting to Aegina; going to the well (the *effect* of thirst) is accidentally associated with going to where the ruffians are; pleasing my palate (the *effect* of the pastrycook's art) is accidentally associated with restoring my health; making a hole (the effect of wishing to plant something) is accidentally associated with finding treasure; an eclipse (the *effect* of celestial motions) is accidentally associated with tomorrow. The only clear example of the first type that we have so far encountered is mentioned alongside the pastrycook example in *Metaph.* vi 2 at 1026b37: a doctor (the *cause* of my health) is by accident a builder.

[7] Some possible objections are considered at the end of the chapter.

[8] I call this lucky event an accident, because lucky events (*apo tuchēs*) are one kind of accident (*kata sumbebēkos*, *Phys.* ii 5, 196b23; cf. b10–17, b20).

i.e. as a case of getting to the wrong destination, that we can say it has gone through a process of coming about (1025a28–30).[9]

With the knowledge that accidents have only accidental causes, we can turn to the chapter that concerns us. I shall start with a translation of the crucial lines of *Metaph.* VI 3.

1027a29   It is obvious that there are origins and causes which can begin or cease to exist without going through a process of beginning or ceasing.

1027a30   For otherwise, all things will be of necessity, if there has to be a cause non-accidentally of what goes through a process of beginning or ceasing. For will this be or will it not? It will, if that happens; otherwise not, and that will happen if something else does. And so it is clear that as time is constantly subtracted from a limited period, one will come to the present. This man, then, will die by violence, if he goes out, will go out, if he gets thirsty, and will get thirsty, if something else. In this way, one will come to what now obtains or to something past. For example, the man will go out, if he gets thirsty, and he will get thirsty, if he is eating something spicy, and this either obtains or does not. Hence it is of necessity that he will die or not die. Likewise, if one jumps over to the past, it is the same story. For that – I mean what is past – already obtains in somebody. So all future things will be of necessity, like the death of what is alive. For something has already come into being, for example, opposed qualities in the same individual.

1027b10   But whether he will die by disease or by violence is not yet [sc. of necessity], but will happen if that does. So it is clear that it runs back as far as a certain origin, but that this origin does not run back to something else. Thus this origin will be the origin of whatever may chance, and there is no further cause of its coming into being.

Metaph. VI 3, and the briefer version of it in *Metaph.* XI 8, both take it as obvious that not every thing happens of necessity (*ex anankēs*), and that it may not yet be necessary that a man will die of disease, or by violence (1027b10–11). But in that case (1027b11–14), it must be possible to have a causal chain which stretches back a certain distance from its terminus in some future event (it runs back as far as a certain origin; this origin will be the origin of whatever may chance), but which stops short without stretching endlessly backwards (this origin does not run back to something else; there is no further cause of its coming into being). For if everything had a (non-accidental) cause, everything would be of necessity (1027a30–2). The important thing is that the causal chain which terminates in the future event should not stretch back as far as the present or past (to the present; to what now obtains or to something past; he is eating something spicy, and this either obtains or does not; jumps over to the past; what is past already obtains in somebody; something has already come into being). The same concern with the present or past reappears in the shorter version in

---

[9] I shall below contrast Jaakko Hintikka's treatment of these passages.

Metaph. xi 8.[10] This is because Aristotle regards the present or past as necessary, because irrevocable (*Cael*. 283b12–14, *NE* 1139b7–9, *Rhet*. 1418a3–5; more controversially *Int*. 9, 19a23–4).[11] Evidently, then, some causal chains do not stretch back as far as the present or past.

If I may import into the discussion a distinction between relative and absolute necessity, Aristotle is allowing a certain kind of relative necessity, although we shall see in Chapter Three that this is not his standard view. He concedes that an effect is necessary, *given* its cause. But this will not give us an absolute (non-relative) necessity, unless the cause is itself absolutely necessary.[12] And the cause becomes absolutely necessary only when it (or its causal ancestry) is past and irrevocable. The situation is parallel to that in logic: as necessity in the premises of a valid syllogism will spread to the conclusion (*An. Pr*. i 15, 34a22–4), so necessity in a cause will spread to the effect. Aristotle's strategy in face of this is to deny that the causal ancestry of future events always reaches back into the past.

But what stops the causal chain reaching into the past? I believe the answer is that an accident features in the chain. That Aristotle is still talking about accidents at the beginning of *Metaph*. vi 3 (contrary to Jaakko Hintikka's earlier suggestion)[13] is clear from several signs. Not only were they the subject of the preceding chapter, but he starts the new one by alluding to the two claims that he makes about accidents. Thus the things he is talking about begin to exist without going through a process of coming into existence (1027a29–30), and but for this they would have a non-accidental cause, and not a merely accidental one (a30–2).

But if Aristotle is talking of accidents, what is the evidence that he thinks of them as entering into the causal chain? This comes at 1027a29, where he describes his accidents which lack non-accidental causes as *themselves being causes* (*archai* and *aitia*). This is the clue we want. I take Aristotle's point to be that certain kinds of accidental conjunction *can enter as causes into a causal chain*, and can stop that chain stretching back any further, because they lack (non-accidental) causes of their own.

The structure of vi 3 seems to be as follows. 1027a29–30 says it is clear

---

[10] *Metaph*. xi 8, 1065a19–20: 'One will come eventually to what obtains, so that since this *is*, . . .'

[11] For the controversy on *Int*. 9, 19a23–4, see below. Modern logicians, until very recently, have ignored the necessity of the past (see Chapter Five, note 29). It is not surprising, then, that commentators should misconstrue references to it as references to some kind of causal necessity. (Margaret E. Reesor, 'Fate and possibility in early Stoic philosophy', *Phoenix* 19, 1965.)

[12] Something parallel is argued for the final cause or goal in *GC* ii 11. Achievement of the goal may make something relatively necessary as a prerequisite. But unless there is some absolute necessity that the goal will be achieved, the prerequisite will not be absolutely necessary.

[13] Jaakko Hintikka (1.3) 1973, 175. He withdraws in (1.4) 1977, 107.

that certain kinds of accidental conjunction can serve as causes. 1027a30 starts defending this by showing that 'otherwise' (*ei gar mē tout'*) determinism would follow, and the manner of someone's death would all along have been necessary. 1027b10–14 protests (*alla*: 'but') that this deterministic consequence is false; the *manner* of a man's death, as opposed to the fact of his death, has not all along been necessary. Thus the chapter is nicely rounded, and the promise made at the beginning, to show that accidents can serve as causes, is fulfilled at the end.

The example in vi 3 can be interpreted as follows. A man eats spicy food, and so gets thirsty, and so goes out to the well, where he meets some ruffians who happen to be passing, and who kill him. They did not come for the purpose of finding him, nor did they lure him there. Now people may misconstrue the man's violent death as having all along been necessary (and I take it that 1027a30–b19 is spelling out the consequences of a *misconstruction*). We can avoid this misconstruction, if we notice that in the causal chain there is a certain kind of accidental conjunction: the man's going to the well at the same time as the ruffians.[14] His going to where the ruffians are causes his death, but it is itself an accident, and so has only an accidental cause, being thirsty.

Aristotle now takes an important further step (1027b12–14): the meeting at the well has no cause at all. 'This origin does not run back to something else . . . and there is no further cause (*aition*) of its coming into being.' This answers our earlier question, whether in these cases Aristotle regards the accidental cause (being thirsty) as a cause of the meeting at all. And the answer is evidently 'no'.

The absence of a cause saves the meeting from being necessary, he thinks (1027a30–2). Thus the chain of causation and necessitation leading to the victim's violent death does not stretch back further than his meeting with the ruffians, and so the determinist is answered.

The briefer version in *Metaph.* xi 8 is less clear, but it too is talking of accidental conjunctions such as there being an eclipse *tomorrow*, and is saying (1065a6–8) that they do not have causes like those of non-accidents. There may in addition be a reference at 1065a14–15 to the argument that these accidents which have only accidental causes can themselves enter into a causal chain and have effects.[15] (It is important

[14] I construe 1027b10–14 as follows: 'But whether he will die by disease or by violence is not yet [necessary], it depends on whether that [the meeting] happens. So it is clear that things run back as far as a certain origin, but this origin no longer runs back to anything further. This origin [the meeting] will be the origin of the chance event [the violent death], and there will be no further cause of its [the origin's] coming about.'

[15] At xi 8, 1065a14–15, Aristotle's opponent talks of a *cause*, which does not yet exist, but which (in his opinion) is in process of being generated. Is this cause the fact of there being an eclipse tomorrow? If so, it will be being treated like the meeting with the ruffians, as an

to notice that the accident which has only an accidental cause is not an eclipse but an eclipse *tomorrow*. Aristotle's handling of phenomena like eclipses in *GC* II 11 and *An. Post.* I 8 suggests that he would not regard them as accidents, since they will *always* recur.)

We are now in a position to assess Aristotle's view that there is no cause at all of the meeting with the ruffians. In order to understand it, I think we must observe that Aristotle thinks of cause as closely connected with explanation. His so-called efficient cause is just one of the four modes of explanation (*Phys.* II 3; II 7). In the present chapter, he rather uncharacteristically adds a second idea into the notion of cause, that a cause necessitates its effect. In claiming that there is no cause, he may seem to be open to an obvious objection. Admittedly (it may be said), the accidental cause, the victim's decision to get a drink from the well, is not *on its own* a cause of his falling in with the ruffians. But why should not the *combination* of that decision with the ruffians' decision to pass by the well be a cause?

This objection has two parts, corresponding to the two elements in the notion of cause he is using. First, why should not the combination of decisions *necessitate* the meeting, at least given the right further conditions? And, secondly, why should it not *explain* the meeting? I do not wish to defend Aristotle against the first line of attack, but instead to take up the second. I believe that the meeting has no proper explanation, and that this is enough to vindicate Aristotle's claim that it has no cause.

One problem is whether we can explain the man's going to the well at *exactly* 2 p.m. But let us suppose that there is an explanation of this, and also an *unconnected* explanation of why the ruffians passed the well at exactly 2 p.m. Does it follow that there is an explanation of why the thirsty man and the ruffians went to the well *at the same time*? Or for the latter, would we need a *connected* explanation of their movements? To take another example, suppose that for each of five airliners we have a *separate* explanation of why it crashed on March 1st: the damaged bolt, the drunken pilot, the terrorist bomb, and so on. Does it follow that we have an explanation of why the five crashed *on the same day*? I think that someone who asked for the latter, would be looking for a *connected* explanation, such as that a group of terrorists planned all five crashes. There may be such a *connected* explanation, but there may only be five separate explanations of the timing. And if we could give only these, I think the man who asked us to explain the simultaneity would be entitled to feel that we had not answered his question. The honest thing to say to him in this case would be that there is no explanation of the simultaneity. And yet it may be the *simultaneity* of the crashes which is the important thing, because it explains a subsequent decision to

---

accident which enters into a causal chain, and has further effects. What Aristotle will reject in the opponent's view is that it has non-accidental causes.

expand the Air Safety Board, just as the *simultaneity* of the parties arriving at the well is what explains the man's violent death.[16]

On these grounds I would deny that coincidences have explanations. But does that justify the further claim that they lack causes? The relationship between cause and explanation is a subtle one. Hart and Honoré have drawn attention to a case in which ascertaining the cause will not supply an explanation to one group of people (although it may to another).[17] Mackie points out that a statement of cause may not be *directly* explanatory.[18] We can say that the cause of an explosion was Tom's movement, but it is not because Tom is Tom that he produced an explosion. And it is only so long as we can assume *other* things about Tom that we get an explanation of the explosion. The same point is made by Aristotle (*Phys*. II 3, 195a32 – b30). The cause of some statue may be specified by naming the sculptor, Polyclitus. But it is not because Polyclitus is Polyclitus that he produced a statue, and it is only *indirectly* explanatory to refer to him. For it is only so long as we can assume *other* things about Polyclitus (e.g. that he is a sculptor) that we get an explanation of the outcome.

Aristotle calls Polyclitus an *accidental* cause of the statue. But he can also be called a cause, because citing the accidental cause at least points the way to something that does explain. The fact of his being a sculptor explains the existence of the statue. And in naming Polyclitus we point the way towards a genuine explanation of the statue, for someone who has the right information, or can gather it. Cause has at least this indirect link with explanation.

The case for saying that an accidental meeting at the well or market place has no cause at all is that there is nothing which plays even this indirect explanatory role. The accidental causes (wanting to go to the theatre, being thirsty) do not, because there is nothing which *directly* explains the meeting, and to which these accidental causes can point. I think this vindicates Aristotle's refusal in *Metaph*. VI 3 (1027b12–14) to treat this particular type of accidental cause as being a cause.

Are we now free to reject the widely held view that every event and state of affairs has a cause? I add 'state of affairs', because although we can say that the simultaneous arrival at the well has been shown to be causeless, the stress is on the *simultaneity*. And simultaneity is more naturally thought of as a state of affairs.

[16] Compare: 'Why did it have to rain *on my birthday*?' – no answer; it was a coincidence. 'Why did it have to rain?' – answerable.

[17] H. L. A. Hart and A. M. Honoré make the point in their excellent book (2.10) 1959, 22–3: when lawyers debate the cause of a fire, they may know the *explanation* already (that it was due to a lighted cigarette being thrown away and a breeze springing up). The question of cause may be a question not of explanation, but of whether the breeze was sufficiently *abnormal* to exonerate the man who threw away the cigarette. Still, even in this case, the factor finally selected as cause would explain the fire to someone else, even if the lawyers are no longer at the stage of seeking an explanation.

[18] J. L. Mackie (2.5) 1974, ch. 10.

Whether every event and state of affairs has a cause can be made to depend on how one counts events or states of affairs. The rules for counting these differ, and it is harder to show for states of affairs than for events that two different descriptions pick out the same one. If, in spite of this, the victim's getting to the well at 2 p.m. is counted as the *same* state of affairs as his getting to the well simultaneously with the ruffians; if the creditor's getting to the market place at 2 p.m. is counted as the *same* state of affairs as his going to where his debtor is; and if getting to the wrong destination is counted as the *same* state of affairs as getting to Aegina, then the conclusion would need to be put differently. Every state of affairs might have a cause; what we should insist on is that it need not have a cause under every description, not, for example, under the description 'getting to the well simultaneously with the ruffians'. Personally, I prefer the stronger formulation that not every state of affairs has a cause. Admittedly, ordinary language does not provide firm criteria. But in a context where our interest was in causation, the very lack of a common cause for getting to the well at 2 p.m. and getting to the well simultaneously with the ruffians could itself be an incentive for calling these different states of affairs.

At one point, Aristotle seems tempted by something roughly equivalent to the claim that getting to the wrong destination is the *same* state of affairs as getting to Aegina (*Metaph.* v 30, 1025a28 – 30).[19] Even so, the conclusion to be drawn would still be striking enough. For we could not say that getting to the well simultaneously with the ruffians had a cause, and Aristotle seems to recognise this.[20] We should have instead to say, for example, that the same state of affairs, differently described, had a cause.

It is a considerable achievement on Aristotle's part to recognise that coincidences do not have causes. But does this refute determinism? It would do, if determinism were simply a thesis about causation, but I defined it in the introduction as a thesis about necessity, not about cause. And Aristotle himself wants to show something about necessity, namely, how to avoid the view that 'all things are of necessity' (vi 3, 1027a31: cf. b8, b10–11; xi 8, 1065a8, a12, a15, a21). As regards this

---

[19] Aristotle's terminology is somewhat different from ours. Without calling them the *same* state of affairs, he does allow at *Metaph.* v 30, 1025a28–30, that getting to Aegina is *a case of* getting to the wrong destination, and that *as such* it has a cause. I take him to be saying: 'Getting to Aegina has not gone through a process of coming about insofar as it is a case of getting to Aegina (*hēi auto*: quā itself), but it has insofar as it is also a case of something else, viz. getting to the wrong destination (*hēi heteron*: quā something different). It has gone through such a process, because there is a cause, the storm, of getting to the wrong destination.'

[20] He does not concede much when he allows the qualified statement that getting to Aegina has a cause, *insofar as* it is a case of something else. For he does not invite us to drop this qualification, and say that it has a cause *simpliciter*. Other passages would agree that it has only an accidental cause (*Metaph.* vi 2, 1027a7–8; xi 8, 1065a6–8; *Phys.* ii 5). And we have seen that in this instance an accidental cause is not a cause.

aim, a determinist could rightly protest that necessitating, i.e. sufficient, conditions are unlike explanations. (By a necessitating condition is meant one which is sufficient and guarantees the outcome, or makes it inevitable; it must not be confused with a necessary condition, which is merely prerequisite.) Sufficient conditions differ from explanations in that, if it is once conceded that there are sufficient conditions for the ruffians being at the well at 2 p.m., and sufficient conditions for the victim being at the well at 2 p.m., then it must be conceded that there are sufficient conditions for what is entailed by this, namely, their being at the well simultaneously. Aristotle has rightly sensed, the determinist may say, that coincidences lack a cause. But he has failed to consider that this might be only because there is no explanation, and not also because there are no sufficient conditions.

I think this objection to Aristotle would be justified. It is not that coincidences have been shown to be necessitated. It is simply that he has not shown that they are not. Yet even in his failure to refute determinism, he enables us to appreciate something of philosophical interest, namely, that if something (an accidental meeting) is necessitated, that is, rendered inevitable, it does not follow that it is caused. A thing can be necessitated without itself having a cause.

Objection based on Davidson's view of cause

It may be objected that my account so far is misconceived. It will be, if it is right to believe a certain bold and original account of causation which has gained widespread influence recently. Donald Davidson has made a battery of claims, the first three of which clash, or seem to clash, with what I have so far said.[21] Those who do not wish to pursue these claims can safely pass on to the next section. (i) First, Davidson maintains that, in a true singular causal statement (i.e. one about a particular occasion), the causal relation asserted holds between events, not between states of affairs, or facts. (ii) Secondly, he bases this conclusion on a complex argument, which involves the idea that if there is a cause of going to *the well*, and the well is where the ruffians are, then we must be able to substitute terms, and say there is a cause of going to *where the ruffians are*. (iii) Thirdly, in order to avoid some apparent counter-examples to this last idea, he draws a sharp distinction between cause and explanation, rejecting statements of causal explanation as not being 'straightforward' singular causal statements. (iv) Fourthly, in place of the idea of explanation, he puts the idea of sufficient conditions and deterministic laws in his account of what a cause is.

These ideas are not immediately obvious. As regards the preference for events over facts, one would have expected to be free to talk not merely of causing an event, but, for example, of causing an event to have

---

[21] Donald Davidson (2.7) 64, 1967, 691–703; exploited further in (2.8) 1970.

a certain character. Again, if terms like 'the well' and 'where the ruffians are' can be freely interchanged, it will not be easy to make fine discriminations about what exactly is caused or causative.

I shall first consider Davidson's second idea: can Aristotle be required to accept the claim that there is a cause of going to where the ruffians are, and would such acceptance be damaging to him? I shall endorse G. E. M. Anscombe's view[22] that claims of the kind in question can be taken in more than one sense, and I shall argue that in the sense in which Aristotle would have to accept it, it would not contradict his view about coincidences. Davidson would probably agree so far, since he would be likely to construe the claim in the same sense.

The idea to be discussed is that in any singular causal statement we can substitute one singular term for another ('where the ruffians are' for 'the well'), so long as it has the same reference.[23] It has been argued by Norman Malcolm[24] that when we speak of something as being *explained*, we are not free in this way to substitute one coextensive singular term for another. Davidson concedes the point about explanation, but denies that it is applicable to cause.[25]

One objection to this last denial can be mentioned, simply to get it out of the way. Let us suppose that there is a fanatic who wants New York to contain the handsomest Irishman, and who brings this about, by choosing the Irish Prime Minister, who happens to be in New York, and killing off all the Irishmen who are both more handsome than the Irish Prime Minister and absent from New York. In a certain sense, the fanatic can be said to have caused the presence in New York of the handsomest Irishman. Someone might then suppose (wrongly) that it was an objection to Davidson that we cannot substitute terms, and say the fanatic has caused the presence in New York of the Irish Prime Minister. But this is, in fact, no objection to Davidson, for the phrase 'the handsomest Irishman' has not yet been used referentially, that is, in order to refer to something. Witness the fact that we cannot say, for example: 'with regard to the handsomest Irishman, the fanatic caused *him* to be in New York'. Let us, then, take a different example, in order to resist Davidson's view.

Suppose the American President causes the presence in New York of the Irish Prime Minister by inviting him there; and suppose that it is a coincidence, without explanation, that the Irish Prime Minister is the

[22] See G. E. M. Anscombe's excellent paper (2.9) 1968.

[23] This thesis goes further, in a way, than the one considered earlier, according to which every event or state of affairs can be ascribed a cause, provided that we choose the right description of it. The new suggestion is that we can vary the description as much as we like, at least insofar as coextensive singular terms are concerned. In another way, Davidson's thesis goes less far, for states of affairs are not allowed to have causes.

[24] Norman Malcolm, 'Scientific materialism and identity theory', *Dialogue* 3, 1964, 115–25.

[25] Davidson (2.7) 702–3, (2.8) 89.

handsomest Irishman. Davidson's substitutions will now yield a claim which is at best ambiguous – that the American President causes the presence in New York of the handsomest Irishman. This latter claim is *false*, if it is taken to mean that the President gets the handsomest Irishman to go to New York *because he is the handsomest Irishman*. It is also false if it is taken to mean that the President behaves like our fanatic. Moreover, the connexion between cause and explanation encourages us to look for some such interpretation; for it is natural to suppose that the description chosen of the visitor will be relevant to the verb of causation, or, as J. L. Mackie says, [26] 'causally relevant'. To obtain a true claim, Anscombe suggests,[27] we should think of that description as insulated from the verb of causation. The insulation could be made explicit by a relative clause in the following manner: 'The American President causes the presence in New York of a certain person, who is (Aristotle might say: who accidentally happens to be) the handsomest Irishman.'

It can now be made clear how Aristotle could respond if anyone claimed that his case was damaged by the need to substitute one expression for another. He need not admit in any damaging sense that there is a cause of the victim going to where the ruffians are. He can say that such an idea is false if the description, 'where the ruffians are', is taken as causally relevant. It will be true, only if that description is understood as insulated from the causal word, in the following way: 'There is a cause of the victim going to a certain place, which accidentally happens to be where the ruffians are.' But if these are the only terms on which the idea is true, nothing important need be conceded. In particular, it need not be conceded that anything causes the victim to go the well simultaneously with the ruffians.

Davidson would probably agree that this need not be conceded. His objection to the discussion would be more radical, and would depend on his first idea, that the causal relation reported in a true singular causal statement holds between events, not facts. His argument for this can be outlined in a footnote.[28] But Anscombe's reply can be indicated very

[26] J. L. Mackie (2.5) 1974, ch. 10. Mackie's is the most useful guide I know to current debate on causation.

[27] Anscombe (op. cit.) suggests another method of insulation, viz. pulling the singular term out into the front of the sentence, away from the verb of causation, as follows: 'With regard to the handsomest Irishman, the American President causes his presence in New York.'

[28] Davidson holds that even if a singular causal statement is phrased, misleadingly, in terms of facts ('The fact that there was a fire in Jones' house caused it to be the case that the pig was roasted'), its real logical form must be given in terms of events ('The fire in Jones' house caused the roasting of the pig'). In a derivative sense, persons, physical objects, states and dispositions can be said to stand in causal relations, thanks to their association with events. (See 'Agency', in *Agent, Action and Reason*, ed. R. Binkley, R. Bronaugh, A. Marras, Oxford 1971, 10 and 15; 'Actions, reasons and causes', *Journal of Philosophy* 60, 1963, pp. 87–8 of the version reprinted in A. R. White (ed.) *Philosophy of Action*, Oxford 1968. I am grateful to Julia Annas for the references.) Davidson concedes that statements

simply. For Davidson's argument depends on the idea that, in his specimen causal statement, coextensive singular terms can safely be substituted for each other.[29] And Anscombe's rejoinder is that, for reasons just
indicated, they cannot be substituted, unless they are so insulated from
the verb of causation as not to form an integral part of the causal
statement.[30]

I shall not discuss separately Davidson's third idea, that the most
straightforward singular causal statements are not explanations; for he
does not offer direct support for that suggestion. But in the next chapter,
I shall explain why I do not agree with his fourth idea, that is, with his
alternative account of how to understand singular causal statements, in
terms of sufficient conditions and deterministic laws.

The supposed connexion of explanation with predictability and laws

The examples of the ruffians and the five aeroplanes have implications
for current theories of explanation. The predominant theory, associated
with the name of Hempel, will be considered more fully in Chapter
Three. It connects explanation with laws and with prediction. In a crude
version, cruder than Hempel's,[31] the covering law theory would say that
to subsume something under a law is to explain it. Further, what can be
predicted on the basis of laws can also be explained on the basis of those
laws. The example of the five aeroplanes casts doubt on these ideas. For
we should not feel that we had any more explanation of why the five
airliners crashed on the same day, if this could be subsumed under the
funny-sounding law, that whenever those five unconnected causes were
operating on the same day, there would be five separate crashes on the

which supply an *explanation* may relate facts, but he dismisses these as not being
'straightforward' singular causal statements. Davidson's argument is that the singular
term 'Jones' house' can be replaced by the coextensive term 'the oldest building on Elm
Street'. But, he continues, there is a logical argument to show that, if we can substitute one
coextensive singular term for another, we ought also to be able to substitute for one of the
component propositions (the pig was roasted) another proposition with the same truth
value (Julius Caesar crossed the Rubicon). This we manifestly cannot do. So there must be
something wrong with the sentence phrased in terms of facts.

[29] This substitutivity is not only a premise of his argument, but also part of what he
means by saying that the relation asserted in a true, singular causal statement holds
between events. The events are thought of as concrete events whose descriptions can
safely be varied.

[30] Another line of reply doubts the validity of the logical argument that if one kind of
substitution is legitimate, so is the other (J. L. Mackie (2.5) ch. 10; R. Cummins and
D. Gottlieb, 'On an argument for truth-functionality', *American Philosophical Quarterly*
IX, 1972, 265–9).

[31] Some of Carl Hempel's main papers on the subject, from 1942 to 1965, are collected in
his *Aspects of Scientific Explanation*, New York and London 1965. In the 1965 paper, after
which the book is named, he leaves it an open question whether every prediction of a thing
based on laws can serve as an explanation of that thing. If, as I have suggested, it cannot, it
would be a major task to specify the circumstances in which it can, and those in which it
cannot.

same day. Secondly, one who could predict, on the basis of laws, the timing of each crash could also predict their simultaneity. But nothing, I have suggested, would *explain* their simultaneity, if the five individual explanations were unconnected with each other. No doubt, the covering law theory of explanation might be refined, so as to avoid these difficulties. Among other things, the notion of a *law* might be explicated in such a way, that the rather quaint 'whenever' statement I cited would not count as a law. If so, the present argument can be viewed as an invitation to define the notion of a law. But the task has proved very difficult.[32] Some of the proposals made would not exclude my bizarre 'whenever' statement, while others exclude it only at the cost of restricting the discussion to 'scientific' laws and 'scientific' explanations.

We shall see in Chapter Three that Aristotle rejected the idea that to subsume something under a law is to explain it. We cannot explain the comparative proximity of the planets by subsuming it under the law that what does not twinkle is near (*An. Post.* I 13, 78a29 – b11; II 16, 98b4–14).

Aristotle's relation to his predecessors on coincidences

If I am right that Aristotle viewed coincidences as neither caused nor necessitated, this casts an interesting light on his relation to his predecessors Democritus and Empedocles. We are told that in connexion with the example of a man finding buried treasure while digging a hole for a plant, Democritus said (or would say) there *was* a cause, namely the digging or the planting of the olive.[33] He is certainly supposed to have held that everything happens of necessity. And one source ascribes to him the view that chance is a cause and is called 'chance' only because the cause is not obvious to the human mind.[34]

This idea, that coincidences are caused and necessitated, is the one commonly attributed to Aristotle as well. What I have been arguing is that in fact Aristotle broke away from Democritus with his argument in *Metaph.* VI 3.

If one thinks with Democritus of coincidences as being necessitated then it is natural to talk in terms of necessary accidents or chance necessities. And in fact such talk is common among Aristotle's predecessors. Plato ascribes it to Empedocles,[35] and Aristotle found, or thought

---

[32] On the definition of law, besides Hempel, see, e.g.: E. Nagel (4.2), 1961, ch. 4; R. B. Braithwaite, *Scientific Explanation*, Cambridge 1953, ch. 9; A. J. Ayer, 'What is a law of nature?' *Revue Internationale de Philosophie*, no. 36, fasc. 2, 1956: W. Kneale (5.1) 1961.

[33] Simplicius, Commentary on *Phys. CIAG p. 330, line 14, quoting Aristotle's pupil, Eudemus (* =Diels *Die Fragmente der Vorsokratiker*, Demokritos A68).

[34] Aëtius I 29 7 (=Diels, Demokritos A66). W. K. C. Guthrie has a good discussion of how to reconstruct Democritus' view, in (17.3) 1969, 418–19. A major, but perplexing, source is *Phys.* II 4.

[35] Guthrie (op. cit. 163–4, 414–15) has collected references from Plato's account of

he found, the ideas of necessity and chance constantly juxtaposed in Empedocles and Democritus.[36] If I am right, Aristotle will have implicitly rejected this way of talking in *Metaph*. VI 3. In view of this, I must, before the end of the chapter, counteract the impression that he endorsed it, in the sense which Democritus intended.

Aristotle's relation to his successors on causelessness

It is also interesting to ascertain Aristotle's relation to his successors. At first sight, his postulation of events or states of affairs without a cause may seem reminiscent of Epicurus' subsequent theory of an uncaused swerve of atoms in the soul, or of the theory from a yet later era of an uncaused act of will. But in fact, Aristotle's idea is far removed from these. For the danger with these later theories is that they make the uncaused event seem mysterious. But Aristotle's examples of going to where the debtor is, or going to where the ruffians are, differ from swerves and acts of will, in that, on reflection, we do not expect that such things will necessarily have an explanation; and to deny them one is not to make a mystery of them.

Aristotle's denial of a cause for accidents differ from later theories in another way, that it is not presented as a means of defending human freedom. It is not even particularly connected with human action, as Ross and others have supposed.[37] That the heavy rains coincided with the highest tides on some occasion could be an example of an accident lacking a cause. And here there is no human agency. In the example of the meeting at the well, the uncaused event does not occur, like Epicurus' uncaused swerve, within the soul of a human being. Epicurus' swerve is quite different: it is presented *inter alia* as a means of defending freedom in Lucretius' Latin exposition. And the objection to which it has often been exposed and from which it has recently been defended,[38] is that, so far from saving human freedom, it destroys freedom by making action random. Aristotle's theory of accidents is not intended to

Empedocles (*Laws* 889A–C), and from the Greek tragedians (Sophocles *Electra* 48 and *Ajax* 485; Euripides *Iphigeneia at Aulis* 511). But sometimes it is merely that chance *creates* some necessity (Aeschylus *Agamemnon* 1042, Plato *Laws* 806A), and sometimes the necessity is merely conditional on whether something else happens (Sophocles *Ajax* 803).

[36] For the ascription of things to necessity by Democritus, see *GA* 789 b3, b13; for the ascription to chance *Phys*. 196a24, *PA* 641b15–23. Similarly, Empedocles is said to ascribe certain things to necessity (*Phys*. 252a5–10, *GC* 334a2—5, *Metaph*. 1000b16), and some to chance (*Phys*. 196a20, 198b29–32; *GC* 333b15; *PA* 640a19–22). Aristotle further complains that Empedocles ascribes the upward movement of aether to chance, but that of fire to nature (*GC* 334a2–5).

[37] Besides the references to W. D. Ross, given in note 2 above, see Richard Taylor, 'The problem of future contingencies', *Philosophical Review* 66, 1957, 1–28, and David Furley (29.2) 1967, 236, n. 8, who compares the Epicurean swerve in the soul which guarantees free will with Aristotle's denial of causation in *Metaph*. VI 3.

[38] David Furley, op. cit. 232–3; A. A. Long (31.9) 1974, 56–61. Defences need to avoid the opposite danger of restoring too large a role to necessity.

save freedom, and it could not, but for a different reason.[39] Even if Aristotle were right that the meeting at the well is not inevitable he says nothing in the present passage against the view that the murder is the inevitable outcome of the meeting. Moreover, the meeting itself, even if not inevitable, still lies outside anyone's control.

Epicurus was some forty-three years junior to Aristotle. Five centuries later again, the Aristotelian, Alexander of Aprodisias, sometimes followed his master in making coincidences causeless. In Chapter Four, I shall argue that he was simply endorsing the doctrine of *Metaph.* vi 3, and not devising some new argument of his own.

Objections to the claim that Aristotle denies that coincidences are necessitated

I have now presented my view that accidents are not caused or necessitated for Aristotle. And I must consider the objections that might be brought in favour of the rival view of Gomperz, Joachim, Owen, Ross and Hintikka. I shall consider first necessity, and then cause, looking for passages where Aristotle might be thought to be ascribing one or other of them to accidents.

(i) One passage in which the ideas of necessity and chance are intertwined is *Phys.* ii 8, 198b10 – 199a8. But here there are two possible reasons for the association. First, Aristotle is discussing his predecessors, and may for that reason be going along with their usage. Secondly, one of the theories he is attacking regards the arrangement of our teeth as the necessary *outcome* of a chance event. This provides a reason for associating chance with necessity, regardless of whether the chance event *itself* is thought of as being necessary.

(ii) There is a group of passages in the biological works, which may create confusion, because Aristotle associates the ideas of accident and necessity.[40] But his point in these passages is not that the necessary occurrence is a *coincidence* (indeed, the existence of spleen or bile in a species is not a coincidence), but that it is not essentially related to *purpose*. Spleen and bile, eye colour and monstrosities are necessary products which serve no purpose themselves, although they may be related to organs and processes which do serve a purpose. It is because their relation to purpose is accidental, and not because they are coincidences, that Aristotle calls them accidental.

The most that can be extracted from the biological works, I think, is that there are certain occurrences which Aristotle calls necessary, and which, if asked, he would have to agree were coincidences. This would be true, for example, of a particular individual's eye turning out blue, or of

---

[39] I am indebted to Myles Burnyeat for pointing out this reason.

[40] *PA* iii 7, 670a30, iv 2, 677a18; *GA* iv 3, 767b8–15; v 1, 778a22 with 35; v 8, 789b19–20. These passages are studied by W. Kullmann (16.2) 1974, 294–7.

a particular birth being monstrous. This falls well short of saying that he recognises the existence of necessary coincidences.

(iii) There is a juxtaposition of the ideas of chance and necessity at *An. Post.* II 11, 95a3–5, which I think is not significant, since the cases of chance and of necessity need not be meant to overlap.

(iv) Ross has another argument: he admits that accidents are regarded by Aristotle as exceptions to what usually happens. But these exceptions, he thinks, do not constitute a breach of necessity. For the exceptions in their turn answer to some regularity. He cites (Commentary, *ad Metaph.* VI 2, 1027a25) Aristotle's remark in that place that although honey water does not always cure fever patients, the exceptions may fall under the rule that at new moon it always or usually fails. He construes this as a recognition that 'there is nothing which is objectively accidental', and that events which 'present themselves as accidents' are 'merely beyond our present knowledge'. He then has to treat the next chapter (VI 3) as going back on this recognition (same commentary, p. lxxxi). But there is no need to attribute this wavering to Aristotle. Kirwan (*ad* 1027a19) correctly points out that Aristotle offers no assurance that there must be a regularity covering the exceptions, and Gomperz had earlier recognised this fact.

(v) Barnes and Joachim[41] cite some further passages to show that among events which happen by nature 'apparent exceptions disappear on closer inspection', and that the appearance is merely due to ignorance. Barnes, however, rightly warns that Aristotle only plays with the idea in certain passages. In one such passage (*An. Post.* I 8, 75b33–6), Aristotle envisages that even though lunar eclipses are exceptions which do not befall the moon all the time they may enter into necessary propositions. He may have in mind that they are everlastingly recurring subjects which always have the same cause. However, Aristotle is not here contradicting the claim of *Metaph.* XI 8, 1065a16, that the coincidence of an eclipse with *tomorrow* is an accident that is not necessitated. He makes clear in 75b35 that he is thinking of lunar eclipses in general as being the subject of necessary propositions, not of particular lunar eclipses, and much less of the coincidence of a lunar eclipse with tomorrow. In another passage (*An. Post.* II 16, 98b2–4; b25–38), he wonders whether a single effect (the fall of leaves) may perhaps be found, in spite of appearances, always to have the same cause (coagulation of sap) without exception, and whether a given cause may always have the same effect. But this attempt to banish certain exceptions is not generalised, as will be argued in Chapter Three.[42]

[41] Jonathan Barnes (27.1) 1969, esp. 136 of the original. H. H. Joachim, *Aristotle on Coming-to-be and Passing-away,* Oxford 1922, xxvii–xxviii.
[42] For the purposes of his syllogistic science, Aristotle is keen in the *Posterior Analytics* to find causes which always have the same effect. But it will be argued in Chapter Three

(vi) It would seem almost impossible to construe Aristotle as allowing that accidents conform to necessary laws, in view of his repeatedly citing them in *Metaph.* vi 3 and xi 8, to show that not everything happens of necessity. Indeed, Ross feels obliged to regard these passages as creating an inconsistency. None the less, Richard Loening[43] has offered to explain the passages away. He suggests that Aristotle is only denying that there is a necessity *in abstracto* for creditors' visits to the market place to coincide with debtors' visits. This would be compatible with any given coincidence of visits being necessitated. But if this were all Aristotle was saying, it would become unintelligible why he should deny (1027b12–14) that some particular event has a cause. And it would be incomprehensible why he should fear (1027a30–1) that Loening's kind of *in abstracto* necessity would obtain, but for the existence of accidents in the causal chain.

(vii) Lastly, a misunderstanding might arise over the distinction between absolute and relative necessity. I have suggested that in *Metaph.* vi 3 he is accepting a relative necessity, while denying an absolute one. It might already have occurred to someone that Aristotle was denying only an absolute necessity. And then, if he understood the absolute-relative distinction in the wrong way, he might conclude that Aristotle was conceding determinism. It will help to dispel this impression, if I say how Aristotle uses the distinction between absolute and relative necessity.

The term he uses for absolute necessity is necessity *haplōs*. It could more accurately be rendered as necessity *without qualification*, while relative necessity is a *qualified* necessity. The qualification in question will be apparent from the context, and will differ from one context to another. There are two main ways in which necessity may be qualified. (a) Sometimes he distinguishes what is necessary, if a certain goal is to be achieved, from what is necessary without this particular teleological qualification.[44] (b) Sometimes he distinguishes the necessity of a conclusion's being true, if certain premises are true, from the unqualified necessity of a proposition's being true.[45] Once (*PA* 677a17) he compares this qualified necessity of a conclusion's being true with the necessity of bile being produced *if* there is a liver.

There is a disagreement whether a third qualification is introduced in *Int.* 9. At 19a23–6, Aristotle says that what is, is necessary when it is, but that we cannot drop the qualification 'when it is', and say that all

---

that he does not in the end claim that this is always a feature of causes. He does not even decide firmly that it is a feature of the example he cites here.

The other suggestion, that a single effect always has the same cause, is qualified at ii 17, 99b4–7; longevity may have one cause in one species, and a different cause in another.

[43] Richard Loening, ch. 18 of (1.2).

[44] *Phys.* ii 9; *GC* ii 11; *PA* i 1, 639b21 – 640a9, 642a1–13.

[45] *An. Pr.* i 10, 30b31–40; *An. Post.* ii 5, 91b14–17; ii 11, 94a21–2; cf. *Cael.* i 12, 281b3–25; *SE* 4, 166a23–31.

that is, is necessary. Traditionally, this has been taken to be the same qualification as that in (b): it is necessary that *if* a thing is, then it is.[46] But the use of the word 'when' may marginally favour a suggestion made at one time by Hintikka,[47] that Aristotle is referring to the irrevocability of the present and past. The point would then be that we can say of all that is that it is necessary when it is present or past, but that we cannot say of all that is that it is necessary without this qualification.

In our chapter, *Metaph*. VI 3, Aristotle does not use these terms. But if he had, he would have treated it as a case of qualified necessity that an effect is necessary *if* its cause occurs. By contrast with this, the necessity of certain particular events that are past would be unqualified. Moreover, if the cause is unqualifiedly necessary, because irrevocable, this unqualified necessity will be imparted to the effect. According to this interpretation, the determinist's necessity of future events is an *unqualified* one.

Three objections might be raised. First, is it not a qualification that past events are necessary *now*, rather than *all along*? I would reply that although Aristotle treats 'when it is' as a relevant qualification (*Int*. 19a23–6), I do not know of his so treating 'now'. A second objection would be that the necessity of future events is a *derived* necessity, since the future events are necessary *because* the past causes are. If the necessity is *derived*, does this not mean that it is *qualified*? Aristotle discusses derived necessity in *Metaph*. v 5, 1015b9–15. But he does not treat it as *qualified*. Although the word *haplous* appears in these lines, it is used in a quite different sense, and has to do with simplicity, not with the absence or presence of qualifications. In fact, Aristotle reserves the idea of qualified necessity for what is necessary *if* so-and-so, or *when* so-and-so, and does not apply it to what is necessary *because* so-and-so. A third objection might be based on the thought that Aristotle reserves the idea of unqualified necessity for one particular kind of case, namely, for the necessity associated with God. But in fact what he counts as unqualified necessity covers a wide range of cases and varies according to the qualification implied in the context. If the word *haplous* has some special connexion with God as *opposed* to other things, this is again in the different sense of simplicity.[48]

It should now be possible to forestall the misunderstanding that was

---

[46] This is the view of the earliest extant commentaries on *Int*.: Ammonius C.I.A.G. 153, and Boethius, 1st commentary 122, 2nd commentary 241–3, ed. Meiser. Alexander of Aphrodisias agrees in his still earlier commentary on *An. Pr. CIAG*. 140,32 – 141,3. It is also the view taken by Leibniz, *Theodicy* §§53 and 132; M. Kneale, in (31.22) 1962, 92; S. Mansion (27.3) 1946 (see p. 317 of 2nd edition, 1976); H. R. Patch (12.3).

[47] Jaakko Hintikka (1.3), 1973, ch. 8, revised from *Philosophical Review* 73, 1964, 461–92. Elsewhere, Hintikka construes the passage differently.

[48] Because God is simple, there is no more than one state possible for him, and so his state is necessary (*Metaph*. v 5, 1015b12; XII 7, 1072b8–13).

expressed in terms of absolute and relative necessity. The insight is correct that in *Metaph*. vi 3, Aristotle is only denying an absolute necessity, while conceding a relative one. But this does not mean that he is conceding the determinist's necessity-of-future-events-because-of-past-causes. On the contrary, the insight that Aristotle is denying an absolute necessity is correct just because the determinist's necessity is an absolute one.

There are three passages to be discussed in Chapter Nine (*GC* ii 11, *PA* i 1, *Phys*. ii 9), where he takes things further. Most events have no kind of necessity other than the relative necessity of kind (a) – necessity if some goal is to be achieved. This would make Aristotle's disagreement with the determinist still sharper, if he stuck to it; but, as we shall see, he does not firmly do so.

Objections to the claim that Aristotle denies that coincidences are caused

I have so far concentrated on objections to my suggestion that for Aristotle coincidences are not necessitated. But there may also be objections to my claim that he regards them as uncaused.

(i) Under the heading 'Chance does not exclude causation' Jaakko Hintikka cites *Phys*. ii 4, 196a13.[49] Here Aristotle agrees with certain of his predecessors that one can refer any lucky accident to some cause. This is one of the ideas that we are told comes from Democritus. But, as Hintikka acknowledges, the passage is a preliminary one in which Aristotle is collecting earlier opinions, without yet fully showing his hand. This is his normal dialectical method. He is not yet committing himself on the question of whether the cause is a cause of going to the market place, or a cause of meeting the debtor, and, if the latter, whether it is only an accidental cause, and whether in such a case an accidental cause is a cause.

(ii) James Bogen[50] cites *Phys*. ii 6, 198a6–13 as showing that what is accidentally caused always has a cause. But I do not think that Aristotle implies more than that, if meeting the debtor has an accidental cause, something *else* – going to the market – is caused. His point is merely that accidental causes are not prior to, but presuppose, non-accidental causes.

(iii) It is possible to be misled by passages in which Aristotle associates chance with cause, if one does not consider whether or not he means the cause in question to be *accidental*. At *Phys*. ii 6, 198a2–3, for example, Aristotle counts chance as an efficient, rather than a final, formal, or material cause. He cannot be expected to be forever repeating the point he has so recently made that, whichever of these kinds it belongs to, it is still an *accidental* cause. Hintikka cites two passages in which, so I have argued, there actually are signs that Aristotle is thinking of accidental cause.[51] Thus at *Phys*. ii 5, 197a15–18, he is

[49] J. Hintikka (1.4) 111–13.   [50] James Bogen, loc. cit.   [51] J. Hintikka, loc. cit.

illustrating the point that chance is an *accidental* cause (197a13). And at *Metaph.* v 30, 1025a26–9, he denies that the coincidence of getting to Aegina can have gone through a 'process' of coming about (i.e. can have had a cause), so long as we take it for what it is (*hēi auto*). In both passages, the causes which he is willing to ascribe to accidents are called 'indefinite' or 'infinite'. Hintikka interprets the meaning of this differently from myself, but it would presumably be agreed that indefiniteness and infinitude are made a mark of accidental cause at *Phys.* ii 5, 196b24–9. And we are in any case told that accidents have only accidental causes (*Metaph.* vi 2, 1027a7–8: cf. xi 8, 1065a6–8; *Phys.* ii 5).

(iv) There is a passage where Ross and Barnes see Aristotle as implying that every event (Barnes), or everything that exists (Ross) has a cause.[52] Both, however, allow that he does not remain consistent on the point, and Barnes cites as an instance of inconsistency Aristotle's view that chance events lack a cause.

The passage is *An. Post.* ii 2, where Aristotle says that to seek whether something exists, or is the case, is to seek whether there is some *explanation* of its existing or being the case. Aristotle's idea is that there is no such thing as lunar eclipse, unless there is some unifying cause of it. To take a modern example, doctors might well come to say that there was no such thing as cancer, if they came to think that the diseases previously labelled cancer were entirely disparate in their causal origins.[53]

I doubt, however, if any conclusion can be drawn about coincidences. For Aristotle probably does not mean to extend his claim to non-scientific subject matters. Now his scientist is not concerned with *particular* events, but only with *kinds* of event. Thus, contrary to some translations, at 90a3, Aristotle would be envisaging someone who asks whether the moon is liable to eclipse, not whether it is *now* eclipsed, or *now* waning. And at 90a4–5, the person would be asking whether there is such a thing as night, not whether it is *now* night. It is, in any case, explicitly said that the scientist is not concerned with coincidences (*Metaph.* vi 2; cf. *An. Post.* i 6, 75a18–27). So we need not suppose that Aristotle would extend to coincidences the idea that whatever exists, or is the case, has an explanation.

Further, it is doubtful in what sense coincidences should be said to have existence or to be events. According to *Metaph.* vi 2 (1026b12–24), coincidences do not exist in the full sense, and do not come into being through a process like ordinary events.

It is not even clear that Aristotle remains consistent within the scientific context, in his claim that to ask whether something exists is to

---

[52] W. D. Ross, *Aristotle's Prior and Posterior Analytics*, Oxford 1949, 611: J. Barnes (27.4) 196. Ross's commentary is a classic, and requires no further commendation. But I should like to say, in advance of review notices, how valuable I have found Barnes' commentary.

[53] The thought is well explained by J. L. Ackrill, in his forthcoming contribution to (27.6).

ask whether there is an *explanation* of its existence. For in *An. Post.* II 9, he suggests that the primitive terms of a science, for example, the unit in arithmetic, must be postulated as existing, even though their existence cannot be explained by reference to something else.

(v) There might be other reasons for expecting Aristotle to say that every event or state of affairs has a cause. For one thing, he inherits from Plato[54] the idea that whatever goes through a process of coming into being has a cause. Indeed, he cites it in the very chapter that concerns us, as well as elsewhere (*Metaph.* VI 3, 1027a31–2; VII 7, 1032a13–14). But the principle is inapplicable to accidental conjunctions, for these do not (VI 2, 1026b22–4; VI 3, 1027a29–30) go through a *process* of coming into being.

(vi) Another causal principle inherited from Plato[55] is that whatever is moved is moved by something (*Phys.* VII 1, 241b34 – 242a49; VIII 4 throughout; *Cael.* II 6, 288a27). The principle is used in proving the existence of a divine Unmoved Mover. But as applied to coincidences, it need only mean that something moves the victim to go to the well at 2, and something else moves the ruffians to go to the well at 2. There need not be a cause that moves them to go to the well simultaneously.

(vii) Finally, Aristotle sometimes appears to have considerable sympathy for the principle of sufficient reason. In *Phys.* VIII 1, he argues against various pre-Socratic cosmologies that motion, and equally change from the rest to motion, must have a cause (251a23–8; b5–10; 252a11–19; 252a32 – b5). And in *Cael.* I 12, he argues the same for a change from existing to not existing, or vice-versa (283a11). Moreover, the cause must explain why the switch to motion or to non-existence occurred just when it did. None the less, this is quite compatible with denying that accidents have a cause: some things call for explanation, others do not.

Resumé

To recapitulate, Aristotle denies that every state of affairs has a cause: coincidences do not. And the link to which he draws attention between cause and explanation makes this plausible. On the other hand, he does not show how to justify his denial that coincidences are necessitated. The discussion brings out that something can be necessitated without being caused, and can be predicted or deduced on the basis of laws without being explained.

[54] Plato *Timaeus* 28A, *Philebus* 26E.

[55] Plato *Timaeus* 57E, implied by *Laws* X 894Bff. When Aristotle finally decides that self-motion is impossible (*Phys.* VII 1, 241b37 – 242a49; VIII 4; VIII5, 257a33 – 258b9), he refines Plato's principle, so that it becomes: whatever is moved is moved by something *else*. For Aristotle's gradual departure from Plato's idea of self-motion, see W. K. C. Guthrie's introduction to the Loeb edition of *On the Heavens* (*Cael.*) Cambridge Mass. 1960.

CHAPTER TWO

Is Cause related to Necessitation or to Explanation?

Is what is caused or explained necessitated?

In the last chapter, it was argued that some things may be necessitated and yet not caused. I shall now argue that some things may be caused without being necessitated. Perhaps some effects are necessitated and others not. If this is true, it has both historical and philosophical significance.

It has historical implications for Ross's claim that in certain contexts Aristotle postulates 'fresh starts'. He cites *Int.* 9, *GC* II 11 and he speaks in similar vein of *NE* III 5.[1] This contrasts with the view he took about Aristotle's treatment of accidents, namely, that it normally involved no breach of necessity.

But if Ross detects 'fresh starts', we must ask whether he means that causation is being denied, as the term might seem to suggest, or only necessitation, or whether both are being denied. Ross does not distinguish,[2] but I believe that in *Int.* 9, *GC* II 11, and *NE* III, Aristotle is only denying necessitation, and that this does not logically commit him to denying causation.

The claim that what is caused need not be necessitated, and the related claim that what is explained need not be necessitated, are philosophically significant, because, if true, they free us from one of the determinist's most ancient and powerful arguments – the argument that if events are not necessitated, they must be uncaused, inexplicable, and hence mysterious.[3] We have already seen that the charge of mysteriousness was levelled against Epicurus' swerve of atoms. And we

[1] W. D. Ross, *Aristotle's Metaphysics*, vol. 1, Oxford 1924, lxxxi, speaks of 'fresh starts' in connexion with *Int.* 9 and *GC* II 11. In *Aristotle*, London 1923, ch. 7 (Meridian Books edition, 1959, 196), he cites *NE* III 5 as the place where Aristotle comes closest, though he does not go all the way, towards postulating free will.

[2] Ross speaks without distinction of a 'breach in the causal nexus', a 'fresh start' (*Metaphysics*, lxxxi) and of a 'breach of necessity' (*Aristotle's Physics*, Oxford 1936, note *ad* II 5, 196b10–17).

[3] The accusation of postulating causeless motion was taken very seriously in antiquity. See Chapters Three and Four. The most recent example of the deterministic move from 'unnecessitated' to 'inexplicable' is in Ted Honderich, 'Causes and causal circumstances as necessitating', *Proceedings of the Aristotelian Society* 78, 1977–8, 76–7.

have noticed how Aristotle could rebut the charge that his accidents were mysterious: that they should be inexplicable is only to be expected and does not make a mystery of them. However, one could not plausibly concede that other kinds of occurrence (say, human decisions) were uncaused and inexplicable, without making them mysterious. It becomes important therefore whether, in claiming that they were not necessitated, we would be implying that they were uncaused and inexplicable. This question goes to the heart of causal determinism.

The determinist draws a further conclusion, equally ancient, from his claim that decisions would be inexplicable. There would then be no moral responsibility, for the agent cannot be praised or blamed for something inexplicable.[4]

In a highly original lecture, G. E. M. Anscombe has argued that events may be caused without being necessitated.[5] Though Anscombe's voice was not a lone one,[6] she was opposing a widespread philosophical tradition, going back at least to the Stoics.[7] Many had been prepared to admit that a cause was not *on its own* a sufficient (i.e. a necessitating) condition. But they had supposed that it would at least be *part* of some sufficient conditions, so that the effect would be necessitated.[8]

The related view that an explanation necessitates the thing explained also has a long pedigree. It is expressed in Plato's *Phaedo*, and a logical necessitation is still postulated by the most widely received account of explanation, the covering law theory.[9] In this chapter, I shall introduce an alternative viewpoint advocated by M. Scriven.

Anscombe took an example originally devised by the physicist A. H.

---

[4] For the ancient evidence, see Alexander of Aphrodisias, *De Fato* 35–7. For modern variants of this argument, see Hume (2.3) 1739, book II, part III, section 2; R. E. Hobart (30.3) 1934; A. J. Ayer, 'Freedom and necessity', *Polemic* 5, 1946 (repr. in his *Philosophical Essays*, London 1954); P. H. Nowell–Smith, 'Freewill and moral responsibility', *Mind* 57, 1948; Moritz Schlick (30.2) 1939.

[5] G. E. M. Anscombe (2.9) 1971.

[6] In the same year, Michael Scriven came out on the same side in 'The logic of cause', *Theory and Decision* 2, 1971, 49–66 (thus retracting his earlier view in his review of E. Nagel's *The Structure of Science* in (6.3) esp. 407). So also did Raymond Martin at about the same time, in 'The sufficiency thesis', *Philosophical Studies* 23, 1972, 205–11, and F. Dretske and A. Snyder in 'Causal irregularity', *Philosophy of Science* 39, 1972, 69–71. See also M. Audi, *The Interpretation of Quantum Mechanics*, Chicago 1973, 86–9, and John Watkins, who develops some thoughts of Popper's, in 'Three views concerning human freedom', in R. S. Peters (ed.), *Nature and Conduct*, Royal Institute of Philosophy Lectures VIII, London 1975, 213. At a much earlier date, Mario Bunge had sketched an example like Anscombe's in passing in (2.2) 1959, 14–15. A similar view based on developments in physics, but without a detailed example, was offered by Max Born, *Natural Philosophy of Cause and Chance*, Oxford 1949, chs 1 and 2; M. Capek, 'The doctrine of necessity re-examined', *Review of Metaphysics* 5, 1951–2, 50. In some of the examples offered, it is hard to be sure whether the thing that is unnecessitated is the very same thing as that which is caused. See, e.g., Watkins, although he may intend nothing to the contrary, since he talks of being 'influenced' rather than of being 'caused'.

[7] For documentation of this view, see below.

[8] For J. L. Mackie's conversion from this view, see below.

[9] For documentation, see next chapter.

Compton, and often repeated in the scientific literature.[10] And she put it
to a new use, in order to show that what is caused need not be necessitated. I shall defend her example from some objections, including those
arising from the usual theories of explanation. And then, diverging
from her view,[11] I shall apply the conclusion to the case of human
conduct, arguing that it too can be caused without being necessitated.

In the scientific example, a lump of radioactive material is placed
near a bomb, in such a way that if an electron is emitted and hits the
triggering device, the bomb will explode. According to most quantum
physicists, the rate and route of radioactive emission is undetermined,
and it is therefore undetermined whether an electron will hit the
trigger.

If this example seems artificial, I suspect that more natural ones could
be described. The arrival of an electron in a vital organ might set off a
chain reaction, which damaged a man's health. Or, if so large an effect
could not be produced directly, then the arrival of an electron might at
least produce a mutation in a gene. And mutations in genes can eventually affect the kind of human offspring produced in future generations,
or the kinds of virus which evolve to attack mankind.

For the purposes of the argument it is not actually necessary to appeal
to large-scale effects such as explosions, failures of health, viral epi-
demics, or the evolution of the species. These merely add to the interest.
It suffices to consider as our undetermined effect the arrival of an
electron at a given point, whether this has large-scale consequences or
not.

What does require care is selecting the right point in the story as an
instance of an unnecessitated effect. We can suppose that a laboratory
technician carelessly leaves out a small lump of radioactive material on
a laboratory bench. And we may then say that the fact of this material
being left out is the cause of an electron reaching the trigger. The latter
will be an unnecessitated effect, provided that the route taken by the
electron is undetermined up to the point of arrival. (If it becomes determined at some earlier point, P, we can simply consider as our unnecessitated effect the arrival of the electron at P.)

Care in choosing the right point in the story will avoid objections
along the following lines. The decay of a particular atom at a particular
instant is admittedly not necessitated, but then it is not caused either.

---

[10] Anscombe cites Richard Feynman, who gave the example in (15.2), a series of lectures
delivered at Cornell University, 1965, 147. The example had earlier been given, along
with others, by A. H. Compton, in (15.1) 1935, 48–52. It is repeated by R. G. Swinburne in
'Physical determinism', in *Knowledge and Necessity, Royal Institute of Philosophy Lectures* III, 1968–9, ed. G. N. A. Vesey, London 1970, 168. For a different purpose, the
physicist Erwin Schrödinger gave a similar example of a cat which may or may not be
electrocuted, according to the undetermined path taken by a particle.

[11] I believe she would reject the suggestion that desires and beliefs cause actions. See,
e.g., p. 25 of her inaugural lecture, and her *Intention*, Oxford 1957.

Conversely, the explosion of the bomb is caused all right by the arrival of the electron, but is also necessitated by that arrival. These challenges to find something that is both caused and yet unnecessitated can be met by selecting the arrival of the electron.

A second objection that can also be met appeals to the possibility that current theories of quantum physics may be proved wrong. But in fact the appeal to a theory currently supported by scientists is only for rhetorical effect. What matters in the above argument is that if we *believe* something to be unnecessitated we do not have to withdraw our supposition that it is caused. This is enough to show that being caused does not *imply* being necessitated, whatever may come to be thought about the particular example used. Later in connexion with human conduct, I shall draw attention to other possible examples, without seeking the support of any scientific theory.

A third objection might be addressed to me *ad hominem*. I have suggested that there is a relationship, perhaps a subtle one, between cause and explanation. And, it may be argued, there is no *explanation* of why an electron hit the trigger, if nothing guaranteed that it would. Can there then be a cause?

In order to reply to this, it is necessary to observe that explanation is relative to the kind of question that needs to be answered. When someone asks for an explanation, he often (not always)[12] has a contrast in mind. He may want one thing explained *in face of* another. This view has been admirably expounded and defended over the years by Michael Scriven.[13] The questioner may want us to explain why an electron hit the trigger, in face of the fact that this amount of material, exposed for this amount of time, would not always irradiate a similarly placed mechanism. If this is the question, there is no answer. On the other hand, the questioner may want us to explain why an electron hit the trigger, in face of the fact that in other rooms, and in this room at other times, levels of radiation are normally zero. In that case, it is a perfectly good explanation to point out that the radioactive material was left out on the bench. That made the difference between the safe rooms that he has in mind and the dangerous one. It distorts the situation to say that there is no explanation of why an electron hit the

[12] Not always: a man might want to learn the explanation of your behaviour and yet find it unsurprising and even to be expected. He might feel that *anyone* would act that way, and yet want to know which of the possible reasons for so acting was your reason. Cases like this are discussed by Sylvain Bromberger, 'Why questions', in *Mind and Cosmos: Essays in Contemporary Science and Philosophy*, vol. 3 in the University of Pittsburgh series in the Philosophy of Science, ed. Kolodny (reprinted in Baruch Brody, ed., *Readings in the Philosophy of Science*, Englewood Cliffs N.J. 1970). I am grateful to G. A. Cohen for drawing my attention to this kind of case.

[13] M. Scriven talks of a 'contrast class', where I have used the phrase 'in face of': review of E. Nagel's *The Structure of Science*, in (6.3) 1964. See also M. Scriven, 'Explanations, predictions and laws', in (6.2) 1962. On cause, however, as opposed to explanation, Scriven did not at that time take the view I am advocating.

trigger. It is only in relation to *certain* questions that an explanation is unavailable.[14]

There may still be a feeling that the explanation is not *complete*. But whether an explanation is complete depends on the question it is meant to answer. Scriven compares how directions to the public library can be complete, without giving the spatial coordinates of every intervening molecule of air, just so long as the directions are geared to the needs of the questioner.[15] If the question is 'Why this room, and not others?', the explanation is complete. And in this case, the complete explanation does not *guarantee* the thing to be explained – the electron's hitting the trigger. In fact, the presence of radioactive material might explain the electron's arrival, even if it would be positively *rare* for that amount of radioactive material, in that amount of time, and in those circumstances, to irradiate a mechanism so placed.

If Chapter One suggested that guarantee by covering laws was not sufficient to provide explanation, the present discussion suggests that it is not necessary either.

Once it has been admitted in one area, that of physics and biology, that it is at least conceivable, and possibly true, that some things are caused without being necessitated, the question arises whether this may not sometimes (not always) be the case in other areas too. In medicine, for example, might catching a cold sometimes be caused without being necessitated? One area of special interest is that of human conduct. Sometimes the case for and against a decision seems equally balanced, but the decision cannot be delayed. We can imagine that a minister of the Crown decides, under these circumstances, to declare some terrorist organisation illegal. If the case for and against really seemed to him equally balanced, we can imagine that, given a few more hours in which to decide, he would have decided the other way, without, however, any new factor having intervened to tip the scales. A determinst would say that there had to be some new factor; but this is a declaration of faith, rather than something which can be proved or disproved. If we believe that the decision could have gone the other way without any difference of factor, does this mean the decision was inexplicable? Admittedly, we could not explain why, in the face of the one set of considerations, he preferred the other. But none the less in the face of other matters, e.g. that no organisations had previously been banned, the decision may well be explicable by pointing to the case, as he saw it, in favour of banning. A more common situation is that in which the case for and against a decision does not seem equally balanced. The case for

---

[14] If the bomb required twenty units of radiation rather than one to set it off, then there would be a further pair of contrasts that a questioner could have in mind: 'Why did we get twenty units rather than nineteen?' (unanswerable). 'Why did we get twenty rather than none?'

[15] Scriven (6.2) 1962, 92–3.

attending some instructive lecture may seem overwhelming, and nine times out of ten in such circumstances a man may act accordingly. But when he does so, we may still feel that his action is not necessitated, just because the tenth time he does not act accordingly, and this not because of some new rival temptation or force. Of course, the determinist will hold that there must be some new rival force; but again this is an expression of faith, rather than a matter for proof or disproof.

If we believe that the tenth time the man might have failed to act, without a new rival force intervening, does this make his action on the other nine occasions inexplicable? No; it can be explained by reference to the case as he saw it. We need not even allow that the man's failure to act on the tenth occasion was inexplicable, so long as there was some disincentive present (say, the effort required) on each of the ten occasions. We can then explain his inaction on the tenth by reference to that disincentive. What admittedly cannot be explained is his succumbing to the disincentive on the tenth occasion *in face of* the fact that he did not on the other nine, or conversely his acting on the other nine occasions, *in face of* the fact that he did not on the tenth. But then ought we to expect that there will be an explanation available corresponding to every contrast that we care to choose?

It may be protested that the desire which wins on any occasion must be the 'stronger' one, and that this will preserve the view that the action which is caused is necessitated. But what does 'stronger' mean? If it means 'winning', we have only the tautology that the winning desire wins, and this tautology will not support any view. On the other hand, if 'stronger' means 'felt as more intense' or 'more approved' or 'thought more important', it just does not seem to be true that the stronger desire always wins, or even that one desire is always stronger. The assumption that the desire which is more approved always wins makes it a puzzle how one can knowingly give in to temptation, but the sad fact is that one can.[16]

The idea I have been attacking, that what is caused is necessitated, featured also in ancient discussions of determinism. The deterministic Stoics held that the same circumstances necessitate the same sequel; and they charged that, if their opponents denied this, they would be denying causation. They also produced the moral argument, that if their opponents denied fate, they would be denying moral responsibility. The

---

[16] Another ambiguous notion that creates trouble here is that of wanting 'more'. Davidson seeks to show that there is a *prima facie* puzzle about how weakness of will is possible by arguing as follows. 'If an agent judges that it would be better to do *x* than to do *y*, then he wants to do *x* more than he wants to do *y*. If an agent wants to do *x* more than he wants to do *y*, and he believes himself free to do either *x* or *y*, then he will intentionally do *x* if he does either *x* or *y* intentionally.' (Donald Davidson, 'How is weakness of the will possible?' in J. Feinberg, ed., *Moral Concepts*, Oxford 1969.) The first claim is acceptable, if the 'more' want is the more *approved* want, the second, if it is the *winning* want. But is there any *single* sense of 'more' in relation to which both claims are true?

Stoic charge and ancient attempts to reply will be discussed in Chapters Three and Four. The attempt to discover unnecessitated causes, it will appear, is not new. What is new is a more effective argument for showing that they are possible.

Implications for causal determinism

The argument so far has implications for causal determinism. For it means that if some of our decisions are not necessitated, it by no means follows that they are uncaused or inexplicable. If this is correct, it should answer the causal determinist's argument that, if some of our decisions are not necessary in advance, they will be inexplicable and mysterious happenings for which we cannot be held responsible. The answer suggested here is that from our decisions being unnecessitated it would not follow that they were inexplicable, or uncaused.

This reply is distinct from the one that has been commonest in recent literature. For it is often conceded to the determinist that decisions do not have causes. And it is insisted instead that decisions have *reasons*, such as desires and beliefs, and that reasons are not causes.[17] I shall be taking a more liberal view than is usually taken of what a cause is. And this will remove some of the grounds for denying that desires and beliefs can be causes of action. Many grounds have been offered in the literature, and I cannot consider them all here.[18] But one objection is merely that desires and beliefs do not conform to the principle of same cause – same effect. And I have already dissented from that principle with the example of radioactive material.

The above reflections have implications not only for the common charge against the indeterminist – that he renders decisions inexplicable – but also for some of the premises that are typically used for establishing the determinist's case. For we have been led to doubt the premises that every state of affairs has a cause (Chapter One) and that whatever is caused is necessitated (Chapter Two).

Even these two premises together would not be enough to yield the determinist's view that whatever happens is necessary *in advance*. To obtain that result, he may appeal to the idea of a *sequence* of causes: each state of affairs has a *prior* state of affairs as its cause. If this seems implausible, because the dent in a springy cushion is caused by the *contemporary* presence of a weight, it will suffice if in any causal chain a *proportion* of the causes are prior. On the other hand, if the determinist allows that a cause is only a *part* of some necessitating conditions, he

[17] That reasons cannot be causes is a widespread view, perhaps most fully argued by A. I. Melden, *Free Action*, London 1961.

[18] For a good statement of other grounds and replies to them, see Donald Davidson, 'Actions, reasons and causes', *Journal of Philosophy* 60, 1963, 685–70, reprinted in A. R. White (ed.), *The Philosophy of Action*, Oxford 1968. He accepts, however, the principle of same cause – same effect.

will have to be willing to argue that the *complete* set of necessitating conditions commonly exists in advance of its effect.

Lukasiewicz has claimed that even this is not enough. For he argues that an infinite series of necessitating causes, with no first member, could be crammed into the infinitely divisible space of a single minute.[19] Certainly a ball progressing across a green for a minute will occupy an infinite number of positions, but I am not clear how to argue from that to a corresponding infinite chain of causes.

Other difficulties for causal determinism

These are the difficulties for the causal determinist that arise more or less directly from the discussion so far. But it is worth reviewing some of the other difficulties that he must confront. One question is whether the necessity of an individual effect is an underived necessity, and, if not, whence it is to be derived. One common view is that it is derived, at least in part, from the necessity of a law of nature. Suppose there is a law of nature that whenever conditions of kind A obtain, an effect of kind B follows. The belief that the law enjoys some kind of necessity is the belief that it is not merely to the effect that you *never* get A-conditions without B-conditions, but that you *cannot* get the first without the second.

What kind of necessity is this? Very recently, it has been suggested by some philosophers that laws of nature may enjoy a *conceptual* necessity. For if we try to imagine them different, we shall find that we can no longer individuate things and their properties.[20] But this is by no means the usual view. On the contrary, it is normally denied that laws of nature possess any *conceptual* necessity, and some philosophers would conclude from this that they have no necessity at all. But William Kneale[21] has argued that this would be to assimilate a law of nature to a mere universal accident, such as 'all mountains are non-golden'. One difference between a law of nature and a universal accident is that in accepting something as a law of nature, one is also accepting an indefinite number of *counterfactual* claims: if conditions of kind A *had* obtained in such-and-such circumstances (where it is implied that they did not), an effect of kind B would *still* have followed. This acceptance of counterfactuals reflects a belief that there is some *necessity* about the

[19] Jan Lukasiewicz's address, as Rector of Warsaw University in 1922, is translated into English from a revised version as 'On determinism', chapter 2 of *Polish Logic 1920–1939*, ed. Storrs McCall, Oxford 1967 (reprinted in *Jan Lukasiewicz, Selected Works* ed. Borkowski, Amsterdam 1970).

[20] Such a view is suggested by Hidé Ishiguro in ch. 4 of (22.7) 1972, and mentioned as a possibility, without endorsement, by Saul Kripke on p. 304 of (22.2) 1972. It is favourably treated in unpublished work by David Wiggins and Sydney Shoemaker.

[21] William Kneale, *Probability and Induction*, Oxford 1949, 73–103; and (5.2) 1950; (5.1) 1961: Kneale is supported by George Molnar, 'Kneale's argument revisited', *Philosophical Review* 78, 1969, 79–89.

law of nature linking A and B. Since the necessity is not *logical* or *conceptual*, we may call it *causal* or *physical*.[22]

Although I find Kneale's argument plausible, there are at least two problems to be mentioned. One is the difficulty of characterising the necessity in a way that brings out the justice of talking of necessity at all. One feels that the justification has something to do with the counterfactuals, with the fact that the law would still have held however much circumstances might have differed. Karl Popper has made suggestions along these lines, although he himself is sceptical about the talk of necessity.[23] His basic idea is that a law of nature would not be changed by any changes, however massive, in 'initial conditions', where initial conditions are particular states of affairs. This idea could be used, although it is not so used by Popper, to justify the talk of necessity. For although a law of nature is not logically incapable of being otherwise, it would take more than a change in initial conditions to make it otherwise. Contrast the absence of golden mountains: this would be made otherwise *either* by suitable differences in initial conditions, *or* by suitable differences in laws of nature.

Unfortunately, subsequent criticism of Popper's idea has shown that matters are not so simple.[24] For we need to ask whether it would count as a change in initial conditions, if we accelerated a particle up to twice the speed of light. Causally impossible changes of initial conditions, such as this, would surely after all involve changes in laws of nature. Popper's basic idea should therefore be reformulated so as to say that a law of nature would not be changed by any *causally possible* changes of initial conditions. And this emendation, though desirable in itself, would be unlikely to satisfy someone who doubted the justice of talking of causal *necessity*. For such a person would also doubt whether any changes could be called causally *impossible*. Perhaps the most we could say to such a person is that at any rate the circumstances under which a law of nature would fail to hold are immensely more restricted than those under which a universal accident would fail to hold.

The second problem is this: the case for treating laws of nature as causally necessary has rested on contrasting them with universal accidents which are not necessary. Yet a determinist would put accidents on the same footing as laws of nature, since he wants to claim that everything is equally necessary. He, therefore, will need to find some *independent* reason for saying that laws of nature are causally necessary.

Suppose he succeeds in establishing, by independent argument, the

[22] I shall interchange talk of 'causal' and of 'physical' necessity. But I shall reserve the name 'natural necessity' for a rather different concept of Aristotle's, for which see Chapter Thirteen.

[23] Karl Popper (5.3) 1960. On p. 438, Popper is hesitant about talking of necessity at all.

[24] The criticism was made by G. C. Nerlich and W. A. Suchting in (5.5) 1967. Popper replied in (5.4) in the same volume and added a note to p. 441 of the 1968 edition of *The Logic of Scientific Discovery*. Suchting replied in (5.6) 1969.

necessity of our law, that when conditions of kind A obtain, an effect of kind B follows. In that case, once conditions of kind A obtain, he can regard an individual effect of kind B as enjoying a derivative necessity. The necessity may be viewed as merely relative: the effect is necessary, *given* the occurrence of such conditions. And this is the more usual view. But if he takes into account that once the conditions have occurred they too enjoy a kind of necessity, since they will be irrevocable, he can regard the effect as absolutely, not just relatively, necessary. For the (absolute) necessity of the conditions will be transferred via the necessary law of nature to the effect.

But so far what is necessary is not the effect with its full range of characteristics, but merely an effect answering to the isolated description 'B'. To overcome this deficiency, the determinist may suggest that we should take into account *all* the laws of nature coupled with *all* the infinitely many states of affairs obtaining in the universe at some earlier moment. Taken together these would supposedly render necessary an effect exactly matching the one that actually occurs.

The appeal to the totality of laws and of initial conditions at some earlier moment brings us closer to the classic formulation of causal determinism by Laplace.[25] But it was not suggested by Laplace, nor is it inherently plausible, that there are necessary laws of nature pertaining to all the social, cultural, judicial, religious and artistic states of affairs. It would be more plausible, and closer to the spirit of Laplace, to suppose that there are laws which render necessary all the *physical* states of all the *physical* particles in the universe. And it might then be argued that if all these *physical* states are necessary, so will be the social and cultural states of affairs, which are merely supervenient upon them.[26]

Many would dispute this last conditional, based, as it is, on the idea of supervenience.[27] But what is still more problematic for the determinist is the meaning of the antecedent. For what is to count as all the physical states of all the physical particles? Laplace considered only the position and momentum of Newtonian point-masses. But this is inadequate, for many other physical states are recognised by science, and every year new sub-atomic particles are being thought of and new states postulated

[25] Pierre Simon, Marquis de Laplace, *Essai philosophique sur les probabilités,* Paris 1814, translated by Truscott and Emory, London and New York 1902, ch 2.

[26] For a related set of ideas, see the interesting paper of Jim Hopkins, 'Wittgenstein and physicalism', *Proceedings of the Aristotelian Society* 75, 1974–5, 121–46. If the claim of supervenience is to be plausible, it is important to consider physical states throughout the universe, and not just in a limited spatio-temporal region. For within the confines of a single human body, the same sequence of physical states could equally represent an act of murder, a surgical operation, or a piece of play acting.

[27] Descartes, for one, would think mental states logically independent of physical states. From a different perspective, Donald Davidson would hold that the same physical situation could legitimately be interpreted in different ways as representing different mental events (2.8) 1970.

for them. Nor are all these other physical states of other particles controlled by the position and momentum of Newtonian point-masses.[28]

One desperate expedient would be to take account of everything that anybody might call a physical state of a physical particle. But it would then become increasingly doubtful that there would be laws to match all these states.

I have so far been assuming that the determinist would derive the necessity of individual events from that of laws. But if the necessity were derived from something else, or treated as underived, many of the same problems would still have to be faced. It would still have to be made plausible that there was such a thing as causal necessity, and the determinist would still have to argue that for every true description of an effect it was necessary in advance that an effect of *just that* description would occur.

Moreover, the current state of physics no longer offers the encouragement that was once expected. By an ambitious extrapolation from the successes of Newtonian mechanics in the field of astronomy, Laplace was able to think of science as on the determinist's side. But the majority[29] of quantum physicists now maintain that their science actually contradicts determinism. For certain micro-events are not made necessary by anything in advance of their occurrence. Sometimes an attempt is made to admit this conclusion, but reduce its interest, by maintaining that indeterminacy at the level of micro-events will not lead to indeterminacy at the level of the large-scale events that concern us in real life.[30] But against this we have already noticed examples of a small-scale indeterminacy being amplified into a large-scale indeterminacy through radio-active material being connected to a bomb or a living organ. The scientific literature repeatedly recognises the possibility of such amplification.[31] And a particularly important example is supplied

---

[28] For a criticism of Laplace along these lines, see Ernest Nagel (4.2) 1961, 281–3. Nagel distinguishes different conceptions of physical state on pp. 285–93.

[29] This is the most widespread interpretation. But Einstein thought the appearance of indeterminacy was merely due to our ignorance, while D. Bohm has argued that the indeterminacy may be reducible at another level of investigation (*Causality and Chance in Modern Physics*, New York 1957).

[30] See, for example, Austin Farrer, *The Freedom of the Will*, London 1958, 3–4; E. Bünning, 'Sind die Organismen die mikrophysikalische Systeme?' *Erkenntis* v, 1935, 337–48; M. Schlick, 'Causality in everyday life and in recent science', *University of California Publications in Philosophy* 15, 1932, 99–126, repr. in H. Feigl and W. Sellars, *Readings in Philosophical Analysis*, New York 1949, see esp. 532.

[31] Besides the example found in Compton, Schroedinger, Feynman and Swinburne, see also: Ralph Lillie, 'Physical indeterminism and vital action', *Science* 66, 1927, 139–44; A. H. Compton (15.1) 1935, 48–52; Niels Bohr, *Atomic Theory and the Description of Nature*, Cambridge 1934, ch. 4, 117 (tr. from the Danish of 1929); Niels Bohr, 'Light and life', *Nature* 1933, 457; Walter Elsasser, *The Physical Foundation of Biology* 1958, 9; Jacques Monod (15.3) 1972, translated from the French of 1970 by A. Wainhouse; P. Jordan 'Quantenmechanik und Grund-probleme der Biologie und Psychologie', *Naturwissenschaften* xx, 815–21; P. Jordan 'Quantenphysikalische Bemerkungen zur Biologie und Psychologie', *Erkenntnis* iv, 1934, 215; M. Capek, 'The doctrine of necessity

by the biochemist Jacques Monod,[32] who maintains that the whole course of evolution is undetermined because of chance at the micro-level. By chance, he explains, he means not only the Aristotelian variety, in which two causal chains intersect, but a complete indeterminacy.[33]

None of this is intended to rule out the causal determinist's view as impossible. I do not know how to do that. But it is meant to place an onus on him to argue for his case, if he wants it to seem at all plausible. I cannot say that I think of it at the moment as having any plausibility. And I should certainly *hope* that it was false. For I believe it is determinism, that rules out moral responsibility and other things we believe in, as I shall explain in Chapter Fifteen. I believe it is a necessary, though not a sufficient, condition of our being morally responsible agents that our actions should not all along have been necessary. I do not think the indeterminacies of quantum physics help in any direct way to preserve moral responsibility. What is important is that, in the different sphere of human conduct, there should be actions which are explicable without being necessitated.

What is a cause?

If the argument at the beginning of this chapter is correct, it will rule out the two most popular definitions of cause. A cause has been thought to be (a) a sufficient (necessitating) condition of its effect (Davidson),[34] or, more commonly, *part* of some sufficient (necessitating) conditions (Mackie).[35] Hume, not accepting that there was any necessitation in the world, substituted (b) the idea of constant conjunction. If A causes B on a particular occasion, this implies that events like A are constantly conjoined with events like B.[36] Proponents of the first kind of definition, (a), sometimes talk of deterministic laws rather than constant conjunctions (Davidson.)[37] If A causes B on a particular occasion, this implies that a deterministic law relates some description of A to some description of B.

Neither of these first two suggestions, (a) and (b), holds true of our

---

re-examined', *Review of Metaphysics* 5, 1951–2, 52. There is a much earlier anticipation of the general idea of amplification in E. Boutroux, *De la contingence des lois de la nature*, Paris 1874.

[32] Jacques Monod, op. cit. 111–12 of the Fontana edition (1974).

[33] Both kinds of chance event are causeless, I believe, but Aristotle fails to show that his kind is not necessitated, if I was right in Chapter One.

[34] Donald Davidson (2.7) 697–9. In spite of holding this view, Davidson is not a determinist in the sense I have defined. For although he believes that every caused event is necessitated, he does not believe that one can take any and every true *description* of the caused event and say it was necessitated that that *description* should be applicable.

[35] J. L Mackie, 'Causes and conditions', *American Philosophical Quarterly* 2, 1965, 254–64.

[36] Hume (2.3) 1739, book I, part III, sections VI and XIV.

[37] Davidson (2.7) and (2.8).

example of radioactive causation, in which the conjunction involved, so far from being constant, might be positively rare. One author who had earlier offered a sophisticated defence of the first view subsequently acknowledged the force of Anscombe's example, and switched to the alternative idea (c) that a cause is a condition necessary (prerequisite) in the circumstances (Mackie).[38] The chief difficulty with this view is well known: it is the possibility of over-determination, that is, roughly speaking, of cases in which if one cause had not operated, another would have done so. To illustrate: suppose that, in our example of the radioactive material, a saboteur with an electron gun had lurked outside, and that he would have fired at the triggering device, if he had not seen the lump of radioactive material already in place. The cause in such cases is only a member of a *disjunction* of conditions (an *either-or* collection), the whole disjunction but no single member being necessary in the circumstances. Worse, the disjunction may be indefinitely large. And by devising a different story, we could show that a cause is not always even a member of a necessary disjunction.[39]

If none of these suggestions works, it may be held that at least (d) a cause makes its effect probable (Jevons).[40] But in our example, the arrival of the electron might have been improbable. Need the dose have become more probable than it would otherwise be, if the radioactive material had been missing? Not necessarily, for suppose the saboteur's electron gun would have been a more reliable source of radiation than the misplaced lump of material. In that case, the misplaced lump would have made the outcome *less* probable than it would otherwise have been.

I should substantiate my claim that the first two of the definitions just considered have been the most popular.[41] The idea that a cause is, or is

[38] Mackie (2.5) ch. 2, candidly expounds the problem of overdetermination and tries to meet it. He acknowledges that, on his view, the fact of a man's dying cannot be caused by the attack on him, if that attack is only one of two alternative attacks, one of which would have occurred, if the other had not. But he argues that at least one attack could still have been a necessary condition, and hence (on his view) a cause, of the man's dying *in a particular manner*. However, as Nigel Carden has pointed out to me, if the *manner* of the two planned attacks was the same, this line of defence could not be maintained, or could only be maintained in a trivial way, by counting the difference of cause as a difference of manner.

[39] Thus suppose something occasionally happens without a reason, although it normally happens only with a reason: in that case, nothing (not even a disjunction) is strictly *necessary* for its occurrence.

[40] W. S. Jevons, *The Principles of Science: A Treatise on Logic and Scientific Method*, 2nd ed., London 1877, reprinted New York 1958, p. 226. Cf. Niels Bohr, as reported by L. Rosenfeld in *Physics To-day*, 16 Oct. 1963, 52, and in *Dictionary of Scientific Biography*, ed. C. C. Gillispie, New York 1970, vol. 2, p. 250.

[41] Two valuable sources of historical information are (2.1) and (4.1). The following references are taken from: Hobbes, *Elements of Philosophy: Concerning Body* (1655) chapter 9; Spinoza, *Ethics* (1677), book I, axiom III; Kant, *Critique of Pure Reason* (1781, and edition B, 1787), book II, chapter II, section 3, 2nd Analogy (edition A 201–2, edition B 246–7); Laplace, op. cit. 1814, ch. 2; Max Born, *Natural Philosophy of Cause and Chance*, Oxford 1949, chs 1 and 2; Mackie 'Causes and conditions' Davidson (2.7) and (2.8).

part of, some necessitating conditions is attributed by Anscombe to Aristotle. I shall dispute her evidence in the next chapter, and claim that Aristotle did not make up his mind on the question. But in Chapter Four, I shall trace the idea back to the Stoics. And it can be found also in Hobbes, Spinoza, and Kant. William Wallace, who has written a history of treatments of cause, regards the heyday of this view as starting with Laplace's *Philosophical Essay on Probabilities* in 1814, which was written under the influence of Newtonian mechanics. Max Born, writing in the light of quantum theory in 1949, suggested that we should instead connect the idea of cause with that of dependence rather than with that of predictability. But none the less Mackie until recently and Davidson have continued to advocate the idea of necessitation.

Hume's idea of constant conjunction made a later start, even though it had been anticipated by a few of Hume's predecessors.[42] It none the less became perhaps the most popular account of cause among the leading philosophers of science – at least among those who continued to acknowledge that there was such a thing as cause. We can cite, for example, Mill, Ayer, Reichenbach, Braithwaite, Nagel and Hempel.[43] In the last few years, however, the constant conjunction analysis has come increasingly under attack, while the necessitation analysis has flourished.

The distinction of these two main lines of analysis, constant conjunction and necessitation, provides a chance of clearing up a possible source of confusion. Some proponents of the constant conjunction analysis do not hesitate to talk of necessary or sufficient conditions, of determinism, and of laws. But the sense they attach to these terms has to be explained in terms of constant conjunctions.[44] A necessary and sufficient condition for them is merely a condition of a kind constantly conjoined with another. Determinism is defined in terms of laws logically determining a unique state. Laws too are regarded simply as a special kind of exceptionless regularity. The concepts thus defined exclude the idea of necessity, and thus differ from the concepts I have been using. The notions of determinism, and of a necessary or sufficient condition, I take to involve the idea of necessity. And I have hitherto treated the notion of a law as including that idea as well, although I shall not always do so.

---

[42] Joseph Glanvill, *The Vanity of Dogmatizing* (1661) 189–90; *Scepsis Scientifica*(1665) 166; Malebranche, *Recherche de la Verité* (1675). See Richard Popkin, 'Joseph Glanvill: a precursor of David Hume', *Journal of the History of Ideas* 14, 1953, 292–303; Mario Bunge (2.2) 1959, 42–3. A remote source of inspiration for such theories was the ancient scepticism of Sextus Empiricus.

[43] J. S. Mill (2.4) 1843, book 3, ch. 5, sect. 2; A. J. Ayer, *Language, Truth and Logic*, London 1936, 2nd ed., p. 55; H. Reichenbach, *The Rise of Scientific Philosophy*, Berkeley and Los Angeles 1951, 157–8; R. B. Braithwaite (20.2) 1953; E. Nagel (4.2) 1961, ch. 4; C. G. Hempel (6.1) 1965.

[44] The full range of concepts is given this sense by E. Nagel in (4.2). For his account of law, see ch. 4; for his treatment of necessary and sufficient conditions p. 74; and for his definition of determinism pp. 281, 292. There are similar treatments of law in Braithwaite op. cit. and Hempel op. cit. 335–47.

If none of the definitions of cause from (a) to (d) is successful, the idea may occur to someone of disjoining the definitions and saying that a cause is what satisfies one or the other of them. But this proposal has the disadvantage of robbing us of any sense of unity in the concept of cause. Rather than looking for variations and permutations of the definitions so far canvassed, let us consider the wholly different approach made by Aristotle.

Aristotle's view of efficient cause as a particular mode of explanation

Aristotle's so-called four causes are best thought of as four modes of explanation, of which the efficient cause is closest to a cause in our sense. The others are the final cause (or purpose), the formal cause (or defining characteristics) and the material cause (or that out of which a thing is made). By an extension, the label 'material cause' can be applied to various things 'out of which' something comes, so that it too is occasionally applied to things which we should recognise as causes.[45]

The four causes are introduced as modes of explanation in the *Physics*.[46] Aristotle's words for explanation are *aitia, aition* (what is responsible, or answerable), and *to dia ti, to di' ho* (the through-what). Each of the four modes of explanation, has its own differentiating mark. The efficient cause is not *any* kind of explanation, but is that which tells us 'whence comes the origin of a change'.[47]

There is one qualification, already noted in Chapter One, to the claim that each of the four causes is a mode of explanation. Citing the efficient cause of a statue as Polyclitus is only to *point towards* an explanation of why a statue has come into existence. It will not help someone who does not know that Polyclitus is a sculptor.[48] A full account would need to introduce other qualifications, as Hart and Honoré make clear.[49]

The word 'explanation' is ambiguous in English. Instead of saying that the efficient cause *is* an explanation, I could say that it is what *provides* an explanation. Michael Frede has argued[50] that the difference between

---

[45] The efficient and material causes are cited together in the biological works at *GA* 731b21–2, 778a35 – b1. At *PA* 677a17, the liver, as a cause of bile, is described in terms appropriate to the material, not the efficient, cause (cf. *An. Post.* ii 11, 94a20–36; *Phys.* ii 3, 195a15–18).

[46] *Phys.* ii 3 (= *Metaph.* v 2) and *Phys.* ii 7.

[47] *Hothen hē archē tēs kinēseōs Phys.* ii 3 (= *Metaph.* v 2). The material cause is that *out of which* a thing comes, and which persists through the process of its coming (*Phys.* i 7, 190a21–31; ii 3, 194b23–6) and by an extension that *out of which* everlasting things (e.g. the stars) are made. Surprisingly, Anscombe uses an 'out of' formula in giving her account of causality (4.1), 7. The final cause is *that for the sake of which*, in one sense the goal, in another the beneficiary (*Phys.* ii 3; *DA* ii 4, 415b2 and 20). The formal cause is the *what it was for so-and-so to be*, in other words, the essence or defining characteristics (*Phys.* ii 3; *Metaph.* i 3, 983a26–b3; vii 7, 1032b1–2; vi 10, 1035b16, b32; viii 4, 1044a36).

[48] *Phys.* ii 3.

[49] See the qualification suggested by Hart and Honoré, noted in Chapter One.

[50] See Frede's illuminating paper, 'The Stoics on cause', forthcoming in (3.3). Originally,

the two senses of explanation was neatly marked in Plato's Greek. In the
Phaedo, the neuter adjective *aition* is used for the things which provide
an explanation, the noun *aitia* for the explanation provided. Some other
writers followed this distinction,[51] but Aristotle did not.

To define cause by saying that, to a suitably placed person, it provides
a particular mode of explanation may seem only to make more acute the
question what explanation is. What does Aristotle have to say about
this? The most popular modern account, Hempel's, connects explanation with deduction from covering laws, but we have already seen that
Aristotle rejects at least part of this account.[52] He has a great deal to say
about how various kinds of explanation work, and we shall study some
of this in Chapters Three and Ten. But he does not try to generalise, so as
to tell us what explanation is quite generally. Talking of the universal,
necessary truths studied by science, he says that to explain them we
must show that they are necessary, by deriving them from necessary
premises (*An. Post.* ɪ 6, 74b26–32), which involve essential connexions
(74b5–12). In this context, he offers us sufficient conditions for explanation. Deciduousness can be explained if it can be deduced syllogistically
from two universal premises whose middle term states the essence of
deciduousness.[53] But he does not claim that particular events have to be
explained in the same way. We shall see in the next chapter that he
thinks they can be explained by invoking regularities which hold only
for the most part.

I take it to be the chief strength of Aristotle's account that he invites us to
think of the efficient cause as what provides a particular mode of explanation. I do not want to deny that he is sometimes attracted by the ideas
found in modern accounts of cause. Indeed, we have just noticed that he
connects *some* explanations with necessity and with universal statements.
We shall see in the next chapter that he once (*Metaph.* vɪ 3) treats an
efficient cause as a sufficient condition, although elsewhere he implies
the opposite. We shall see that he also associates efficient cause explanation with probability (*Poet.* 10), and with what happens for the most
part (*Metaph.* v 30), which is closely associated with probability. But his
account differs from modern ones, in that these appeals are given some
unity, by all being connected to the fact that a cause is a particular kind
of *explanation.* It is the reference to *explanation* that goes into his
definition of the efficient cause. If some efficient causes are connected
with probability, some with necessity, some with universal statements,

Frede points out, the terms were legal. The *aition* thing would have been the guilty person,
the *aitia* the accusation *that* he did so-and-so. Plato's usage preserves some of the original
idea, since the *aitia* is still a proposition *that* something is the case, while the *aition* is an
entity like mind or bones and sinews.
    [51] Diocles of Carystus, fragment 112 in Wellmann: the *aitia* is a proposition (*logos)*
concerning the aition. But Galen explicitly says he will use *aition* and *aitia* interchange-
ably (ɪx, 458, 7 in Kühn).
    [52] In *An. Post.* ɪ 13, 78a29 – b11: see Chapter One.   [53] *An. Post.* ɪɪ 16, 98b16–24.

and some with for-the-most-part regularities, this is because such things can be *explanatory* of various different subject matters.

Of course, it would have been satisfying if he had been able to give a perfectly general account of what explanation is. Since he does not, his account of efficient cause may to that extent be considered incomplete. But it would be wrong to deny that it is illuminating. For the reference to explanation shows how the various criteria for causation offered by modern philosophers are relevant – they are relevant just insofar as they are features which in one context or another can contribute to explanation. Any incompleteness in Aristotle's account of cause will not rehabilitate the modern accounts just considered. They may have the advantage of completeness, but this is nullified if they can be shown to be erroneous. The account of cause which has aroused most interest recently dissociates cause very sharply from explanation, and plumps for laws and sufficient conditions (Davidson). But another minority account has stressed the link with explanation (Scriven; cf. Meyerson).[54]

Other aspects of Aristotle's efficient cause

This is a convenient point to explain more fully what Aristotle means by efficient cause. The efficient cause is defined by reference to change: it is that whence comes the origin of change, *hothen hē archē tēs kinēseōs*. (The simpler phrase, 'origin of change', *archē tēs kinēseōs*, can be applied to other 'causes' besides the efficient; while a variant, 'that whence the change comes', *hothen hē kinēsis,* seems to be used for the efficient cause at *Metaph.* v 4, 1014b18–20.)

Aristotle is fairly liberal in what he selects as that whence comes the origin of change.[55] Sometimes it is a substance like the sculptor as the cause of a state,[56] but sometimes it is the art of sculpting.[57] Another favourite example is a raid as the cause of a war.[58] He also cites hard work as the cause of fitness,[59] the soul as the cause of motion,[60] and the inner nature of a thing as a cause.[61] A variety of further possibilities is catalogued in *Phys.* ii 3. This liberality is, I think, a merit. Aristotle, in citing a raid, does not think it necessary, in Davidson's manner, to treat it as an event rather than a fact. What he might concede to Davidson is that an efficient cause does *involve* an event in some way. For, in his view, a thing can come into existence or begin to move, or grow, or

---

[54] D. Davidson (2.7) and (2.8); M. Scriven, 'Causation and explanation', *Nous* 9, 1975, 3–16. Scriven's remarks are, however, like mine, merely programmatic. Causation was closely connected with explanation, though also with law, by E. Meyerson, *Identity and Reality*, New York 1930 (translated from *Identité et realité*, Paris 1908), 9–10; 43–7; *De l'explication dans les sciences* vol. 1, Paris 1921, 53.

[55] This point is made also in a forthcoming paper by Julia Annas.

[56] *Phys.* ii 3, 195a34, b5–6, b26–7.   [57] *Phys.* ii 3, 195a5–8, b24.

[58] *Phys.* ii 7, 198a19; *An.Post.* ii 11, 94a36.   [59] *Phys.* ii 3, 195a9–11.

[60] *DA* ii 4, 415b21–3.   [61] *PA* i 1, 641a25–8.

change in quality, only if some prior *motion* occurs (*Phys* viii 1,251a8–b10; viii 7, 260a26–261a26; *GC* ii 10, 336a14–b17). Indeed, this would supply a reason, although it is not the stated reason, why Plato's changeless forms are repeatedly held inadequate to account for the beginning of a change. Events, then, and in particular motions, may be required for such beginnings; and efficient causes, which have already been differentiated as the source of beginnings, can be further differentiated by their dependence on prior motion. But this still allows Aristotle to designate very various kinds of entity as the efficient cause.

Aristotle's liberality in these canonical chapters is worth emphasising, because it has been denied. W. Wieland maintains that the efficient cause is normally a thing, not a process, and so also is the effect.[62] A strange restriction on effects was attributed to Aristotle in antiquity. What is caused is not a predication (*katēgorēma*), such as being built, being melted, being cut, as the Stoics thought, but an appellation (*prosēgoria*), such as a house, a ship, a cut, a burning, a melting.[63] There is no basis for this, so far as I know, in any surviving Aristotelian text.

It was the Stoics who first tried to get some order into the subject. Their standard view, though not their only one, was that every cause is a body which is a cause to a body of something being predicated of it.[64] As Frede has argued, this is less restrictive than it might seem at first, since *qualities* would be counted by the Stoics as bodies.[65] Another standard Stoic requirement, discussed by Frede, was that something can act as a cause only by doing something.[66] This makes bodies suitable candidates, but propositions unsuitable candidates, for being causes.

If Aristotle's more liberal attitude is to be regarded as one merit in his account, we can also draw attention to another. He shares Hume's interest in what distinguishes cause from effect,[67] a question that was acute for Hume, once he had related cause and effect by constant conjunction rather than by necessitation. Hume's suggestion is that the cause must precede its effect.[68] But Aristotle is aware, despite some occasional wavering,[69] that a cause may be either precedent or simultaneous.[70] In seeking another way of distinguishing cause from effect,

[62] W. Wieland, *Die aristotelische Physik*, Göttingen 1962, ch. 16, p. 226, translated in *Articles on Aristotle* vol. 1, ed. J. Barnes, M. Schofield, R. Sorabji, London 1975, 150.

[63] Sextus *Outlines* iii 14, Clement of Alexandria *Stromateis* viii 9, 26, 4. I owe these references to Frede's paper, cited above.

[64] Sextus *Against the Mathematicians* ix 211. For alternative hypotheses see Clement *Stromateis* viii 9. The Stoic restriction of causality to one kind of entity was compatible with their distinguishing many kinds of cause, as will be seen in Chapter Four: necessary and inactive, necessary and active, sufficient, intensifying, joint causes, etc. For this, see Clement *Stromateis* viii 9 and Cicero *Topics* 58–60.

[65] M. Frede, op. cit., forthcoming.

[66] Seneca *Epistles* 65, 4: the cause is *id quod facit*.

[67] *An. Post.* i 13, 78a29 – b11; ii 16, 98b4–24.

[68] Hume (2.3) 1739, book i, part iii, section 2 and 14.

[69] *An. Post.* ii 11, 94b23–6.

[70] *Phys.* ii 3, 195b16–21; *An. Post.* ii 12, 95a14–24; cf. *DA* iii 2, 426a20–6.

he actually uses an example in which they are simultaneous: lunar eclipse and the interposition of the earth between sun and moon. In insisting that the cause has a certain priority,[71] then, he does not mean temporal priority, but we shall have to consider in the next chapter whether he means an ontological or an epistemological priority. On one very natural reading, it will emerge, he means that the cause is prior in the order of understanding. This sensible view certainly ought to be taken by someone who thinks that a cause provides an *explanation* of the effect. But there is at least one complication; for sometimes, as Aristotle recognises,[72] we get cases of *reciprocal* explanation, in which the effect provides a teleological explanation of the cause. In these cases, either term can be prior in understanding, depending on the kind of explanation invoked.

Resumé

The main themes of this chapter have been that what is caused and what is explained need not be necessitated. This provides an answer to the causal determinist, but not the usual answer which concedes to him that indeterminism leaves actions without causes, while pleading that it leaves reasons intact. A different account of cause from the usual one will also be required. And Aristotle's approach of connecting it with a particular mode of explanation is recommended as at least more promising than the familiar alternatives.

[71] *An. Post.* II 16, 98b4–24; cf. I 2, 71b30; *Cat.* 12, 14b12.
[72] *Phys.* II 3, 195a8. To take an un-Aristotelian example: the presence of the heart in a species could explain the circulation of the blood by being its cause, while the circulation of the blood explained the presence of the heart by being its function.

CHAPTER THREE

Necessitation and Law in Ancient Accounts of Cause and Explanation

In modern philosophy, four concepts have been associated with each other in various ways: necessitation, law, cause and explanation. It has been thought that necessitation implies laws, and that cause and explanation are associated not so much with each other, but each with laws and necessitation. We have already encountered and criticised examples of these views in the doctrine that what is caused is necessitated, and in the doctrine that to explain something is to exhibit it as an instance of a covering law. The latter idea introduces one kind of necessitation, for it is held that the thing to be explained is logically necessitated by a set of statements which includes a covering law.

The main aim of this chapter will be to show that this whole set of ideas was not immediately self-evident to Aristotle or to the Greeks, and to trace its gradual development. Some of the interconnexions began to commend themselves sooner than others, but I shall suggest that the biggest step was taken by the Stoics. I shall start with the idea of explanation, rather than cause. And among accounts of explanation, I shall start with the covering law theory, because this has become the orthodox view, thanks largely to the exposition of Carl Hempel.[1] Later I shall consider other ways in which explanation has been thought to involve necessitation.

Explanation as necessitation through covering laws

The covering law theory distinguishes two factors in the explanation of a particular state of affairs. First, there is a statement that certain particular conditions obtain, and then there is the statement of a law that whenever such conditions obtain, so will a state of affairs like the one to be explained. The conclusion that such a state of affairs will occur can actually be *deduced* from the other two statements combined. This is the point at which necessitation enters: the premises necessitate the conclusion. Hempel does not regard either premise as being necessary

---

[1] Hempel's main papers on the subject from 1942 to 1965 are collected in 6.1 For a summary of variations on Hempel's view, see Bas C. van Fraassen, 'The pragmatics of explanation', *American Philosophical Quarterly* 14, 1977, 143–50.

on its own, since he thinks of a law not as involving necessity, but only as being a special kind of exceptionless regularity.[2]

Hempel was bold enough to extend this account of explanation outside the physical sciences, and to say that this is the form taken by explanation even in such fields as history. Explanations need not actually be presented in this form. But they must be re-expressible in this form, or they will be inadequate. Within the physical sciences, the same pattern of explanation is used for explaining laws, as well as particular states of affairs. The so-called laws of planetary motion, for example, are explained by deducing the corresponding law-statement from a statement of some more general laws of motion, coupled with statements about the particular situation of the planets. Again, a law can be explained by deducing the corresponding law-statement from two other law-statements.

Two major qualifications are introduced into the theory. First, in place of a universal law, Hempel is willing to accept in his premises a statistical law, according to which the state of affairs specified follows only with a high frequency upon the conditions specified. This qualification makes a big difference to the explanation of a particular state of affairs. It means that a statement announcing the occurrence of such a state of affairs can no longer be deduced from the other two statements combined, in the case where the law is statistical, but can only be rendered probable by them. The second qualification appears in Hempel's later publications.[3] He acknowledges that there may be examples in which the deductive pattern is not after all explanatory. But he is not able to say how the covering law theory ought to be revised in the face of this.

Deduction from universal truths not sufficient for explanation

On turning to Aristotle, someone who starts with his treatise on scientific method, the *Posterior Analytics*, may think he is being offered very much the same theory of explanation. Certainly, this has been claimed in one recent account.[4] But Baruch Brody's more careful study makes clear that Aristotle denies that the covering law pattern is enough on its own to explain.[5] Aristotle is concerned in the *Posterior Analytics* with syllogisms in which the premises explain the conclusion,[6] and in particular the middle term (the one occurring twice in the premises) explains.[7] He points out that deduction from two universal premises will not always give us an explanation. For example, if all non-twinkling

---

[2] Hempel (6.1) 335–47.   [3] Hempel (6.1) 366–75.
[4] Max Hocutt (7.3) 1974, 389.   [5] Baruch Brody (7.2) 1972.
[6] *An. Post.* i 2, 71b29 – 72a5.
[7] *An.Post.* i 6, 74b32; i 33, 89a16; i 34, 89b15; ii 2, 90a7; ii 8, 93a7–8; ii 11, 94a23, a31, a35, b7; ii 12, 95a11; ii 16, 98b10.

lights are near, and all the planets are non-twinkling lights, we can deduce that the planets are near; but we will not have *explained* their nearness. The middle term, non-twinkling lights, is not explanatory. On the other hand, if all the planets are near, and all near things are non-twinkling, we can both deduce that, and explain why, all the planets are non-twinkling.[8]

It is worth comparing also Aristotle's treatment of Democritus. In one passage, Democritus is said to have argued that no further explanation is possible of things that happen *always*.[9] In another passage, he is said to have spoken as if it is explanation enough of why something happens to say that it *always* happens.[10] And this (to use terms foreign to Democritus) looks like a particular version of the view that deduction from a covering regularity is sufficient to explain. In this guise too, Aristotle rejects the covering law theory of explanation.

Brody goes wrong, I believe, only when he specifies how Aristotle would deal with the example of the non-twinkling planets. He quotes two passages which he takes to be giving the answer that deduction from laws cannot be expected to yield an explanation, if the laws do not specify either the cause (i.e. the efficient cause) or the essence of the thing explained. In fact, I believe Aristotle is not talking about efficient cause in the first passage, but rather about explanation in general.[11] What is true is that explanation must be by one or other of the so-called four causes. As for essence, Brody is right that Aristotle's answer to the problem has something to do with that. But for Aristotle's explicit discussion we must go to a passage not cited by Brody, ɪɪ 16, 98b4–24.

An explanation is *prior* to the thing explained (cf. ɪ 2. 71b31; *Cat.* 12, 14b12). In the particular example under discussion, Aristotle is able to make a very specific suggestion about how the explaining factor is prior.

That eclipse is not the explanation of the middle term, but the middle term of eclipse is obvious (*phaneron*). For the middle term is in the *definition* of eclipse, so that it is clear (*dēlon*) that eclipse is known (*gnōrizetai*) through the middle term, not the middle term through eclipse (98b21–4).

Applying this to the example of the planets, we get the result that, if nearness enters into the definition of non-twinkling, but not vice versa, then nearness, as the prior term, can explain non-twinkling, but not vice versa.

---

[8] *An. Post.* ɪ 13, 78a29 – b11; ɪɪ 16, 98b4–24.

[9] *GA* ɪɪ 6, 742b17 – 743a1.   [10] *Phys.* vɪɪɪ 1, 252a32 – b5.

[11] In the first passage, ɪ 13, 78a26 – b4, where Brody sees a reference to cause, Aristotle does not seem to be explaining why the premises about non-twinkling provide no explanation. He simply takes it as obvious that they do not. Much less does he account for their non-explanatoriness by reference to there being no mention of the efficient cause. The word used (*aition*) is a general one for any kind of explanation, not just for the efficient cause, and later in *An. Post.* ɪɪ 11 he will say that *any* of the four causes may feature in an explanatory syllogism.

It is not clear whether Aristotle is laying it down as a *general* requirement that the middle term (the one repeated in the premises) must enter in this way into the essence of the major term (the predicate of the conclusion). Such a requirement would be far stricter than Aristotle's normal practice, and his point may merely be[12] that, since the particular example under discussion happens to meet this much stricter condition, it is obvious and clear (*phaneron* and *dēlon*) that it meets any less strict condition on which he would insist. As to whether his less strict condition is an epistemological or an ontological priority or both, there is room for different interpretations. On what is perhaps the smoothest reading, Aristotle explicitly states his less strict condition in 98b24: the explanandum must be known (*gnōrizetai*) through the explanans. The priority required will then be epistemological, and one certainly feels it is true in some sense that an explanation comes before the thing explained in the order of understanding. At the same time, it should be noted that *Cat.* 12, 14b12, assigns to the explanation (*to aition*), and *Top.* vi 4, 141b28, to the essence, an *ontological* priority.

The passage on essence to which Brody turns is *An. Post.* i 6, 74b5–12, to which might be added 75a28–37. Here Aristotle requires that for purposes of scientific understanding and scientific explanation, we need premises which state *essential* connexions, because only these will state *necessary* connexions. Aristotle thus has two distinct requirements. The premises must state essential connexions (Brody's point from i 6), and the middle term must be *prior* in the right way (ii 16). The planetary syllogism is probably viewed by Aristotle as failing on the second requirement, rather than on the one to which Brody draws attention.

Universal, necessary truths and deduction not necessary for explanation

So far Aristotle has disagreed, rightly, with one half of the covering law theory of explanation. Deduction from covering laws is not *sufficient* to yield explanation. But does Aristotle accept the other half of the covering law theory – that deduction from laws is a *necessary* condition of explanation? Again this is a matter of controversy. Against Max Hocutt's view, that Aristotle is simply offering us the covering law theory, stands the view of Richard Rorty and Allan Gotthelf, that in place of explanation by reference to laws, Aristotle puts explanation by reference to things and their natures.[13]

Certainly, Aristotle's aim is to show that scientific explanations can be set out in the form of syllogisms. And in one way, he seems to be

---

[12] I owe this interpretation, and the 'smooth reading' which follows, to Jonathan Barnes.

[13] Richard Rorty, 'Genus as matter: a reading of *Metaphysics* Z – H', in *Exegesis and Argument* (Studies Presented to Gregory Vlastos, *Phronesis* supp. vol. 1) ed. E. N. Lee, A. P. D. Mourelatos, R. M. Rorty, Assen 1973, 415. Allan Gotthelf (18.3) 1976, 232–4. Contrast Max Hocutt, loc cit.

putting forward a stronger requirement than Hempel's. For in the *Posterior Analytics,* he looks not merely for deductions from exception-less generalisations, but for deductions from exceptionless generalisations which are themselves necessary.[14] This goes beyond Hempel, because, although Hempel talks of deductions from law-statements, he thinks he can avoid defining law-statements as *necessary* truths.

In more detail, Aristotle's requirements are as follows. First, there must be *deduction.* One cannot explain why something (a species? an individual?) breathes by saying that it is an animal, since not every animal breathes.[15] Next, this passage and others imply that explanation requires truths which are universal, in the sense of applying to *every* case.[16] Thirdly, in order to be explanatory, the deduction must be from *necessary* premises.[17]

Aristotle reaches the requirement of necessary premises by stages. First, he argues in I 2, 71b9–12, that the *conclusion* will be necessary. He is here describing the ordinary conception (*oiometha*) of scientific understanding (*epistēmē*). According to this conception, we have scientific understanding of a thing, when we know its explanation (*aitia*), and know that the thing to be explained cannot be otherwise.[18] When Aristotle refers to knowing that the thing cannot be otherwise (in other words, that it is necessary), he is not talking about *all* forms of understanding. For he believes that non-necessary things can be understood, for example, particular contingent events, or generalisations which hold for the most part. The examples which he cites show that he is talking of *scientific* understanding, and his paradigms of scientific understanding are drawn, in the preceding chapter and throughout the first ten chapters of the *Posterior Analytics,* from the *mathematical* sciences. This, I suggest, is why the ordinary conception of such understanding includes the idea that the thing understood cannot be otherwise.

It is an inference from the fact that in scientific contexts the thing to be understood is necessary that the explanatory premises will have to be necessary in their turn. This inference is drawn in I 6, 74b26–32 and 75a12. In a case where scientific understanding is possible, Aristotle says, one will not know the explanation (*dihoti, dia*), unless one knows that the thing to be explained follows from necessary premises.

It can now be seen that the scientific context of the *Posterior Analytics* creates an important restriction. For although Aristotle's scientist is

---

[14] *An. Post.* I 4; I 6; I 33, 88b31.   [15] *An. Post.* I 13, 78b22–3.

[16] *An. Post.* I 24, 85b24–6; I 31; II 2, 90a26–30. A stricter sense of 'universal' is introduced at I 4, 73a34 – b5, b16–28: in order to belong universally, a predicate must attach not only *kata pantos* (to every instance and at all times, 73a28–34), but also *kath' hauto* (by definition) and hence necessarily.   [17] *An. Post.* I 6, 74b26–32, 75a12.

[18] I take it that '*this* cannot be otherwise' (71b12) means that the *thing to be explained* cannot be otherwise, not that the *explanatory factor* cannot be otherwise. The latter is something which Aristotle thinks it necessary to *infer* from the former in I 6.

sometimes concerned with explaining particular events,[19] on the whole, his interest is confined to explaining universal, necessary truths. And the argument just cited from *An. Post.* ɪ 6, 74b26–32, that explanation calls for necessary premises, actually hinges on the presupposition that the thing to be explained is itself a necessary truth. As if to rub in that he is not laying down requirements for explanation quite generally, Aristotle twice repeats that he is talking of cases in which scientific demonstration is possible (74b28; 75a12).

That not all explanation requires universal or necessary premises is made clear by Aristotle's recognition that in natural science it is not always possible to obtain exceptionless generalisations. Often a predicate will attach to members of the kind only *for the most part.*[20] In *An. Post.*, he is not confident that broadness of leaf, or coagulation of sap, will have its effect of making the leaves fall in every instance.[21] Twice, therefore, he discusses degenerate scientific syllogisms in which the predicates attach *only for the most part* to their subjects (*An. Post.* ɪ 30, 87b19–27; ɪɪ 12, 96a8–19). In these syllogisms, the thing to be explained will be a truth that holds for the most part, and the explanatory premises will be neither necessary nor universal, but again true only for the most part.

The recognition that one may be able to obtain only generalisations that hold for the most part has an even more radical implication. It means that for explaining *particular* events, so far from always being able to use premises which are universal and necessary, one will not always be able to use the *deductive* pattern at all. For premises which hold only for the most part cannot *entail* the conclusion that a particular event of some type occurs. Like Hempel's statistical laws, they could at most render the occurrence of such an event *probable*. This possibility of explaining a particular event by showing an event of that type probable, or in accordance with what is usual, is recognised by Aristotle at *Poet.* 10, 1452a18–21 and *Metaph.* V 30, 1025a21. What matters is that this explanation is not a *deduction* of such an event's occurrence.

In one kind of case, Aristotle actually says that the deductive pattern cannot be used for explaining a particular event (*An. Post.* ɪɪ 12, 95a27 – b1). Suppose the causal origin (*archē*, 95a28) for some event has already occurred. Its occurrence will presumably *explain* the eventual occurrence of the sequel. But, Aristotle argues, a *syllogism* cannot be constructed to show that the sequel has occurred (it may still lie in the future), nor that it will occur (one cannot switch tenses in mid-syllogism). And he draws the same conclusion for cases in which the origin and sequel both lie in the future.

I have made two points: the *Posterior Analytics* does not lay it down as

[19] E.g. *An. Post.* ɪɪ 11, 94a36 – b8; ɪ 31, 88a1–4.
[20] *GA* 727b29, 770b9–13, 772a35, 777a19–21; *PA* 663b28; *An. Pr.* 25b14, 32b4–13.
[21] *An. Post.* ɪɪ 16, 98b2–4, b25–38.

a requirement for *all* explanation that there should be deduction, nor that there should be universal or necessary truths available to supply the explanation.

Universal, necessary premises are not required – so Jonathan Barnes has pointed out – even for scientific purposes, in Aristotle's earliest account of scientific demonstration (*apodeixis*) in *Top.* ɪ 1.[22] That this account is early he establishes by pointing out that the *Topics* is not yet aware of all the rules of syllogism which were later to be woven into the theory of scientific method.

Outside the logical works, as is notorious, the syllogistic theory of explanation scarcely appears. Instead, the main theory of explanation is that of the four causes: formal, final, efficient and material.[23] I must now examine this theory, to see whether it brings in necessitation in a different way. So far, we have considered the logical necessitation of a conclusion by premises. But it needs to be asked whether explanation by reference to the efficient cause, for example, involves some other kind of necessitation by the efficient cause of its effect.[24]

Does efficient cause, or explanation by efficient cause, involve necessitation?

The efficient cause is Aristotle's nearest equivalent to cause in our sense. Efficient causes certainly *can* necessitate their effects, but we

[22] Jonathan Barnes, 'Proof and the syllogism', forthcoming in (27.6), is supporting the earlier hypothesis of Friedrich Solmsen in (27.8).

[23] For the theory, see *Phys.* ɪɪ 3 (slightly reworded in *Metaph.* v 2), and ɪɪ 7. A historical background and rationale for the classification is supplied in *Metaph.* ɪ 3–10.

[24] On final and formal cause, see Chapter Ten, note 2. On the material cause, Aristotle wavers both as to how far it is explanatory, and as to whether it is necessitating. On the whole, however, where he treats it as explanatory, he also treats it as necessitating though not (*GA* v 8, 789b2–20) vice versa. For denials of explanatory value see Chapter Nine, note 18; for wavering Chapter Ten, notes 62 and 63. The denials are themselves sometimes nuanced: e.g. at *GA* v 8, 789b20, the word 'through' (*dia*) seems to allow physiological causes explanatory value in producing biological parts in those cases where the parts serve no purpose; and even when the causes produce useful parts, they can be called explanations of the material kind (*hōs hulē aitia*, 789b8). Cf. *Phys.* ɪɪ 9, 200a6, a9–10: things do not occur 'through' (*dia*) material causes, 'except in the sense of occurring through matter' (*plēn hōs di' hulēn*). For denials that the material cause necessitates, see *Phys.* ɪɪ 9. The evidence that it can after all necessitate is scattered. Thus at *Phys.* ɪɪ 3, 195a15–18 (= *Metaph.* v 2, 1013b17), the example given of a material cause is the premises of a conclusion. The example is repeated at *Phys.* ɪɪ 7, 198b7–8, and *An. Post.* ɪɪ 11, 94a20–36, without the name 'material cause'; but the *An. Post.* passage cites the example to illustrate one of the four causes at the point where we should expect the material cause to be mentioned. What premises have in common with other material causes is presumably that they are that 'out of which' something (the conclusion) comes. The phrase used in *An. Post.* to characterise the relation of premises to conclusion ('when something holds, it is *necessary* that this does', 94a24) is close to that used in *PA* ɪᴠ 2, 677a17, where the presence of a *liver* is said to necessitate the presence of *bile*; the liver seems here to play the role of material cause. Again, the material cause is associated with the efficient cause, and both are linked with necessitation at *GA* ɪɪ 1, 731b21–2 (in connexion with why some embryos are necessarily female) and v 1, 778a35–b1 (in connexion with why some eyes are necessarily blue).

52 *Necessity and Cause*

need to ask two questions. Does Aristotle think that every efficient cause necessitates its effect, as has recently been suggested?[25] Or again does he think that every efficient cause is at least *part* of some necessitating conditions? W. D. Ross implies that he thinks the latter, when he ascribes to Aristotle the view that any exceptions to honey-water alleviating fever will themselves fall under a law.[26] Thus although the administration of honey-water does not *on its own* necessitate alleviation, it presumably does, on Ross's interpretation, in conjunction with attendant circumstances other than those covered by the law about exceptions. The idea that every effect is necessitated could be derived either from the stronger view that the efficient cause *on its own* necessitates, or from the weaker view that it is *part* of some necessitating conditions.

I know of only one passage where Aristotle implies unequivocally that every effect is necessitated. And there, surprisingly, he goes the whole way, and implies that the efficient cause *on its own* necessitates the effect. The passage is the one familiar to us from Chapter One: *Metaph.* VI 3. It is because Aristotle here thinks of causes as necessitating their effects that he sees no other way to avoid determinism but the denial of causation in certain instances.

There is another passage which, in combination with further texts, may seem to imply that every cause is at least *part* of some necessitating conditions. In *Metaph.* IX 5, Aristotle is talking of *dunameis* or *abilities*. Aristotle's claim about *dunameis* is that, when the circumstances are right, it is necessary (*anankē*, 1048a6, a14) that they should be exercised. He distinguishes between irrational *dunameis*, such as the ability of what is hot to transmit heat, and rational *dunameis* such as the ability of the doctor to heal. Rational *dunameis* differ, in that one who has the ability to heal also has the ability to withhold health, since he knows what is needed for health, and so his ability can be exercised in opposite ways, depending on what outcome he wants. None the less, the exercise of his ability is just as much necessitated, when the conditions are right; the chief difference is that the conditions will include his having certain desires.

This passage is cited by Anscombe[27] to show that Aristotle believes that what is caused is necessitated. It is also cited by Hintikka[28] as one of

---

[25] So Max Hocutt, op. cit. 386–7.
[26] W. D. Ross, ad *Metaph.* VI 2, 1027a25, in *Aristotle's Metaphysics*, vol. 1, Oxford 1924, 361.
[27] G. E. M. Anscombe (4.1) 2.
[28] J. Hintikka (1.3) ch. 9 cites *Metaph.* IX 5, 1047b35 – 1048a21; IX 7, 1048b37 – 1049a18; *Phys.* VIII 4, 255a30 – b31 (cf. II 8, 199b18, 26); *Long.* 3, 465b14–16; *Mot.* 4, 699b29 (cf. 8, 702a10–17 and *GA* II 4, 740b21–4). In (1.4) 38 Hintikka adds *Rhet.* II 19, 1392b19–20. But here Aristotle is merely advising how by special pleading you can pin guilt on a man by saying that all men do a thing when they are able and wish to do it, if nothing hinders them.

a group of passages which exhibit a deterministic strain. The passages concern *natural tendencies*, such as the ability of earth to fall and fire to rise. Although there is only one other passage in the group in which Aristotle uses a modal expression equivalent to 'necessary',[29] he often says that, when the conditions are right, action follows, or follows at once, 'unless something prevents it'. On the other hand, the claim that the skilled man's work is produced of necessity is apparently contradicted, as we shall see, in a chapter of the *Posterior Analytics*. Further, as Hintikka allows, Aristotle is talking about special cases.

Certainly, the examples of action described in *Metaph.* ix 5 are special cases. Not every action is the exercise of a rational ability like medicine. And in ix 7, 1048b37 – 1049a18, Aristotle distinguishes the ability of a seed, once implanted in the womb, to become a human being, from the mere possibility that a seed not so implanted will one day turn into a human being, or a piece of elemental earth into a bronze statue. There must be many stages in the process by which a piece of earth turns into a bronze statue. We have not yet been told that every effect in this long sequence represents the necessitated exercise of an ability.[30]

The idea that the right conditions will necessitate the exercise of a *dunamis* only becomes more significant, when we put it together with certain other ideas. Thus an efficient cause is distinguished as that whence comes the origin of a change. And change in its turn is defined in *Phys.* iii 1[31] as involving the activation of a *dunamis*.[32] If we put these ideas together, it looks as if all efficient causation involves the activation of a *dunamis,* while *dunameis* are activated *of necessity*, once the conditions are right.

It does not look, however, as if Aristotle had put all these ideas together and recognised this conclusion. And even if he had, it falls short of the conclusion that whatever is caused is necessitated. For he has not ruled out the possibility that *dunameis* might sometimes be activated *before* the necessitating conditions are assembled.

I conclude that we still have only the one passage (*Metaph.* vi 3) implying that whatever is caused is necessitated. But two other lines of thought need to be considered. One comes at *GC* ii 10, 336a26–9, where he argues that if, instead of the sun approaching and retreating during the year, there were only a single motion, that motion could not cause both creation and destruction. For these results are opposites, and a

---

[29] *Long.* 3, 465b14–16.

[30] Nor need all the effects which escape from this category fall into the opposite category, which involves necessitation in the different sense of being produced by force contrary to nature.

[31] *Phys.* iii 1, 201a10, a27, b5.

[32] Moreover, Aristotle has a theory that whenever something comes to be by nature or by human skill, when, for example, it comes to be hot or a human being, it is brought to that state by something which is already hot or a human being, and it must at the start have the *dunamis* for being hot or a human being (*GA* ii 1, 734b21 – 735a4).

single thing, if it remains in the same circumstances, naturally produces a single result. But Aristotle does not here make any use of the
principle that the same cause in the same circumstances must always
produce its result. All he needs is the weaker principle, enunciated by
Plato in the *Phaedo*, that a single thing cannot produce *opposite* results.
And this is how he puts the point elsewhere, if he is the author of *Meteor*
IV 6, 383a7–8.

As a final piece of evidence, we may recall that in the *Posterior
Analytics* Aristotle is interested in premises which are necessary, and
sometimes obtains his necessary premises by taking an example of an
efficient cause which necessitates its effect. Thus at II 8, 93b7–14, he
may have in mind a syllogism that runs as follows: noise belongs to the
quenching of fire; quenching of fire belongs to the clouds; therefore noise
belongs to the clouds.[33] Here the first premise is necessary, presumably
because the quenching necessitates the noise. And in case we have any
doubt about this, Aristotle says at *An. Post.* II 11, 94b32–3, that the noise
when it thunders, is made necessary by the quenching. Again in *An.
Post.* II 16–17, he is concerned with whether the efficient cause, coagulation of sap, makes it necessary (*dei*, 98b36–8) that the leaves will fall in
every instance. The scientific context gives him an interest in effects
which are necessitated. But we have seen that we cannot safely generalise from the special interests of the scientific context. It does not fully
cover, for example, the explanation of *particular* events. And we shall
shortly see that the *Posterior Analytics* itself supplies examples of
unnecessitated effects.

Let us turn to the evidence on the other side. First, there is evidence
that Aristotle associated explanation by efficient cause not simply with
what happens always and necessarily, but also with what happens for
the most part. This is Christopher Kirwan's good suggestion about
Metaph. v 30 and VI 2.[34] At v 30, 1025a21, Aristotle moves from the idea
that planting is not necessarily, nor for the most part, connected with
finding buried treasure to a conclusion (*hōste*) about the planter's discovery of treasure not being *because of* (*dihoti*) his planting. Are we to
infer that if only planting led *for the most part* to the discovery of buried
treasure, it would not be debarred from explaining the discovery? If so,
this would allow explanation without necessitation.

The suggestion is confirmed at *Poet.* 10, 1452a18–21.[35] The events in

[33] The second premise is relevant to a question to be discussed in Chapter Twelve,
whether Aristotle's necessary premises are about kinds or all their members, or both. He
would like to say 'both', but in the present example, he can hardly believe that quenching
of fire attaches to *every* cloud.

[34] Christopher Kirwan, *Aristotle's Metaphysics Books Γ, Δ, E*, Clarendon Aristotle
Series, Oxford 1971, 181. Cf. Willie Charlton, *Aristotle's Physics Books I and II*, Clarendon
Aristotle Series, Oxford 1970, 116.

[35] I am grateful to Myles Burnyeat for this confirmation. Incidentally, I think this
passage belies Kirwan's suggestion (124) that Aristotle does not raise Hume's problem as
to the difference between 'post hoc' and 'propter hoc'.

a tragedy should occur because of (*dia*) each other, not merely one *after* another. And to secure this, what is needed is that they should arise out of what went before either of necessity *or with probability* (*eikos*). Probability is elsewhere defined in terms of what happens *for the most part*.[36]

Admittedly, Aristotle does not go so far in these passages as to recognise an example like that of the radioactive material which would only *rarely* irradiate a similarly placed mechanism. But he does recognise that we can explain something by reference to an efficient cause, while appealing only to what happens *for the most part,* not to what happens necessarily.

Another example is provided by his treating honey-water as alleviating fever (*Metaph.* vi 2, 1027a19–26). It does not always alleviate and Aristotle does not say that on the occasions when it does succeed, it is part of some necessitating conditions. What is more, even if it were part of some necessitating conditions, he does not think that we have to cite the necessitating conditions, in order to be able to offer it as the efficient cause, and hence as the explanation, of a particular alleviation.

But so far I have been talking of *explanation.* It will perhaps be admitted that *explanation* does not always involve necessitation, for Aristotle, and that an efficient cause is defined as something which provides an *explanation.* But, it may be asked, might not Aristotle demand of efficient causes that, in addition to their explanatory role, which evidently does not call for necessitation, they meet certain further requirements? And might not one of the further requirements be that they necessitate their effects, or form part of some necessitating conditions? We have already seen that *Metaph.* vi 3 does make the stronger of these requirements. What I now want to say is that other passages imply that neither requirement is correct. The clearest evidence comes in some passages to be discussed in Chapter Nine, where Aristotle is tempted by the view that, with few exceptions, nothing that comes into being does so of necessity (esp. *GC* ii 11, *PA* i 1, *Phys.* ii 9). In spite of the attraction that this view has for him, he is not tempted to deny that there are efficient causes of coming to be. A man or a house does not come into being of necessity, but there is an efficient cause of its doing so – the father or the builder. In other words, the existence of a man or a house is caused, but not necessitated. The same point is implied about artifacts in *An. Post.* ii 11, 95a3–5, where Aristotle says that a house or a statue never comes into being of necessity.[37] Yet a cause is not denied; on the contrary, each is said to be the result of planning (*apo dianoias*). This is the passage which apparently contradicts the claim of

[36] *An. Pr.* ii 27, 70a5; *Rhet.* i 2, 1357a34; ii 25, 1402b16, 1403a1.

[37] Someone might object that the necessity ruled out here is only one kind of necessity, namely, that associated with chance. But it is doubtful that Aristotle is associating necessity with chance here. He may be mentioning them as separate things. And even if he is not, the context suggests that he is concerned not with one kind of necessity, but with necessity in general.

Metaph. ɪx 5, that the activation of a rational ability can be necessitated. Finally, the same chapter, *An. Post.* ɪɪ 11, implies that an efficient cause is not in every case *on its own* a necessitating condition, when it makes such necessitation the distinguishing mark of a different one of the four causes (94a24–36).[38]

I conclude that Aristotle does not firmly stick to the view that every effect of an efficient cause is necessitated. The fact that he sometimes allows unnecessitated effects will help us later in interpreting some crucial passages in the *Ethics*. For it releases us from supposing that when he denies that voluntary actions have been necessary all along, he must be envisaging a failure of causation.

I must add that Aristotle's reason for allowing efficient causes, and efficient cause explanations, without necessitation is not the same as mine. It is not due to a sense that explanation is relative to the needs of the questioner. On the contrary, at least within the sphere of science, he maintains that some things are better fitted *by nature* than others to provide understanding (*An.Post.* ɪ 2, 71b33 – 72a5; *Top.* vɪ 4). It is rather that, in the nature of things, many events and things are not necessitated, and for these a different kind of explanation is appropriate.

The relation of syllogism to the four causes

I have now considered two different kinds of necessitation: the logical necessitation of the conclusion in a syllogism and what we should call the causal necessitation associated with efficient causes. I shall not yet consider necessitation in connexion with Aristotle's other three causes. (It will later emerge in connexion with the *material* cause that necessitating forces need not be explanatory.) For the present I shall state more clearly how explanation by the four causes relates to the syllogistic theory of explanation.

The theory of four causes is the more comprehensive theory. Aristotle maintains that the four causes are the *only* modes of explanation (*Phys.* ɪɪ 3, ɪɪ 7; *Metaph.* ɪ 10), whereas he does not maintain that all explanation has a syllogistic structure. At most, he argues in *An. Post.* ɪɪ 11 that any of the four causes can feature in a syllogism as the middle term (the term that occurs twice in the premises) and can explain the conclusion. If the syllogism is a scientific one, the premises will be necessary like the one already cited: noise belongs to the quenching of fire. Here the necessity seems to be a causal necessity of the kind we have just been considering (quenching causally necessitates noise), although this would not always be the case. Curiously enough, when Aristotle comes to illustrate the role of the efficient cause in an explanatory syllogism, he is hard put to find even one satisfactory example. His illustration is

[38] 'When something holds, it is necessary that this does' (94a24). The final cause can *also* necessitate, but in a different way: not *when* it exists, but *if it is to* exist.

probably meant to run: 'All aggressors are warred on; the Athenians are aggressors; therefore the Athenians are warred on' (94a36–b8). Here, once it is acknowledged, as it ought to be, that aggression as an efficient cause provokes war at best only *for the most part*, the conclusion cannot even be represented as following, let alone as following from necessary premises. The example illustrates how unsatisfactory is the attempt to extend a syllogistic pattern of explanation to too wide a range of cases.

Aristotle's concern with generality

What I have said so far will be misleading if it has given the impression that Aristotle does not in any way share Hempel's interest in generalisation. Certainly, he does not think that all explanation requires *exceptionless* generalisation, but then neither does Hempel. Both, however, would consider that some degree of generality is required. The individual Polyclitus can explain the coming into being of a statue as its efficient cause, but only because he is a sculptor, and there is a generalisation linking sculptors to the creation of statues.[39]

There is another way in which Aristotle shows himself interested in *generality*. Just as Hempel thinks that an explanation becomes better, the more comprehensive the theory in which it is embedded, so Aristotle would like, ideally, to derive all the things to be explained within a given science from as small a group of first principles as possible. Not only does Aristotle argue in *An. Post.* that explanatory syllogisms are better, the more universal their premises;[40] but his preference for generality is clear from his actual scientific practice. In *Meteor.* ii 3, 357a24 – 358a27, for example, Aristotle asks why the sea is salt, and rejects Empedocles' analogical explanation that the sea is the sweat of the earth. Instead of resting content with the analogy, he goes back to the material and efficient causes which lie behind both the saltness of the sea, and the saltness of sweat. The common factor, according to his theory, is that matter which heat fails to digest, or otherwise master, is salty. He thinks that such matter is left over both in sweat by the digestive processes and by heating processes in the dry vapour which is included in rain. As G. E. R. Lloyd comments,[41] in such examples, Aristotle shows that the particular cases compared are instances of the same *general laws*.

The point at which Aristotle and Hempel diverge is that Aristotle would not be content with generalisation, unless it introduced one or other of his four causes. After all, his predecessors had already been willing to generalise. In explaining various cases of motion and aggregation, some had cited not just a single analogy, such as, 'birds of a

[39] This point is well made in a forthcoming paper by Julia Annas.
[40] *An. Post.* i 24; cf. i 4, 73b38 – i 5, 74b4; and i 9, 76a18–22.
[41] G. E. R. Lloyd, *Polarity and Analogy*, Cambridge 1966, 378; 413.

feather flock together', but the generalization, 'like is attracted to like'.[42] A generalisation of this kind, however, devoid of reference to the four causes, would not have impressed Aristotle.[43]

How rigid is Aristotle's theory?

There is one further respect in which Aristotle may appear akin to Hempel. Both of them are trying to formulate requirements for explanation in science which will not vary according to the needs of the individual questioner. But Aristotle's reasons for attempting this go beyond Hempel's. As remarked above, he thinks that in science *nature* dictates what will be genuinely explanatory (e.g. *An. Post.* I 2, 71b33 – 72a5; *Top.* VI 4). This imports a host of ideas quite foreign to Hempel: it is essences which are ultimately explanatory in this sphere. Moreover, Aristotle expected that scientific investigation could in principle be completed, and formulated once and for all, in a finite set of theorems corresponding in structure to nature. This belief in turn encouraged his elaborate rules of axiomatisation.

The points in the last paragraph have been very well brought out by Myles Burnyeat.[44] They give to Aristotle's treatment of scientific explanation a certain kind of rigidity. In a different way, however, Aristotle's thought can be seen as comparatively flexible. Thus he does not view necessitation by a covering law as the *ideal* of explanation in fields outside science, such as history or tragedy, an ideal to which we fail to attain. For in the nature of things, many particular events are not necessary, and many subject matters do not admit of exceptionless laws, so that here necessitation by a necessary covering law would be a quite inappropriate mode of explanation. Again, while Hempel's stress is on

[42] The subject is well discussed in F. M. Cornford's inaugural lecture, 'The laws of motion in ancient thought', Cambridge 1931. For examples, of the generalised formulation, see Empedocles fragment 22, Democritus fragment 164, both in H. Diels, *Die Fragmente der Vorsokratiker* (cf. Aristotle's reports of these thinkers *GC* 323b10–15; *DA* 409b23–8, 416b33–5). Similarly Plato *Timaeus* 81A.

[43] Aristotle's preference for generalisations, and for generalisations which introduce one of the four causes, would distinguish him also from another modern philosopher of science: Norman Campbell. Writing in 1920, Campbell, accepted a deductive account of explanation to the extent of saying that a law was explained by a theory, if it could be *deduced* from it. But he added that such explanation was scientifically worthless, unless it incorporated an analogy, leaving some of the points of comparison to be ascertained, rather than spelling them out in a generalisation (Norman Campbell, Physics, *The Elements*, Cambridge 1920, ch. 6; repr. in Dover edition entitled *Foundations of Science*). Aristotle, by contrast, does not think that we have any explanation, until we *replace* Empedocles' analogy with a reference to one or more of the four causes. That the mere statement of analogy is not yet explanatory on its own comes out again in his repeated insistence that the four causes are the *only* modes of explanation. And it comes out also in his warnings (*An. Post.* I 2, 71b33 – 72a5; I 13, 78a26–30) that appeal to what is *familiar* will not necessarily be explanatory.

[44] See Burnyeat's forthcoming contribution to (27.6).

the uniformity of all explanation, Aristotle is equally interested in diversity. Within the syllogistic pattern of explanation, any one of the four causes may be invoked (*An. Post.* ii 11). And we shall see in Chapter Ten that, under the heading of final cause alone, Aristotle distinguishes three different types of explanation in biology (*PA* i 1, 640a33 – b4). Finally, outside the sphere of science, Aristotle is very ready to accept Plato's point that different classes of people are concerned with different explanations: the maker is interested in the material cause of his product, the user in the formal (*Phys.* ii 2, 194a36 – b7).

Plato on explanation and necessitation

Before we leave the relation between explanation and necessity, it will be instructive to consider Plato's position. The most thorough treatment of explanation prior to Aristotle's is that at the end of Plato's *Phaedo*. Plato there states or implies several important principles of explanation, one of them bearing on necessitation.

In a passage already mentioned (98c – 99b) Plato claims that a mere prerequisite is not explanatory. In the same part of the *Phaedo*, he lays down three further requirements for explanation, all having to do with opposites. First, a thing cannot be explained by something that has characteristics opposite to its own.[45] Secondly, a single thing cannot explain opposites,[46] and, thirdly, a single thing cannot be explained by opposites.[47]

It is sometimes thought that the second principle calls for an explanation to provide a *sufficient* (necessitating) condition, and the last for it to supply a *necessary* (prerequisite) condition.[48] But then there is surprise when Plato later endorses explanations invoking conditions that are sufficient without being necessary: fever explains sickness, fire heat, and snow cold.[49] In fact, Plato's requirement is weaker. The creation of two cannot have two *opposite* explanations. But this is not yet to say it cannot have two *different* ones. When we come to sickness, it presumably can have *different* explanations.

What is clear, is that Plato is looking for explanations which give *sufficient* (necessitating) conditions. But this is clear not from his point about opposites, but from his treatment of fever, fire, and snow as 'necessarily' bringing on sickness, heat and cold respectively.[50] This insistence on necessitation is stronger than anything in Aristotle.

[45] Plato *Phaedo* 101a–b; cf. 105d–e; *Parmenides* 131c–e.
[46] *Phaedo* 101a–b.
[47] *Phaedo* 96e – 97b.
[48] E.g. D. Gallop, *Plato: Phaedo*, Clarendon Plato Series, Oxford 1975, 183, 185, 210, 211.
[49] *Phaedo* 103c – 105c.
[50] See *Phaedo* 104d for the talk of necessity.

The divorce between necessitation and laws

So far I have considered how Aristotle and his predecessors related cause and explanation to necessity and laws. Now let us consider how they related necessity and laws to *each other*. I shall argue that they did not connect them as much as we might expect.

Modern philosophers connect the idea of an event being necessary with the idea of laws. If some conditions jointly necessitate an event of a particular kind, this implies a law that if exactly similar conditions recurred, an exactly similar event would occur. Conversely, if there is a law to this effect, and if the law is itself necessary, this implies that the occurrence of an exactly similar event will be necessary, once the relevant conditions recur. The necessity may either be absolute, or relative to the recurrence of the conditions, for reasons explained in Chapter Two.

The 'laws' I have just referred to are very unspecific ones. But, as will be noted again later in the chapter, when philosophers talk of laws, they often have in mind laws with a much more specific content. An example would be Newton's law that for every action, there is an equal and opposite reaction. One idea is that all the necessary laws of nature, discovered and undiscovered, taken together and coupled with all the infinitely many 'initial conditions' that obtain in the universe at a given instant, jointly necessitate, for every subsequent event, that an event of exactly that description should occur. And again the necessity can be thought of as absolute, or as relative to the occurrence of the initial conditions.

The links between necessity and laws were far less obvious to Aristotle and his predecessors. He recognises, of course, many kinds of necessity, as a glance at the catalogue in Chapter Thirteen will show. One kind of necessity he does admittedly associate with exceptionless laws: the necessity of everlasting things (*aïdia*). But this necessity is confined, as I shall argue in Chapter Eight, to things which exist or recur everlastingly. He denies that such necessity belongs to individual events (*GC* II 11). Certain broadly specified *types* of event recur everlastingly, for example, showers of rain or eclipses.[51] Hence one can say it is necessary that showers and eclipses will occur. But the birth of Mr Smith does not recur everlastingly, and so is not necessary in this way. Even about eclipses Aristotle is rather grudging elsewhere.[52]

---

[51] Though less ready than modern philosophers to connect necessity with exceptionless regularity, Aristotle here goes further than most modern philosophers, by arguing from exceptionless regularity to necessity, rather than the other way about. This will be the subject of Chapter Eight.

[52] The coincidence of an eclipse with *tomorrow* is a mere accident (*Metaph.* XI 8, 1065a16). And one cannot have scientific knowledge of the proposition that the moon is *now* eclipsed, or that it is *sometimes* eclipsed, since in neither case does the attribute attach to the subject *always* (*An. Post.* I 8, 75b33–6). It was of great interest to mediaeval philosophers in what sense there could be scientific knowledge of lunar eclipses. For their

In connexion with other events, Aristotle sometimes recognises two kinds of necessity: necessity in accordance with and necessity contrary to nature (*An. Post.* ii 11, 94b37 – 95a3). In neither case does it occur to him to suggest that there must be an exceptionless law at work. Necessity in accordance with nature is illustrated by the case of a stone's falling down. The downward motion is in accordance with its nature, and Aristotle thinks of nature as something which may produce its results either invariably *or only for the most part* (references in note 20). Thus a stone does not *invariably* fall through the air: it may get thrown upwards. There is no attempt to argue that, in the cases where natural necessity is in play, nature behaves invariably. The second kind of necessity, that contrary to nature, is illustrated precisely by the case of a stone's being thrown upwards. The upward motion, being contrary to its nature, is actually *contrary* to what happens always or for the most part. Others might say that if its upward journey is necessary, then such a body would invariably travel upwards given the same circumstances. But invariability is the very opposite of what Aristotle notices in the situation.

Plato is like Aristotle in divorcing natural necessity from invariability. A classic statement comes in the *Timaeus* at 46E, where he talks of the causes which belong to things that are moved by others and *of necessity* set yet others in motion. These causes, he says, produce chance results without order (*to tuchon atakton*). And again necessity is contrasted with reason and associated with the 'wandering' (*planōmenē*) cause at 48A. I would not go so far as those who say that necessity is here being connected with the *exceptional*. The reference to chance, lack of order and wandering probably has to do, as others say, with lack of purpose.[53] None the less, when Plato speaks of necessity here, he cannot be associating it with perfect invariability. For he states emphatically in the *Republic* (530B) and *Statesman* (269D–E) that what is bodily cannot always behave in the same way without alteration.[54]

The *Republic* passage is particularly interesting, because Plato suggests that, if the motions of the heavenly bodies do not conform to mathematics, this shows that there is something wrong with the bodies,

suggestions, see William A. Wallace (2.1) vol. 1, 1972, index s.v. 'eclipse'. I presume there are two factors which make scientific knowledge possible, in Aristotle's view: first, lunar eclipses exist always, in the sense of being everlastingly recurrent; secondly, they are produced always and only by interposition of the earth.

[53] So F. M. Cornford (17.1) 1937, 161–77; Glen Morrow in (17.2) 1965. For the 'unforseeable' interpretation, see G. Grote, *Plato and the Other Companions of Socrates*, London 1888, vol. 3, ch. 36, and for a modified version, A. E. Taylor, *A Commentary on Plato's Timaeus*, Oxford 1928, 300-1.

[54] Admittedly, in the *Statesman*, where the universe is made to reverse its direction of spin periodically, because bodies cannot always behave in the same way, it is none the less implied that there is some proper time period during which the revolution is in the direction dictated by God (269C, 272E). But if this gives some overall regularity to the irregularity, Plato does not make this point.

not with the mathematics.[55] This is contrary to the spirit of those who believe that nature obeys exceptionless laws, and who would seek ever to improve their mathematical formulae, to approach closer to the laws.

Not everything is subject to law, even if it is subject to necessity

I believe that Greek philosophers before the Stoics did not make everything subject to law or regularity, even in those cases where they made it subject to necessity. It may be wondered whether what I am saying can be right, in view of Gregory Vlastos' account of early Greek Philosophy in *Plato's Universe*.[56] For he says that all the early *physiologoi* (those who studied nature) would agree that 'solar regularities are either themselves absolutely unbreachable or else any given breach of them will admit of a natural explanation as a special case of some other, still more general, regularity which is itself absolutely unbreachable'. Generalising, he maintains that for these thinkers, 'nature remains the inviolate all-inclusive principle of explanation', which 'leaves no room for anything else', and the nature of a thing 'is always the same wherever it turns up and conforms to the same highest-level regularities'.

W. D. Ross sought to read a rather similar view into Aristotle's remarks about honey-water sometimes failing to cure fever. All exceptions, he thought, would come under some higher level regularity. But we saw that the view was not in the text. And I have suggested that Aristotle does not postulate that every event conforms to high-level regularities. I doubt if Plato does either. What about the earlier philosophers of whom Vlastos is talking?

Admittedly, they postulate many regularities. Vlastos focuses on the passages about reparations in Anaximander (fragment 1), and about measures in Heraclitus (fragments 30 and 94). Useful examples are assembled by Cornford in his inaugural lecture, 'The laws of motion in ancient thought'.[57] But if Democritus and others explained some motions by the 'law' that like was attracted to like, did they also express the idea that every motion is covered by some law? And would such laws deal with the speed and direction of each motion? It is easy for us to think that Democritus must have thought this, if he held that every collision and rebound of every atom (and hence by implication the speed and direction of every rebound) is necessary. But the question is whether he associated this necessity with the idea of exceptionless laws of motion and velocity. I believe that, on the contrary, he applied the notion of necessity much more widely than the notion of law. Certainly, the laws of motion Democritus cites would not cover every rebound, much less its velocity, and I do not know of his expressing the thought

[55] *Republic* 529D – 530B. I am indebted to Myles Burnyeat for pointing this out.
[56] Gregory Vlastos, (3a.1) 1975, ch. 1, pp. 9–10, 20–2.
[57] F. M. Cornford, 'The laws of motion in ancient thought', Cambridge 1931.

that there are other laws that would. The idea is not an obvious one, and if it seems obvious to us, that may be because we live in the age of Newton.

The legal metaphor

The legal metaphor in modern talk of laws of nature is virtually dead. This is especially true for modern philosophers like Hempel who think of laws of nature as being exceptionless regularities, but not as involving any kind of *necessity*. In comparing ancient views with modern, therefore, I shall not be concerned with ancient applications of legal terminology to nature, except insofar as they imply a belief in necessity or in regularity.

Legal terminology is already applied to nature by Anaximander, in the sixth century, when he says of the elements (fragment 1): 'They make amends and pay reparation to each other for their injustice, according to the ordinance of time.' Here a certain regularity is implied: encroachments by any one element will be counteracted. But there is no attempt to represent every detail in nature as an instance of some regularity. And by the mid-fifth century legal terminology would not have suggested regularity to the Greeks quite so readily as it does to us. For at that time, the sophists began to *contrast nomos* (law or convention) with *phusis* (nature), as being more subject to local variation and therefore less universal. It was consequently a deliberate paradox when, in the fourth century, Plato twice combined the words *nomos* and *phusis*, and talked of a law of nature (*nomos tēs phuseōs*). On neither occasion did he mean what would nowadays be meant by a law of nature.[58]

The growth of the idea that nature can be thought of as having laws has been studied by Klaus Reich.[59] He cites Epicurus' idea that there are essential combinations of atomic shapes (*sunkriseis ousiōdeis*, *On Nature* 14), i.e. the ones which alone are viable in all possible worlds. He also cites the laws of nature (*nomoi phuseōs*) of the Peripatetic Critolaos of Phaselis (*c.* 240 – *c.* 155 B.C.), who insists that men can never have sprung up fully grown, but must always have required a certain time period for their growth (*ap.* Philonem Alexandrinum, *On the Indestructibility of the World*, 11 – 13). Both these concepts, Reich suggests, influenced Lucretius' references to the compacts of nature (*foedera naturae*), in his Latin exposition of Epicurean thought. However, none of these authors is suggesting that every single detail can be shown to be an instance of an exceptionless or necessary regularity. And the

---

[58] At *Gorgias* 483E, Callicles is made to argue that when the stronger subjugate the weaker, though not following a law made by us, they are following the law of nature. At *Timaeus* 83E, Plato remarks that sometimes our blood is replenished not from food and drink, but contrary to the laws of nature.

[59] Klaus Reich (3a.2) 1958. I am grateful to Charles Kahn for this reference, and for discussing the legal metaphor with me.

Epicureans, as indeterminists, would positively have resisted such a suggestion.

The Stoic innovation in linking causation, and hence every event, with exceptionless regularity

For the idea that absolutely *everything* happens in conformity with regularity, we have to wait till the Stoics. Their innovation was to associate exceptionless regularity with *cause*. Since every event, in their view, had a cause, this linked every event with exceptionless regularity.

The kind of regularity which interested the Stoics, however, was not a law of nature like the laws of Newton, or of the early Greek philosophers. These were laws with a specific content, which might be instantiated many times a day, such as 'like is attracted to like', or 'for every action, there is an equal and opposite reaction'. It was Laplace's incautious extrapolation from Newton's successes which led to the idea that everything conforms to specific laws of this kind. The Stoics, less extravagantly, were concerned with a more abstract kind of law, which might be called a law of causation. Let us turn to them as introducing a new development into the subject.

It will help if I introduce some of the main figures. The first two belong to the dialectical, not the Stoic, school. Diodorus Cronus taught in the late fourth century B.C., largely between the death of Aristotle and the founding of the Stoa. His death has recently been put around 284 B.C.[60] His pupil Philo was a friend of the man who founded the Stoa around 300 B.C. The founder was Zeno of Citium (not to be confused with the earlier Zeno of Elea who propounded the paradoxes). Zeno's successors as head of the school were Cleanthes and Chrysippus, and the latter's dates were approximately 280–206 B.C. Zeno's contemporary Epicurus set up a rival school in Athens in 307–6 B.C.

Let us consider the fullest formulation of the Stoic law of causation, which comes in Alexander *De Fato* ch. 22. He says the Stoics postulated many causes. As we know from elsewhere,[61] some were self-sufficient on their own, some were joint causes and only *jointly* sufficient, some merely eased or intensified the effect, some were mere necessary conditions, while some necessary conditions did not *do* anything and so[62] were not really causes at all. With regard to each of these causes, Alexander says, the Stoics maintained that when all the circumstances (*peries-*

[60] By a *tour de force*, David Sedley had established that Diodorus and Philo belonged to the dialectical, not the Megarian school, and that Diodorus died around 284 B.C., not, as previously believed, in 307 B.C.: (10.1) 1977.
[61] Clement of Alexandria *Stromateis* VIII 9. See O. Rieth (3.1) 1933; M. Pohlenz (3.2) 1940; M. Frede (3.3) forthcoming.
[62] Seneca *Epistles* 65, 4.

tēkota) surrounding the cause and effect were the same, it would be impossible for things to turn out now one way, now another. The word *periestēkota* and its cognates recurs in nearly all the accounts. Judging from this fullest version, what the Stoics envisaged was a repetition of the *totality* of circumstances, both the cause and all its surroundings. Then, they maintained, the effect would be the same.

The point that the same circumstances will have the same outcome is recorded by many sources.[63] And it is incorporated into the very idea of causation. For the Stoics maintained that causation implied the outcome would be the same. If anyone allowed the possibility of an event's happening differently in the same circumstances, he would be denying that event a cause, but there cannot be a causeless event.[64] In this way, both causation and each particular event are associated with regularity.

There was a special reason why the Stoics should think of particular events as connected with exceptionless regularity. For the exact repetition of circumstances was for many of them not an abstract possibility, but something they positively expected. They thought that whatever happens will be exactly repeated in unending cycles.[65] There is an interesting contrast with Aristotle's view. He is prepared to allow that what happens always in unending cycles is necessary, not because of causation, but just on the basis of its happening *always* (*GC* II 11). On the other hand, he does not think, as Zeno and Chrysippus do,[66] that a particular event can be so repeated. He only allows that certain broadly specified types of event, like eclipse and rainfall, are repeatedly instantiated.[67] He therefore has no incentive for asking, in regard to events like the birth of Mr Smith, what would happen *if* there were an exact repetition of the attendant circumstances.

Later in antiquity, the Stoic view had prevailed sufficiently for one Aristotelian author, Alexander or whoever wrote the relevant section of the *De Anima Mantissa*, to allow that proper causation is linked with

---

[63] Nemesius *On the Nature of Man* 35; Alexander of Aphrodisias *De Fato* 10 (176 21–2), 15 (185 8–9), and 22 (192 22–3); Plutarch *De Stoicorum Repugnantiis* 1045B–C; Alexander of Aphrodisias (?) *De Anima Libri Mantissa CIAG* p. 171, lines 20–7; cf. 174 3–5 and 170 4–5. (On the disputed authorship of this part of the *Mantissa*, and for a translation, see Robert Sharples (31.12) 1975.)

[64] Alexander *De Fato* 15 and 22 as in preceding note; Plutarch *De Stoicorum Repugnantiis* 1045B – C; cf. Alexander (?) *Mantissa* 174 3–5 and 171 20–7.

[65] The view is also ascribed to Pythagoreans by Aristotle's pupil Eudemus of Rhodes, in Simplicius' commentary on Aristotle's *Physics CIAG* p. 732, line 26, and is endorsed in a work of the Aristotelian school, *Problems* 916a18–39. The ascriptions to Chrysippus and other Stoics are collected by Hans von Arnim in *Stoicorum Veterum Fragmenta* Leipzig 1921, vol. 2, fragments 596–632 and vol. 1, 109.

[66] Zeno, *ap.* Tatianum *Adv. Graec.* ch 5 = SVF I 109 Chrysippus *ap.* Alexander *Comm. in An. Pr. CIAG* 180 = SVF II 624.

[67] But see also his view that inventions are endlessly rediscovered (*Metaph.* XII 8, 1074a38 – b14; *Pol.* II 5, 1264a1–5; VII 10, 1329b25–35; *Meteor.* I 3, 339b27). Furthermore, there is a Great Year, with prolonged wintry and summery epochs (*Meteor.* I 14).

what happens everlastingly and always in the same way.[68] He only pleads that some events have only accidental causes, and concludes that these events at least are not linked with exceptionless regularities.

So far we have noticed that the Stoics linked causation, and hence each particular event, with exceptionless regularity. But did they also make any link between cause and *necessity*? The answer is 'yes', because all the sources use modal words. If the same circumstances are repeated, it is *necessary* that the same outcome should recur, and it is not *possible* for there to be now one outcome and now another.[69] Moreover, from this is inferred the deterministic conclusion that we *cannot* do otherwise than we do.[70]

I have been arguing that the Stoics made a big stride towards modern accounts of cause, by linking it with exceptionless regularity and necessity. It might be wondered, then, whether I was congratulating them. But in this instance I do not believe that the latest is the best. I argued in Chapter Two that effects need not always be necessitated, or linked to attendant circumstances by exceptionless laws. A. A. Long has commented on the Stoic belief that if circumstances are exactly repeated, the same outcome will occur. He had a distinguished philosophical tradition on his side when he claimed that the theory is 'true, but trivial',[71] I attempted to argue in Chapter Two that it was significant, but (hopefully) false. An electron, in the example given there, would not always reach the trigger, even if the attendant circumstances were all exactly similar.

The idea that what is caused is necessitated was a subject of explicit controversy. Chrysippus actually discussed a suggestion like one of mine, that the considerations for and against a course of action might be equally balanced, and that in that case a man could equally decide either way. Chrysippus denied that this was possible. Rather, he said, there must be some cause and some difference which leads the person's impulse in one direction rather than the other. And he applied this view equally to the fall of dice, or the tipping of a balance.[72] The view is, however, what I have called merely a declaration of faith.

The belief in necessitation *appears* to be more than a declaration of faith, so long as it can be supported by a certain argument. It is suggested that, if you deny that the man's action, or the tipping of the scales

[68] Alexander (?) *Mantissa* 171 20–5.
[69] Nemesius, *On the Nature of Man* 35; Alexander, *De Fato* 10 (176 21), 22 (192 22); Alexander (?) *Mantissa* 170 4, 171 24–5; cf. 174 5.
[70] Alexander, *De Fato* 15 (185 9–10).
[71] A. A. Long (31.7) 1971, 188. He adds (189) that the theory of eternal recurrence does not say anything which is relevant to action now, but merely denies the possibility of acting differently at the same point in the next cycle. I should like here to acknowledge my debt to the writings of Long, as well as of Frede, Donini, Sharples and Mignucci. I must also thank Long, Frede, Sharples and Mignucci for valuable criticisms of an earlier draft.
[72] Plutarch *De Stoicorum Repugnantiis* 1045B–C.

is necessitated, you will be making what happens inexplicable, or causeless. This is just the charge that certain Stoics pressed, and it has been
well documented by Robert Sharples.[73] They claimed that their opponents were committed to postulating 'causeless motions'.[74] And the
claim has been made by modern philosophers too.[75]

The Stoics' opponents sometimes responded, in effect, by looking for
ways in which something could be caused without being necessitated.
Their methods of doing this were not very successful. They insisted that
their unnecessitated effects were not causeless, but rather had a special
kind of cause. We can distinguish several positions. (a) Sometimes they
said the causes were *internal*. Faced with the same *external* circumstances, we may choose the pleasant, the admirable, or the useful aspect
of things, and so *we* or our *decisions* are the cause.[76] (b) Sometimes the
distinction was made between necessary and sufficient conditions: the
father is only a *necessary* condition of the child.[77] (c) Sometimes there
was an appeal to fortuitous or accidental causes of chance phenomena.
The lucky discovery of treasure has a merely *accidental* cause in the fact
of one's digging in the garden.[78] (d) It was sometimes urged that in the
various cases cited, there is not an *everlasting* chain of causes.[79]

Although I do not think that any of these arguments succeeds, I think
they are right *in spirit*: cause need not involve necessitation or uniform
regularity. What I tried to do in Chapter Two was to formulate a better
explanation of why it need not.

Did Chrysippus undo the link with necessity?

An objection may be raised to my account of the Stoic view. It will
perhaps be agreed that the Stoics connected cause with exceptionless
regularity: the same circumstances have the same outcome. But how
can I claim quite generally that the Stoics linked cause with necessity?
For is it not notorious that Chrysippus and others tried to escape from
commitment to necessity?[80] For one thing, Chrysippus suggested that
certain statements which looked like conditionals were not genuine

[73] Robert Sharples (31.12) 1975.
[74] Cicero *De Fato* 23–5, 28, 34–6, 46–8; Alexander *De Fato* 8 (173 13 – 174 28); 15 (185 7 – 186 12); 20 (190 19 – 26); 22 (192 8 – 25); 24 (193 30 – 194 25); Alexander (?) *Mantissa* (173 31 – 175 32); Plutarch *De Stoicorum Repugnantiis* 1045b–c; Ps-Plutarch *De Fato* 574e.
[75] Ted Honderich, op. cit. 1977–8, 63–86, esp. 68, 76–7.
[76] Cicero *De Fato* 23–5; Alexander *De Fato* 15 (185 7 – 186 12), 20 (190, 19–26); Alexander (?) *Mantissa* (173 31 – 175 32).
[77] Cicero *De Fato* 36, Alexander *De Fato* 24 (193 30 – 194 15).
[78] Cicero *De Fato* 19, 28; Alexander *De Fato* 8 (173 13 – 174 28); 24 (194 15–25).
[79] Cicero *De Fato* 34; Alexander (?) *Mantissa* 171 8.
[80] Alexander *De Fato* 10; Cicero *De Fato* vi 12 – viii 16, xvii 39 – xix 45; Augustine *City of God* book v, chs 9 and 10; Epictetus *Dissertationes* 2 19 1–5; Plutarch *De Stoicorum Repugnantiis* 1055d–e; Plutarch *Epitome* i 27 (Aëtius *Placita* i 27 in Diels, *Doxographici Graeci* 322).

conditionals, but only negated conjunctions, or, in modern terms, material implications. That is, instead of having the form 'if p, then q', they would have the form, 'not both (p and not q)'. They would then involve no necessary link between antecedent (p) and consequent (q). Michael Frede and S. Sambursky have both suggested that Chrysippus would view as material implications any statements in which the link between antecedent and consequent was empirical rather than logical.[81] This would place the Stoic law of causation in a new light. We have been construing it as saying that if circumstances (*periestēkota*) are exactly repeated, the same outcome will occur. On the view of Frede and Sambursky, we have a choice: either circumstances and outcome must have a logical connexion, or the law of causation must be reconstrued as a material implication. It will then read: 'It is not the case both that the same circumstances are repeated and that the same outcome does not occur.' No *necessary* link between circumstances and outcome would then be implied.

In a forthcoming paper,[82] Frede has explored the possibility of ascribing to the Stoics a *logical* link between circumstances and effect. Indeed, he has gone further and concentrated on just *one* of the causes distinguished by the Stoics, namely, the one which is indifferently called perfect (*autotelēs, perfecta*) or consolidating (*sunektikē, continens*). We are told that these were capable of producing the result self-sufficiently by themselves (*autarkōs di' hautōn poiētika*).[83] In the case of a cylinder's rolling, or of a man's assenting, Chrysippus would probably distinguish the *internal* state of the cylinder or of the man as the 'perfect' cause,[84] although perfect causes do not *have* to be internal. If the link between cause and effect is here to be represented as *logical*, perhaps the idea will be that if one understood the internal state sufficiently fully, one would see that the rolling or the assent was *logically* implied. It is, however, only a conjecture that Chrysippus thought in this way. Moreover some examples of perfect causes make one doubt whether Chrysippus can really have meant that every perfect cause on its own necessitated its effect, logically or otherwise. Thus a teacher is a perfect cause of someone's learning, fire of something's burning, and cautery of pain.[85] In each of these cases, something is required not only of the agent, but also (one would think) of the patient, before an effect can ensue. Sharples has suggested to me that in calling 'perfect' causes *self-sufficient*, the Stoics do not mean that they always necessitate their effects without further preconditions, but only that they rely on no further *causes* for their effects.

The view of Frede and Sambursky allows only two alternatives: either

---

[81] M. Frede (31.22) 1972, 80–93; S. Sambursky (31 16) 1959, 79.
[82] M. Frede (3.3).   [83] Clement of Alexandria *Stromateis* viii 9.
[84] See Cicero *De Fato* 41–4, where, however, the point is not quite explicit.
[85] These examples are taken from Clement loc. cit. and Cicero *Topics* 58–60.

Chrysippus made the link between circumstances and outcome a logical link (which is difficult to show), or he represented it merely by a material implication, and hence not as a *necessary* link at all. I believe that we need not accept either alternative. For in the next chapter I shall argue that Chrysippus' use of material implication was not connected with the distinction between the empirical and the logical. None the less, the idea of material implication was used in another context, along with a selection of other devices, for trying to escape from commitment to necessity, and this may suggest that the connexion made by the Stoics between cause and necessity is not as firm as I have suggested. I shall argue that in the end none of these arguments was successful, so that the general picture of the Stoic view which I have been presenting need not be revised.

Resumé

Aristotle thinks of cause in terms of explanation, and this may well be fruitful. But the modern tendency has been to relate cause and explanation to necessity and laws, and necessity and laws to each other. The Greeks did not at first regard these relations as self-evident; and Aristotle, though recognising some such links, makes his account more nuanced – rightly, I believe – than many modern ones. It was the Stoics who first connected causation emphatically with necessity and laws.

CHAPTER FOUR

Stoic Embarrassment over Necessity

I must substantiate the claim made in the last chapter that the Stoics committed themselves to postulating that all events occur of necessity. This was certainly the view of them taken in antiquity. Moreover, their own words make this interpretation virtually inescapable. Chrysippus wrote in the first book of his treatise on Fate that all things are held fast by necessity and fate, though he tried in the second book to deal with some of the difficulties that that created for human conduct.[1] Not only do the words for necessity and necessitated recur in the reports,[2] but the Stoics had a battery of other words for inevitability which they applied to this all-embracing Fate: *aparabatos, atreptos, anekpheuktos, anapodrastos, aniketos, anekbiastos, akolutos, aparallaktos, ametabletos, ametathetos*; in Latin: *insuperabilis, indeclinabilis, non posse mutari*.[3] To Zeno and Chrysippus is ascribed a comparison with a dog tied to a cart. If it is willing to follow, it follows, combining its own consent with necessity. But if it is not willing, it will be subjected to necessity anyhow.[4] Nor is any detail exempt from the necessity of Fate.[5]

The necessity which the Stoics postulated arose from causation. In one comparison, fate was conceived as a rope or chain of *causes*.[6]

---

[1] Diogenianus, apud Eusebium *Evangelica Praeparatio*, book VI, chapter 8, pp. 262a, 265d. This is reproduced in Hans von Arnim *Stoicorum Veterum Fragmenta* (*SVF*) Leipzig 1921, vol. 2, nos 925, 998. Similar is Plutarch *De Stoicorum Repugnantiis* 1049F – 1050D, 1056C; Alexander of Aphrodisias *De Fato* 7, *CIAG* 171 26; Aulus Gellius *Attic Nights* VII 2.

[2] *Ananke, katenankasmenon, necessitas, necesse, necessarius*. For reports, some interpreting, some quoting direct, see *SVF* II 913, 914, 916, 918, 923, 926, 937, 939, 942, 943, 963, 975, 997, 1000, and Aulus Gellius *Attic Nights* XIII 1 2; Marcus Aurelius 12 14 1; Boethius, 2nd commentary on Aristotle's *De Interpretatione*, ed. Meiser, Leipzig 1877, 194; Nemesius *On the Nature of Man* 35. It is also the standard interpretation of Alexander of Aphrodisias *De Fato* 1, 7, 8, 9, 11, 13, 14, 15, 22, 28, 30, 31, 34, 36.

[3] See *SVF* II 202, 528, 913, 914, 917, 918, 923, 924, 1000, and Aulus Gellius *Attic Nights* XIII 1 2; Marcus Aurelius 12 14 1; Cornutus *Theologia Graeca* 13, ed. Lang, Leipzig 1881, 13; Alexander *De Fato* 2, 10; Nemesius *On the Nature of Man* 35. Sharples has suggested to me that this plethora of words may represent a desire to avoid the naughty word 'necessary'. But for instances of the naughty word and its synonyms, see the preceding two notes.

[4] Hippolytus *Philosophumenon* 21, in Diels, *Doxographici Graeci* 571 (= *SVF* II 975).

[5] This is implied by the references in note 1, and by Plutarch, *De Communibus Notitiis* 1076E.

[6] Cicero *De Divinatione* I 127, Aulus Gellius *Attic Nights* VII 2.

In view of all this, it is not very surprising that the ancient sources regard as unsuccessful the Stoic attempts to escape from saying that all events happen of necessity.[7] Indeed, for those Stoics who explicitly postulate necessity, the only possible strategy would presumably be to introduce two or more senses in which events can be necessary, and to argue that they are not committed to events being necessary in *every* sense.[8] The task would then be to find a *morally significant* sense in which it can be denied that all events are necessary. By a morally significant sense, I mean one whose invocation will allow us to continue holding people morally responsible, and to continue applying our other moral categories.

The Stoic retreat from necessity constitutes one of several strategies for avoiding the unfortunate implications of determinism for morality; and it deserves a chapter to itself for that reason as well as for the light it sheds on the Stoic concept of causation. Moreover, we can distinguish no less than eight attempts to retreat from necessity, which have not, I believe, been adequately distinguished from each other. Although I doubt whether these attempts succeeded, what I do think remarkable is that once again they come very close to certain modern attempts of the same kind.

Some of the arguments bear not directly on necessity, but on the related concept of possibility, and are designed to show that there is room for alternative possibilities. This is how Cicero describes Chrysippus' position (*De Fato* 13)

But you do not want this at all, Chrysippus, and it is especially on this very point that you have a struggle with Diodorus. For he says that only that can happen which either is, or will be, true; and that whatever will be must necessarily happen, while that which will not be cannot happen. But you say that things which will not be are also capable of happening. For example, this jewel can be broken, even if it never will be, and it was not necessary that Cypselus should reign at Corinth, although that had been announced a thousand years before by the oracle of Apollo.

The first two attempts: reply to Diodorus' Master Argument

The first four Stoic arguments are defensive. They are intended to rebut certain *particular* attempts to saddle them with a deterministic account of possibility. Diodorus Cronus, the dialectician, had defined possibility in a way that, suitably interpreted, was deterministic. For he said that nothing *else* is possible other than what is or will be (or what is or will be true). Moreover, he produced a famous argument, the Master

---

[7] Cicero *De Fato* 12–16, 39; Plutarch *De Stoicorum Repugnantiis* 1056c, 1055d–e; Alexander *De Fato* 10; Aulus Gellius *Attic Nights* vii 2 15.

[8] Alexander mentions the denial of necessity in the same breath as he uses one of the words for inevitability (*aparabatos: De Fato* 10).

Argument, in support of this account of possibility. We are told the premises of the argument by Epictetus.

I shall for the moment postpone trying to explain the argument. My present interest is merely in the fact that Cleanthes and Chrysippus sought to avoid the deterministic conclusion. Cleanthes did so by denying the premise that what is past and true is necessary, Chrysippus by denying the premise that the impossible does not follow from the possible.[9] Cleanthes chose the right point of attack, I believe, provided that Diodorus' argument is construed in the manner that A. Prior has suggested, and which will be discussed in Chapter Six. But Chrysippus who attacked the *other* premise, chose a strange example in order to do so.[10] If you are talking in Dion's presence, 'Dion is dead' (which is possible) entails 'this man is dead' (which is impossible, since the 'this' would have no reference, if Dion were dead).

The third attempt: Cicero De Fato vi 12 – vii 14

At this point, Cicero conducts an imaginary argument with Chrysippus, which evidently represents earlier debates.[11] He doubts whether Chrysippus can succeed in escaping from Diodorus' determinism. For first, Chrysippus accepts one of Diodorus' premises, namely, that the past is irrevocable and hence necessary. Secondly, he also accepts divination, and would therefore have to accept the claims of astrologers, for example: if Fabius was born at the rising of the Dogstar (antecedent), he will not die at sea (consequent).

Putting these ingredients together, Cicero argues that what is mentioned in the antecedent, Fabius' birth at the rising of the Dogstar, is past and hence necessary. Moreover, the necessity of the antecedent will spread to the consequent: Fabius will not die at sea.

Chrysippus' reply is that necessity does not always spread from antecedent to consequent. Why not? It has been suggested that he would appeal again to the example concerning Dion. For if we rearrange the materials of that example, we get a reply relevant to Cicero's argument. 'This man is not dead' (necessary, because the 'this' requires a living referent) entails 'Dion is not dead' (non-necessary). Here is an example in which Chrysippus would claim that the necessity of the antecedent ('This man is not dead') does not spread to the consequent ('Dion is not dead').[12]

I am satisfied with this interpretation. It makes the present argument into a version of the preceding one. But it would be challenged by

---

[9] Epictetus *Dissertationes* 2 19 1–5.
[10] Alexander of Aphrodisias, commentary on Aristotle's *Prior Analytics*, *CIAG* 177.
[11] Cicero *De Fato* vi 12 – viii 16.
[12] For this interpretation, see M. Kneale (31.21) 1962, 127, followed by P. L. Donini (31.14) 1973; M. Frede (31.22) 88.

someone who argues, as does Mario Mignucci,[13] that the Stoics take the necessary to be *always* true. For if they do, they cannot view as necessary, 'This man exists', since, as they see it, the 'this' may sometimes lack a reference, and then the claim is neither true nor false. In Chrysippus' terminology, the claim 'perishes',[14] when the word 'this' lacks a reference, and hence it is not *always* true.

Mignucci's argument is interesting and original. But on the other side I would urge that it is Diodorus, rather than the Stoics, who comes close to defining the necessary in terms of what is *always* true, and even he does not go all the way.[15] Moreover, I doubt whether the Stoics ever transferred their allegiance to the Diodorean definition.[16] The *Stoic* definition of the necessary is that it is that which is true (they do not say: *always* true), and which does not admit of being false, or (a clause not needed for our purposes) which admits of being false, but is prevented from being false by external circumstances.[17] By the first two tests in this definition, 'This man exists' ought to qualify as necessary. For, said with reference to some man, it is true, and it will 'perish' sooner than admit of being false.[18]

I rest content, then, with the orthodox interpretation of the third argument. Before recounting the fourth, Cicero interposes a little sally against Chrysippus, which is left unanswered, but which has some intrinsic interest. He complains that, if there is a natural cause of Fabius' not dying at sea, then it is not possible that he will. He evidently expects Chrysippus to agree, and also to accept that there must be a natural cause. Presumably, he expects the latter because of the view

[13] M. Mignucci, 'Sur la logique modale des Stoiciens', in J. Brunschwig (ed.), *Les Stoiciens et leur logique*, Paris 1978.

[14] Alexander, comm. on *An. Pr.* 177 25 – 178 5.

[15] For convenience, I shall render his definition of 'necessary' as 'always true', where the nuances do not matter. But in fact Boethius gives the definition as: 'that which, being true, will not be false' 2nd comm. on *Int.*, ed. Meiser, 234.

[16] Mignucci cites two passages in support of the suggestion that the Stoics regard the necessary as *always* true. But in one (Cicero *De Fato* 14), all that need be implied is the Stoic view that what is true and does not admit of being false is necessary. As for the other passage (Alexander *De Fato* 10 177 7–15), rather than disbelieve our other sources about the Stoics, it is easier to suppose that the argument was devised *ad hominem* by a Stoic against a Diodorean view, and that it incorporates a (slightly loose) rendering of the *Diodorean* definition of necessity.   [17] Diogenes Laertius vii 75.

[18] A second reason for expecting Chrysippus to treat 'This man *does* exist' as necessary is that he undoubtedly treats as impossible 'This man does *not* exist'. To this second argument Mignucci has a reply, namely, that when we follow out the implications of the Stoic definitions of modal terms, we find that 'not possibly not' does not entail 'necessarily'. This is because calling something necessary is said to carry the implication that it is *true*, while calling its negation impossible is not said to carry a corresponding implication that the negation is *false*. Interesting as this observation is, I am not entirely convinced of its force, since I am not sure that the non-entailment is an *intended* feature. It is not one to which the ancient commentators drew attention, and Frede has suggested that the purpose of adding the implication 'is true' is merely to make clearer the relation of the Stoic definitions to rival ones (M. Frede, op. cit. 111–13).

common to himself and the Stoics that things can be foreknown, only if
there are natural causes of them.[19]

I shall return to this argument about natural cause in Chapter Six.
Can we reconstruct how it went in the original sources from which
Cicero is drawing? If speculation is allowed, perhaps I may suggest that
Cicero has recorded the argument in the wrong order. Chrysippus may
first have sought to divest statements about astrological evidence of any
necessitarian implications by offering the argument which Cicero post-
pones until *next* – the argument that such statements are only material
implications. Someone may then have reminded him of his view that
where there is an astrological sign, there will also be a cause, and
complained that the corresponding *causal* statements could not be
treated as mere material implications.

Be that as it may, Cicero leaves Chrysippus without a reply to the
argument about natural cause, and goes on to record a *fresh* attempt by
him to prevent necessity spreading from antecedent to consequent in
the original example about Fabius. This is the attempt that turns on
negated conjunction, or material implication.

The fourth attempt: Cicero De Fato viii 15 – 16

Instead of saying, 'If someone was born at the rising of the Dogstar, he
will not die at sea', the diviners ought merely to use material implication. They ought to say, 'It is not the case both that someone was born at
the rising of the Dogstar and that he will not die at sea.' Because the
second form of words uses material implication, necessity will not
spread from the first clause to the second.

Philo the dialectician had suggested that all conditional statements
could be reduced to material implications, and some Stoics followed him.
As Frede well argues, Chrysippus probably denied that any could, and
maintained instead that in a genuine conditional the denial of the
consequent actually 'conflicts' (*machetai*) with the antecedent.[20] Without wishing to commit myself at all on the nature of this 'conflict', I shall
for convenience follow a common way of talking, and put the point by
saying that antecedent and consequent have a *necessary* connexion. In

---

[19] Cicero *De Divinatione* i 127, ii 15 and 17, ii 25. For the Stoic view, see *SVF* ii 939–44.

[20] Sextus Empiricus, *Outlines of Pyrrhonism* ii 110–12, distinguishes four theories,
ascribing the first to Philo. Cicero, *Academica Priora* ii 143, tells us that Philo and
Chrysippus disagreed. M. Kneale suggests that Chrysippus' theory was that the denial of
the consequent is in conflict with (*machetai*) the antecedent ((31.21) 129). This would fit
with Cicero's use of the notion of conflict (*pugnare*) in reference to Chrysippus (*De Fato* vi
12), and with Diogenes Laertius' ascription of the 'conflict' view to the Stoics (vii 73). For
evidence that some Stoics none the less preferred Philo's view, see Sextus *Outlines* ii
104–5; *Against the Mathematicians* viii 245–7, 447, 449; Simplicius commentary on
Aristotle's *Physics*, CIAG 1299 36. Here Sextus seems to ascribe Philo's view quite
generally to the Stoics, and he bases one of his criticisms on the assumption that they took
it (*Outlines* ii 115–18; *Against the Mathematicians* viii 268, 449–51).

that case, by treating the astrologers' statements as equivalent merely to material implications, he shows that he does not regard them as genuine conditionals. Why not?

It is at this point that Michael Frede, in line with S. Sambursky, offers his alternative. Chrysippus insists on material implication, he suggests, because the link between time of birth, and place of death is *empirical*. Chrysippus, on this interpretation, would have wished to confine genuine conditionals to stating logical, not empirical, connexions. The 'conflict' between the antecedent and the denial of the consequent will have been a *logical* one.

Frede is most candid in acknowledging difficulties in this interpretation, and there are a good number of them. One important one is that the distinction between empirical and logical was not a favoured one in antiquity. For another thing, Cicero clearly does not think that material implication was recommended for empirical connexions in general, since he implies that Chrysippus did not consider treating as a material implication the connexion, which is surely empirical, between a quickened pulse and fever. Indeed, Cicero speaks as if Chrysippus formulated no general principle as to which conditionals were genuine and which not.[21]

Frede acknowledges yet another difficulty. A sign is defined by the Stoics as the antecedent in a certain kind of conditional, the thing signified being the consequent.[22] And we have just seen that the Stoics generally gave the antecedent a *necessary* connexion with the consequent in a genuine conditional. Yet the sign and thing signified, which have this necessary connexion, appear in several of Sextus' examples to be related *empirically*, or at least not with a *logical* necessity. Thus milk in the breasts is a sign of having conceived, blushing of shame, sweat of pores in the skin, a viscid bronchial discharge of a wound in the lungs, bodily movements of the presence of soul, smoke of fire, a scar of a wound, and a puncture in the heart of imminent death.[23]

This evidence that empirical connexions may for the Stoics be necessary might be discounted by someone who followed Sextus. For in the very passages which concern us, Sextus defines the Stoic conditional without reference to there being a *necessary* link between antecedent and consequent (*Outlines* ii 104, *Against the Mathematicians* viii 245). But at the same time, he shows himself aware that the definition was a matter of dispute among the Stoics, and Frede himself has argued convincingly that the normal Stoic definition did postulate a necessary connexion.

[21] He implies that Chrysippus had not explained why we should not treat as a material implication the (logical) connexion between two lines being greatest circles on a sphere and their intersecting each other.

[22] Sextus, *Outlines* ii 104, *Against the Mathematicians* viii 245. I am grateful to Malcolm Schofield for drawing my attention to this.

[23] Sextus *Against the Mathematicians* viii 152–5, 173, 252; *Outlines* ii 100, 102, 142.

Frede recognises the difficulty, and allows that after all there were Stoics who treated some empirical relationships as stateable in genuine conditionals and as involving a necessary connexion. His only plea is that these Stoics may have been later than Chrysippus.[24] Part of his evidence is that the distinction between 'indicative' and 'commemorative' signs, which enters into this discussion, may have been a late one. But this evidence is called into question by Jacques Brunschwig, who has found very early traces of it.[25]

There is a further difficulty which seems to me still more significant. Cicero has just earlier introduced the idea of a 'natural cause', and he assumes Chrysippus will have to agree that, if there is a natural cause of Fabius' not dying at sea, it is not *possible* that Fabius will die at sea. He does not record Chrysippus as having answered the objection by employing the idea of material implication. Why not? For Chrysippus would be able to escape, if he could argue that we have only a material implication, and not a genuine conditional, in the proposition that if such a natural cause of immunity already exists, then Fabius will not die at sea. In fact, however, Chrysippus is represented as leaving the objection unanswered, and as employing the idea of material implication not in connexion with statements about the natural cause of Fabius' immunity, but only in connexion with statements about the *astrological evidence* for that immunity.

Chrysippus' silence could be explained away, if it could be made out that, in his view, cause and effect have a *logical* relation. We could then understand why he does not offer to analyse a statement of natural cause by means of material implication. But, as I indicated in Chapter Three, it is not easy to see how cause and effect could be represented as always having a logical link.

I think that on the whole the evidence is against Frede's suggestion. An alternative has been offered by P. L. Donini.[26] His hypothesis is that time of birth is a mere *sign* of place of death, and that this is why the two are related only by material implication. On this view, although the Stoics treated the existence of astrological signs as a proof of the existence of necessitating causes,[27] they will not have thought there was any necessary connexion involved when one reported the sign, rather than the cause, of the eventual outcome. It might seem to support this interpretation that Aristotle himself, who had earlier cited milk in the breasts as a sign of having conceived, seems to waver on the question of whether a sign can be necessarily linked to the thing signified.[28] But

[24] M. Frede, op. cit. 89.

[25] Jacques Brunschwig, 'Proof defined', in (3.3).

[26] P. L. Donini (31.15) 1974–5.

[27] See, for example the section on divination as a proof of the necessity of fate in *SVF* ii 939–44.

[28] Aristotle normally recognised that there could be a necessary link and gave the example, later used by the Stoics: if she has milk she has conceived. Plato *Menexenus* 237E;

this suggestion runs into the same difficulty as the preceding one. For if a sign is the antecedent in a genuine conditional, it *will* have a necessary connexion with the thing signified, and their relationship cannot be represented by material implication. Moreover, it might in any case be doubted that a sign *never* has a necessary link with the thing signified. For one example of a sign is the premises of a valid and conclusive syllogism.[29] And in these the conclusion follows by necessity.[30]

A modification of Donini's suggestion would exploit the Stoic distinction between two kinds of sign commemorative (*hupomnēstikon*) and indicative (*endeiktikon*).[31] The commemorative sign signifies something temporarily non-evident, and works, as its name suggests, by *reminding* us of what it has been observably correlated with in the past. The indicative sign, on the contrary, signifies something which is non-evident by nature, and which cannot therefore have been *observably* correlated with anything encountered in the past. Instead, it makes us *reason* to the existence of the thing signified, not on the basis of memory, but by the force of its own nature and constitution. To illustrate: if sweat flows through the skin, this is an *indicative* sign of there being invisible pores, but an astrological conjunction must be a *commemorative* sign of the manner of Fabius' future death. The new suggestion would be that Chrysippus postulates material implication because time of birth is a merely *commemorative* sign of mode of death. But this suggestion also violates our evidence; for Sextus clearly intends to place indicative and commemorative signs on the *same* footing, when he says in *Outlines* ii 101 that a sign is the antecedent in a conditional; and he goes on to give a *single* account (even if not the expected account) of how the Stoics understand conditionals (ii 104).

I would suggest tentatively that it is more likely that Cicero is right. On his view, Chrysippus had not worked out when to treat something as a material implication rather than a genuine conditional. Another interesting instance of the resort to material implication comes in the formulation of the Sorites argument: if two is few, three is few; if three is few, four is few; if four is few, . . . and so on.[32] The Stoics who related this argument converted it to the form: 'not both (two is few and three is not few)', perhaps because they felt uncertain about the exact relation between antecedent and consequent, and were confident only that you

---

Aristotle *An. Pr.* ii 27; *Rhet.* i 2, ii 25; Sextus *Outlines* ii 106, *Against the Mathematicians* viii 252). But at one point, he introduces an uncharacteristically strict criterion for necessity, so that there is necessity only where there is a definitional connexion (*An. Post.* i 4, 73a34 – b5; i 6, 74b12; 75a20–2, a31). And in this context, he seems to imply that sign and thing signified are not linked by necessity, even if linked invariably (i 6, 75a31–4).
    [29] Sextus *Outlines* ii 96, 122, 131, 134; *Against the Mathematicians* viii 180, 277.
    [30] Sextus *Against the Mathematicians* viii 304; *kat' anankēn.*
    [31] This was suggested to me by Myles Burnyeat. For the distinction, see Sextus *Outlines* ii 99–102, *Against the Mathematicians* viii 151–5.
    [32] Diogenes Laertius vii 82, and see David Sedley (10.1).

would not get the first without the second. In other cases, it is hard to discern why material implication is used.[33]

The Stoic arguments considered so far are designed to ward off certain particular dificulties. It remains for Chrysippus to show how his whole treatment of fate can leave room for alternative possibilities.

The fifth attempt: possibility as aptitude in Philo

One argument to allow for alternative possibilities might be based on Philo's definition of the possible. For Philo said that it was possible for a piece of wood at the bottom of the ocean to be burnt, in virtue of the bare *fitness* of the subject (*epitēdeiotēs*), and some Stoics evidently followed him. External obstacles to its being burnt are ignored in assessing possibility. By this test of possibility, alternatives would be possible, even if fate ensured that obstacles prevented one of the two outcomes from being realised.

But it is doubtful that the Stoics can in general avail themselves of this argument. For most sources[34] expressly distinguish their definition of possibility from Philo's, by saying that it lays down *two* necessary conditions for possibility, *not only* something corresponding to Philo's 'fitness', *but also* the absence of external obstacles. The possible is that which admits of being true, there not being opposition from external obstacles.

The difference from Philo's definition is easily obscured. The most serious difficulty, though not the only one,[35] is that the grammatical construction in some of the formulations is ambiguous. Is the absence of obstacles meant to be a second prerequisite for *possibility*, as I have claimed, or merely a prerequisite for the possible thing actually being *true*? This makes all the difference.

The ambiguity helps to account for the disagreement among interpreters, several of whom assimilate the Stoic definition to Philo's.[36] One translates the Stoic definition in such a way that the absence of obstacles appears as a prerequisite of truth, not of possibility.[37] Another does

[33] Alexander, *De Fato* 35 and 37, oscillates between the two forms, without any obvious reason, in his report of some Stoic arguments.

[34] Diogenes Laertius vii 75 explicitly refers to the Stoics. Boethius, 2nd commentary on Aristotle's *Int.*, ed. Meiser, 234, cites Philo and the Stoics. Three other sources contrast the definitions without attributing them: Simplicius, commentary on Aristotle's *Cat. CIAG* 195–6; Alexander *Quaestiones* i 4, p. 9 lines 5–7, p. 12 lines 5–12; Ps–Plutarch *De Fato* 571A.

[35] Another difficulty is that one of the two conditions is occasionally cited without the other, something like Philo's condition being attributed by Plutarch to the Stoics (*De Stoicorum Repugnantiis* 1055D–F).

[36] So Benson Mates, *Stoic Logic*, Berkeley, 2nd ed. 1961, 41; I. M. Bochenski, *Ancient Formal Logic*, Amsterdam 1951, 87; Margaret Reesor (next note).

[37] Margaret E. Reesor, 'Fate and possibility in early Stoic philosophy', *Phoenix* 19, 1965, 291.

the opposite, and attributes both definitions to Philo, construing the absence of obstacles in one account of Philo's definition as a condition of possibility, not of truth.[38] Yet another interpreter suggests that the Stoics recognised two separate senses of each modal term on the grounds that two criteria are cited in the Stoic definition of necessity.[39] But since it is agreed that there is no mention of two senses in the corresponding definition of possibility, it is easier to suppose that in each case there is a single sense defined by *two* necessary conditions.

That the normal Stoic definition was not Philo's is clearly implied by Boethius. That the insistence on absence of external obstacles is an *additional* precondition of possibility over and above fitness is implied by Alexander, Simplicius, and the author of the *De Fato* of pseudo-Plutarch.

This finding is amply confirmed by Frede.[40] In a careful study, he takes the Stoic definitions of four modal terms, as they are recorded by Diogenes Laertius, and he places two constraints on any interpretation. First, the terms (possible, impossible, necessary, non-necessary) should come out as far as possible having the right relation to *each other*. Secondly, Diogenes' word 'admitting of' (*epidektikon*) should come out having the same sense in each of the definitions where it appears. It emerges that these two reasonable requirements can be conveniently met, only if the absence of external obstacles is taken in the manner suggested above, namely, as an *additional* prerequisite for something's being possible.

We should ask, however, what would have happened if the absence of external obstacles had not been made an extra prerequisite for possibility, and if the normal Stoic definition of possibility had appealed, like Philo's, to mere fitness. Would they then have been able to allow for alternative possibilities in a morally significant sense? I think not; for it is hard to believe that bare fitness to act otherwise than one does would give one a morally significant possibility of acting otherwise. If this fitness is frustrated by external obstacles, could one then be blamed for anything? None the less, there have been comparable arguments in the modern literature, to the effect that we can escape from determinism, by insisting that, in something like Philo's sense, we have a capacity or aptitude for acting otherwise than we do.[41]

The sixth attempt: internal causes

A sixth Stoic argument seems to have been based on a distinction between internal and external causes. But it is hard to be sure what the conclusion of the argument was. Three authors report it in turn: Cicero,

---

[38] S. Sambursky (31.16) 74.   [39] M. Kneale in (31.21) 122–6.
[40] M. Frede, op. cit. 107–17.
[41] See M. Ayers, *The Refutation of Determinism*, London 1968.

Aulus Gellius and St. Augustine, and the last two had both read Cicero's account. According to St. Augustine, the aim of the argument was to show that our wills are not subject to necessity at all.[42] The other two accounts are more nuanced, although some phrases in Cicero, taken in isolation, could well have suggested the Augustinian interpretation. Thus Chrysippus is said to reject necessity, to aim at escaping necessity while retaining fate, and to side more with those who want the mind to be free from necessity of motion.[43]

In order to decide what the conclusion was, we should first consider the premises, to see how they drew the distinction between internal and external causes. Zeno had made causes into sufficient conditions, by saying that it was *impossible* (*adunaton*) for a cause to be present and that which it caused to be absent.[44] But Chrysippus drew a distinction between causes.[45] External conditions are only necessary and never sufficient to produce human action. Among the external necessary conditions, one of the most important is the sensory appearance (*phantasia*) which is presented to the agent. From the *external* necessary conditions of action we should distinguish the *internal* efficient causes, some of which produce their results necessarily (*necessario*), some not.[46] The most important of these are assent (*sunkatathesis*) and impulse (*hormē*), and we are told by one source that every impulse actually is an assent.[47]

If we move back a stage, and ask what is the cause of assent, we find that the external sensory appearance (*phantasia*) is again merely a necessary condition. The internal cause of assent is the character and quaility of our minds. Chrysippus compares a cylinder rolling down a slope. The external necessary conditions needed for its rolling is the agent who pushes it, but the internal cause is its own character and nature.[48]

With the distinction of internal and external causes now outlined, I am in a position to distinguish three interpretations of Chrysippus'

[42] Augustine *City of God* v 10.

[43] These phrases are taken from Cicero *De Fato* 39 and 41.

[44] Stobaeus *Eclogues* I (= Diels, *Doxographici Graeci* 457; *SVF* I 89).

[45] For the fullest account of Chrysippus' distinctions, see Clement of Alexandria *Stromateis* VIII 9, Cicero *Topics* 58–60. For their application to human conduct, see Cicero *De Fato* 39–45; Alexander *De Fato* 13–14; Aulus Gellius *Attic Nights* VII 2; Origen, extracts in *SVF* II 988 (esp. p. 288, line 23), 989 (esp. p. 289, line 12); Plutarch *De Stoicorum Repugnantiis* 47, 1055F – 1056D.

[46] Cicero *Topics* 59–60.

[47] Stobaeus *Eclogues* II (= *SVF* III 171). They differ in that the assent is directed to a proposition, the impulse to the action which it mentions. Alexander (*De Anima, CIAG* 72 13 – 73 1) rejects the idea that every assent is an impulse, but not the idea that every impulse is an assent. Plutarch, however, gives us the weaker formulation that an impulse cannot exist without assent (*De Stoicorum Repugnantiis* 1057A), and other passages the still weaker one that an impulse *culminating in action* cannot exist without assent Cicero *Academica Priora* II 24; Plutarch (*De Stoicorum Repugnantiis* 1057B).

[48] Aulus Gellius *Attic Nights* VII 2 11; Cicero *De Fato* 42–3.

conclusion. On one view, the distinction of causes is meant to show that our assent is not subject to necessity. That is how Augustine takes it. It is suggested by some of Cicero's phrases, and we shall see that there were others besides the Stoics who hoped to escape from necessity by relying on *internal* causes. On the other hand, it is baffling how the argument could in fact establish that our assent is not necessitated. Why should it not be necessitated, for example, by our own inner state?

An alternative has been suggested by Donini.[49] According to this, Cicero misunderstood Chrysippus, who was not making a point about necessity at all. Allowing all things to be necessitated by fate, and fate to include all causes, he none the less looked for a way in which moral responsibility could be preserved. It can be, in Chrysippus' view, if the distinction between internal and external causes is used in order to define a sense in which things can still be up to us or in our power (*in nostra potestate* will be the Latin translation of *eph' hēmin*: see Cicero *De Fato* 41, 43, 45; Aulus Gellius *Attic Nights* VII 2 15). Donini takes it that this sort of account is intended by Gellius.

A third interpretation has been suggested to me by Frede. This alternative takes its start from the fact that Cicero says Chrysippus tried to adopt a *middle* position.[50] He was between those who said that all things happen by fate in such a way that fate exercises the force of necessity, and those who said that our minds move without any fate at all, although he sided more with those who wanted our minds to be free from any necessity of movement. It would be possible to assign Chrysippus a *middle* position, if we do two things. First, we should emphasise that Chrysippus is sometimes described as denying not necessity (*tout court*), but the necessity of *fate* (*necessitas fati,* Cicero *De Fato* 39). Again, he attacks those who attach necessity to *fate* (§ 42), as his opponents are said to do (§ 40). We shall be obliged to reinterpret the references to Chrysippus' denying necessity as elliptical allusions to his denying the necessity of *fate*. Secondly, we should take fate to consist only of *external* causes. In denying the necessity of *fate*, he would then not be denying the *existence* of necessity, but only making a point about its *source*. Necessity would not be derived from fate, i.e. from *external* causes.

But what would be the point of arguing this? It would be to draw a conclusion about what is 'in our power'. Impulse (§ 41) and assent (§ 43) are in our power. For their perfect cause is the character and quality of our minds, which may be compared with the inner nature of the rolling cylinder (cf. Aulus Gellius *Attic Nights* VII 2 7–11). What matters about this perfect cause is that it is *internal*;[51] and, for the purpose of assessing

---

[49] P. L. Donini (31.15).   [50] Cicero *De Fato* 39.

[51] Contrast the sensory appearances, which are *external*. But they do not stop assent from being in our power, because they are not *perfect* causes of assent, but only *auxiliary* causes (*adiuvantes* is the Latin translation of the Greek *sunerga*, §§ 41–2).

whether something is in our power, Chrysippus simply does not consider
whether it is necessitated, but only whether it is necessitated by *external* causes. We shall see that this is exactly the view attributed by
Alexander of Aphrodisias to his Stoic opponents.[52]

If either of the last two interpretations is correct, then the present
argument does not after all belong with the other ones we have been
discussing. For there will be no attempt to deny that everything is
necessitated. The strategy will rather be to find room for moral responsibility in spite of necessitation.

A difficulty for the third interpretation is that it makes Chrysippus
identify fate, not with the sum total of causes, but only with the external
ones. Whether he did so is hard to determine. Cicero believes that he
did.[53] Moreover, this is mentioned by Plutarch as a possible interpretation of Chrysippus, though not as his explicit contention.[54] Aulus Gellius also speaks at times as if the character of our minds exercised a
causal influence independently of fate.[55] A number of modern commentators, therefore, accept that fate is confined to *external* causes.[56] On the
other side, however, Plutarch complains that if Chrysippus does mean
to confine fate to external causes, he will be contradicting what he says
elsewhere. For according to Plutarch, Chrysippus claims that nothing
rests or moves in the slightest degree except in accordance with the
reason of Zeus, which is identified with fate, while fate is identified with
an inevitable necessity, not with a mere necessary condition which can
be overriden.[57] Gellius also reports that for Chrysippus *all* things are
compelled by a necessary and principal reason and are bound together
by fate. Moreover, he quotes Chrysippus' definition of fate as a natural
order of *all* things, following one another in succession from everlasting
with an unavoidable interconnexion.[58] Cicero agrees that, for Chrysippus, *all* things happen by fate.[59] One source records that the inner
impulse (*hormē*), which is apparently an assent, is given to us by fate in
Chrysippus' opinion.[60] Indeed, it was the common view of Stoic theory in
general, and of Chrysippus' theory in particular, that the necessity of

[52] Alexander *De Fato* 13, 26; cf. *Quaestiones* II 4, *CIAG* p. 50, line 30.
[53] Cicero *Topics* 59, *De Fato* 41 and 43.
[54] Plutarch *De Stoicorum Repugnantiis* 1056B.
[55] Aulus Gellius *Attic Nights* VII 2 7–8 and 11.
[56] For modern endorsements of this interpretation see the notes *ad loc.* of H. Cherniss to
(31.20) 1976; W. Theiler (31.17) 1946, p. 64, note 1; M. E. Reesor, 'Fate and possibility in
early Stoic philosophy', *Phoenix* 19, 1965, 285–97.
[57] Plutarch, *De Stoicorum Repugnantiis* 1056B.
[58] Aulus Gellius *Attic Nights* VII 2, 3 and 7.
[59] Cicero *De Fato* 21.
[60] Nemesius *On the Nature of Man* 35 (= *SVF* II 991). M. E. Reesor, op. cit., 287, seeks to
disarm this reference by suggesting that what is given us by fate is not impulse, but
merely the power of giving or withholding assent. Her evidence is that impulse is elsewhere said to be in our power. But this will not serve as evidence if, as we are told
elsewhere, the Stoics were willing to argue that things can be in our power (or up to us) in
spite of being fated and necessitated.

fate applied to every detail.[61] The third interpretation, then, must saddle Chrysippus with a *volte-face* about the comprehensiveness of fate.

On any interpretation, the argument does not seem to me a happy one. On the first interpretation, it tries like the others, but fails, to reject necessity. On either the second or the third, it takes a view which I do not myself believe, but which has been popular in modern times, that moral responsibility is compatible with universal necessitation.

Whatever Chrysippus' position in the present argument, it is not the same as the appeal by Philo and certain Stoics to possibility as aptitude in the preceding one. This will be clear enough if Chrysippus is not denying necessity at all. But even if he is denying it, and allowing for alternative possibilities, he still differs from Philo. For unlike Philo he recognises that external circumstances can restrict possibilities by failing to supply a necessary condition.

The seventh attempt: epistemic possibility

Two final Stoic attempts to escape necessity, and to allow for alternative possibilities, are recorded by Alexander of Aphrodisias, in his *De Fato*, ch. 10, although he does not himself tell us who devised the arguments. The opening moves of the first argument are best given in a footnote.[62] What matters is that, at a certain point, the Stoics, who are presumably the authors of the argument, try to establish that alternatives are not prevented, by pleading that we often do not *know* what factors prevent the things which fail to occur. But Alexander protests that this cannot be accepted as a proof that they are not prevented. And he adds that, if anyone pressed the plea of ignorance further, and it is not clear that anyone did, he would end up with a merely epistemic sense of possibility. He would be saying that, even if everything happens in accordance with fate, alternatives are still possible as regards the future; and he would mean merely that they are compatible with the limited state of our knowledge.

Certainly this can be a useful way of talking, but in spite of Tony Long's spirited defence of the Stoics,[63] my sympathies lie with Alexan-

[61] All the sources in notes 1 and 5 above, except Alexander, mention Chrysippus in particular.

[62] The argument starts from the Stoic definition of the possible as what is prevented by nothing from occurring. If this is to be faithful to the Stoics' intentions, Alexander must be referring to prevention whether by intrinsic unfitness, or by external obstacles. The idea is mooted by the Stoics that the opposite of what happens by fate is not actually *prevented* from happening, and is therefore possible. To this the objection is raised that the causes which make one thing happen in accordance with fate equally cause its opposite not to happen; for, on the Stoic view, it is impossible for the same circumstances to be attended by opposite results. The Stoics try to establish that alternatives are *not* prevented, by means of the epistemic argument cited in the text.

[63] See A. A. Long (31.8) 1970, 257.

der. For a merely epistemic sense of possibility would not help with any of the moral problems that concern the Stoics. If the question is how praise and blame can be appropriate, it cannot help to say that there is an *epistemic* sense in which a person has the possibility of acting otherwise than he does.

The eighth attempt: non-necessity as ceasing to be true

In the other argument cited by Alexander, an appeal is made to the definition of a necessary proposition as one which will *always* be true. This looks slightly closer to Diodorus' requirement that a necessary proposition will never be false than to the Stoic requirement that either it does not admit of being false or else it is prevented from being false by external circumstances.[64] If the argument was devised by a Stoic, then it may have been intended as an *ad hominem* argument against Diodorean determinism. But in fact the argument can be adapted so that it applies equally to a Stoic or to a Diodorean definition of necessity.

The argument is that it cannot be a necessary proposition that there will be a sea battle tomorrow. For this proposition, with its future tense, cannot remain true once the battle is over. (Indeed, it might be added, it will then become false.)

At least two doubts should be raised about this argument. First, were the Stoics and Diodorus right to agree, as they did, that a change from truth to falsity would prove a proposition not to be necessary? After all, the proposition that Scipio will die is like the proposition that there will be a sea battle tomorrow, in containing a future tense, which will prevent it from being true after the event. Yet, for all that, Scipio's contemporaries could justifiably regard it as a necessary proposition that he would die.

Then there is the question whether propositions do change from truth to falsity. Diodorus evidently maintained that the proposition that Scipio will die cannot so change.[65] He presumably had not considered the problem created by the future tense 'will'. A modern logician would deal with this problem by saying that there is not a *single* proposition that Scipio will die, which changes its truth value from true to false. Rather, each time the sentence 'Scipio will die' is used, it expresses a *different* proposition. One speaker expresses the proposition that Scipio's death is later than his utterance; another speaker expresses the different proposition that Scipio's death is later than his quite *different* utterance. Of these two propositions, the first is changelessly true and the second changelessly false. There is not a *single* proposition which changes from true to false.

[64] For Diodorus, see Boethius, 2nd comm. on *Int.*, ed. Meiser, 234; for the Stoics, Diogenes Laertius vii 75, both cited above.
[65] Cicero *De Fato* 17–18.

The Stoics are now confronted with a dilemma. Either their test for necessity prevents it from being a necessary proposition that Scipio will die. Or, if they avail themselves of modern logic, in order to avoid that result, their test will make *all* propositions necessary, even the proposition that there will be a sea battle tomorrow. For *no* propositions will change from true to false.

Resumé

I hope it will have been of some use to distinguish these eight arguments, for they are not always sharply distinguished. The fifth has been assimilated to the sixth,[66] the seventh to the fifth,[67] and the third to the fourth.[68] In particular, I would dissent from the view that the Stoics allow *only* an epistemic possibility so that other arguments must be seen as versions of the seventh.[69]

My conclusion is that the ancients were right to regard as unsuccessful the various Stoic attempts to escape from commitment to necessity. In that case, my earlier comparison of Stoic with modern views can stand: they did relate causation firmly both to exceptionless regularity and to necessity.

Positions adopted in the ancient debate on causal determinism

To conclude, I ought to make clear that Chrysippus' strategy of trying to retreat from commitment to necessity was only one of many adopted in the ancient debate on causal determinism. I can usefully distinguish five others. In doing so, I have been much helped by the lucid publications of Robert Sharples.[70]

(i) Surprisingly, those Stoics who looked for a sense in which they could deny necessity came close to a certain group of their opponents. Their opponents denied from the start the every event occurred of necessity. But they were then embarrassed, as we have seen, by the charge that changes which occurred not of necessity would be causeless. To escape this charge, we saw some of them insisting that they were not postulating causeless changes, but only changes with a special kind of cause: a fortuitous cause, an internal cause, or a mere necessary condition.

[66] M. E. Reesor, op. cit. (endorsed by A. A. Long (31.7), footnote 55 to p. 189), ascribes to the Stoics a definition of possibility like Philo's and then relates that definition closely to the fifth argument about internal causes.

[67] The authors of the argument for epistemic possibility (the seventh) quote in their support something like Philo's definition from the fifth.

[68] P. L. Donini remarks on this conflation, in (31.14).

[69] A. A. Long (31.7) 176, 189, note 15; (31.8) 248, 256: 'Possibility exists to the extent that, but only to the extent that, men are ignorant of the future.'

[70] See his (31.12) Section 4, 'The problem of uncaused motion', 44–6, and his references below relating to 'hard' determinism.

The net result of this manoeuvre was that both parties were looking for a way of showing that something could be caused without being necessitated. The difference between their conclusions would only be that those Stoics who had committed themselves to acknowledging the necessitation of all effects would need to distinguish a sense in which they were necessitated and a sense in which they were not.

(ii) The claim to have found a special kind of cause was not the only line taken against the Stoics. A less common reply to them was that events could occur without a cause. I have already argued that Aristotle denies in *Metaph.* vi 3 that coincidences have causes. This should help us to understand some remarks of Alexander of Aphrodisias which have been found puzzling. Once in the *De Fato*, and once in the *Mantissa* (if he is the author of the relevant section), Alexander slips from arguing for a special sort of cause into arguing for no cause at all.[71] And in this, he need not be devising a fantastical argument of his own, as has been suggested,[72] but simply following the opinion of Aristotle in *Metaph.* vi 3. The best known attempt, however, to introduce causeless events is that of Epicurus with his uncaused atomic swerve.[73]

(iii) The Stoics too had more lines of argument. One line no longer seeks a sense in which necessity can be denied. Indeed, necessity is asserted,[74] and it is claimed that our ordinary concepts of morality and conduct are compatible with the necessity of all things.[75] We have already encountered this as an alternative interpretation of one of the earlier arguments. The most important moral concept is that of an action's being up to us (*eph' hēmin*). It is claimed that an action is up to us, if it is in accordance with our impulse (*hormē*), and occurs *through* us (*di' hēmōn*). And it is explicitly denied that an action's being up to us implies the possibility of alternative actions.[76] In one way, this is reminiscent of Moritz Schlick's account of freedom, that a man is free so long as he does not act under compulsion, where compulsion is defined as the hindrance of natural desires by external factors or by unnatural internal ones.[77] However, Schlick's idea differs from the present one in that he does not admit the necessity of all things.

(iv) In one version, the last line of argument goes over to the offen-

---

[71] Alexander *De Fato* 8 174 3–11: spontaneous events lack causes. Alexander (?) *Mantissa* 170 2 – 171 27: an accidental cause is not a cause (171 13–14), and therefore some events lack causes (170 7–8, 172 9). See Sharples (31.12).

[72] Alexander need not be guided by the rather disreputable argument which A. A. Long rightly deplores in (31.8) 251.

[73] Lucretius *De Rerum Natura* ii 216–93; Cicero *De Fato* x 22–3; *De Finibus* i 6 19; *De Natura Deorum* i 25 69; Diogenes of Oenoanda, fragment 32 ii – iii (Chilton).

[74] Alexander *De Fato* 13, 34, 36; Diogenianus *ap.* Eusebium *Praeparatio Evangelica* vi 8, 265d (= *SVF* ii 998).

[75] Diogenianus loc. cit. 265d – 267a; Alexander *De Fato* 13–14, 33, 35–8; Nemesius *On the Nature of Man* 35.

[76] Alexander *De Fato* 13, 26; cf. *Quaestiones* ii 4, *CIAG* p. 50, line 30.

[77] Moritz Schlick (30.2) 1939.

sive. In a style reminiscent of certain modern authors (Hobart, Schlick)[78] it argues that our ordinary conceptions about conduct actually require fate (which Alexander, in his report, still associates with necessity). Without fate, there would be no law, no right or wrong, no virtue or vice, no good or bad, nothing praiseworthy or blameworthy, no honour or punishment, no reward or correction, no wisdom, and no knowledge of right or wrong.

(v) The rarest view in antiquity was that which William James has called *hard* determinism.[79] The hard determinist not only maintains that everything is necessary, *but also* accepts that, because of this, there is no moral responsibility. The first Stoic, Zeno, has an argument with which a hard determinist would agree, though it is unlikely that he himself, with his strong moral views, was a hard determinist. If the thief pleads it was fated that he would steal, we can reply it was fated he would be thrashed.[80] Where does this argument come from? The earliest instance I know of the same pattern of argument appears in a non-philosophical context. In Aeschylus' *Choephoroe*, Clytemnestra seeks to excuse herself for the murder of Agamemnon by blaming fate. Orestes replies that fate now has something in store for her.[81] Subsequently, Zeno's contemporary and rival Epicurus anticipated, and objected to, an analogous argument which 'assigned chance necessity to our admonishing and being admonished'.[82] Presumably, Epicurus envisaged a determinist who was faced with the difficulty that necessity would remove the justification for admonishing people, and who replied by saying that, justifiable or not, the practice of admonition was necessitated. There are signs of a similar move in Eusebius, and Robert Sharples has drawn my attention to two other examples in Manilius and Galen.[83] But the strategy is comparatively rare, and in any case does not go quite all the way to denying the existence of moral responsibility, or the justifiability of our moral practices.

To summarise the history of the controversy, as I see it: in Aristotle's time, determinists were not differentiated into the hard, who denied moral responsibility altogether, and the soft, who claimed that it was compatible with determinism. On the contrary, Aristotle addresses himself to undifferentiated determinists, and raises against them objections, which will be discussed in Chapter Fifteen, to show that determinism is incompatible with normal ways of thinking about conduct. The

---

[78] Alexander *De Fato* 35–7. Cf. R. E. Hobart (30.3) 1934, and Moritz Schlick op. cit.

[79] William James, 'The dilemma of determinism', *Unitarian Review* 1884, reprinted in *The Will to Believe and Other Essays*, London 1897.

[80] Diogenes Laertius VII 1 23.   [81] Aeschylus *Choephoroe* 909-11.

[82] Epicurus, *On Nature*, ed. Arrighetti, 2nd edition, 34.27. 'For if someone assigned *tēn kata to automaton anankēn* to admonishing and being admonished, . . .' I learnt of this passage from David Sedley.

[83] Eusebius *Praeparatio Evangelica* VI 6 15 (244A); Manilius *Astronomicon* IV 106–18; Galen *Quod Animi Mores* 11 init.

'soft' reply, that there is no incompatibility, did not come until much later, perhaps with Chrysippus, the third head of the Stoic school. The 'hard' reply, that, thanks to determinism, there is indeed no moral responsibility, probably had little appeal. But quite early Zeno, the founder of the Stoic school, and Epicurus, his contemporary, were conscious of an attitude which hard determinists share, namely, that punishment and admonition are inevitable, whether or not justifiable.

PART II

NECESSITY AND TIME

CHAPTER FIVE

Tomorrow's Sea Battle: an argument from past truth (*Int*. 9)

Aristotle's most famous treatment of determinism in *De Interpretatione* 9 is not concerned with causation at all. And indeed it is often not appreciated that he ever concerned himself with *causal* determinism. For the determinist to whom he replies in *Int*. 9 makes no explicit appeal to causality. Instead he reaches his conclusion that things happen of necessity apparently by reference to the premise that of two contradictory predictions one is true (18b7), is earlier true (18b10), has always been true (18b10–11), and has been true for the whole of time (19a1–2). The well-known example of the occurrence or non-occurrence of a sea battle tomorrow comes a little later in the chapter. It is not explained how this determinist moves from considerations about truth to a claim of necessity. There are any number of suggestions in the modern literature about what may have motivated him.[1] I shall consider in Chapter Eight Hintikka's suggestion that he is moved by the 'always' in 'always been true'. But I think his argument looks most plausible, if it is based on the 'earlier' of 'earlier true'. His idea will then be that, whatever is happening now, it was true earlier, say, at noon yesterday, and indeed ten thousand years ago, that it would be happening. But in that case, it was no good my deliberating at one o'clock yesterday afternoon whether to make it true. For it was by then true already, and since the past cannot be altered (as Aristotle admits in a different connexion elsewhere in the chapter) it was by then too late for me to prevent its having been true. The only influence I could hope to have would be as the agent who made it to have been true. I would have no hope of making it to have been false.

I shall discuss at the end of the chapter whether this deterministic argument would be sound. But if the determinist is arguing in this way

---

[1] A fairly full bibliography is given by Hintikka in (8.9) 1973, ch. 8, and a fuller one by R. Gale in (8.8) 1968. On why the move is tempting, we may cite, besides Hintikka himself, G. Ryle, *Dilemmas,* Cambridge 1954, ch. 2; R. Taylor, 'The problem of future contingencies', *Philosophical Review* 66, 1957, 1–28; R. Albritton, 'Present truth and future contingency', *ibid*. 29–46; C. Strang, 'Aristotle and the Sea Battle', *Mind* 69, 1960, 447–65; G. E. M. Anscombe (8.2) 1956; D. Frede, *Aristoteles und die Seeschlacht, Hypomnemata* vol. 27, Göttingen 1970; O. Becker (10.3) 1960. The only reliable English translation is that of J. L. Ackrill (8.1) 1963.

from the unalterability of the past, one way of answering him would be
to deny that every prediction is *already* true or false before the time of
the thing predicted. And this has in fact been denied in two different
ways. Many modern logicians think of truth and falsity as predicates
which attach *timelessly* to a proposition. For present purposes, it would
not be enough to say that the truth of a proposition attaches to it at *all*
times, for that would imply that it attached in the past, which is what
the determinist seeks to exploit. It must be maintained instead (and this
requires some extra argument, which is seldom given) that it makes no
sense to speak of truth and falsity as attaching at any *times*. Or at least
such talk must be reconstrued. The other way of denying that predictions must be already true or false is to say either that they are not true
or false at all, or that they only become true or false at the time of the
thing predicted, or when that thing becomes inevitable. A solution of
this kind has often been attributed to Aristotle. So let us consider what
the grounds are for attributing it to him.

   In 19a39 – b2, Aristotle concludes his discussion of predictions by
saying: 'so it is clear that it is not necessary that, of every affirmation
and opposite negation, one should be true and one false'. This is qualified in 19a39, on one natural interpretation, by saying that neither half
need 'yet' (*ēdē*) be true or false. Aristotle concedes that some predictions
are true in advance of the thing predicted, e.g. predictions about things
that are always going on or recurring (19a35–6), such as the prediction
that the sun will move or that summer will come. He does not explicitly
say whether other kinds of prediction would become true in advance, if
the thing predicted became inevitable in advance. But at any rate, many
predictions are not true or false in advance, on this interpretation. And
the conclusion is not confined, as is sometimes supposed, to predictions
about human actions.[2] Admittedly, some of the examples involve
human action, but even this is not clearly true of the example concerning something being white (18a39 – b25).

   For convenience, I shall refer to this interpretation of Aristotle as the
traditional one, although this is something of a misnomer, in view of my
theme below that there are rival interpretations just about as old. None
the less, I shall call it such, because it was the interpretation of Aristotle
taken by the Peripatetics (i.e. the Aristotelian school) according to
Simplicius.[3] And without mention of the 'yet' (*ēdē*), the same view was
ascribed to Aristotle by the Stoics, according to Boethius.[4] Moreover, the
denial of truth value, with or without the qualification 'yet', was
accepted as being a correct view in itself, necessary for avoiding deter-

   [2] *Pace* W. D. Ross, *Aristotle's Metaphysics*, Oxford 1926, vol. 1, lxxxi; R. Gale (9.2) 1968,
136.
   [3] Simplicius, Commentary on Aristotle's *Categories*, ed. Kalbfleisch, *Commentaria in
Aristotelem Graeca* (*CIAG*) 407 6–13.
   [4] Boethius, 2nd Commentary on Aristotle's *De Interpretatione*, ed. Meiser, Leipzig 1880,
208.

minism, by Epicurus, by the Platonist Nicostratus, and probably by the Aristotelian Alexander of Aphrodisias, while being rejected by the Stoic Chrysippus, by the Academic Carneades, and by Cicero.[5] In modern times, the majority of authors have accepted the traditional interpretation as giving a correct account of Aristotle, and some have added that Aristotle was right to take this view, either in order to avoid determinism, or for other reasons. Lukasiewicz explains in some lucid and penetrating papers how he was led by reflection on the problem of future contingents and the desire to avoid determinism, to introduce values other than true and false into modern formal logic, and to create the so-called many-valued logics, and he adds a valuable appendix on the history of the problem in antiquity.[6]

None the less, this is by no means the only interpretation of the chapter. Boethius mentions others,[7] and he himself explicitly denies what we have called the traditional interpretation,[8] and along with Ammonius, the other main ancient commentator on the *De Interpretatione*, endorses a different one. According to this, all predictions are for Aristotle true or false, but not 'definitely' true nor 'definitely' false. Boethius says that the qualification 'definitely' has to be understood,[9] and that the lack of definiteness is not a function of our ignorance, but is due to the nature of the propositions.[10] In spite of the obscurity of the word 'definitely', this interpretation was influential among mediaeval philosophers, and it is not surprising that Rescher is able to give a long list of mediaeval philosophers who dissented from what I have called the traditional view, although I would not agree that Al Farabi was the first

[5] Epicurus, *ap.* Cicero *De Fato* ix 18, x 21, xvi 37–8; *Academica* ii 30 97; *De Natura Deorum* i 25 70. Nicostratus *ap.* Simplicium, Commentary on Aristotle's *Categories* 406 13–16. Alexander of Aphrodisias *De Fato* 10 (177 7 – 178 7 in *CIAG*); 16 (187 22); 17 (188 3); 27 (197 12–17); but see below for a possibly different view in the *Quaestiones* attributed to him, i 4. For Chrysippus, Carneades and Cicero himself, see Cicero *De Fato* x 20–1, xii 27–8, xvi 38; *Academica Pr.* ii 95; Diogenes Laertius vii 65; Ps-Plutarch *De Fato* 574f.

[6] Some of the originals of Jan Lukasiewicz's papers of 1920, 1922 and 1930 are hard to find. But they appear in English translation as (8.3). The paper of 1930 has the historical appendix, on pp. 63–5 of McCall. Lukasiewicz was followed by A. Prior (8.4) 1953, who, however, changed his mind about how best to treat future contingents in a series of later publications, culminating in *Past, Present and Future*, Oxford 1967. For other endorsements of the denial of truth and falsity, see C. D. Broad, *Scientific Thought*, London 1923, 74, 83; R. Taylor, op. cit.; S. Cahn, *Fate, Logic and Time*, New Haven Conn. 1967, ch. 3; Storrs McCall (8.5) 1966; and (in connexion with the epithet 'correct') G. Ryle, *Dilemmas*, Cambridge 1955, ch. 2.

[7] Boethius, 2nd Commentary, ed. Meiser p. 215, mentions one which (running flat against 18b17–25) makes Aristotle treat each of two contradictory predictions as false.

[8] Boethius, 2nd Commentary, ed. Meiser, 208, line 7.

[9] Boethius, 1st Commentary, ed. Meiser, 125, line 20.

[10] Boethius, 2nd Commentary, ed. Meiser, 245. For the general view, see Ammonius, Commentary on *Int.*, *CIAG*, e.g. 130 23, 131 3–4, 138 17 – 139 20, 141 20, 154 11. Boethius, ed. Meiser, e.g. 1st Commentary 104 5 – 108 11, 124 23 – 126 21; 2nd Commentary 13 15, 199 28 – 201 2, 208 1 – 209 6, 215 21–6, 235 14–17, 245 10–12, 246 12, 247 28 – 250 14. Robert Sharples (31.13) has pointed out that the same view appears in *Quaestiones* i 4, which is ascribed, perhaps wrongly, to Alexander of Aphrodisias, *CIAG* 12 18, 13 4.

dissenter.[11] There have been plenty of modern dissenters too, who have expanded the range of alternatives in interesting ways.[12] Many think that Aristotle is not making a point about truth at all, but only about necessity.

As an interpretation of Aristotle, the traditional account fits well with the way in which the determinist's argument is presented. Aristotle seems repeatedly to say that the deterministic consequences follow if every affirmation and opposite negation is true or false (18a34, a37), or one true one false (b27–9), without giving any warning that he thinks the inference from premise to conclusion invalid. This leads us to expect that it is the premise which he will deny. None the less, there are difficulties for the traditional interpretation, of which I shall state two main ones. First, it seems to make Aristotle deny the law of excluded middle (p or not-p), which he affirms not only in *Metaph.* IV and XI, but even in this very chapter. But several answers have been suggested to this complaint. First, it has been suggested[13] that what Aristotle denies is only the principle of bivalence (every proposition is true or false), not the law of excluded middle (either p is true or not-p is true). Although these two principles may look alike, they will differ, if we allow that there are neuter truth values, and that in the case where p is neuter, not-p is true. In that case, the principle of bivalence would be violated, but the law of excluded middle would still hold. A second suggestion is that the principles which Aristotle recognises are not formulated by him in terms of *truth* and *falsehood*. Thus his formulations of the law of excluded middle are in terms of being (or coming to be), and not being (or coming to be), and again of affirming and denying, but are not in terms of *true* and *false*. And it might be argued that he did not recognise himself as committed to formulations of this last kind. This fits with the fact that in 19a27–32 he can happily affirm, 'It is necessary that there will be a sea battle tomorrow or that there will not be', shortly before he goes on (on the traditional interpretation) to deny that either disjunct is yet *true* or *false*. Unfortunately for these first two suggestions, Aristotle

[11] N. Rescher, in *Studies in the History of Arabic Logic*, Pittsburgh 1963, ch. 5, and in 'Truth and necessity in temporal perspective', in R. Gale, ed. (8.8) 1968. In the latter, he classifies Ammonius and Boethius, wrongly I should say, as being on the traditionalist side.

[12] A. Becker, 'Bestreitet Aristoteles die Gültigkeit des "Tertium non Datur" für Zukunftaussagen?', *Actes du Congrès international de Philosophie Scientifique* 6, Paris 1936, 69–74; L. Linsky, 'Professor Donald Williams on Aristotle', *Philosophical Review* 63, 1954, 250–2; R. J. Butler, 'Aristotle's Sea Fight and three-valued logic', *Philosophical Review* 64, 1955, 264–74; G. E. M. Anscombe, op. cit. 1956: C. Strang, op. cit. 1960; P. Wolff, 'Truth, futurity and contingency', *Mind* 69, 1960, 398–402; N. Rescher, op. cit. 1963; J. Hintikka (8.9) ch. 8, revised from *Philosophical Review* 73, 1964, 461–92.

[13] That Aristotle is denying the principle of bivalence, without denying the law of excluded middle, was suggested by Jan Lukasiewicz, op. cit. 1930. This interpretation is lucidly expounded by Martha Kneale, in (8.6) 1962. The same position is ascribed by Cicero to certain later Epicureans (*De Fato* XVI 37–8). And it has been endorsed as a valid position (in spite of the scorn of Cicero and of Quine) by Storrs McCall, in (8.5).

does seem to endorse the principle of bivalence (which is formulated in terms of truth and falsehood) at *Cat.* 4, 2a8; 10, 13b2 (cf. *Int.* 4, 17a2). But there is a third and more effective reply offered by defenders of the traditional interpretation,[14] namely, that Aristotle does not regard himself as rejecting the principle of bivalence, but only as qualifying it with a 'yet'. This fits with the fact that at 19a36–7 he says that it is necessary that each disjunct should be true or false, while immediately going on (on the traditional interpretation) to say that it is not yet (*ēdē*, 19a39) true or false. The word 'yet' at 19a39 certainly suits this interpretation. Admittedly, it does not make it mandatory, for opponents of the traditional interpretation can follow Anscombe in denying that 'not yet' has temporal force (it might mean: 'but that does not yet mean that . . .').

The other main objection to the traditional interpretation turns on 18b17–25, where the determinist is allowed to rule out the suggestion that neither member of the contradictory pair is true. But the suggestion ruled out differs from the one that traditionalists ascribe to Aristotle in three ways. First, it is taken as implying that both the contradictory predictions are *false* rather than neuter (18b18–20); next, there is no qualification about not *yet* being true; and finally, presumably because of these first two differences, it is taken in a sense which implies that the sea battle will neither happen nor not happen.

For opponents of the traditional interpretation I may also mention two main difficulties. First, there is Aristotle's final claim in 19a39 – b2 that it is not necessary for every contradictory pair that one should be true and one false. A. Becker found this so embarrassing that he suggested it should be excised as an addition made by someone who did not understand the argument.[15] Secondly, it is not clear what the relevance is of the preceding lines from 19a23–39 where Aristotle rejects various arguments for necessity.[16] Those opponents of the traditional interpretation who think that Aristotle is talking here and in the following lines about necessity rather than about truth are in danger, as Ackrill has pointed out,[17] of preventing Aristotle from addressing himself anywhere

[14] The point that the principle is not so much abandoned as qualified by a 'not yet' is made very clear by J. L. Ackrill (8.1) 1963, 133, 140–2, but was already indicated by Lukasiewicz in the appendix to his 1930 paper, p. 64 of McCall.

[15] A. Becker, op. cit. Anscombe, however, interprets '*tēn men . . . tē de*' as meaning: it is not necessary that *this* one should be true and *that* one false.

[16] Here Aristotle says first that what is is necessary when it is, but that one may not drop the qualification 'when it is', and declare it necessary *tout court* (19a23–7). Next, he says that it is necessary that *p* or not–*p*, but that one cannot divide and say that *p* is necessary, or that not–*p* is necessary (19a27–32). Finally, he says that it is necessary for each member of a contradictory pair to be true or false (at least eventually, on the traditional interpretation), but that it is not necessary for either particular member to be true, or for it to be false, nor consequently (on the traditional interpretation) need either be already true or false.

[17] J. L. Ackrill, op. cit. 139–40.

in the chapter either to the premise or to the inference of the determinist. They make Aristotle allow the determinist's premise, if they accept that the premise is that all predictions are already true or false, or that they always have been true or false. And they also make Aristotle ignore the determinist's inference, unless they can show that the confusions Aristotle is here exposing somehow motivate that inference. Admittedly, even for the traditional view, the relevance of lines 19a23 to 39 may not be immediately obvious. But it has been plausibly maintained by Ackrill[18] that Aristotle's strategy is as follows. He accepts the determinist's inference that *if* every prediction is earlier true or false, then everything is of necessity. But he then turns round and argues that since many future events are not yet necessary (19a7–32), therefore the corresponding predictions are not yet true or false (a32–9).

So far as the interpretation of Aristotle is concerned, the traditionalists and their opponents each have their difficulties, and given the enormous variety among the opposition, I cannot indicate how they would all try to cope. I shall simply state my belief that the traditional view can cope better than any alternative I know of, and pass on to the philosophical question of how the determinist ought to be answered, if he argues in the way outlined.

The determinist's argument hinged on the idea that, whatever happens, it already *was* true in advance that that thing would happen. Two lines of reply were mentioned, Aristotle's and the one that made truth timeless. It was important for the latter reply that truth should be timeless rather than merely omnitemporal (belonging at *all* times), in order that talk of '*was* true' might be impugned. Against this reply, many of our idioms seem to connect truth with particular times. We say, for example, that something *changes* from being true at one time to being false at another, and *vice versa*. Aristotle draws attention to this way of talking and endorses it (*Cat.* 5, 4a23–8), and Arthur Prior has introduced a whole logic of tenses based on it.[19] But others think that such ways of talking are improper or misleading.

There are various cases in which we talk of a change from true to false. The sentence, 'The decisive battle lies in the future' is no longer true, when the decisive battle is over. Nor is the general's continuing belief that the decisive battle lies in the future. Besides sentences and beliefs, we can also introduce a proposition by means of a 'that'-clause, and say it is no longer true *that* the decisive battle lies in the future. It makes no difference whether we take the sentence-type, or the sentence-token, that is, a particular spoken or written *instance* of the sentence-type. For the written sentence-token which the general displays outside his tent, 'The decisive battle lies in the future', will also cease to be true. And if we

    [18] J. L. Ackrill, op. cit. 140.
    [19] Arthur Prior, *Time and Modality*, Oxford 1957; id., *Past, Present and Future*, Oxford 1967.

think of this written sentence-token, or of the sentence-type, as expressing a single proposition, that proposition will cease to be true as well.

These examples in which something ceases to be true provide ample opportunity for the determinist to introduce his use of 'was true', and to say it *was* true that there *would* be a battle. There are other reasons too why we talk in this way. Sometimes when we say that a prediction *was* true, we use the past tense only to indicate that the prediction was made in the past. Sometimes, without commenting on a prediction that has actually been made, we are trying to reconstruct the historical situation at some moment in the past. At the time of Queen Elizabeth's birth, the Battle of Britain had not yet taken place. We may correct someone's impression that it had, by saying it was true at that time that there *would* be such a battle, but not yet true that there *had* been. Here we use the past tense 'was true', simply because the time we are thinking about, the time of Queen Elizabeth's birth, is earlier than our present utterance.[20]

If there are all these opportunities for saying that it *was* true in advance that something *would* happen, how can it be objected to the determinist that truth is timeless? One line of objection, which seems to me unsuccessful, trades on the fact that changes from true to false are only made possible by the existence of token-reflexive expressions. And it was at one time a widespread view among logicians that token-reflexive expressions could be eliminated without loss. Examples of token-reflexive expressions are the tenses of verbs and the terms 'past', 'present', 'future', 'now', 'tomorrow', 'yesterday', 'three days *hence*', 'three days *ago*'. These expressions were called 'token-reflexive' by Reichenbach, because he considered that they could all be defined in terms of the phrase 'this token', a token being a written or spoken *instance* of an expression.[21] For example, someone who says on a particular

---

[20] Our use of tenses here is most lucidly explained by Hans Reichenbach, in (9.1), 1948, § 51. He points out that there are three times in question, not two: the time of Queen Elizabeth's birth, the time of the present speech act, and the time of the battle. Our utterance is intended to make clear the relation of these three times to each other. Three such times are always logically distinguishable in our use of tenses, Reichenbach suggests, even if one coincides with another in many cases.

[21] Hans Reichenbach, op. cit. § 50. Reichenbach was developing a view expressed by Russell in 'The experience of time', *Monist* 25, 1915, that 'now' means: simultaneously with this sense datum. That all temporal token-reflexives, and not just the tenses, would have to be removed, in order to get rid of changes from true to false, is clearly stated by W. V. O. Quine (9.5) 1960, 194. It does not much matter what noun we use: this token, this utterance, this sense experience, this event. The important point is that token-reflexive expressions are all equivalent to some expression employing the word *'this'*, and that the past, for example, is time earlier than *this* time. We might as well put this by saying: 'time earlier than (the time of) *this* utterance'. The fact that the 'this', not the noun, is important obviates Prior's objection that, when we say, 'thank goodness that's over', our relief is not at the fact of the nasty situation being earlier than some utterance (A. Prior, 'Thank Goodness' That's Over, *Philosophy* 34, 1959, 17). I shall discuss other objections in a book now in preparation on ancient treatments of time.

occasion, 'There will be a battle', means, 'There is (tenselessly) a battle later than *this* token', or, as we might say, to simplify things, 'later than *this* utterance'. 'Tomorrow' would mean, 'the day after *this* utterance'. If token-reflexive designations of time were eliminated, we should be left with such sentences as, 'There is (tenselessly) a battle on 1 January 1976', or 'There is (tenselessly) a battle on the day following Sorabji's 30,000th utterance',[22] and these will not change from true to false. We could no longer say,'There *will* be a battle', or 'There *will* be a battle tomorrow', or 'There is (tenselessly) a battle (a day) later than *this* utterance'. I do not agree, however, that nothing would have been lost, if token-reflexive designations of time were eliminated in this way, and I shall give one argument, derived from Richard Gale,[23] to show why not. If I say, 'A hand-grenade is (tenselessly) thrown into your room on 1 January 1980', this would not serve to guide your actions and emotions, unless you were able to make for yourself a judgement involving token-reflexives, such as '1 January 1980 is today', or '1 January 1980 is four years hence'. If you did not know whether it was a thousand years hence or a thousand years ago, I would not have guided your emotions or actions.

Another attempt to represent truth as timeless suggests that uses of *'was* true' are improper.[24] I am not sure how they could be shown actually improper, but a more modest claim, sometimes associated with this one, is that such uses are not *basic*, and need to be reconstrued. If they can be paraphrased into talk which does not even appear to carry deterministic implications, then the determinist cannot exploit them. Can such paraphrasing be achieved?

We might, for a start, paraphrase talk of *ceasing* to be true, and with it one set of uses of *'was* true', in the following manner. The method can be set out in three steps. First, it may be said that a written sentence-token such as, 'The decisive battle lies in the future', expresses a different proposition at each successive reading, and that the sentence-type expresses a different proposition every time it is used to make a spoken announcement. For the proposition expressed on a given occasion is that the battle is later than that *particular* act of reading or speaking, and the proposition expressed on the next occasion is that the battle is later than that *different* act of reading or speaking.

[22] These formulae are based on ones advocated by Quine, loc. cit., and by Nelson Goodman, (9.6) 1951, ch 11.

[23] R. M. Gale, 'Tensed statements', *Philosophical Quarterly* 12, 1962.

[24] Replies to the determinist along these lines are presented by M. Kneale in (8.6) 1962, 45–54, and by A. J. Ayer, 'Fatalism', in *The Concept of a Person*, London 1968, both well worth reading. Mrs Kneale, whose account is particularly detailed and lucid, also presents what I take to be the weaker view that uses of *'was* true' are not *basic*, and she suggests some paraphrases. Both Ayer and Kneale take the proper (or basic) subject of the predicates 'true' and 'false' to be a proposition. Aristotle's comments at *Int.* 1, 16a9–11, suggest the different view that thoughts in the mind are the primary bearers of truth-value.

The next step in the argument is that the proposition expressed on a given occasion, if true, is *changelessly* true, even though it would have to be expressed at a later date by a differently tensed sentence: 'The decisive battle *lay* in the future.' A doubt may be raised as to whether two differently tensed sentences can express exactly the same thing. The answer surely is that there is a common core of meaning and reference. Each is used to express the idea that the battle is later than a certain time, and the time referred to is the same time. On the other hand, different designations of the time are used, and these carry different implications and different action-guiding force.[25] If we switched to a non-token-reflexive designation of the time, there would be different implications again and no action-guiding force, though still the common core of meaning and reference.[26] Now the suggestion before us is that no matter which designation of the time is used, and no matter whether the designation is token-reflexive or not, what is expressed is *changelessly* true, if true at all.

The final step is to say that talk of something's *ceasing* to be true can be paraphrased in terms of changeless truth. If a person says that it is no longer true that the decisive battle lies in the future, this must be taken to mean something like this: 'The proposition which would have been expressed by an earlier spoken use of the sentence, "The decisive battle lies in the future", is *changelessly* true, but the proposition which would be expressed by a present spoken use of the same sentence is *changelessly* false.' Thus talk of *ceasing* to be true, and the accompanying use of '*was* true', need not be taken to carry deterministic implications, it is suggested. For it can be paraphrased in terms of 'is changelessly true', which obviously has no such implications.

Other uses of '*was* true' can also be paraphrased. When we say that a prediction *was* true', using the word 'was' merely to indicate that the prediction was made in the past, we could again say instead without loss that the past prediction *is changelessly* true. And when we are trying to reconstruct the situation at the time of Elizabeth's birth, instead of saying that it was true that there would be a battle of Britain, we can simply say that at that time there *was going to be* such a battle.

But here already the programme of paraphrasing receives a setback. For the last paraphrase only eliminates talk of *truth;* it does not eliminate the '*was*', on which the determinist's argument hinged. And there is a further setback. For the other paraphrases employ the idea of *being changelessly* true, and the determinist might say that that gives him exactly what he wants. The propositions and predictions which are changelessly true are presumably true at *all* times, and therefore *inter*

---

[25] The use of one tense implies that the time is that of the current utterance; the use of the other implies that it is earlier than a different current utterance.

[26] One advantage of a non-token reflexive designation is that the same one can be used at a later date to express the common core.

alia in the *past*. So his use of '*was* true' is vindicated. Can the determinist be answered? His opponents want to say that changelessly true propositions are not true at *all* times, but *timelessly*. In other words, it does not make sense to talk of them as being true *at times*. But I am not sure how this is to be shown. It seems to make sense, even if paraphrasable or derivative sense, to say of certain entities that they are true at some times, but not at others. So why should it not make sense to say of these changelessly true entities that in contrast they are true at *all* times?

There is a further difficulty. It was hard to find something changelessly true, because it would not for ever be true to say, using the present tense, 'The decisive battle *lies* in the future'. To find something changelessly true, it was necessary to look for something that could be expressed first by a present tense 'lies', later by a past tense 'lay', and at any time by a tenseless 'lies in 1975'. But what is there that can be expressed by all of these? Only what I called the common core of meaning and reference, which excludes token-reflexives. But to maintain that this is all we express to ourselves or to others is in effect to revert to the view already rejected, that token-reflexives are eliminable without loss. The defect of this view was that it ignored the action- and emotion-guiding force of token-reflexives. In what follows, I shall prefer a different reply to the determinist.

Aristotle's own line of reply attacks the determinist's use of 'was true' by saying that predictions about contingent matters only become true or false at the time of the thing predicted, unless perhaps in those instances where the outcome is settled in advance, in which case they may become true or false earlier. Presumably, it is important to be clear what it is that becomes true at the time of the predicted event. It is not the sentence 'there will be a sea battle tomorrow' that becomes true at the time of the battle. And Aristotle would be wrong if by *logoi* in 19a33 he meant sentences, or at least if he meant sentence-types, rather than the spoken instances of a type. For if the sentence-type, with its future tense, is to be true at any time, it will have to be true on the day preceding the battle. But various other entities could be said to become true at the time of the battle. On one view, the proposition expressed by the use of the sentence on the preceding day becomes true, although at the time of the battle that proposition would have to be expressed by a differently tensed sentence. Storrs McCall suggests that what becomes true is a tenseless proposition, expressed by a tenseless sentence.[27]

What ought we to say about Aristotle's solution? There is a sloppy use of the word 'true' to mean 'fixed', 'inevitable'. And it must naturally be admitted that, in this sense, a prediction will not become true until the thing predicted occurs or becomes inevitable. But I presume the determinist is not trading on this use of the word 'true' to mean 'fixed', when

[27] Storrs McCall, in (8.5).

he declares that whatever happens, it was *true* in advance that it would happen. Or else he would merely be begging the question in favour of determinism. He is presumably using the word 'true' in its normal sense, whatever that may be. Perhaps we might paraphrase it as 'corresponding to the facts'. And Aristotle's view can be seen as a recommendation that, even in the normal sense, we should not regard a prediction as being true until the thing predicted occurs or becomes inevitable.

Such a recommendation seems to me possible, but not desirable. For one thing, we are being asked to abandon our ordinary ways of talking, and before we do that, we shall want to be assured that there is something to be gained. Ordinarily, we are prepared to say, for example, 'It was true that there would be a decisive battle.' Moreover, I suggested several different reasons why we want to use this kind of locution: there were considerations about ceasing to be true, about referring to the time of some past prediction, and about reconstructing the historical situation at some past time. Further if our normal use of 'true' really can be paraphrased as 'corresponding to the facts', then it ought to be possible for propositions about the future to be true in advance. For this purpose, they merely have to correspond to the facts. Perhaps someone will protest that the facts in question are facts about the future, or even that they are future facts. Without approving this talk of 'future facts', I need only say that, if it is adopted, propositions about the future can *still* be true in advance, just so long as they correspond to *future* facts.

Of course, our customary ways of talking can be abandoned, if they really carry undesirable deterministic implications. But we shall be taking all this trouble to no purpose, if it can be shown that those ways of talking do not carry such implications after all. And this much more economical line is the one for which I would argue.

Aristotle is like the believers in timeless truth in attacking the determinist's use of '*was* true'. My claim is that we can allow that use, and still remove the sting from his argument, if we can show that the use of 'was' carries no deterministic implications. It seemed to carry such implications because after the horse *has* bolted, it is no good shutting the stable door. And by analogy it seemed that once it *had* been true that I was going to swim, it would be too late for me to deliberate whether to make it to have been false; the past cannot be affected or altered. But is it so clear that the two cases are analogous? After the horse has bolted, I have no power to prevent it from having bolted. But when we say that something has been true about my future, do we imply that I have no power to prevent it from having been true, or only that I am not, as it happens, going to exercise any such power? Speaking of the future, we allow that even if I am going to swim later, I still now have the power to refrain. If I am going to swim, this is because I am not, as it happens, going to exercise the power of refraining. The suggestion is that analogously, even if it has already been true that I am going to swim, I still retain the power to make it to have been false instead. If it has been true, this is because I am not, as it happens, going to exercise that power.

A moment ago, I recalled some of the purposes that motivate our use of '*was* true'. I think it can be seen that these purposes can be served, without our having to treat '*was* true' as analogous to 'The horse *has* bolted'. Since our purposes do not require us to imply anything about irrevocability, I doubt if we should, and I doubt if we do, imply any such thing.

If there are no implications of irrevocability, when we talk of predictions being true in advance of the thing predicted, we must restrict the maxim that we cannot affect or alter the past. It will not apply in the same way to past truth about the future. The maxim is in general a sound one: after the horse has bolted, I cannot prevent it from having bolted. And this is not, as is sometimes supposed,[28] the mere tautology that I cannot make the past fit the description of being 'other than it was'. Such a tautology would apply equally to the future: I cannot make the future fit the description of being 'other than it will be'. The idea is rather that the past has already happened in a certain way (call it f), and I have no power now to make it fit the description 'not-f'. This fact about the past has no analogue as regards the future. The future will happen in a certain way (call it g), but it does not follow that I now lack the power to make the future not-g. So far the maxim that the past cannot be affected or altered is a good one, though modern logicians are only just beginning to recognise the necessity of the past.[29] But there are certain ways in which we can affect the past. For a start, the suicide can make his most recent birthday to be his last, because this is only to make it have no successor. And I can make a past prediction to be true, because this is only to make it correspond to the facts, which I can do by making the facts correspond to it. This is possible because 'last' and 'true' are both relational terms, one implying a relation to successors, the other to facts. But not only can we make something past to be true, or to be the last member of a series. The preceding two paragraphs suggest that we

[28] Anthony Kenny sees only this tautology in the maxim that we cannot *change* the past. On the other hand, he observes correctly that (with certain exceptions) we cannot *bring about* things in the past, and from this it follows (the exceptions apart) that when the past has happened in way f, I have no power any longer to make it fit the description 'not-f'. (Anthony Kenny, 'Divine foreknowledge and human freedom', in A. Kenny, ed., (12.9) 1969, 266–8.)

[29] David Wiggins has done so in 'Towards a reasonable libertarianism', his contribution to *Essays on Freedom of Action*, ed. Ted Honderich, London 1973. He there offers (p. 46) a general definition of necessity designed to include the necessity of the past. It is necessary at time t' that p, if and only if p holds in every possible world whose history is indistinguishable from the history of the actual world up to, but not necessarily including, time t'. Similarly David Lewis in *Counterfactuals*, Oxford 1973, 7. On the other hand, the three commentators on Iseminger's paper see no appropriate sense in the idea that the past is necessary (12.8) 1976.

can say we are making it to *have* been true, or to *have* been the last. This is more startling; it implies that the relation of being true has already existed in the past, and that in turn might *seem* to imply that we lack a certain power (the power to make the prediction to have been false). But what the paragraph before last maintained was that it implies not the absence of this power, but only the absence of its exercise. Consequently, we have the following control over the past: when a prediction is already true, we may possess not only the power to make it have been true, but also the power (unexercised) to make it have been false.

The suggestion is that we can answer the determinist, without joining Aristotle or the believers in timeless truth in attacking his use of '*was* true'. What we need is not to attack that use, but to understand it.

CHAPTER SIX

Other Arguments from the Necessity of the Past

Diodorus' Master Argument

The deterministic argument of *Metaph.* vi 3 is explicitly based on the necessity of the past. This basis is not made explicit in the deterministic argument of *Int.* 9, though I have argued that it is there. But Diodorus Cronus, Aristotle's younger contemporary or near-contemporary, is explicitly said to have used this same basis for a famous deterministic argument of his own.

Actually, the argument was presented not directly as a defence of determinism, but as a proof of Diodorus' definition of possibility.[1] But that definition seems to imply determinism, and was taken in antiquity to imply it, and to be intended to do so.[2] The definition says that the possible is that which is or will be, or alternatively that which is or will be *true* (there are two formulations),[3] and what seems to imply determinism is the suggestion that nothing else is possible. Whether this suggestion really implies determinism depends on how it is interpreted,

[1] So Alexander of Aphrodisias, Commentary on *An. Pr.*, ed. Wallies, *CIAG* 184; Epictetus, *Dissertationes*, ed. Schenkl, ıı19 1.

[2] Alexander of Aphrodisias (Comm. on *An. Pr.* 184, line 1) stresses the deterministic implication, when he puts Diodorus' view as being that *only* (*monon*) what is or will be is possible. And similarly Epictetus (loc. cit.) phrases the conclusion of the Master Argument in terms of nothing *else* being possible (other than what is or will be true). Cicero says (*De Fato* vıı 13, ıx 17–18) that Diodorus' treatment of possibility was connected with his view that whatever happens will do so of necessity. Plutarch (*De Stoicorum Repugnantiis* 46, 1055ᴇ) considers that by refusing to accept Diodorus' definition of possibility, Chrysippus was betraying the determinism to which he was otherwise committed. Finally, Boethius reports (2nd comm. on *Int.*, ed. Meiser, 235) that, in Diodorus' view, if anyone dies at sea, it was not possible for him to die on land.
A dissentient view is that of Robert Blanché. He argues that Diodorus' interest was in logic rather than in determinism. He wanted to produce an extensional logic, and to accommodate modal terms (possible, necessary, impossible) in it, by reducing them to temporal ones (some time, always, never). It was others, on Blanché's view, who said that this committed Diodorus to determinism, and Blanché argues that in a way they were wrong, because the necessity which Diodorus is committed to postulating is a necessity which has been rendered harmless by being reduced to temporal terms (Robert Blanché (10.5), 1965).

[3] The definition is given by Alexander of Aphrodisias, in *An. Pr.* 183–4; Boethius, 2nd Commentary on *Int.*, ed. Meiser, 234; Cicero *De Fato* vıı 13, ıx 17; Plutarch *De Stoicorum Repugnantiis* 46, 1055ᴇ.

as will emerge later. But at least it *appears* that if no alternative to tomorrow's events is possible, then tomorrow's events are necessary. In some way or other, this deterministic conclusion about what is possible in the future was based on the premise that what is past and true is necessary.

The argument is preserved only by Epictetus (loc. cit. note 1 above). It was known as the Master Argument, and was one of the famous named arguments of antiquity.[4] Epictetus tells us little about it other than its premises. One was the premise that whatever is past and true is necessary. Diodorus may have wanted to infect the future with the necessity which belongs to the past. And for the purpose of spreading the infection, he may have used his second premise, that the impossible does not follow from the possible.[5]

On this tantalisingly sketchy evidence, it is impossible to reconstruct the argument with certainty. But there are several able and ingenious reconstructions current. The one which has gained most support recently, causing two people to withdraw their earlier conjectures, is that of Arthur Prior,[6] who represents Diodorus as making explicit the kind of thinking that I suggested lay behind the determinist's argument in Aristotle's *De Interpretatione* ch. 9. This makes it desirable to say something about the relation of Diodorus to Aristotle.

Diodorus' two premises can both be found in Aristotle. The idea that the past is necessary we have already encountered both in *Metaph.* vi 3 and probably in *Int.* 9, 19a23–4, and it can be found elsewhere as well,[7] while the idea that the impossible does not follow from the possible is put forward in many places.[8] On the other hand, Diodorus' deterministic conclusion about possibility, as Alexander of Aphrodisias points out (loc. cit., note 1 above), is directly opposed to Aristotle's. For Aristotle believed that some things are possible (e.g. the cutting up of a particular cloak, *Int.* 9, 19a12–16), even though they neither are nor will be. When we bear in mind that Diodorus was considerably younger than Aristotle, it is natural to think that he may have been borrowing premises from

    [4] Another named argument will be encountered in Chapter Fifteen: the so-called Lazy Argument.

    [5] I am here treating Diodorus' definition of possibility as a conclusion which is meant to follow from these two premises. I do not think this involves any distortion; but I should warn that Epictetus presents things differently, giving the negation of Diodorus' definition as a third proposition, which helps to create an inconsistent triad when added to the other two premises.

    [6] Prior's reconstruction is developed in a series of publications from 'Diodoran modalities', *Philosophical Quarterly* 5, 1955, 205–13, to *Past, Present and Future*, Oxford 1967. It is endorsed by O. Becker (10.3) 1960, and M. Kneale (8.6) 1962, 117–28. Becker thus retracts his 'Über den "Kyrieuon Logos" des Diodorus Kronos', in *Rheinisches Museum für Philologie* 99, 1956, 289–304, and M. Kneale recants Martha Hurst, 'Logical and metaphysical necessity', *Proceedings of the Aristotelian Society* 38, 1937–8, 253–8.

    [7] Aristotle *Cael.* i 12, 283b12–14; *NE* 1139b7–9; *Rhet.* 1418a3–5.

    [8] Aristotle *An. Pr.* 30b4–5, 32a18–20, 34a5–7, a25–b2; *Phys.* 256b10–12; *Metaph.* ix 3, 1047a24–9; ix 4, 1047b6–16.

Aristotle, in order to turn them against him. The relationship between the two will have been even closer, if (as Prior's reconstruction suggests) Diodorus was sharpening up the deterministic argument that lies behind *Int.* 9.

This view of Diodorus, as responding to Aristotle, is by no means the only one that has been taken. Scholars are not agreed on who, if either, was responding to whom.[9] It has been questioned how much of Aristotle's work would have been available to Diodorus at the time he thought out his view on possibility. It is usually taken that Diodorus' work came after a comparatively late passage: Aristotle's attack on certain Megarian philosophers in *Metaph.* IX 3. But, surprisingly, there is disagreement as to whether it also came after Aristotle's treatment of the sea battle in *Int.* 9. For some have regarded the *De Interpretatione* as a late work, or have taken chapter 9 to be later than some others.[10] And though Düring has made a good case for treating the *De Interpretatione* as a whole as early,[11] some scholars have urged (without much evidence) that it would not at first have been known outside Aristotle's Peripatetic school or that at least the final lines of the chapter would not have been known, since (on one interpretation of the chapter) they have to be viewed as a spurious addition. It has even been maintained that Diodorus would not have known *Int.* 9, nor Aristotle the Master Argument,[12] but this seems a very uneconomical hypothesis.

A flood of light has been thrown on the subject in a challenging article by David Sedley. As well as rebutting the universal view that Diodorus was thought of as belonging to the Megarian school, he has brought down his date of death from 307 B.C. to about 284 B.C.[13] His age at death is not known, but since Aristotle died in 322 B.C., thirty-eight years earlier, his period of work is not likely to have overlapped much with Aristotle's. Assuming, as is only reasonable, that one is responding to

---

[9] Diodorus is taken to be replying to Aristotle's handling of the sea battle, e.g., by O. Becker (10.3) and J. Hintikka (10.4), ch. 9. The opposite view, that *Int.* 9 is a reply to the Master Argument, is taken by P. M. Schuhl, *Le Dominateur et les Possibles*, Paris 1960; K. von Fritz, review of Schuhl, *Gnomon* 34, 1962, 147.

[10] *Metaph.* IX is now widely considered to be fairly late. *Int.* has been considered late by H. Maier ('Die Echtheit der Aristotelischen Hermeneutik', *Archiv für Philosophie* XIII 1, N.F. VI 1, 1900, 23–72), and by E. Zeller (*Aristotle and the Earlier Peripatetics*, vol. 1, tr. Costelloe and Muirhead, London 1897, 66–7, 154–8). In spite of the late date he assigns to *Int.*, Maier doubts if the Master Argument had by that time reached its final formulation. D. Frede allows that some of *Int.* is early, but regards *Int.* 9 as late (*Aristoteles und die 'Seeschlacht'*, *Hypomnemata* 27, Göttingen 1970, § 19, 26).

[11] I. Düring, *Aristoteles*, Heidelberg 1966, 55.

[12] For these three views, see Von Fritz (loc. cit.), A. Becker ('bestreitet Aristoteles die Gültigkeit des "Tertium non datur" für Zukunftaussagen?', *Actes du Congrès international de Philosophie Scientifique* 6, Paris 1936, 69–74), and D. Frede (loc. cit.). The motive for Becker's suggestion has been explained and challenged in Chapter Five.

[13] Zeller relied on a story that Diodorus committed suicide because he was unable immediately to solve a puzzle in the presence of Ptolemy Soter, who conquered Megara in 307 (Diogenes Laertius II 22). His dating has been challenged by David Sedley (10.1) 1977.

the work of the other, the dating makes it likely that Diodorus is responding to Aristotle. This will be even more likely, if there is a link between the Master Argument and *Int.* 9, since I am persuaded that this chapter, including its final lines, fits into its context, and that the surrounding context represents a comparatively early work of Aristotle's.

On Prior's interpretation, Diodorus exploits the fact (if it is a fact) that whatever is now, or will be, true, it has already been true in the *past* that it was going to be that way. Thus whereas there were several formulations of the determinist's premise in Aristotle's *Int.* 9, Diodorus has confined himself to the one which appears at 18b10, according to which if something is white now, it was true *earlier* (*proteron*) to say that it would be white. Moreover, Diodorus combines this with the idea which Aristotle makes explicit only in a different part of the chapter (19a23–4) that the past is necessary, and any alternative to it impossible. The rest of the argument can easily be worked out from there: any alternative to tomorrow's events is not possible, because it implies an impossibility, namely some alternative to what has already in the *past* been true about tomorrow's events. In Prior's example, if a certain shell will never be seen, the supposition that it will be seen tomorrow is not merely false, but impossible. For it implies an impossibility, namely that it has not in the past been true that the shell will never be seen. The latter is impossible, because it has already in the *past* been true, and therefore is necessarily true, that the shell will never be seen. Diodorus thus makes explicit some of the moves which Aristotle had not fully articulated in the presentation of the determinist's argument in *Int.* 9.

An apparent difficulty for this reconstruction is that it makes Diodorus ignore Aristotle's objection that predictions about the future need not be already true or false. But this difficulty could be met, if by the time of Diodorus' argument it was already being supposed that Aristotle intended to deny, not truth, but only *'definite'* truth, to the predictions in question. In any case, in Cicero *De Fato* 18, Diodorus is credited with an *argument* to show that propositions about the future are already true or false. He may, then, have thought that Aristotle had been *answered*, if he believed the contrary. A related difficulty for Prior is why Epictetus does not record that it is a premise of Diodorus' argument that predictions are always true or false in advance. This would seem to call for mention because Epicurus was later to deny it.[14] But a possible answer would be that Epictetus has only troubled to pick out those premises which were challenged by his fellow-*Stoics*.

If Prior is right about how Diodorus argued, then the flaw in his very

[14] For this criticism of Prior, see Nicholas Rescher, 'A version of the "Master Argument" of Diodorus', *Journal of Philosophy* 63, 1966, 438. For Epicurus' denial that all predictions are true or false, see Cicero *De Fato* ix 18, x 21, xvi 37–8; *Academica* ii 30 97; *De Natura Deorum* i 25 70.

plausible argument will be the same as that in the deterministic argument of *Int.* 9. As I maintained in Chapter Five, although it is in general
true that the past enjoys a certain kind of necessity, this does not apply
to past truths about the future.

The other outstanding interpretation of Diodorus' Master Argument
is Hintikka's.[15] His reconstruction makes Diodorus trade on the fact
that what is now future will *eventually* be past, and hence necessary.
Thus suppose that there will be no sea battle tomorrow, Tuesday. Then
on Wednesday it will be necessary (because past) that there was no sea
battle on Tuesday, and impossible that there was one. But in that case a
person who says on Monday that it is then possible for there to be a sea
battle on Tuesday is wrong. For from this supposedly possible thing (the
Tuesday sea battle) there would follow the thing that we have agreed to
be impossible on Wednesday, namely that there should have been a sea
battle on the preceding day.

If this is how Diodorus argued, his mistake will have been to overlook
the difference between being possible or impossible at a particular time
and being possible or impossible (*tout court*). He will have shifted from
his original premise (that the impossible does not follow from the possible) to the illegitimate premise, that what is impossible *on Wednesday*
does not follow from what is possible *on Monday*.

These are the two best reconstructions I know. Some ingenious alternatives have been offered since, on which I shall not dwell.[16] Can we
decide between the two described?

Hintikka frees Diodorus from the error of ascribing necessity to all
past tense statements. His first premise will only mean that true propositions about past occurrences are necessary. But it is not clear that this
gives Hintikka's interpretation an advantage. For if Diodorus' premise
is as acceptable as that, it becomes less clear why Cleanthes should have
disputed it.

Hintikka's interpretation is more economical in its ascription of premises to Diodorus. But again it is not clear whether on balance this is an

[15] Jaakko Hintikka (10.4) 1973, ch. 9.

[16] Nicholas Rescher (op. cit.) takes Diodorus to be asserting not the Aristotelian premise, that the impossible does not follow *logically* from the possible, but the un-
Aristotelian premise, that the impossible does not follow *chronologically* after the possible. Hence if it is impossible on Wednesday that there should have been a sea battle on
Tuesday, it cannot have been possible on Monday that there was going to be one. For this
would involve a shift from first being possible to later being impossible in the proposition
that there is [tenselessly] a sea battle on Tuesday. A minor disadvantage of this reconstruction is that Diodorus' premise, so interpreted, no longer connects with Aristotle. A
major doubt is whether Diodorus would have got anybody to believe the premise that what
is once possible never becomes impossible. A further feature of Rescher's interpretation,
which reduces its historical probability, is that it treats Diodorus' propositions as *tenseless*. This last feature is retained in an ingenious contribution by F. S. Michael ('What is
the Master Argument of Diodorus Cronus?', *American Philosophical Quarterly* 13, 1976,
229–35). For reconstructions earlier than Prior's, Rescher has assembled a useful bibliography.

advantage. For when Prior ascribes to Diodorus the extra premise that all predictions are already true or false, he thereby connects the Master Argument with *Int*. 9, giving it topicality, and providing for it a natural genesis. He also supplies a motive for Epicurus' subsequent denial of that premise.

Epicurus was worried that, if propositions about the future were in every case true or false, he would have to admit determinism. Moreover, Cicero tells us of Epicurus' worry in close connexion with a discussion of Diodorus (Cicero *De Fato* 17–21). This increases the likelihood that Prior is right, and that Diodorus' argument, like the one which subsequently worried Epicurus, exploited the idea that propositions about the future can be true in advance. Indeed, in reporting Diodorus' premises, Epictetus explicitly mentions truth ('Whatever is past and *true* is necessary'). It is therefore some disadvantage in Hintikka's reconstruction that it makes no use of the notion of truth.

I conclude that, despite the elegance of Hintikka's interpretation, Prior's supplies more historical interconnexions, and is therefore marginally more plausible.

Past truth about the future and the necessity of the past in the treatises De Fato *of Cicero and Alexander*

Deterministic arguments based on considerations of past truth about the future continued to flourish after Diodorus, and so did arguments based on the necessity of the past. It is not clear how far the two classes of argument overlapped, but Cicero's *De Fato*, written in 45–54 B.C., is an important source for both, and in this section, I shall record both kinds of argument. The necessity of the past may be being exploited in three arguments. Two of the three are directed against Chrysippus' attempts to evade necessity, while the other is an argument which Epicurus found threatening. All three are discussed in connexion with Diodorus Cronus, but it is not clear that any is identical with the Master Argument. One would expect the ultimate source of inspiration to be Aristotle's *Int*. 9, but in fact Cicero is much more concerned with Diodorus than with Aristotle, about whom he seems to know little. Indeed, he mentions Aristotle as a determinist (§ 39), which may be a sign that he is wrongly assuming that Aristotle endorsed the deterministic argument of *Int*. 9.

Cicero supplies some of the Diodorean background in §§ 17–18. He reveals that there had been discussion of Diodorus' definition of the necessary, which is given by Boethius as 'that which, being true, will not be false' (2nd Commentary on *Int*., ed. Meiser, 234). Evidently, Diodorus argued that propositions about the future are perfectly capable of being true in advance. Moreover, if true, they will not change to being false. Hence they can satisfy Diodorus' two requirements for being *necessary*.

The argument seems to be influenced by a reading of Aristotle's *Metaph.* vi 3. For Diodorus argues that necessity will attach not only to 'Scipio will die', but just as much to 'Scipio will die by violence in his bedroom at night'. When we hear that Diodorus makes these two propositions equally necessary, we cannot help recalling *Metaph.* vi 3, 1027b8–11, where Aristotle contrasts as *not* equally necessary 'He will die' and 'He will die by violence'.

That 'Scipio will die by violence in his bedroom at night' was *true in advance* is argued on the basis of the fact that that is how he eventually died. That what is true will not *change* to being false is obvious in the case of 'Scipio *has* been killed'; it is merely less apparent in the case of 'Scipio *will* be killed'. Evidently, Diodorus did not anticipate the objection, mentioned in Chapter Four, that the future tense of 'will' will make this proposition change to falsity after the event.

So far, Diodorus' interest has been in past truth about the future; not in the necessity of the past. But Cicero now informs us of an argument which may have been concerned with *both*. *Epicurus* had been afraid of a deterministic argument based on the assumption that every proposition, including every proposition about the future, is either true or false. Consequently, Epicurus had sought to deny the assumption (§§ 18–19, 21, 37–8). The deterministic argument draws a conclusion both about necessity and about causation. In one version (§ 21), it claims that, if, of two contradictory propositions, one has been true from everlasting (*ex aeternitate*), then that one is certain (*certum*), and hence necessary (*necessarium*), so that necessity and fate (*necessitas* and *fatum*) are confirmed. The reference to being true *'from everlasting'* recurs in close connexion with Epicurus in § 37. It is not said how the argument moves from past truth, or everlasting past truth, to necessity. But the move is similar to that made by Aristotle's determinist in *Int.* 9, and by Diodorus in the Master Argument, both of whom were probably exploiting the necessity of the past. We see here, then, Aristotle's influence exerted either directly or *via* Diodorus.

Cicero himself (§§ 19, 28, 32, 37–8) accepts the view that every proposition is either true or false, and further accepts Diodorus' position that propositions about the future do not change from true to false, but wisely maintains that all this proves nothing about causation, but is only a point about the meanings of terms.

He records, however, an argument by Chrysippus which insists on causation rather than necessity (§ 20–1). Evidently, Chrysippus had argued strenuously for the claim that every proposition (*axiōma*) is either true or false. He thought this both necessary and sufficient for maintaining that everything happens by fate and from everlasting causes.

This last argument does not mention the necessity of the past, nor any kind of necessity. And this may be significant, for, as was seen in

Chapter Four, one of Chrysippus' devices for preserving moral judgments was to deny necessity, while insisting on causation and fate. Indeed, there are two arguments recorded by Cicero (§ 14), and discussed in Chapter Four, which seek to force Chrysippus to go further and admit necessity against his intentions. And these two arguments do both trade on the necessity of the past, which Chrysippus is said to have accepted in the form: 'everything true in the past is necessary' (§ 14).

In the first argument, it is urged that Chrysippus ought to agree with Diodorus' deterministic conclusion, if he once accepted the conditional 'if Fabius was born at the rising of the Dogstar, he will not die at sea'. For the antecedent of this conditional (Fabius was born at the rising of the Dogstar) is necessary, because it is already past. Hence, if the whole conditional is correct, the consequent (he will not die at sea) must be necessary also.

The second argument appeals, not to an astrological sign, but to a 'natural cause' of Fabius' not dying at sea. I suggested that it may have been designed as an improvement on the first argument. Someone might have reminded Chrysippus of his view that, where there is a sign, there is a cause.[17] He will then have argued that in the conditional whose antecedent mentions a past cause, necessity will attach to the antecedent and spread from there to the consequent. If the consequent mentions Fabius' not dying at sea, while the antecedent mentions the past cause of that immunity, then Fabius' not dying at sea will already be necessary.

On this reconstruction, the second argument is similar in form to the deterministic argument of *Metaph*. vi 3; for there too the necessity of a past cause is transmitted to a future effect.

Skipping two and a half centuries, we come to the great Aristotelian Alexander of Aphrodisias, whose *floruit* may be placed around A.D. 205. In *Quaestiones* i 4, dubiously attributed to him, there is an explicit argument from prior truth to necessity (*CIAG* 10 32 – 13 8). Regrettably, the discussion strays into a debate over whether there is prior '*definite*' truth (*aphōrismenōs*), which was not the original question (12 18 and 13 4). In the indubitably genuine *De Fato*, Alexander makes no mention of 'definite truth', but two or three times seeks to commit his opponents to belief in necessity, by using an argument based simply on prior truth (187 22, 188 3, perhaps 177 25–7). The last mentioned passage is one in which Alexander records an attempt to escape necessity: a correct prediction of tomorrow's sea battle is not necessary (*anankaion*), it is alleged, because its future tense will make it change to falsity after the battle is over. Alexander replies by conceding that the proposition is not necessary (*anankaion*), but insisting that the event it reports may still happen of necessity (*ex anankēs*, 177 7 – 178 7).

The deterministic arguments of *Metaph*. vi 3, of *Int*. 9, of Diodorus

---

[17] See the references collected in *SVF* ii 939–44.

Cronus, of Cicero's *De Fato* and of Alexander's *De Fato* and *Quaestiones* can be seen as the first of a series. For arguments from the *necessity of the past* have continued to be popular with determinists.

An argument from the necessity of the past and foreknowledge

Arguments based on the necessity of past *truth* receive a powerful twist in the tail when they are converted into arguments based on the necessity of past *knowledge*. An argument of the latter kind, expounded and attacked by St. Thomas Aquinas, has been discussed in several papers recently.[18] The idea is in part that God's foreknowing that we will do so-and-so entails that we will do it. But if God *already* foreknows, then his foreknowledge has the kind of necessity that belongs to the past. And this necessity will be transferred to what is entailed, that is, to our action. This is in some ways more persuasive than the arguments based on past truth. What ought we to say about it?

It is necessary to divide up the idea of God's foreknowledge into its component parts. If God foreknows that I will do something, then first he believes in advance that I will do that thing, second it is true that I will do that thing, and third he is presumably infallible, i.e. incapable of error. To say that God's *foreknowledge* has the kind of necessity that belongs to the past is too simple. It is his prior *belief* that has that kind of necessity. In other words, if he or any other predictor already has a given belief, it is irrevocable that he has that belief. On the other hand, past *truth* does not have the kind of necessity that attaches to the past, so it was argued in Chapter Five. For in the case of an ordinary prediction, I suggested, we can talk of having the power to affect its past truth value. So far, then, it would seem that although God's *belief* is past and therefore necessary, the *truth* of his belief cannot be proved necessary on the grounds of its pastness. If we want therefore to establish that God's foreknowledge as a whole is necessary, we must appeal to some extra consideration, and a suitable one would be God's infallibility.[19]

[18] Aquinas *Summa Theologiae* 1a 14 13 2; *De Veritate* question 2, article 12, section 7. For recent literature, see A. N. Prior, Gary Iseminger, A. Kenny, Nelson Pike and J. R. Lucas in the select bibliography § 12. I have profited from a helpful discussion of Iseminger's paper with Iseminger, John Watling and Peter Cave.

[19] My account differs from some of the others that have been given. First, many of those who discuss deterministic arguments from divine foreknowledge do not see the arguments as being based on the necessity of the past. We shall shortly see that this is true of many ancient sources. It seems to be true also of the recent discussions by Steven Cahn (*Fate, Logic and Time*, New Haven 1967, ch. 5) and Susan Haack ('On a theological argument for fatalism', *Philosophical Quarterly* 1974). Secondly, some do not appreciate the need for a second premise, such as God's infallibility. This is true of Aquinas himself, of Arthur Prior (12.6), Gary Iseminger (12.7), Susan Haack and Steven Cahn. It results, in some cases, from not splitting up the concept of knowledge into its component parts, and it produces the conviction in some cases (Haack, Iseminger) that no specifically *theological* premise is needed. John Lucas (12.9), however, and Nelson Pike (12.4 and ch. 4 of 12.5) observe the

We cannot now influence what God's belief shall have been. What infallibility adds is that we cannot affect its truth value either. The combination of infallibility with prior knowledge then really would make our actions inevitable in advance. And in face of this, one modern author prefers the view that God's foreknowledge is, like ours, fallible.[20] What must be noticed is that the inevitability of our action would arise not merely from the pastnesss of God's belief, much less from the pastness of its truth value, but from the pastness of the belief coupled with the very peculiar supposition of infallibility. It would remain to say just what made the predictor infallible, what, in other words, made it impossible for us to falsify his prediction. Until this was made clear, it would not be clear what kind of inevitability attached to the predicted action.

Not all foreknowledge, however, would be incompatible with our freedom. For when we talk of knowledge not in connexion with divine beings, we do not normally wish to imply infallibility, i.e. the *impossibility* of error; we mean rather to imply that the *risk* of error is negligible in relation to the purposes in hand, and in addition, as a distinct (though easily confusable) requirement, that error has not *in fact* occurred. Neither of these two requirements is tantamount to saying that error was actually *impossible*. I believe, then, that although the ability to falsify predictions is incompatible with their infallibility, it is not incompatible with their amounting to knowledge.[21] When a person predicts what we will do, provided the risk of error is negligible, and provided (as a second requirement) we do not in fact exercise our power to render his prediction false, he can be said to have had foreknowledge. This prior knowledge is like past truth, in that it does not enjoy the kind of necessity, or unaffectability, that attaches to other aspects of the past. Rather, by refraining from falsifying a prediction, we can bring it about in the present that the prediction amounted to knowledge in the past. The prediction in any case had the requisite unriskiness; all it needed, in order to qualify as knowledge, was for us to allow it actual truth.

---

need for both premises. Third, some do not notice that describing a past *belief* as necessary is more acceptable than describing past *truth* as necessary (John Turk Saunders, 'Of God and freedom', *The Philosophical Review* 1966). The last two oversights can produce the conviction (Haack, Cahn) that the argument from prior *knowledge* constitutes no advance over the argument from prior truth. In general, failure to recognise the two premises involved (irrevocability and infallibility) can lead (Haack) to underestimating the force of the determinist's argument.

[20] John Lucas, *The Freedom of Will*, Oxford 1970, 75–6.

[21] I am oversimplifying since there are special cases in which true belief with negligible risk of error is not sufficient for knowledge (suppose one's grounds include misinformation which by mere luck does not increase the risk). None the less all I require is that the conditions stated are commonly sufficient for knowledge. Arthur Prior protests (12.6) 35–6, that the prediction cannot amount to knowledge, if we can falsify it, because there will be no ground for the prediction's correctness. Admittedly, there will be no *infallible* ground. But the risk of error could be negligible, either with a less-than-infallible ground, or (see p. 122) with no ground at all.

An argument from the necessity of the past and the Special Theory of Relativity

Deterministic arguments from the necessity of the past have continued to find supporters in modern times. Many people have thought that the Theory of Relativity has implications for determinism. H. Bondi and M. Capek have held that it supports indeterminism,[22] H. Reichenbach that, under a certain interpretation, it implies determinism.[23] I shall confine myself, however, to those deterministic arguments which seek to exploit the necessity of the past. One such argument has recently been erected on the basis of the Special Theory of Relativity.[24] Let us imagine that one observer shoots past another at a very high speed, travelling in a rocket, and that, as they pass, the two observers synchronise their watches. They also speculate about the occurrence of a distant event which neither of them has yet witnessed. We must imagine this distant event to be in what is called their *regions of topological simultaneity*. My present region of topological simultaneity is a region of space-time in which events are so distant, or so soon, or so recent, that there is now no time for causal influence to travel between me and them, since nothing can travel faster than light. Because of this, I cannot now influence such events, nor can they now influence me or be perceived by me. None the less, if I wait until the light signal reaches me from such an event, I can calculate retrospectively when it occurred.

The interesting thing about our two observers is that when they finally receive a light signal from the distant event about which they were speculating, their retrospective calculations may give different results.

[22] H. Bondi argues, mistakenly I believe, that the finite speed of light implies that some events will be undetermined (Letter in *Nature* 169, 1952, 660). M. Capek's point is that the Laplacean determinist can no longer formulate his premise, which has to do with predictions based on knowing the state of the whole universe at a given instant. For Einstein shows that there are different answers, relative to different frames of reference, to the question what states exist in the universe simultaneously at a given instant. The appropriate reply for the Laplacean determinist, however, would seem to be that, whatever frame of reference is chosen, it is predictable what will be happening at any later time which is specified in relation to that same frame of reference. (See M. Capek, 'The doctrine of necessity reexamined', *The Review of Metaphysics* 5, 1951, 11–54; 'Eternal return' in (14.2); and 'The theory of eternal recurrence in modern philosophy of science', *Journal of Philosophy* 57, 1960, 289–96).

[23] H. Reichenbach holds that Minkowski's representation of the space-time continuum implies determinism, by excluding dynamic, token-reflexive, time-conceptions like 'now' (14.4) 1956, 11. I agree with him that, if we could not use these conceptions, we would be incapable of planning or action (see Chapter Five above). But I am not clear that the exclusion of the dynamic concepts would imply that events were *necessary* rather than contingent. What is true is that the Theory of Relativity gives an incomplete account of time, insofar as it ignores these concepts.

[24] References in § 13 of the bibliography. Answers to the deterministic argument are offered by McCall, Stein and Lango. I have introduced the word 'fixed' into the discussion, in preference to the word 'real', whose meaning and connexion with determinism are unclear.

One may calculate, perfectly correctly, that the distant event occurred *before* their meeting, and the other, perfectly correctly, that it occurred *after*. This is because they are making a judgment about the temporal relation of two events, the distant event and their meeting, and such judgments, according to the Special Theory of Relativity, are relative to the state of motion which is presupposed. Our two observers have widely different states of motion.

The determinist seeks to exploit this situation. An event which is still future for me can evidently be past, and therefore fixed, for another observer. Nor need that other observer actually exist; it is enough to say that the event can be past in relation to a different frame of reference. If every event is past, and therefore fixed, in relation to some frame of reference, can there be any events which are genuinely unfixed?

I believe this argument can be given an answer in three parts.[25] First, there is a merely relative sense in which the distant event is already fixed for both our observers, even for the one for whom it still lies in the future. For it is already too late for *him* to influence the event. But this point does not imply a deterministic conclusion, since nothing follows about its being too late for someone nearer the scene of the event.

Secondly, both observers must admit that for a person near the scene of the distant event there is a time when it is not too late for him to have an influence. The only disagreement concerns how that time is to be related to the time of their own meeting. In other words, the disagreement concerns the relationship between two widely spaced situations — their own meeting and the distant person's having an opportunity to act. That he has an opportunity is not in question.

Finally, if the two observers consider, not a very distant event, but one in their own vicinity, then if one calculates that he still has plenty of time to influence that event, the other must agree with his calculation.

I conclude that the determinist has failed, since his desire was to show that all events lack futurity, and that all must be regarded as having the necessity of things past.

Argument from returning to the past

There is, however, a further situation arising out of Relativity Theory which may appear to have deterministic implications.[26] The two observers in our last example did not agree in all their judgments of simultaneity or temporal order. This fact is sometimes expressed by saying that there is no objective, that is, no commonly shared, lapse of time. In

[25] I am very grateful to Professor Clive Kilmister for his patient answers to my questions about the situation.

[26] I am grateful to John Jupp and Alison How for raising the question in a seminar whether there were deterministic implications, and to Clive Kilmister, who gave the seminar with me, for his discussion of the question.

1951, Kurt Gödel sought to confirm this conclusion, against some attempts to define an objective lapse of time.[27]

We can represent someone's movements on a piece of paper by a line. Such lines are commonly known as world lines. As the line climbs from the bottom of the page to the top, so the person moves forward in time. As the line slopes to the left or right, so he moves in space away from his original position. Normally, one would keep the piece of paper flat, in order to represent a person's movements. But Gödel argues that the mathematics of Relativity Theory allows some very strange movements to occur, when sufficiently high velocities are attained, and certain further conditions are satisfied. These movements might be represented by curling the paper and pasting it back on to itself, so that it formed a cylinder. The result of this curling is that as the world line advances up the page it also approaches the bottom of the page. This implies that the man who leaves spatial position A at time t_0 and travels towards position B will eventually find himself back at position A and time t_0: he will have returned to his past.

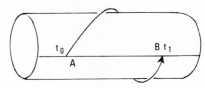

Hans Reichenbach had already presented travelling backwards in time as a logical possibility, though not a possibility implied by Relativity Theory, in 1928. And R. P. Feynman in 1949 offered it as a way of picturing the behaviour of certain electrons and positrons. Hilary Putnam has defended its possibility in the light of all these arguments.[28] These writers have used a variety of different diagrams to illustrate their idea. I shall not stop to discuss the peculiar features of each; but Putnam's can be displayed in a footnote.[29]

A great deal more would need to be said, I believe, in order to convince us that what the diagrams represent can still be called *time*. For the

[27] Kurt Gödel (14.6) 1951. Some particularly useful contributions to the subsequent debate are: Hilary Putnam (14.7) 1962, John Earman (14.8) 1967, Howard Stein (14.9) 1970.

[28] Hilary Putnam, op. cit. Hans Reichenbach (13.3) 1928 (English translation 1957, 139–43), and (14.4) 1956, 36–40. R. P. Feynman (14.5) 1949.

[29] If we read Putnam's diagram in the conventional way, taking entries lower on the page to represent earlier times, and entries higher on the page to represent later, we will see that it represents the movements of three separate men, each called Oscar. Two are suddenly created at t_1, and two suddenly annihilated later at t_2. But Putnam suggests that the careers of Oscar$_1$, Oscar$_2$ and Oscar$_3$ might be so connected that we wanted to think in terms of their being one man, and of the N as being his world line. For this purpose, he suggests, we should need to introduce a distinction between proper and objective time. Progress in objective time is represented by progress up the page; progress in proper time

diagrams suggest that what is past, or earlier than x, is also future, or later than x. Where one time is later than another, the times can still be the same. Where one time is between two others it is also before and/or after them. The question of how long someone has been living or travelling invites several different answers. It may reduce confusion to distinguish between proper or personal and objective or shared times, as Putnam does in his diagram. But even so both are still being called *times*, and we shall need to be convinced that it is not self-contradictory to treat times as standing to each other in these relationships.

Other concepts are affected too; for the problems which affect the use of the word 'time' will equally affect the talk of 'motion'. And Putnam brings in causation too, allowing a person to be causally affected by events which in objective time are yet to come.

It is not my task, however, to assess the coherence of these suggestions, but rather to try and understand them sufficiently well to see whether they would imply determinism. In connexion with the cylindrical diagram, it certainly looks as if the man's future movements are fixed. For suppose he is at spatial position A at time t_0, and at spatial position B at the later time t_1. This later time t_1 turns out after all to be the *same* time as t_0, since the times are represented on the diagram side by side. In that case, as soon as he leaves position A, the fact that he will be at position B is already a fact about his *past*, and therefore irrevocable. Although the diagram may be intended to represent only his *movements*, all his *other* future experiences will also be fixed. For if at t_0 he *will* have a toothache at t_1, that future time is already present.

It might be wondered whether he could not complete the journey represented on the cylinder, and thereafter continue freely on a more normal journey. But he seems to have no hope of completing this journey; for even when he is at position B and time t_1, the journey is represented as lying in his future.

Now it may be asked whether the fixity of this individual's future fixes the future of *other* entities. If, for example, he is inevitably to visit

---

by movement along the world line starting from spatial position A and time t_0. Progress along this line when it plunges down the page represents a return to the objective past.

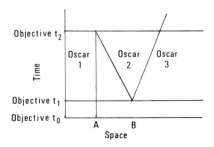

me in his future, it might seem that I must suffer a corresponding fate: I will inevitably be visited by him. But the main conclusion that Gödel draws in his paper is that there is no objective, that is, no commonly shared, lapse of time. This presumably means that my past and future cannot necessarily be put in relation to his. Even though the visit to me is irrevocably past at any time in the *man's* career, it does not follow that the visit is yet irrevocably past in *my* time.

Gödel appears unaware that he has introduced any fixity into his man's career.[30] Putnam is readier to acknowledge that his diagram restricts the future. But in four respects, I think he does not recognise the extent of the restrictions. (i) For one thing, an event lying in his man's *proper* future may lie in his *objective* past, and such events can no longer be prevented. Putnam recognises here only the weaker principle that such events cannot be prevented, if they are *known* about; and (ii) he seeks to play down the significance of this weaker principle by claiming, mistakenly, I believe,[31] that it is merely the analogue of the principle that, if you know that something will happen in the future, then, try as you may, you will not succeed in forestalling it. (iii) For another thing, Putnam does not observe that even when an event lies both in the objective and in the proper future of his man, it may already ᵢn his objective past have exercised a causal influence on him, according ₒo the story as he tells it. Consequently, an event may already be irrevocable, in spite of lying in both futures.

(iv) Finally, there is a man represented on Putnam's diagram who is free to go where he likes, once the period of time travel is over in both objective and proper time. Does this not mean that the time traveller will eventually be able to resume free movements? Only if we can make sense of the idea that the time traveller is the *same person* as the one who is represented as subsequently journeying freely. But against the proposed identification is the fact that these persons are represented as

[30] Gödel gives the impression that his man is perfectly free, when he says: 'It is possible in these worlds to travel into any region of the past, present, and future, and back again, exactly as it is possible in other worlds to travel to distant parts of space.' In fact, Gödel goes out of his way in according freedoms to his man. For he envisages the objection that the man could visit his former self, and do to his former self something which he never suffered (561). His reply (that the velocity required for this is not likely to be in practice attainable) concedes that the theory allows the logical possibility of such a thing. But it should surely have been denied that the theory allows this particular freedom. In allowing the possibility of a return to the past, the theory need not allow the possibility of doing in the past anything that was not done before.

[31] Putnam's discussion is on p. 247 (= 669 of the original). I do not think the analogy holds, because I have argued, and shall be arguing again, that ordinary human foreknowledge that you will do something does not on its own imply that you *cannot* forestall it, but only that you *will* not. Knowledge that you *have* done something, by contrast, implies that the thing is past, so *cannot* now be undone. The disanalogy is obscured if, with Putnam, we imagine our man failing after a *struggle* to forestall something. Failure after a *struggle* may imply inability to forestall, but foreknowledge does not.

being at the same objective time in different places, travelling to different destinations, and possessed of differerent experiences.

I conclude that if beings could be involved in these abnormal time journeys, their futures would be fixed.

Ancient theories of return to the past

There were theories in antiquity which would imply fixity in much the same way. It was thought by various groups that events will be repeated in the same order in endlessly recurring cycles. The Stoics combined this theory of endless recurrence with determinism, because they held that when the same causes recur, the same effects must follow. But our present question is whether the repetition itself would imply determinism, without the aid of this extra causal thesis.

The ancient theorists were puzzled about identity. Some held merely that people just like ourselves would be born, and would hold exactly similar conversations. Some held that we ourselves would be reborn, and would hold the very same conversations. Some, we are told, held that the time itself would be the same.[32] Again, I am not concerned primarily with the coherence of these theories, but with whether, in so far as they can be understood at all, they imply determinism. The last theory, that the times will be the same, seems similar to Gödel's in a crucial respect. It implies not merely that our future conversation has an irrevocable *past* occurrence, but also that its *future* occurrence is irrevocable. For the time of its future occurrence is represented as a past time.

Diodorus again

That concludes my survey of deterministic arguments based on the necessity of the past. At the beginning of this chapter, I said that Diodorus' definition of the possible seemed to imply determinism, and was taken in antiquity to imply it, and to be intended to do so. I must now explain that whether it really implies determinism depends on how it is interpreted. There are two formulations; according to the first, the

[32] For this view, see Eudemus' report on the Pythagoreans, *ap*. Simplicium, Commentary on *Phys*., *CIAG* 732–3. Others who held that the very same people and conversations will recur are the Stoics, Zeno (*ap*. Tatianum *Adv. Graec*. 5 = *SVF* i 109) and Chrysippus (*ap*. Alexandrum, Commentary on *An. Pr.*, *CIAG* 180 = *SVF* ii 624). But the Stoics evidently debated whether it would be numerically the same person (Simplicius on *Phys*. 886 11 = *SVF* ii 627): some said that it would be a person exhibiting no changes, but not the same one (Origen *Against Celsus* iv 68 = *SVF* ii 626), while some allowed small changes, e.g. in respect of freckles (Origen *Against Celsus* v 20 = *SVF* ii 626; Alexander on *An. Pr.* 181 25). The pseudo-Aristotelian *Problems* 916a18–39 considers a theory of endless recurrence, but denies that numerically the same people, as opposed to similar ones, could appear. It is more favourable to a view which represents time as one big circle, so that it will not make sense to say that the Trojan warriors are anterior to ourselves. For a discussion, see Pierre Duhem (14.1).

possible is that which is or will be. If this formulation is to imply
determinism, it must be applicable to everything, not only to sea battles
in general, but also to particular sea battles, such as a sea battle
tomorrow. It must be permissible to say that a sea battle tomorrow is
only possible if it is or will be. But the 'is' here seems redundant.
Naturally, we cannot say that a sea battle tomorrow *is* taking place; so
the only live issue is whether it *will* take place. If it will not, can we
declare it impossible by Diodorus' definition? Only so long as we are
willing to make the redundant statement that it *neither* is *nor* will be.
The awkwardness of this way of talking becomes more apparent, when
we switch from Diodorus' definition of the possible to the equivalent
definition of the necessary, as that which is and always will be. Can we
ever say that by this definition the absence of a sea battle tomorrow is
necessary? Only if we are willing to talk yet more awkwardly, and to say
that this absence exists and always will exist.

Diodorus' other formulation is in terms of *truth*, and declares that the
possible is that which is or will be *true*. Boethius records corresponding
definitions which Diodorus gave of other modalities: the necessary, for
example, is that which is true and will not be false.[33] If this is to imply
determinism, Diodorus must be very careful about the kind of entity
which he regards as being true or false. If he has sentences in mind, for
example (that is, sentence-types rather than sentence-tokens), it will
turn out to be easier than he would wish to find sentences which will at
some time be true, and which therefore ought for Diodorus to express
possibilities. Equivalently, one could say that it is harder than he would
wish to find sentences which will never be false, and which therefore
will for Diodorus express necessities. 'There will be another sea battle'
will become false, if there is a last one; 'There will be a sea battle
tomorrow' is often false; even 'There will be a sea battle in A.D. 1990' can
be regarded as false after the event is over. Certain Stoics seem to have
raised this difficulty in connexion with, 'There will be a sea battle
tomorrow', saying that it will cease to be true after the battle is over
(Alexander of Aphrodisias *De Fato* 10, *CIAG* 177.7). We get the same
result if we take a certain kind of proposition that was discussed in
Chapter Five. For if it is true now that there will be a sea battle in 1990,
we can say that it will cease to be true after the battle is over that there
will be such a battle. If Diodorus is to obtain deterministic implications
from his definition of necessity, he would do well to say that it applies to
non-token-reflexive propositions, such as, 'There is [tenseless] a sea
battle in 1990'. To make this point might well have been beyond
Diodorus' resources.

I conclude that Diodorus' definitions need to be carefully interpreted,
if they are to imply determinism, as they were apparently intended to.

[33] Boethius, 2nd Commentary on *Int.*, ed. Meiser, 234.

CHAPTER SEVEN

Other Arguments from Foreknowledge

In the preceding chapter, we encountered one argument for determinism from divine foreknowledge. But there are many other less good arguments to the effect that foreknowledge implies determinism. I shall consider some of the most important, along with the three main replies offered in antiquity. My account will be brief, because Aristotle's influence on these arguments is much less direct. None the less, it is not negligible; and in any case, it is so easy to confuse the good argument of the last chapter with the other ones, that this alone makes it desirable to spell them out. At the same time, we shall be able to study the growth of one line of reply which eventually came to be deployed against the good argument itself.[1]

One *caveat* must be entered at the outset. There are two ways of considering the compatibility or incompatibility of foreknowledge and freedom. One may ask; given that God has foreknowledge, how can we be free? But one may also ask: given that we are free, how can God have foreknowledge? It was the latter question which occupied many of the earlier writers, and so their arguments will need to be adapted, if they are to be made relevant to the former question, which concerns us.

(1) The first argument suggests that foreknowledge depends in some way on necessitating causes. Carneades, head of the Platonic Academy from 137 to 131 B.C., supposed that in order to foreknow something, one must know the causes which necessitate it.[2] The Stoics, followed by Cicero, disagreed: humans, unlike gods, will not know the causes of everything; it is enough if they know the *symptoms* of those causes.[3] But this still connects foreknowledge with causes, and indeed the Stoics appealed to human divination in order to prove causal determinism.[4]

---

[1] I am particularly indebted to two sources for the references that follow. One is Robert Sharples (12.1) forthcoming, along with the relevant section of his doctoral dissertation, *Studies in the De Fato of Alexander of Aphrodisias*, 1977, deposited in the library of Cambridge University. The other source is the doctoral dissertation of P. T. M. Huber (12.2) 1976.

[2] Cicero *De Fato* xiv 32–3.

[3] Cicero *De Divinatione* i 127. Cicero appears to agree: ii 17 ('neither *causa* nor *nota*'). Nelson Pike, however (12.5) 1970, 64, assimilates Cicero's view to Carneades'.

[4] See *SVF* 939–44.

In his beautifully clear book, *God and Timelessness*, Nelson Pike objects that a crystal-ball gazer, whose predictions were always right, would be thought to have foreknowledge, even if he used no grounds at all, not even the grounds of his own past success (which might in any case be concealed from him).[5] But in reply, the determinist who wanted to connect foreknowledge with causation might argue that we would not think the crystal-ball gazer had foreknowledge, unless we thought that some unknown factor was *causing* his predictions to tally with the subsequent events.

All I would say in reply to the determinist's insistence on causes is that the causes need not be such that it is *inevitable* that the outcome is as predicted. It will suffice for foreknowledge if they are such that the risk of error is *negligible*. Further, as regards *God's* foreknowledge, we need not suppose that it would depend on causes in any of the three ways suggested.

(2) A second mistaken view is that God's foreknowing actually *is* a kind of causing. There were philosophers in antiquity who consciously assimilated God's foreknowing to causing, but there were others who rightly declared this an error.[6] It is, however, easy to slip from a discussion of foreknowing into a discussion of fore-ordaining; and to slip in this way is to do unconsciously what some ancient philosophers tried to do consciously.

(3) One reason for supposing that foreknowledge implies determinism is a confusion about what is governed by the word 'necessary'. The answer to this confusion was given by Leibniz, by Aquinas and by Boethius; and the distinction on which the answer is based has been traced back earlier still to Ammonius. But it is less generally recognised that the distinction is made by Aristotle himself, though probably not in the passage where Boethius and Ammonius think they find it.[7]

[5] Pike, op. cit., 55. In spite of disagreeing below on points of detail, I would strongly commend Pike's lucid book.

[6] Proclus *De Dec. Dub.* 8 32–5 ties foreknowledge closely to causing. Cf. Aquinas *Summa Theologiae* 1a, question 14, article 8, and objection 1 with the reply to it in article 13; *Summa contra Gentiles* 1 67. The assimilation is rejected by Alexander of Aphrodisias *De Fato* ch. 30, 201 14; ch. 31, 203 1; Origen *On Prayer* vi 3, and an extract from his Commentary on *Genesis* iii, preserved as chapter 23 in the anthology of his works called *Philocalia*, and by Eusebius in *Praeparatio Evangelica* vi 11, 283c – 284a; Ammonius, Commentary on *Int. CIAG* 136, 25; Boethius *Consolation* v 3; John of Damascus *An Accurate Exposition of the Orthodox Faith* 2 30; Augustine *De Libero Arbitrio* 3.

[7] The confusion is answered by Boethius *Consolation* v 6; by Aquinas *Summa Theologiae* 1a 14 13, reply to objection 3; *Summa Contra Gentiles* I 67; *On Truth* q.2, a.12, reply to objection 4; and by Leibniz *Theodicy* § 37, *5th Letter to Clarke* § 5. The distinction between compounding and dividing is made by Aristotle at *SE* 4, 166a23–31: while a man is sitting, he has the power to walk, but he does not have the power to walk-while-sitting. Boethius and Ammonius, followed by Leibniz, think, probably wrongly, that the same distinction is made by Aristotle in *Int.* 9, 19a23–6. The reference there to something's being necessary *when it is*, is taken by them as a reference to the necessity of the *compound* statement that a thing is-if-it-is (Ammonius in *Int. CIAG* 152, 33 – 154, 20; Boethius in *Int.*, 2nd comm., ed. Meiser, 241–3; Leibniz *Theodicy* § 53; cf. § 132). Courcelle, Patch and Huber trace back

It is one thing to say that the following *compound* is necessary: if you know that someone will walk, he will walk. But suppose we *divide* the compound up, and take 'He will walk' in isolation: nothing follows about the walking *on its own* being necessary. This is the mistake that some determinists make; they think the future walking is necessary, when it is only the *compound* that is so. This is an example of what Aristotle calls the fallacy of compounding or composition (*sunthesis*).

(4) Alongside the argument from the necessity of *past* foreknowledge, Aquinas records an argument from the necessity of *everlasting* foreknowledge.[8] He is here trading on an idea to be criticised in the next chapter, and which is found in Aristotle, for example at *Cael.* I 12, that what is *everlastingly* the case about an everlasting subject is *necessarily* the case about it. From that unwarranted premise, the argument proceeds in parallel to the argument from the necessity of *past* foreknowledge. If God has foreknown that this thing will be, then it will be. If he has foreknown *necessarily*, because everlastingly, then the thing will be *necessarily*.[9]

(5) Aquinas records also a more general threat to God's infallible foresight, a threat which concerns all contingent truths. The idea is that because contingently true propositions are *capable* of being false, there is always a possibility of error about them, while in regard to necessarily true propositions there is no possibility of error, because they are *incapable* of being false.[10] If this were really so, the truths that God infallibly knows would have to be necessary. But, in fact, the argument confuses a question about the knower, whether he is capable of being deceived, with a question about the proposition known, whether it is capable of being false.

Ancient solutions to the arguments from foreknowledge

We can distinguish three main lines of reply that were offered in antiquity to the move from divine foreknowledge to determinism, over and above the replies, already recorded, to individual arguments. Some denied that a god could foreknow contingent events, except in the sense of knowing that they might turn out either way.[11] This might seem to

the distinction no further than these commentaries by Boethius and Ammonius (Courcelle, 'Boèce et l'école d'Alexandrie', *Mélanges de l'École Française de Rome* 52, 1935, 185–223; H. R. Patch (12.3) 1935; P. T. M. Huber, op. cit., 1976).

[8] Aquinas *Summa Theologiae* Ia 14 13 objection 2; *On Truth* 2 12, difficulty 8.

[9] At this point in the two parallel arguments, Aquinas in effect supports Chrysippus' account of conditionals as against Philo's (see Chapter Four). The antecedent *conflicts* with the denial of the consequent, or, in other words, there is a necessary connexion between antecedent and consequent. This is why it cannot be denied that necessity will spread from antecedent to consequent (*Summa Theologiae* Ia 14 13, reply to objection 2; *On Truth* 2 12, reply to difficulty 7).

[10] Aquinas *On Truth* 2 12, difficulty 6.

[11] Carneades, *ap.* Ciceronem *De Fato* 32; Cicero *De Divinatione* II 18 and 105–6; Cal-

detract from God's omniscience, but it does not, if to be omniscient is to know everything that *can* be known, and if future contingents *cannot* be known. Certainly, Alexander of Aphrodisias maintains that they *cannot* be.[12]

But how can it be established that future contingents *cannot* be known? It would be a mistake to suppose that their being foreknown would prevent them from being contingent. An argument that might have appealed to Alexander as an Aristotelian, and which has been used by Arthur Prior, is that propositions about contingent matters in the future are not yet true or false, whereas propositions can only be known, if they are true.[13] But there are at least two difficulties about this. First, in Chapter Five, I argued against Aristotle's suggestion that propositions about future contingencies are neither true nor false. Secondly, if Aristotle's suggestion were accepted, we might well revise the usual definition of knowledge, to allow for knowing propositions that will *become* true.

A second line of solution was introduced by the neo-Platonist Iamblichus (died *c*. A.D. 330). He argued that knowledge takes its character from the knower, not from the thing known, so that although future contingents are indefinite, divine knowledge of them can be definite. This view was endorsed by others in the Platonist tradition. It is sometimes added that a future contingent is indefinite in itself, and definite only as known to a god.[14]

According to a *third* solution, what God knows is in time, but God himself is not in time, and he therefore sees future events not as future, but as present. The whole of time is present to God. It is wrong, then, to describe his knowledge as *fore*knowledge. And since it is not *fore*knowledge, it no more imposes necessity on an event than our seeing of an event imposes necessity on it.

It is interesting to see this third line solution slowly being separated

cidius *Commentary on Plato's Timaeus* 162; Alexander of Aphrodisias *De Fato* 30; Porphyry *ap.* Proclum, *Commentary on Plato's Timaeus* 29c–d, ed. Diehl I 352 12; Calcidius *Commentary on Plato's Timaeus* 162. The view is ascribed to the Peripatetics (the Aristotelian school) by Proclus *De Providentia* 63.

[12] Alexander *De Fato* 30.

[13] Sharples points to several passages in Alexander's *De Fato* which suggest that he endorsed Aristotle's denial that predictions about future contingents need yet be true or false. See Chapter Five. For A. Prior, see (12.6) 1962. Cicero, however, rejected the idea that predictions are neither true nor false (*De Fato* 27–8, 38), *pace* N. Pike, *God and Timelessness*, 67.

[14] Iamblichus, as recorded and endorsed by Ammonius, Commentary on *Int.*, *CIAG* 135 14–19, 136 11–12; Proclus Diadochus *De Decem Dubitationibus Circa Providentiam*, question 2, §§ 7–8, *De Providentia et Fato* §§ 63–4; Boethius *Consolation* v 4 and 6. At a later date, the same view is given by Michael Psellus, *De Omnifaria Doctrina* 17, Bonaventure, *Commentarium in I Librum Sententiarum*, dist. 39, article 2, question 3, and Aquinas (see below). For the point taken up by Aquinas, that a future contingent is indefinite in itself, but definite as known by a god, see Ammonius 136 30 – 137 1. I shall return to Iamblichus in a projected book on ancient problems of time.

out from the second, and gradually getting deployed with more and more effect. Proclus, and after him Ammonius, who says he takes his inspiration from a much earlier discussion in Iamblichus, are aware of a dilemma: either the gods do not have definite knowledge of future contingents, or the future is fixed and necessary.[15] Both bring up the solution of divine knowledge being timeless; but they do so more in connexion with the first horn, in order to show how the gods can have definite knowledge. Moreover, Proclus offers the timelessness of God's knowledge merely as one example to illustrate the second solution, that knowledge takes its character from the knower, not from the known.[16] Ammonius adds more detail: to the gods nothing is past or future; everything is in an eternal present. But the point about timeless knowledge is introduced first, merely in order to show that they can have definite foreknowledge, and then to confirm the general point that the character of their knowledge is superior to that of the thing known.[17] We must wait until Boethius in order to find the idea of timeless knowledge connected more closely with the problem of determinism.[18] It is he who adds the reflection that knowledge which is not foreknowledge need not render the thing known necessary any more than seeing so renders the thing seen. But Boethius did not recognise what Aquinas brought out later, just *how* the pastness of God's knowledge is important to the determinist's case, namely, by implying *irrevocability*. So it is only when we reach Aquinas that we fully appreciate how the substitution of timeless knowledge for foreknowledge could meet the determinist's case. Even Aquinas, however, still combined this third solution with the second, and further used the third in reply to other arguments besides, that based on irrevocability.[19]

However successful the appeal to timeless knowledge might be in meeting the deterministic argument from irrevocability, it raises fresh problems of its own. For one thing it may be wondered whether it preserves God's omniscience (his knowledge of *everything*). For if he has not a position in time, he cannot know any tensed propositions such as that there *will* be a sea battle. For someone who has this thought must be thinking of the battle as *later* than his thought, and God's thoughts, on the present view, are not in time. God would at best know the *tenseless* proposition that there is (tenselessly) a sea battle on such and such a date, and that was argued in Chapter Five to be a *different* proposition from the tensed one. He could also know that some human

---

[15] The deterministic horn of this dilemma appears at Proclus *De Providentia* 62 and *De Dec. Dub.* 6; Ammonius *Comm. in Int., CIAG* 132 10 and 135 7–11.

[16] Proclus *De Providentia* 64, *De Dec. Dub.* 7, 29.

[17] Ammonius *Comm. in Int., CIAG* 133 16–30 and 136 15–25. As Sharples has pointed out to me, Ammonius makes it very clear that his use of the present is tenseless, 136 21–5.

[18] Boethius *Consolation* v 6.

[19] Aquinas *Summa Theologiae* I 14 13, reply to objection 2, *On Truth* 2 12, reply to difficulty 7. See also in each article his general reply.

judged that there would be a sea battle in his (the human's) future, i.e. later than his (human) judgment. But God still could not know whether the human's judgment lay in the past or future, i.e. earlier or later than his *own* (divine) thought.

Nelson Pike has sought to answer this kind of difficulty by saying that the very same fact which we express with token-reflexive words like 'now' could be known by a timeless being. For if we judge, 'Our hour of need is *now*', a timeless being could express the same fact without using token-reflexive expressions at all.[20] In Chapter Five, I explained why even *tenses* must be regarded as token-reflexive,[21] so the timeless being would have to be confined to judging, for example, 'Their hour of need (tenselessly) is on the 12 May 1977'. But as explained in Chapter Five, such ways of talking cannot express the same fact as we do with our utterance 'Our hour of need is *now*'. For unless the timeless being can employ token-reflexives, and judge 'The 12th of May is *now*', he cannot know when to help us or pity us. Perhaps the latter information would be useless to him in any case, but the point is that, useful or not, it would be unavailable. The token-reflexives carry some extra action- and emotion-guiding information, which he could not have.

Discussion of the first difficulty, that God would not be omniscient, has already drawn attention to a second: God's ignorance of tensed propositions would have serious consequences for us. If he cannot know that a sparrow is falling to the ground *now*, he cannot know that it needs his concern *now*. Nor again could he know when to intervene in human affairs, when, for example, to send his son, or to answer a prayer. These consequences might, however, have been expected by those who believe that God's perfection requires him to be changeless.

Third, it might reasonably be thought that knowledge is the sort of state which inevitably has duration, and which could not therefore belong to a timeless being. And the same might reasonably be thought about many other of God's attributes, such as his compassion. Activities also, such as the activity of creation, seem to require a location in time.[22]

Finally, some of those who accepted that God knows everything as *present* thought that this itself created a deterministic threat. St. Bonaventure, for example, was worried by the deterministic objection that what is present is irrevocable. In effect, he fell back on the second line of reply, arguing that the presentness characterises God's knowledge, not the thing known.[23] Similarly, Anselm had earlier been worried by the determinstic objection that what is eternal cannot be

[20] N. Pike (12.5) ch. 5, summarised 95.

[21] *Pace* Pike, who treats the tenses *differently* from 'today', on p. 88.

[22] For difficulties of this third sort, see Pike (12.5) 105–7, 127. Difficulties of both the second and the third sort, however, have been the subject of some ingenious solutions, and I shall need to return to them in my next book (note 14).

[23] Bonaventure loc. cit.

changed. He replied that the very same thing which, as eternal, is immutable, is also in time, and hence mutable.[24]

Aristotle's influence on the arguments from foreknowledge

Aristotle's influence on the arguments from foreknowledge is not direct, since his own God has no awareness of contingent matters. None the less, his influence is important, notably through his supplying the premise for the only good argument, by insisting on the necessity of the past. Moreover, his discussion in *Int.* 9 of tomorrow's sea battle provides the context in which Ammonius takes up the arguments from foreknowledge to determinism. Both Ammonius and Boethius find in *Int.* 9 a reference to the fallacy of composition, which certainly is expounded elsewhere in Aristotle, and which Boethius uses to disarm one deterministic argument from foreknowledge. Finally, Aristotle's denial in *Int.* 9 that statements about future contingencies need yet be true or false may have encouraged Alexander to believe that he could square God's lack of foreknowledge with his omniscience.

In rejecting arguments from foreknowledge to determinism, I have been extending a theme of the opening two chapters. It was there maintained that being explainable does not go hand in hand with being necessitated, or being predictable on the basis of laws. The new point is that being predictable does not imply being necessary. I shall not discuss the converse thesis that determinism, or rather causal determinism, implies predictability, although this thesis too has been the subject of dispute.[25]

[24] Anselm *De Concordia Praescientiae et Liberi Arbitrii* qu. 1, ch. 5.

[25] It has been disputed by Karl Popper, 'Indeterminism in quantum physics and classical physics', *British Journal for the Philosophy of Science* I, 1950, 117–33 and 173–95; D. M. Mackay, 'On the logical indeterminacy of a free choice', *Mind* 69, 1960, and 'Choice in a mechanistic universe: a reply to some critics', *British Journal for the Philosophy of Science* 22, 1971, 275–85.

CHAPTER EIGHT

Deterministic and Indeterministic Accounts of Possibility (*Int.* 9, *Cael.* ɪ 12, *GC* ɪɪ 11, *Metaph.* ɪx)

The principle of plenitude

I have maintained that Aristotle would have rejected the deterministic account of possibility according to which nothing is possible other than what is or will be. But Ross and Sambursky have represented Aristotle as more or less sympathetic to this deterministic definition, and their interpretation has been endorsed and richly elaborated by Hintikka.[1] The root idea that whatever is possible is or will be has been called by Arthur Lovejoy 'the principle of plenitude'.[2] I shall argue that in his account of possibility Aristotle remained firmly opposed to the determinists on this issue. He accepted the principle of plenitude only for a very restricted range of cases, while denying it for other cases, as I shall now try to show. But if I disagree with Hintikka, I think this disagreement less important than the fresh insight he has provided by drawing attention to suggestive interconnexions between widely scattered texts.

In *Int.* 9, Aristotle distinguishes between something like a cloak and things which (like the stars) exist for ever and are for ever active (19a9–18). A cloak is (for a finite time) capable of being cut up, even if it is never cut up, but wears out first. With the stars, however, which last, and whose capacities last, for the whole of time,[3] possibilities cannot thus remain for ever unactualised. If the sun and stars were capable of stopping their motion, then, given the whole of time, they would at some time stop. This is presumably what Aristotle has in mind at 19a9, when he says that the dual possibility of being and of not being does not apply to what is for ever active. The same example of what is for ever active is

---

[1] Jaakko Hintikka, 'Necessity, universality and time in Aristotle', *Ajatus* 20, 1957, 65–90 (reprinted in *Articles on Aristotle*, vol. 3), and (1.3) 1973, esp. ch. 5. S. Sambursky (31.16) 1959, 73. W. D. Ross, *Aristotle's Metaphysics*, a revised text with introduction and commentary, Oxford 1924, vol. 2, 244. Hintikka has extended his argument in (1.4) 1977.

[2] Arthur O. Lovejoy (11.1) 1936.

[3] The sun and stars last for the whole of time, and for Aristotle the whole of time is an infinite amount of time. One would expect, on the other hand, that an infinite amount of time (e.g. the past) need not add up to the whole of time; but at *Cael.* ɪ 12, 283a10, Aristotle says of time which is infinite only in one direction that it is infinite only 'in a way'.

given, among others, at *Metaph*. ɪx 8, 1050b20–30, and there it is repeated that, since the motion of sun and stars is everlasting, it is not capable of stopping.

There are several related principles here: the claim (i) that if stopping is possible, it must at some time be actual, has a corollary (ii) that if stopping is never actual, it is not[4] possible, and this in turn is equivalent to saying (iii) that if motion occurs always, it occurs necessarily. These relationships have been very clearly explained by Hintikka. The idea that what goes on always goes on necessarily can be found in a chapter to which we shall be returning (*GC* ɪɪ 11, 338a1–3), and there again the sun's motion is relevant (338a17 – b5). A *proof* is attempted in *Cael*. ɪ 12, 281b3–25, where Aristotle argues that if something were at all times sitting, it would be incapable of standing, and that what always exists is incapable of perishing. How does the argument go?[5]

Aristotle concedes (i) that a man can possess simultaneously the two abilities of sitting and standing (281b15–18). Elsewhere he makes the related point (ii) that he has the ability, when he is sitting, to stand (*SE* 166a23–31). Both passages, however, affirm (iii) that he lacks the ability to stand-while-sitting. He has only the ability to stand at *one* time and sit at *another*.

Aristotle takes (iii) to have implications for a thing which is *always* sitting or *always* in being. Such a thing cannot have the power to stand or to be non-existent, Aristotle thinks. If it could, then nothing impossible should result from the exercise of the power. But something impossible would result, namely, that it was standing and sitting at the *same* time, or existing and not existing at the *same* time, contrary to what was allowed under (iii).

The answer to this ought to be that no such impossibility would result, because in the imagined circumstance the thing would *not* be sitting and *not* existent. Aristotle has not allowed enough under (i) and (ii). He should recognise that even if a man will be sitting at some future time he may now have the ability to be standing instead of sitting at that very *same* time, not merely the ability to be standing at a *different* time.

Once again Aristotle's argument is not applied to transient things like cloaks, but only to everlasting things, and their everlasting capacities. Thus they are described as sitting, or as existing, for ever, and at 281b18–19 the hypothesis under discussion is that something might for an infinite time have more than one capacity, for example, the

---

[4] But we must add a complication: if, as we are suggesting, Aristotle insists on actualisation only in the case of *everlasting* capacities, the corollary is that what is never actual is not *everlastingly* possible. We need the extra premise that, if a stellar halt is not everlastingly possible, it is not possible at all, before we can reach Aristotle's conclusion that stellar motion is necessary.

[5] The passage has been very carefully expounded and criticised by C. J. F. Williams, who finds a second, even more muddled, argument in 282 a 5–25 (11.3) 1965. Hintikka offers a further diagnosis (11.2) 1973, 210–13.

capacity to sit and the capacity to stand, or the capacity to exist and the capacity not to exist. However, given the unsatisfactory character of Aristotle's argument, it is hard to see how he could resist, if somebody extended it, contrary to his intentions, to transient cloaks. For although a cloak which has been burnt up does not continue to possess the capacity to be cut up, it does for ever possess the negative property of not being cut up. Aristotle allows that things can continue to possess negative properties after they have ceased to exist (*Cat.* 13b26–35, *Int.* 16b11–15), and this should be enough to enable someone to apply Aristotle's argument. For if in the whole of time it will not be cut up, there should, on Aristotle's reasoning, be no time left at which a capacity to be cut up could be actualised; and so the cloak should be *incapable* of being cut up.

The appeal of the principle of plenitude

An aside is worthwhile at this point on the general appeal of the principle of plenitude. It has already become clear that, under suitable interpretations, the principle must be accepted by a determinist, and conversely, if accepted, commits the holder to determinism. It might seem that, apart from this, the principle would neither have much interest nor prove very persuasive. But in fact this expectation is shown to be wrong on both counts by Lovejoy's book, which is devoted to the subject. The principle has proved remarkably popular throughout the history of western philosophy, and has been seen to have innumerable implications.[6]

Although the principle of plenitude has appealed to many people, its plausibility, once it is subjected to scrutiny, will tend to vary according to the kind of possibility one has in mind when he evaluates it. Sometimes when we call something possible, we mean merely that it is compatible with the laws of logic (logical possibility), or with what we happen to know (epistemological possibility). It is not at all plausible that whatever is possible in these senses will at some time be actual. A causal determinist, however, who says that whatever is possible happens, will mean something different by 'possible', perhaps 'compatible with the laws of nature and with earlier initial conditions'. In this form the principle of plenitude is likely to seem more plausible. Again, however, we might take 'possible' simply in the sense of 'compatible

---

[6] The ramifications of the principle are enormous. Lovejoy has traced its implications for God's creation of the world, his freedom, the problem of evil, political conservatism, the evolution of species, the extent of space, and the diversity of its contents. The principle gets its name from the implication that God would have to stuff the universe full (plenitude meaning fullness) with specimens of every possible kind of creature. Yet other implications are pointed out by Hintikka, *Time and Necessity*, 94–100, and 'Leibniz on plenitude, relations and the "reign of law"', in *Modern Studies in Philosophy*: Leibniz, ed. H. Frankfurt, Garden City N.Y. 1972. For references to plenitude in Hume, Hobbes and others, see M. R. Ayers, *The Refutation of Determinism*, London 1968, 16, 90, 96.

with the laws of nature', and then the principle of plenitude can only begin to seem plausible, if it is held in a very restricted form. So much is compatible with the laws of nature that not all of it can happen: my being a racing-car driver, or a judge, my sitting now, my standing now, there being a golden mountain now, there not being a golden mountain ever. The principle becomes slightly less implausible, if it is restricted, as Aristotle restricts it, to the everlasting capacities of everlasting things to be in particular states. For example, if matter is everlasting, and if it is compatible with the laws of nature that matter should form itself into a golden mountain, there will eventually be a golden mountain. People are often persuaded to believe a similar idea, that unending relays of monkeys hammering randomly at a typewriter would, given an infinite amount of time, type out the works of Shakespeare. They may believe that this is guaranteed by the laws of probability and chance. Karl Popper was once inclined to suggest that all events and processes compatible with the laws of nature are somewhere at some time realised in the universe. It is a corollary that if some event or process never occurs (if, for example, a golden mountain never arises), it is not compatible with the laws of nature that it should. Yet we might protest that the non-occurrence of a golden mountain could be a mere accident. And Popper himself eventually changed his view, under criticism from William Kneale, and acknowledged the need to recognise the possibility of such universal accidents.[7]

Yet another context in which the principle of plenitude is still a live issue is the discussion of whether modal concepts can be reduced to temporal ones. Diodorus Cronus in effect suggested that they could be, when he defined the possible and the necessary in terms of some time and always. And recently Arthur Prior has found these definitions sufficiently interesting to hunt for a modal system that would incorporate them.[8]

The principle is applied by Aristotle only to everlasting things

When we return from the appeal of the principle of plenitude to Aris-

---

[7] Karl Popper, 'A note on natural laws and so-called contrary-to-fact conditionals', *Mind* 58 N.S. 1949, 62–6; *The Logic of Scientific Discovery* (5.3) 1959; William Kneale (5.1) 1961; and *Probability and Induction*, Oxford 1949. A distinction is sometimes made (rightly, I believe) between three kinds of universal statement. Some express logically or conceptually necessary truths, e.g. (a) '2 + 2 =4'; others express causally or physically necessary truths, e.g. (b) 'the velocity of light *in vacuo* is independent of the velocity of the emitting source'; others again express universal accidents, e.g. (c) 'there are no golden mountains'. The effect of Popper's original view was to deny that (c) can express a universal accident. Others, following Hume, have denied that physical necessities exist. It is admittedly difficult to define the physical necessity involved in (b), so as to distinguish it both from the logical necessity in (a) and from the universal accident in (c). But see on this subject Chapter Two.

[8] These attempts culminate in A. Prior, *Past, Present and Future*, Oxford 1967.

totle's own position, the important thing to stress is that Aristotle refuses to apply the principle of plenitude to things of finite duration. The evidence for this abundant. We have already noticed that at *Int*. 9, 19a9–18, he distinguishes between things which are for ever active and things like a cloak. The latter is capable of being cut up, even if it never will be. We have also observed that the argument for plenitude in *Cael*. I 12 is not *intended* to be applied to transient things, even if Aristotle's oversights would leave room for an unintended application. A further striking piece of evidence comes to light when we examine the passages which Hintikka cites for versions of the principle of plenitude.[9] For in nearly all of them, certainly in all the non-controversial ones,[10] the idea that what is always true of something is necessarily true of it is explicitly applied to *everlasting* things. And the converse idea that what is possible is at some time actual is applied to transient things only in the special case of failure to exist. Naturally Aristotle holds that what can fail to exist will at some time fail (otherwise it would be an *everlasting* thing with a never actualised capacity for non-existence). But this is not to imply that the capacities of transient things, *other* than the capacity for non-existence, will eventually be actualised. Aristotle's view is stated particularly clearly, though representatively, at *Phys*. III 4, 293b30: 'In *everlasting things*, there is no difference between being possible and being the case.'

This I think, is evidence enough, but a further indication can be gained by considering the opening chapters of *An. Post.* In I 6, Aristotle implies that a predicate will attach of *necessity* to a subject only if subject and predicate have an '*in-itself*' relation (74b12, 75a20–2, a 31), that is, only if one is definable in terms of the other (I 4, 73a34 – b5). He carefully distinguishes predicates which attach to their subjects in every instance and at all times (I 4, 73a28–34), but *without* having a definitional connexion. The implication is that attaching *always* is no guarantee of attaching necessarily. If this last piece of evidence is less conclusive, this is because, as will be seen in Chapter Twelve, Aristotle's requirements for necessity are somewhat stricter in this passage than elsewhere.

Hintikka's response

Hintikka is, of course, well aware of Aristotle's treatment of a cloak. But

[9] Hintikka cites: *Metaph*. XIV 2, 1088b23–5; IX 3, 1047a12–14; IX 4, 1047b3–9; IX 8, 1050b7–8 and 20; XII 6, 1071b18–20; v 30, 1025a33; VI 2, 1026b27–37; *Phys*. III 4, 203b30; IV 12, 221b25 – 222a9; *Cael*. I 12; *GC* II, 338a1–4; *Int*. 9, 18b11–15; 19a9–11; *Top*. II 11, 115b17–18; v 1, 128b16–18.

[10] I would count as controversial at least the following: the passages in *Metaph*. IX 3 and 4 to be discussed below; the passage in *Int*. 9, also to be discussed below, where Aristotle speaks of a prediction '*always*' having been true; and two passages where '*always*' is joined to a modal expression only by the word 'and' (*Metaph*. VI 2, 1026b27–37; *Top*. v 1, 128b16–18).

he claims that Aristotle would still apply the principle of plenitude in a way to non-everlasting things, such as particular sea battles and cloaks. And he suggests that Aristotle could have done this by treating the statement that there can be a sea battle tomorrow, or that a particular cloak can be cut up, as an elliptical statement about sea battles and cloaks in general, that at least one sea battle will be fought, and at least one cloak cut, some time or other.[11] I am not sure that I see convincing evidence that Aristotle intended this (Hintikka cites *An. Pr.* ɪ 13, 32b4ff.). But at any rate the important thing is that such a use of the principle of plenitude would no longer mean that Aristotle was 'adopting . . . by implication anything like a deterministic doctrine' (*Time and Necessity* 201). So used, the principle would not authorise us to argue in deterministic fashion from the possibility that this cloak will be cut at noon tomorrow, or that a sea battle will take place then, to the conclusion that this cloak will then be cut, or that a sea battle will then take place. We could only argue in non-deterministic fashion to the conclusion that some time some cloak will be cut, and some sea battle will take place.

None the less, having made Aristotle accept the principle of plenitude, in a restricted form, even for cloaks, Hintikka also expects that Aristotle will be drawn, against his will, in the direction of the determinist's argument in *Int.* 9. Hintikka construes the determinist as arguing not, as we supposed, from the 'is earlier true' of 18b10, but from the 'has *always* been true' of 18b10–11. And having ascribed to Aristotle the principle of plenitude, he expects Aristotle to accept the determinist's move from 'has *always* been true' to 'is *necessarily* true'.[12] Moreover, Hintikka does not think that Aristotle replies to the determinist by denying that certain predictions have been true or false; on the contrary, he thinks Aristotle must accept that some have always been true. The problem then is, for Hintikka's view, how Aristotle can escape agreeing completely with the determinist's conclusion that the sea battle is necessary. Hintikka makes him escape only by ascribing to him a thoroughly unsatisfactory move. Aristotle 'forgets or disparages', he suggests, future-tense sentences of the kind that have *always* been true, or *always* false, such as, 'There will be a sea battle in 1990', where the last two words specify the date independently of the time of utterance (*Time and Necessity* 159–61). Instead, he makes Aristotle concentrate on sentences like, 'There will be a sea battle *tomorrow*', which have not *always* been true nor *always* false.

Hintikka further suggests that Aristotle actually picks out sentences

[11] The treatment of the cloak is recognised, and the principle of plenitude restricted in the way we have suggested on pp. 100–1 of (11.2) and slightly differently on p. 75 of the earlier article in *Ajatus* 1957. The different suggestion that the principle of plenitude is still applied in a roundabout way to cloaks and sea battles is made on pp. 161–2, 167, 172–4 (cf. 113) of (11.2).

[12] Hintikka (11.2) 105, 152–3, 167.

which contain a phrase specifying the date independently of the time of utterance, and concedes that, if true, they are necessarily true. This, at any rate, is how I believe he construes 19a23 (*Time and Necessity* 151–3, 158–9; *Aristotle on Modality and Determinism* 32, 38), where Aristotle allows that everything is of necessity, *when* it is. Elsewhere (*Time and Necessity* 183) Hintikka, like myself, takes this as merely conceding the necessity of the past and present. But here I believe he takes Aristotle's talk of 'what is, when it is' as being a reference to sentences like, 'there will be a sea battle in 1990'. Because these specify the time by means of a calendar date, rather than by an expression like 'tomorrow', and because they are couched in the future tense, and are about something still future, they have *always* expressed a truth, if they have expressed one at all. Somehow (I am not sure how) we are to take the talk of 'what is, when it is' as referring to sentences like this, and as conceding that they express a necessary truth.

For at least three reasons,[13] I cannot accept Hintikka's positive suggestion about 19a23–6. But the more important question is whether his interpretation is in general plausible, whatever we make of those particular lines. A major difficulty, as it seems to me (the converse of one stated in note 13), is that there are plenty of sentences lacking a calendar date (or equivalent) which would nevertheless meet the requirement that concerns us. That is, if they have been true or false at all, as Hintikka assumes, they must *always* have been true, or *always* false. And this creates a fresh problem for Hintikka: how can he protect Aristotle from conceding to the determinist that these sentences are necessarily true or necessarily false? We may instance such sentences as, 'There will be a sea battle at such-and-such a (specified) place', 'A philosopher king who makes cloaks will be born', 'The first cloak made by a philosopher king will not be cut up'. If these sentences have always been true, or always false, then, on Hintikka's interpretation, Aristotle ought to concede to the determinist that they are necessarily true, or necessarily false. Yet he makes no such concession, and it surely will not

[13] First, I do not see how we can construe the concession that everything is of necessity, when it is, as bearing the meaning that Hintikka ascribes to it. The phrase 'when it is' does not draw our attention to calendar dates or their equivalents. Secondly, I doubt if Aristotle is concerned with *sentences* at all in 19a23–6, or with other bearers of truth value. He does not seem to reach that until 19a32. Thirdly, if he were interested in sentences, and in ones which have always been true or always false, it still would not suit his interest to pick out sentences with a calendar date (or equivalent), for there are many such sentences which have not always been true or always false. These are sentences with a tense (no matter which tense) and with a past date: 'There was a sea battle in 1945', 'There is a sea battle in 1945', 'There will be a sea battle in 1945'. These, though dated, have not always been true, nor always false, and, as Hintikka rightly points out (11.2) 150, what goes for the sentence also goes for the thought, and for any other bearer of truth value, in Aristotle's opinion. It cannot even be claimed, for the present and future-tense sentences, that they will always be true in the future. Hintikka pleads (11.2) 152, on behalf of the future-tense ones that at least they have been true for an infinity of past time. This cannot be claimed, however, for the present and past-tense ones.

be maintained that this is because he forgets or disparages these sentences too.

On my view, Aristotle may have felt that if he once conceded '*already* true', he would have to concede 'necessary'. But he would have had no general disposition to move from '*always*' to 'necessarily', as Hintikka maintains. For he accepted the principle of plenitude only in connexion with such things as the heavens, their motions, and the resulting seasons, not in connexion with a battle, or, for that matter, with the truth about a battle. Even where that truth may have lasted for the whole of past time, it is not clear that it belongs on a list with the heavens, their motions, and the seasons.[14] I conclude that, in his treatment of the sea battle, Aristotle is not pulled in the way that Hintikka supposes towards the position we find in Diodorus, that is, towards determinism and the principle of plenitude.

Deterministic interpretations of Metaphysics ix

To complete our picture of Aristotle's attitude towards deterministic accounts of possibility, we need to consider another work of his, *Metaph*. ix, which has been deterministically interpreted. Here Aristotle is talking about the capacities of things, and in ix 3, he rejects a definition of capacity devised by some Megarian philosophers. As it has now been made doubtful that Diodorus was known as a Megarian (see Chapter Six), and as the rejected definition seems in any case to be more extreme than that of Diodorus, we cannot safely infer anything about Aristotle's attitude to the latter. The Megarians in question are said to hold that something has the capacity of acting only when it does act (1046b29–30). This statement is ambiguous; it might be a simple statement of Diodorus' kind of determinism. If I build a house on three occasions in my life, my capacity is for building only on those three occasions, and presumably for refraining only on other occasions. I cannot build, or refrain, at other times. However, this is not how Aristotle interprets the Megarian view. He first interprets it as meaning that, in between the occasions of building, one loses one's capacity, and he asks how one gets it back (1046b30 – 1047a10). He then suggests that one loses the capacity of ever building again, and objects that things would be stuck changelessly in their present state (1047a10–17). He complains that such a view collapses capacity into actuality (1047a17–24). Clearly, Aristotle takes himself here to be combatting a very extreme view, so that we cannot decide on this basis what he would have said about simple determinism.

---

[14] It would be no good pleading that the argument of *Cael*. ı 12 would be applicable to such a truth, no less than to the heavens; the argument of *Cael*. ı 12 is a bad one, and, if pressed, would be applicable to an individual cloak, in a way which is agreed to be contrary to Aristotle's intention.

In the sequel, Aristotle makes various suggestions of his own, which Hintikka has construed as positively favouring Diodorean determinism. But once again I do not believe that Aristotle commits himself. In several passages, Hintikka interprets Aristotle as endorsing, like Diodorus, the principle of plenitude. But since, in connexion with the hardest passage (ix 4, 1047b3–9) Hintikka candidly cites the rival interpretation of Martha Kneale and G. E. L. Owen (*Time and Necessity* 107–9), I can make my comment brief.

On ix 4, 1047b3–9, Hintikka can claim the support of W. D. Ross. But Kneale and Owen suggest that Aristotle is not objecting to a denial of the principle of plenitude, but only to a certain moral misguidedly drawn from that denial. The mistaken moral is that what never happens is *in every case* possible, so that, for example, it is possible to find a common measure for the diagonal and side of a square, and indeed impossibility is abolished. As S. Mansion points out,[15] if the passage is interpreted in this way, it actually goes against the ascription to Aristotle of the principle of plenitude. For in resisting the idea that *all* things which fail to happen are possible, Aristotle will be allowing that *some* things which never happen are none the less possible.

Hintikka also cites as an endorsement of the principle of plenitude ix 3, 1047a12–14. But the claim there that impossibility means never being the case, need only mean that it *entails* never being the case, not that there is an equivalence of meaning. If Aristotle were speaking of an equivalence, the natural interpretation would in any case be that his Megarian opponents were committed to the equivalence, not that he himself was.

Finally, in ix 8, 1050b7–8 and 20, the principle of plenitude is endorsed, but only in connexion with everlasting things.

More significant than the remarks in chapters 3 and 4 is the analysis that Aristotle goes on to give in ix 5 of certain kinds of capacity, and of their relation to the actual. For this analysis is not merely compatible with determinism, but has actually been used by modern determinists. Aristotle claims that to say that something *can* act is to say that it *will* act, but only *if* certain conditions are satisfied. (The Megarians ignored the 'if'.) In the case of capacities which involve reason, the agent *will* act, if, among other conditions, he *wants* to act. Twentieth-century determinists have reinvented this analysis with the aim of showing that determinism is compatible with moral responsibility. They claim that, in spite of the truth of determinism, an agent *can* act otherwise than he does, so long as 'can' means something like 'will, if he wants'. I shall return to this view in Chapter Fifteen.

What matters for the moment is that the appearance of an analysis favoured by modern determinists might be misconstrued as supporting the deterministic interpretation of Aristotle. And Hintikka has for

[15] S. Mansion (27.3) 1946, 2nd ed. 1976, new note 13.

different reasons cited this passage as a sign that 'in one of his moods at least he thus comes fairly close to Diodorean determinism'.[16] Hintikka groups the passage with an interesting collection of others which were discussed in Chapter Three,[17] to show that Aristotle often thinks of capacities not as bare possibilities, but as natural tendencies which necessarily realise themselves, once the circumstances are right, or unless something is actually preventing the realisation. I explained there why I did not accept that the passages were genuinely deterministic. The assembling of the right conditions may depend on coincidences which Aristotle does not regard as necessitated. Moreover, there is nothing to rule out these tendencies sometimes being realised *before* all the normal conditions have been assembled, on which occasions their realisation will not have been necessitated.

Gomperz and Loening

So far I have considered only a modified deterministic interpretation. Hintikka's view is that there are many elements in Aristotle's thought which drive him, against his will, towards determinism. A more radical position is adopted, and eloquently supported, by Theodor Gomperz and Richard Loening.[18] Gomperz only calls Aristotle nine-tenths a determinist, but Loening is prepared to go further. In his admirable book on Aristotle's *Ethics* (reprinted in 1967) he maintains that for individual future events Aristotle fully accepts causal necessity. There was at that time, in Loening's view, no controversy between determinism and indeterminism, in relation to which Aristotle would have thought of himself as taking sides, but none the less only determinism was thinkable for him.[19] In *Int.* 9, according to Loening,[20] Aristotle's quarrel with his opponent only concerns the suggestion that the cutting up of cloaks, or the occurrence of sea battles, is necessary in the same way as the circular motion of the stars is necessary. Aristotle thinks this stellar motion necessary simply in virtue of the fact that it *always* happens. According to Loening, he is here merely protesting that cloaks are not *always* cut up, and sea battles do not occur *every* day. The necessity of what always happens is not the same as causal necessity, as Loening rightly says (contrast Taylor and Strang),[21] and so if Aristotle is only denying that the cutting up of cloaks is necessary in this way, he leaves

[16] Hintikka (11.2) 201–2; cf. 199, and *Ajatus* 1957, 73.

[17] *Metaph.* ix 7, 1048b37 – 1049a18; *Phys.* viii 4, 255a30 – b31 (cf. ii 8, 199b18, 26); *Long* 3, 465b14–16; *Mot.* 4, 699b29 (cf. 8, 702a10–17); cf. *GA* ii 4, 740b21–4.

[18] Theodor Gomperz (1.1) ch. 10 and 16, tr. 1912, from the German of 1896. Richard Loening (1.2) 1903.

[19] Loening, op. cit. 318.

[20] Loening, op. cit. 293.

[21] R. Taylor, 'The problem of future contingencies', *Philosophical Review* 66, 1957, 1–28; C. Strang, 'Aristotle and the Sea Battle', *Mind* 69, 1960, 458.

himself free to say that the cutting up of any given cloak is causally necessary.[22]

It must be acknowledged that Aristotle does seem to be talking about the necessity of what always happens at various points in the chapter (18b8–9, 19a9, a19–20, a35–9). But this need not be because he regards his opponent as believing in this kind of necessity. It may rather be that this is one of the main kinds of necessity that Aristotle himself recognises, and he thinks that if he once supplies a reminder that this kind of necessity cannot be ascribed to everything, his opponent will not be able, on the basis of his present argument, to find any other kind. The causal necessity, discussed in *Metaph.* vi 3, would be quite irrelevant to this chapter. Only two other cases of necessity are mentioned for the opponent's consideration. One is the necessity of the present or past (so I construe 19a23–4), and one is the necessity of some form of the laws of excluded middle or of bivalence (19a28, 30, 32, 36), but Aristotle thinks he has a direct answer to his opponent's attempt to exploit these.

Loening apparently thinks that Aristotle regards his opponent as seriously intending to ascribe to everything the necessity of what always happens, as if cloaks were always cut up, just as the stars always move. But it is hard to see why anyone should think this conclusion at all tempting, or why they should think a premise about being already true should lend it any plausibility. Certainly, Loening believes that Aristotle contents himself with rejecting this particular kind of necessity. But in 19a12–16 he does not seem to be saying merely that *some* cloaks are cut up, while *others* wear out first. He seems rather to be arguing that a *particular* cloak enjoys the dual possibility of being cut up or not. And in 18b8–9, he does not say merely that what is as chance has it happens equally often either way; he concludes from this that (in a *particular* case, presumably) it might equally well happen or not happen. If Aristotle were only denying that cloaks are always treated the same way, he would not need so elaborate an argument. The opponent's view could be briefly expounded, and Aristotle's reply could finish at 19a22. There would be little point in going on to consider other cases of necessity in 19a22–39, and he would have lost his main motivation for denying (if he does) that certain predictions yet have a truth value. Indeed, if Aristotle once conceded to the determinist that all predictions were in *some* way necessary all along, he would hardly feel entitled to deny that they yet had a truth value. Nor would he have established his claim (18a33–4) that they were in the relevant respects different from all other propositions. Fortunately, Loening himself does not in the end

[22] Compare Robert Sharples, who finds in the Aristotelian Alexander of Aphrodisias, and to some extent in Aristotle himself, a confusion of the question whether a thing's behaviour varies from one occasion to another, according to circumstances, with the question whether, on each occasion taken individually, its behaviour is determined, (31.11) 1975.

go so far as to say that *from the very beginning* a particular deliberation, for Aristotle, admits of only one outcome. He only claims that the outcome is *eventually* necessitated, and we can agree that Aristotle thinks this true at least of some cases. But Loening does not explain how Aristotle can escape saying that the outcome has *all along* been causally necessary, if he really allows, as Loening believes, that each of its causal antecedents was causally necessary. It is easier, then, to accept the usual view that Aristotle is denying any necessity to future contingents.

Retrospect

If we now look back over the first eight chapters, we can distinguish different kinds of reason for believing in determinism. The first four chapters were concerned with arguments from causation, the next two with arguments from the irrevocability of the past, and the seventh with arguments from foreknowledge. The present chapter has uncovered a possible, rather than an actual, further source of motivation. If someone for independent reasons came to define possibility in Diodorus' manner, he might find himself driven to determinism. This was not the direction of Diodorus' own thought, so far as one can tell from the structure of his Master Argument; rather his belief in determinism and in the principle of plenitude appear as joint products of reflection upon the necessity of the past. None the less, considerations about possibility constitute a further possible source of belief in determinism. Reflection on Aristotle has then, I hope, proved its value in a further way, by making us consider such a wide range of grounds for determinism, grounds which are usually treated in separate works by separate authors.

Throughout, I have been resisting deterministic interpretations of Aristotle. I have denied that he thought coincidences to be necessitated,[23] or that he was driven towards the deterministic account of possibility given by Diodorus Cronus,[24] or towards the deterministic conclusion of the sea battle argument.[25] In Chapter Fourteen, I shall further deny that Aristotle's account of *action* is deterministic.[26] I have not in general disputed Hintikka's view that there were pressures driving Aristotle in the direction of determinism. But I believe there were fewer than Hintikka maintains, and I have emphasised that, whatever the pressures, Aristotle resisted them.

In the next three chapters, I shall, however, resist an indeterministic interpretation which goes to the opposite extreme. It has been thought that among natural processes Aristotle allowed practically no causal necessitation, perhaps in order to make room for his purposive explana-

[23] Gomperz, Ross, Joachim, Owen, Hintikka, Long, Bogen, Etheridge (Chapter One).
[24] Ross, Sambursky, Hintikka (Chapter Eight).
[25] Hintikka, cf. Loening (Chapter Eight).
[26] Loening, Gauthier, Allan.

tions. It has been further thought that he denied causation both in the sphere of natural processes, and in the sphere of human action. In Chapters Nine to Eleven and Fourteen, I shall argue that this interpretation goes too far.

PART III

NECESSITY AND PURPOSE IN NATURE

CHAPTER NINE

Necessity in Nature (*GC* ii 11, *PA* i 1; *Phys*. ii 9)

Aristotle sometimes denies necessity without denying causation

Before confronting the indeterministic interpretations of Aristotle, I want to return to a theme of Chapter Two: the divorce between causation and necessitation. In his philosophy of nature, I believe that Aristotle denies necessity at certain points, without denying causation. But I shall have to answer the arguments of W. D. Ross and David Balme, both of whom speak of 'fresh starts'. The phrase suggests that causation is being denied.

The passage in which Ross detects fresh starts is *GC* ii 11. This Chapter is strikingly different from *Metaph*. vi 3, in that Aristotle recognises only one kind – a different kind – of absolute necessity. He equates *always* being or coming into being with *necessarily* doing so (337b35 – 338a3). If the heavens always exist, they exist necessarily and if rain always recurs after a pause, then rain necessarily recurs. This idea has already been encountered in Chapter Eight above. The equating of 'always' with 'necessarily' in such cases is argued for in *Cael*. i 12, 281b3–25. Aristotle concludes from his equation in *GC* ii 11 that, if we consider coming into being (as opposed to being), it can be necessary only for cyclically recurring states of affairs; for only these can be said to come into being *always*. The most important cyclical occurrence is the motion of the heavens, and in particular the annual advance and retreat of the sun. As the preceding chapter *GC* ii 10 explains,[1] this influences the other cyclical occurrences: the seasons, the birth of a new generation and the decay of an old one, the transformation of the four elements, evaporation followed by rain, and the motion of winds. Such things recur *always* and hence necessarily. The same cannot be said of Mr Smith, and so his coming into being is not necessary (*GC* ii 11, 338a4 – b19).

What interests me for the moment about *GC* ii 11 is the status it assigns to the coming into being of an individual, seeing that this does not recur everlastingly. How are we to think, for example of the coming

[1] See also *GA* 777a31 – 778a12, 767a1, 738a20, 737a3; *Meteor*. i 9, ii 4; *Cael*. ii 3, 286b2.

into being of a house? Aristotle recognises a hypothetical necessity: foundations are necessary *if* the house is to come into being. However, there is no unhypothetical necessity, that is, no necessity unqualified by 'if so-and-so is to be'. In this chapter, then, Aristotle recognises very few cases of coming into being which possess unhypothetical necessity. Indeed, the question he asks is not whether any coming into being is contingent, but whether any coming into being is necessary (337b1–3). What is striking is that he does not even consider the source of necessity which he is anxious to remove in *Metaph.* vi 3. In that chapter, he is worried that if every causal chain stretches back into the present or past, then the earlier members of the chain will have an unalterable fixity which they will transfer to future members of the chain. Of this worry there is no trace in *GC* ii 11. The chapter recognises only the hypothetical necessity of what is needed for an end, and the absolute necessity of what happens always. The coming into being of a particular house has no unhypothetical necessity.

Ross is right, then, to say that *GC* ii 11 recognises a breach of necessity. But it would be wrong to suppose, as his talk of 'fresh starts' might suggest, that when coming into being is not necessary, it is also uncaused. David Balme has argued that Aristotle does postulate such 'fresh starts' in nature.[2] He cites as evidence the origins (*archai*) mentioned in *GA* 778a7, which prevent births and deaths being perfectly synchronised with celestial motions, and which are often causes (*aitiai*) of things turning out contrary to nature. But these origins need not be uncaused; I shall argue in Chapter Fourteen that lack of an earlier cause is not implied by the meaning of the word *archē*. Nor is it true that elemental motion would come to an end without the intervention of uncaused starts. *GC* ii 10 explains that elemental motion is kept going by the approach and retreat of the sun (337a7–15). So I think the situation is that necessity is denied, causation is not. At least, the denials that natural coming into being is necessary do not seem to be accompanied by denials that it is caused. The coming into being of a man is not necessary, but it has a cause in the father.

Aristotle's denials of necessity

The main problem concerning Aristotle's philosophy of nature, and the main problem to be discussed here, is not the status of causation, but the status of necessity. Chapters such as *GC* ii 11 have suggested to commentators ancient and modern[3] a very radical kind of indeterminism.

    [2] D. M. Balme, 'Greek science and mechanism I', *Classical Quarterly* xxxiii, 1939, 132–4, 137–8; with (18.1) 1965, 24; and (1.6) 1972, 82 and 96.

    [3] D. M. Balme (1939) 134; (1972) 80, 82. In *CIAG*, see e.g. Philoponus on *GC* 337b22; Simplicius and Philoponus on *Phys.* 198b5–6; Michael of Ephesus on *PA* 640a4. See also Boethius, 2nd Commentary on *Int.*, ed. Meiser, pp. 244–5; S. Sambursky (31.16) 1959, 71–3; id. (1.5) 1956, 46–8; W. D. Ross, *Aristotle's Physics*, Oxford 1936, 43; I. Düring,

Aristotle's position has been variously expressed as being that there is only hypothetical necessity in nature, or among things that come to be, or in the sublunary region, or in biology. Some have gone further and concluded that, since this doctrine was applied to the whole of the sublunary region, it impeded the progress of science, and the attempt to find laws that would apply throughout the universe.[4]

These formulations cannot all be quite right as they stand. Let us try to get the thesis formulated a little more accurately. For one thing, Aristotle makes a sharp distinction between being and coming to be. It is with regard to coming to be that *GC* II 11 is particularly reluctant to allow unhypothetical necessity. And the same is true in other passages where necessity is denied (*PA* I 1, 639b24–5, 642a6: *Phys.* II 9, 200a1, a16, a19). In *GC* II 11, he makes it clear that he is thinking not only of the coming to be of substances, but also of the coming to be of states of affairs; in other words, he is thinking of events in general, and he mentions heavenly motions, solstices, the arrival of seasons, and of rain. The chapter opens by explaining (337a34–5) that he is concerned with change in general. It is not quite right to say that unhypothetical necessity is altogether disallowed in connexion with changes in the sublunary region or in biology; for among the comings-into-being declared everlasting and necessary in *GC* II 11 are the cycle of evaporation and showers (cf. *An. Post.* II 12, 95b37), and the cycles of death and birth, and their various accompaniments. (He does not mean *individual* showers or births.) *Metaph.* IX 8 adds the movements (i.e. the comings-to-be in a given place) of the four elements, earth, air, fire and water (1050b28–30). If we now turn to being, instead of coming into being, it is still less true that unhypothetical necessity is altogether denied. For many things can be said to be (or exist) everlastingly and hence necessarily, in Aristotle's view: not only the heavens, but also the natural kinds in the sublunary region.

It is, incidentally, just as well that the chapter makes these concessions, or else it would be in conflict with Aristotle's whole programme in the *Posterior Analytics* for expounding scientific discoveries. For he there thinks that scientists should prove with regard to various affirmative predicates that they belong everlastingly and necessarily to the various natural kinds.[5] And he also thinks it a precondition of this that

---

[footnote continuation] 'Aristotle's method in biology', in S. Mansion (ed.), *Aristote et les Problèmes de Méthode*, Louvain and Paris 1961, 215; A. Preus, *Aristotle's Biological Works*, Hildesheim 1975, ch. 4; Helene Weiss, *Kausalität und Zufall in der Philosophie des Aristoteles*, Basel 1942, 75–93; W. Wieland, *Die aristotelische Physik*, Göttingen 1970, 264–6 (translated in *Articles on Aristotle*, vol. 1; W. Kullmann (16.2) 1974, 292–3, 337.

[4] Sambursky and Düring.

[5] For Aristotle's programme, see: *An. Post.* I 2, 4, 6, 8; II 3, 90b24; II 17, 99a22; *NE* VI 3 and 6; *DA* I 1, 402b16 – 403a2. I have tried to explain and defend certain aspects of the programme in the misleadingly entitled paper, 'Aristotle and Oxford philosophy', *American Philosophical Quarterly* 6, 1969, 127–35, which was in fact a consideration of definition and necessity in Aristotle's philosophy of science. See also Chapter Twelve.

the natural kinds should *exist* everlastingly and necessarily.[6] What, then, is the necessity that Aristotle is denying in *GC* II 11? To put it in our terminology, what he is denying about the coming into being of a particular house, or of Mr Smith, is that it is made necessary by causes. In general, in art and nature, particular changes are not causally necessitated.

In other chapters, he appears to speak similarly. There are two such passages in *PA* I 1, where again he is talking about coming into being (639b24–5; 642a6). In the first (639b21 – 640a9), he says that unqualified necessity characterises things that are everlasting, while hypothetical necessity (does he mean *only* hypothetical necessity?) characterises things that come into being. He goes on to ban from natural science explanations which take the form, 'since this exists or has come into being, that of necessity exists or will come into being'. In the second passage (642a1–13), he says that for things which come into being there is hypothetical necessity, but not either of the two kinds of necessity defined in the philosophical works. These two kinds are, on the one hand, the necessity associated with force (*bia*) when we throw a stone up against its natural tendency, and on the other hand either the necessity associated with everlasting things, which does not admit of being otherwise (this is suggested by *Metaph.* v 5, 1015a34; vi 2, 1026b28–9), or the necessity with which a stone falls downwards, when there are no obstacles (as is suggested by *An. Post.* II 11, 94b37 – 95a3; cf. *Rhet.* I 10, 1368b35).

Aristotle talks in the same spirit (again about coming to be, 200a1; a16; a19) in *Phys.* II 9. He says that the necessity which is to be found in nature is the necessity connected with the matter (200a30–2), and he here means by that a merely hypothetical necessity, as he says at 200a13, adding that the goal achieved (*telos*) is not itself a necessary outcome.[7] *Int.* 9 fits in with the other passages cited, insofar as it considers other kinds of necessity, but omits mention of the necessitation of a cause by an effect. And it is tempting to add to the catalogue *An. Post.* II 12, 95a29 – b1, where Aristotle denies that we can infer a later event from an earlier one.

Aristotle's affirmations of necessity

All this suggests a fairly radical indeterministic view. But it is time to call a halt; for on the other side are numerous passages where Aristotle speaks as if certain events do happen from some kind of necessity. The

[6] *An. Post.* I 8; *NE* vi 3, 1139b22–4; *Metaph.* vii 15, 1039b27 – 1040a2. Natural kinds include not only kinds of substance, such as animal species, but also kinds of event such as thunder and eclipse. The latter occur only intermittently, and it seems to be thought adequate that instances of the kind should be everlastingly and necessarily recurrent (*An. Post.* I 8, 75b33–6; *GC* II 11, 337b32–4.

[7] Elsewhere, however, he allows that matter can necessitate. See Chapter Three n.24.

most useful discussion of this that I know is by David Balme (*op. cit.*, 1972), whose sizeable collection of examples from Aristotle's biology will be cited in a little while. But even without the biological examples, we have already encountered a good number of others. In *Metaph.* VI 3, Aristotle was quite ready to allow that a man's death by violence might eventually become necessary. All he wanted to deny was that it had *all along* been necessary. In Chapter Fourteen, we shall encounter four passages which describe certain human actions or animal movements as necessitated (*NE* 1147a27, a30; *Metaph.* IX 5, 1048a14; *Mot.* 9, 702b24; *Poet.* 7–10). We have noted (Chapter Three) a group of references, collected by Hintikka, to certain natural tendencies which realise themselves (Aristotle twice says necessarily), once the circumstances are right, unless something actually prevents it. One of these passages, *Metaph.* IX 5, was especially disconcerting, because, taken in conjunction with certain others, it implied that all efficient causation involves the activation of a *dunamis*, while *dunameis* are activated *of necessity*, once the conditions are appropriate (Chapter Three). We saw in the same chapter, that in the context of discussing scientific method, Aristotle has a particular interest in efficient causes which necessitate. One example was the quenching of fire which necessitates noise (*An. Post.* II 8, 93b7–14), another the coagulation of sap which may necessitate the fall of leaves (II 16, 98b36–8). In *An. Post.* II 11, 94b27–95 a3, Aristotle says that there are very many (*pleista*) events (*ginesthai*) which are necessitated. And he illustrates the point by the old example of a noise necessarily being produced when fire is quenched. He makes clear that this is no merely hypothetical necessity, for he cites two kinds of necessity, neither of them hypothetical: the violent necessity with which a stone is thrown upwards contrary to its natural tendency, and the natural necessity with which a stone falls downwards, the latter being the one, presumably, which is applicable to the noise of quenching.[8]

These examples are ones which we would class as cases of causal necessitation. This is not one of Aristotle's categories. But he too groups many of the cases together, under the heading of 'natural necessity'. The tendency of a stone to fall, and the doctor's skill which tends to issue in action, are grouped by him along with the other natural tendencies cited by Hintikka.[9]

It makes the clash all the sharper that often the examples of necessitation come from passages very close to those which appeared to be

---

[8] I am disinclined to add a passage cited by H. Happ, *Hyle*, Berlin 1971, 719ff., namely, *Phys.* II 8, 198b16–21. For Aristotle is probably citing his *opponents'* views here, when he says that it rains *of necessity*, because what goes up *must* cool, and what cools, on becoming water, *must* descend.

[9] For the doctor's skill alongside other tendencies, see *Metaph.* 1047b35 – 1048a21. The stone's tendency to fall is grouped with other natural tendencies at *Phys.* VIII 4, 255a30 – b3. For the classification of various examples under the heading of natural necessity, see *An. Post.* II 11, 94b37 – 95a3; *PA* I 1, 642a34 – b2.

removing necessity from the sphere of natural coming to be, passages such as *PA* ɪ 1, *Phys.* ɪɪ 9, and *An. Post.* ɪɪ 12. Thus *PA* ɪ 1 finishes (642a31 – b2) by describing respiration as taking place through the natural necessity of hot and cold streams of matter pushing each other this way and that. And this necessity is distinguished from a merely hypothetical one.[10] *Phys.* ɪɪ 9 is preceded by two chapters which recognise that it may be 'necessary that *this* comes from *this*' (ɪɪ 7, 198b5–6), and that a seed invariably develops in the same sort of way, if nothing prevents it (ɪɪ 8, 199b18, b26). *An. Post.* ɪɪ 12 is preceded by the chapter which describes the necessity of a stone's falling, and of quenched fire making a noise.

The question is how these examples of what we should call causal necessitation can be squared with Aristotle's suggestion that in natural events there are only two kinds of necessity: the necessity of what recurs everlastingly, and the merely hypothetical necessity of certain prerequisites, if a certain goal is to be achieved. Can the examples of causal necessitation really be accommodated under one or other of these two restrictive headings?

Ross' reconciliation

The attempt has been made. For a start, W. D. Ross hints at an assimilation of the necessity of a stone's falling to the necessity which is found in everlasting things. At any rate he thinks that Aristotle is making the *same* contrast, when he contrasts certain other kinds of necessity now with one and now with another of these two.[11] But in fact the cases are different, for Aristotle is talking about the falling of an *individual* stone, and this is not the kind of example he has in mind when he talks of the necessity of the *everlasting*. He is prepared to allow that the cycle of births and deaths, or of evaporation and rain, is necessary, because it is *everlastingly* recurrent (*GC* ɪɪ 11). But he is not talking of *individual* births and showers. Again, he considers that earth is necessarily heavy, but then it is *everlastingly* so, whereas an *individual* stone cannot be *everlastingly* falling. There are many further differences between the cases. For one thing, whereas all earth is heavy, according to Aristotle, not every stone falls. A stone has a natural tendency to fall, but other conditions may cooperate with this tendency or frustrate it. The stone may already be at ground level, or it may be caught on a ledge. Sometimes conditions are such that its natural tendency will necessarily be

[10] It is hard to be sure what kind of necessity this pushing illustrates. There was a general reference to necessity in 642a32, followed by a distinction of two particular kinds. The pushing might illustrate the most recently mentioned kind, the natural necessity of 642a34; or it might simply fall under the general heading of necessity, illustrating neither kind. What seems to be ruled out, by the order of presentation as well as by considerations of sense, is that it illustrates hypothetical necessity, the variety which Aristotle distinguishes first.

[11] Ross *ad Metaph.* v 5, p. 299, comparing *PA* 639b24 with *An. Post.* ɪɪ 11, 94b37 – 95a3.

fulfilled, or necessarily frustrated. On other occasions, no doubt, things could go either way: a gust of wind, occurring by accident at the right moment, could trap it on a ledge. The possible sources of interference cannot always be predicted. Aristotle does not try to enumerate them, but speaks very loosely, as, for example, when he says that a heavy thing falls, 'if nothing prevents it'.[12] Nor, in spite of a suggestion made by Ross, does *Metaph*. vɪ 2, 1027a19–16, imply that the cases of interference would fall under exceptionless rules, if only we could discover them.[13] Admittedly, many modern philosophers would see an *indirect* link with the everlasting. It is not that stones fall in everlasting cycles, but that, when a stone does fall of necessity, we may infer that it would *always* fall, if it were in exactly the same circumstances. We noted in Chapter Three, however, that Aristotle does not make this particular connexion between 'necessarily' and 'always'.

Balme's reconciliation

The alternative strategy is that of Balme, who has now been followed by Kullmann and Preus.[14] Balme suggests that we can view the necessities which abound in Aristotle's biological writings as disguised hypothetical necessities, i.e. as things necessary if some end is to be achieved. The examples which he cites from the biological works can be divided into several groups. First, there are the cases most favourable to his suggestion in which Aristotle is only claiming that if an eye is formed at all in a given specimen, then it will necessarily be a blue eye. And similarly, if hair is formed, it will necessarily be thick; if an embryo, it will necessarily be female, and if teeth, the front ones will necessarily grow first.[15] But even here the necessity of an eye's being blue seems to be being distinguished from a hypothetical necessity at *GA* 778b16–19. Next are the examples in which Aristotle maintains that while some things exist to serve a purpose, other things occur of necessity because of the end-serving things. The liver, for example, serves an end, but the bile in the gall bladder is thought by Aristotle to be merely a residue from the liver, and to occur of necessity because of it; and something analogous is said of the spleen.[16] Balme argues that the bile has a sort of indirect hypothetical necessity, for it is bound to be present, if the liver's job is to

[12] There are similar unspecific provisos in connexion with a seed's developing, a man's being healed, knowledge being exercised, fire burning something, and a thing's expanding to its full size: *NE* vɪɪ 3, 1147a30–1; *Mot*. 701a16; 702a16; *Rhet*. 1392b20–1; *Metaph*. ɪx 5, 1048a16–21; ɪx 7, 1049a7, a 13; *Phys*. vɪɪɪ 4, 255b3–31; ɪɪ 8, 199b18.
[13] The example under discussion here is the one discussed in Chapter Three of honey water alleviating fever, except in certain circumstances.
[14] D. M. Balme, op. cit., 1972, 76–84; A. Preus, op. cit. ch. 4; W. Kullmann, op. cit. 333, 337 (cf. 286–93).
[15] *GA* 788b9 – 789a4, 766a14–30, 767b8–13, 778a16 – b19, 781b30 – 783b8.
[16] *PA* 670a30, 676b16 – 677a19; cf. *GA* 767b14.

be done. But against this we must presume that the indirect hypothetical necessity only exists because there is some *other* kind of necessity that the liver should produce a residue. And it looks as if it is this other kind of necessity to which Aristotle is referring, or else he would not *contrast* necessity with serving an end. Sometimes as Balme points out, Aristotle describes the matter in the body as coursing along of necessity, and according to the direction it takes, being turned into teeth, tusks, horns, beaks, spurs, claws, webs or long legs. Similarly, milk teeth and horns are shed of necessity, women of necessity form menstrual fluid and milk, man's head is hairy of necessity, ink is squirted of necessity in fear, the omentum and the mesentery are formed of necessity, and fish eggs grow larger of necessity after being discharged, one part of the embryo is softened and another hardened of necessity, and a membrane of necessity forms round it, the air circulates of necessity in respiration, and changes in the primary sex characteristics necessarily affect the secondary characteristics.[17] Within this group all the things that happen serve an end. But the necessity that is mentioned is *contrasted* with serving an end, and is pretty clearly not the relation of being hypothetically necessary for an end. Nor does that relation seem to account for the non-biological examples that were cited earlier.

It might be wondered whether the necessities just cited from the biological works could be treated as hypothetical, on the grounds that they are dependent on the occurence of the cause. But first, this suggestion would not solve the original problem. For Aristotle's idea in *GC* II 11, *Phys.* II 9 and *PA* I 1 is that the necessity of coming to be in nature is hypothetical in a quite *different* way. Coming to be is necessary if a goal is to be achieved, not necessary because of the occurrence of causes. In any case, it was argued in Chapter One that necessity because of the past occurrence of causes is not viewed by Aristotle as merely hypothetical, but as an unqualified necessity.

If any doubt remains, we may recall that two of the passages which speak of necessity specify the kind they mean. Thus *PA* I 1, 642a31 – b4 distinguishes the necessity involved in respiration from hypothetical necessity. And when Aristotle says in *An.Post.* II 11, 94b27 – 95a3, that many events are necessitated, he makes it clear that the necessity involved is the same as that of a stone's falling – a case which it would be hard to assimilate to hypothetical necessity.

Explanation of the clash

In spite, then, of Balme's intriguing suggestion, I see no way of reconciling Aristotle's many references to necessity with the statements which

---

[17] *GA* 789a12–14, 766a28–30, 743a36 – b18, 739b26–30, 755a21–5, 776a15 – 777a3, 738 a33 – b9; PA 642a31 – b4, 663b14, 679 a 27–30, 677b21–36, 658b2–13, 663b22 – 35, 694a22 – b12, 678a3–6.

severely limit the occurrence of necessity. The best I can do is to offer some sort of explantion of the clash. There are several comparatively modest points that Aristotle wants to make, and he may have been led on from some of these to his too sweeping denials of necessity.

(i) In *Phys.* II 9 and *GC* II 11, some of his examples suggest only the limited point, which he also makes elsewhere (*PA* I 1, 640b4–29; *Metaph.* 983b6–11), that we cannot exhibit a result as necessary, if we merely refer, as the Presocratics did, to matter or material cause; bricks do not *necessitate* a house.

(ii) Nor yet do they *explain* a house (*Phys.* II 9, 200a6, a9). Aristotle repeatedly casts doubt on the explanatory value of the material cause, on which he thinks his predecessors relied too much.[18]

(iii) *GA* v 8, 789b2–20 is particularly interesting in this regard. For it allows after all that the material cause can necessitate. What it denies is not the *existence* of necessitating causes, but their *explanatory value*, at least where teleological explanations are available. In such cases, the necessitating causes show *how*, but not *why*, the result is achieved.

(iv) There are other things too whose explanatory value he thinks has been misjudged. In the process of embryonic development, the stages take place as they do because of what the final product is. The final product is not explained by the stages (*PA* I 1, 640a10 – b4).

(v) In *Phys.* II 8, 198b10–16 (cf. *Metaph.* I 4, 985a10–23), Aristotle's initial objection to his predecessors is not that they explained things in terms of necessitation, but that they paid so little attention to any *other* kinds of explanation.

(vi) He does go on to object to one *particular* use of the notion of necessity (*Phys.* II 8, 198b18–20, b24). The arrangement of our teeth might be represented, in Empedocles' manner, as the *necessary* outcome of a *chance* event. And the chance event itself might be regarded by Democritus and Empedocles as a necessary one.[19] Aristotle attacks these ideas, but it is the appeal to *chance* which concerns him most. It is chance that he thinks particularly antagonistic to purpose (199a3–5).[20] It is exclusively in terms of chance that, after the first few lines, he describes his opponents' view.[21] And his reply in 198b34 – 199a8 applies

---

[18] *Metaph.* I 3, 984a16 – b22; I 4, 985 b19–22; I 10; *GA* II 1, 734 b 28 – 735 a 3; v 8, 789b2–15; *PA* I 1, 640a10 – 641a17; 642a13–30; *GC* II 6, 333b4–20; 335b7 – 336a12; *DA* II 4, 416a9–18. Cf. Plato *Phaedo* 98c – 99b.

[19] See Chapter One for evidence that many of Aristotle's predecessors thought of chance events as necessitated. It is commonly believed that Aristotle himself held this view, since he defined a chance event as the intersection of two independent causal chains. In Chapter One, however, I argued that Aristotle tried to break away from the idea that chance events were necessitated.

[20] Chance is actually defined in *Phys.* II 5–6 as operating merely 'as if' for a purpose (196b22, b34–5, 197a3–5, a35, b19, 198a6).

[21] Things are ascribed to accident (*sunebē*, 198b29), or to two of its species, chance and spontaneity (*apo tuchēs, apo tou automatou*, 198b30, b36, 199a1, a5). Aristotle also uses a group of words different from those which we have been rendering by 'accident'. *Sum-*

only to the hypothesis of chance, not to that of necessity: he protests that chance events are by definition exceptional, so that the normal arrangement of our teeth cannot be ascribed to chance.[22] His repeated emphasis that nature acts always or for the most part in the same way (198b34–6; 199b18; b24–6) counts against the appeal to chance, but might positively encourage those who appeal to necessity.

(vii) Turning to *An. Post.* II 12, we find Aristotle's discussion not strictly incompatible with the belief in widespread causal necessity. For his points are merely *epistemological*. For example, when we are dealing with the past cause of a particular effect, we cannot construct a syllogism to show that the effect *has* occurred (it may lie in the future), nor that it *will* occur (one cannot switch tenses in mid-syllogism). When the points reappear, however, in *PA* I 1, 640a4–8, they are associated with the metaphysical claim that (only?) hypothetical necessity attaches to coming into being. Has Aristotle been led on from the more limited epistemological claim to the denial of necessity?

(viii) Finally, Aristotle sometimes seems to be saying only that a necessity of coming into being does not exist until near the moment of the event (e.g. *Metaph.* VI 3).

If he had confined himself to points such as these, then, whether we agreed with him or not, we would have found no major conflict among his ideas. But he may have been led on from some of these more modest claims to the rather sweeping denial of unhypothetical necessity.

I have left the conflict unresolved, and accepted that, inconsistently with what he says elsewhere, Aristotle recognises the widespread occurrence of what we should call causal necessity. But I have not yet stated Balme's main reason for saying that the denial of such necessity must be taken more seriously. Balme concedes (1972, p. 80) that *PA* I 1 is not on its own decisive. But he thinks that what clinches the matter (1972, pp. 79 and 80; 1939, p. 133) is that such necessity would rule out Aristotle's teleological talk of things in nature being for an end or purpose. Balme's study of Aristotle's teleology is particularly valuable because of the rich knowledge he brings to bear of Aristotle's actual practice in biology.[23] And he has now received impressive support from Jonathan Barnes, whose commentary on the *Posterior Analytics* has made that work so much more accessible, and from Anthony Preus.[24]

---

pesein and apo sumptōmatōn (198b27, 199a1, a3, a4–5) might perhaps be rendered by 'coincidence'.

[22] The justice of this objection will be considered in Chapter Eleven.

[23] I regret that his excellent inaugural lecture on the subject, though printed, was not published. There are copies in the libraries of King's College and University College, London. There is a briefer discussion on pp. 93–100 of the 1972 commentary.

[24] Jonathan Barnes (27.4) 1975, 222, agrees with Balme that explanation of something by a necessitating cause and explanation of the same thing by purpose are incompatible. He also accepts Balme's suggestion that Aristotle dealt with the supposed incompatibility by banning unhypothetical necessity. Similarly Anthony Preus (op. cit. ch. 4). Others who accept that there is an incompatibility between Aristotle's purposive explanations and

None the less, I am not able to agree that teleological explanation is incompatible, or is thought by Aristotle to be incompatible, with the existence of necessitating causes.

Showing that it is not in fact incompatible is a task for the next chapter. It will require us to analyse how Aristotle's teleological explanations in biology actually work. That Aristotle does not *think* there is an incompatibility, however, can be shown without delay. He implies that there is no incompatibility in *An. Post.* ɪɪ 11, 94b27 – 95a3, when he says that very many (*pleista*) events occur *both* of necessity *and* for a purpose. It is now legitimate for me to add the impressive collection of passages made by Balme and cited earlier in the chapter (notes 15 and 17). For in the great majority of these, something is described as serving an end, and yet is said to occur by a necessity which I have now argued not to be merely hypothetical. Horns, to recall one example, are shed *both* of necessity *and* for a purpose.

How could the opposite interpretation of Aristotle's opinion be sustained? One possible source of confusion is Aristotle's denial that necessitating causes have explanatory value, where purposive explanation is available (*GA* v 8, 789b6). This must not be taken as a denial that necessitating causes *exist* in such circumstances; indeed, 789b4 makes clear that they *do* exist.

But what, it may be asked, about *Phys.* ɪɪ 9? For here the very existence of necessitating causes seems to be denied. And might this not be because of the interest in purposive explanation which he expressed in the preceding chapter, ɪɪ 8?

I think it would be a mere speculation that Aristotle's denial of necessitating causes in ɪɪ 9 is due to a belief that their existence is incompatible with purposive explanation. He does not say that. As argued above, it is chance, not necessity as such, which is said to be incompatible with purpose in ɪɪ 8. Even Aristotle's predecessors, who relied so much on necessitating causes, did not think of them as excluding purpose. For they made a half-hearted appeal to purpose, and Aristotle's initial complaint is merely that they failed to pursue it (ɪɪ 8, 198b10–16).

I conclude that Aristotle sees no incompatibility between purposive explanation and the existence of necessitating causes. In this, I think he was right, and the only matter for regret is that he did not consistently recognise that there is also no incompatibility with their having explanatory value. But before I turn to the task of explaining this, I can profitably make my position in this chapter a little clearer, by relating it to a comment of Anthony Preus (loc. cit.). He maintains that Aristotle does not use the concept of a mechanical necessity. With this I have already implied agreement, by saying that causal necessitation is not

explanation by reference to necessitating causes are Helene Weiss (op. cit. 75–93) and Harold Cherniss (*Aristotle's Criticism of Presocratic Philosophy*, Baltimore 1935, 257).

one of Aristotle's categories; instead he groups the necessities in question under the heading of *natural* necessity. All I have been maintaining is that they are necessities which *we* should class as causal, and that they must be viewed as distinct from Aristotle's cyclical or hypothetical necessities.

CHAPTER TEN

Purpose in Nature

In this chapter I shall consider Aristotle's treatment of purpose in nature quite generally, so that the question raised and left unanswered, in the last chapter will be only one of the questions tackled. That question was whether explanation by reference to purpose in nature is incompatible with the existence of necessitating causes.

In order to answer this, and to throw light on other questions, it will be necessary to distinguish some of the very varied ways in which Aristotle's purposive explanations work. I shall start by drawing some of these distinctions.

Different patterns of purposive explanation

An important part of Aristotle's account of explanation by reference to purpose in nature is summarised at *PA* I 1, 640a33 – b4.

This is why we should for preference say (A) that man has these [parts] because this is what it is for a man to be. For without these parts he cannot be. Failing that, the next nearest thing: that is, either (A') that it is altogether impossible otherwise, or at any rate (B) that it is good this way. And these [parts] follow.

But (C) because he is such and such, his development must happen so and be such; which is why this part develops first, then that. And thus similarly with everything that is composed naturally.

The first paragraph here is concerned with explaining why animal species have the *parts* they do; the second with explaining the *processes* by which an individual's parts are formed.

It may well be simplest to suppose that (A') simply repeats (A), and that Aristotle is talking in each case about showing that parts are necessary for human existence. The best alternative interpretation of (A'), I believe, is Kullmann's, that it refers, for example, to the explanation of bile or of the spleen. These are not considered by Aristotle to be necessary prerequisites for the realisation of the human form, but merely inevitable byproducts of some such prerequisites: bile is a byproduct of the liver.[1]

[1] W. Kullmann (16.2) 1974, 37. For the examples of bile and spleen, see *PA* 676b16 – 677a19, 670a30.

(B) can cover two different kinds of case: a part may be shown to be necessary, not for human existence, but for some other good, such as our greater comfort, or the promotion of the intellectual life. This is the alternative which Aristotle actually illustrates elsewhere.[2] Alternatively, a part may be shown to contribute to human existence, but not as being *necessary* for securing it, merely as *one* good way of securing it.

'And these parts follow' refers (again?), as Balme suggests, to organs like the spleen. I shall postpone consideration of (C).

The explanations with which Aristotle is here chiefly concerned are commonly called *teleological,* presumably because in each case a part or process is explained by its contributing to, or permitting, the realisation of a *goal*. The Greek word *telos*, from which our word 'teleological' comes, meant an end or goal.[3] The comparison with a consciously sought goal is no more than an analogy; Aristotle certainly does not want to suggest that the goal in these cases is consciously sought.

How do Aristotle's teleological explanations work? The first type (A) can be illustrated by what Aristotle says about the camel's extra stomachs (*PA* 674a28 – b15). The camel needs to eat tough and thorny food, and therefore it has an extra series of stomachs for digesting. This explanation is teleological because the existence of the camel is viewed as a goal. The explanation seems to work by taking the existence of the camel, together with certain characteristics, such as the thorny diet, as given. Once these things are given, extra stomachs are *only to be expected*.

The characteristics which Aristotle is willing to take as given are the essential ones, i.e. the ones which enter into its definition. But in the case of an animal species, this covers quite a wide range of characteristics, since he would define a species by a large number of differentiae, and is willing to consider (i) parts of the body and their shapes, (ii) activities, including bodily functions, (iii) the way of life, e.g. feeding habits, (iv) psychological character.[4] His idea is that once the *other* essential characteristics are taken as given, the possession of extra stomachs is only to be expected.

For such an explanation to work, it is only necessary that the essential characteristics should be taken as given *for the purposes of discussion*. But Aristotle has some special reasons of his own for being willing to take these characteristics as given. Not believing in evolution, he

---

[2] *PA* 670b23, 675a19, b23, 654b22; *GA* 717a15–31. The other alternative would supply us with a fresh example of explanation without necessitation (on which see Chapter Three).

[3] There is no need for the goal to lie in the *future*: the existence of the species need not be thought of as *subsequent* to the part or process. I would not agree with Mackie's suggestion (2.5) 274–5, that a case of backwards causation (cause coming after effect) would provide the purest case of teleology. A cause that acted backwards would not necessarily be analogous to a goal, nor is a goal very like a cause; quite commonly it is instead an *effect*.

[4] *HA* ɪ 1, 487a11, with *PA* ɪ, 2–4.

thinks they have always been there; moreover, as will be seen in Chapter Thirteen, he thinks the camel's essential characteristics belong to it of necessity.

It may be wondered why front teeth in both jaws would not have done the job just as well as extra stomachs. A lazy answer would be that the absence of extra teeth may be one of the things that is taken as given, and when it is given, the stomachs can be represented as indispensible. But Aristotle does not in fact rely on this. Rather, he says that extra teeth are less necessary than extra stomachs, presumably because they would not on their own have been adequate.

The explanation, as so far described, depends on showing that the extra stomachs are *only to be expected*, when certain things are taken as given. But here I must confess to embarrassment, because showing that something is *only to be expected* is not always to explain it. A fall of the barometer shows that rain is only to be expected, but does not *explain* the imminence of the rain.[5] And yet in many cases to show that something is only to be expected is to explain it. I confess I do not know how to distinguish the cases, and can therefore only record my conviction that in this instance showing that the camel's extra stomachs are only to be expected can serve to explain them.

If we turn to explanations of type (B), some would simply be a weaker version of type (A). If it is shown that a part is present because it provides *one* good way of securing the existence of a species, it is shown that some such part, either this one *or an equivalent*, is only to be expected. It is the reference to equivalents which makes this version weaker.

Some explanations of type (B), however, follow a pattern quite unlike that of (A). For sometimes an animal part is explained as being necessary not, or not only, for the existence of the species, but for some *other* good. Aristotle, following Plato, talks of existing for the sake of the *better* or the *good*.[6] I have elsewhere spoken of organs which exist *only* for the sake of some good other than existence as *luxury* organs.[7] Aristotle's examples cover two kinds of case. First, and of less interest to us, is the use of the tongue and breath for communication, the use of sight and hearing for providing the basis of theoretical and practical knowledge, and the use of the long-range senses, in animals that can move, to give advance warning of predators and prey.[8] Aristotle speaks of these things

[5] I am grateful to G. A. Cohen and John Watling who first drew my attention to this kind of case. The barometer example was related to me as having been used by Peter Downing. It appears also in M. Scriven, 'Explanation and prediction in evolutionary theory', *Science* 130, 1959, is discussed by A. Grübaum in *Philosophical Problems of Space and Time*, 2nd ed. (*Boston Studies in the Philosophy of Science* 12) Dordrecht 1973, and is referred to by Bas C. van Fraassen as a classic example) 'The pragmatics of explanation', *American Philosophical Quarterly* 14, 1977, 143–50).

[6] *PA* 654b22, 670b23; *GA* 717a15; *DA* 420b19–22, 434b22–9, 435b17–25; *Sens.* 436b13–437a17. Cf. Plato *Timaeus* 74E – 75E.   [7] Sorabji (20.9) 1964.

[8] *DA* 420b19–22, 434b22–9, 435b17–25; *Sens.* 436b13 – 437a17.

as existing partly or wholly for the sake of the *good,* because not all animals need them, but only the higher forms of life. Yet surely they are needed for *existence*; for men could hardly exist as men, if there were no speech and no theoretical or practical knowledge. Nor would mobile animals like ourselves survive without long-range senses. So the parts in question are needed for existence, if not by *all* animals, at least by those species which possess them. Moreover communication and knowledge are not the *sole* function respectively of the tongue and breath and of sight and hearing. The relevant parts have additional functions more obviously connected with existence. Because of the connexion with existence, the presence of such parts can often be explained in manner (A).

There is, however, a more interesting group of organs and arrangements which exist for the sake of the good. Aristotle believes that the function of testicles is to loop the seminal canals, so that seed is emitted less frequently, and similarly the function of the convolutions in our gut is to delay excretion, so that replenishment is needed less soon.[9] The second idea is taken from Plato,[10] and if Aristotle is faithful to him, his thought will be that the arrangement gives us more time for the characteristic higher human activities. Similarly, the kidney's job of cleaning the bladder, and the ball and socket's job of increasing flexibility, promote our *comfort,* but are not considered by Aristotle necessary for *existence.*[11]

How does it explain the presence of an organ to show that in this way is does some good, without however promoting existence? The explanation could not easily follow the first pattern (A). For it would be hard to maintain that the existence of the human species, together with its essential characteristics, show that the ball and socket joint is *only to be expected.* Perhaps at a pinch we could explain the convoluted gut in the style of a weaker version of (A). For if man's leisured way of life is one of his essential characteristics, then we can take it as given, and so represent the convoluted gut, or some *equivalent,* as only to be expected. But if the kidney, or ball and socket, really produced no more than *comfort,* this would seem to Aristotle too accidental a characteristic for him to want to take it as given. How, then, does the appeal to comfort explain? Aristotle does not say; so we shall have to go beyond him.

Explanation, it was maintained in Chapter Two, is relative to the needs of the questioner; and we can imagine one context in which it would be explanatory to allude to the comfort produced by an organ. Suppose the questioner takes as given, not the existence of the species and its essential characteristics, but instead a teleological rule – the rule that organs usually do some good. (Compare Aristotle's teleological rule that 'nature does nothing in vain'.) The kidney and the convoluted

[9] *GA* 717a15–31, 787b19 – 788a16; *PA* 675a19; b23.
[10] Plato *Timaeus* 73ᴀ, *Gorgias* 494ʙ.   [11] *PA* 654b22, 670b23.

gut may look like a potential exception to the rule. If this is what motivates the call for explanation, we can explain the organ's or the arrangement's presence by showing that it does do some good after all, and so is not an exception to the rule. We explain their presence in this case by showing that after all it is *not surprising*. Such explanations have been called 'how-possibly' explanations.

A *caveat* is in order again. To show that something is unsurprising is not always to explain it. We may show that it is after all unsurprising that a certain man is a cheat by revealing that he is also a thief, but that will not *explain* his cheating.

This pattern of explanation is radically different from anything in (A). It takes as given not the defining characteristics of the species, but a teleological rule about the beneficial character of organs. And it appeals to the frame of mind of a questioner who believes that the rule may have been violated. None of this is consciously recognised by Aristotle; but he may none the less have been trading on it, when he claimed that the kidney or ball and socket are there because they promote our comfort.

To summarise, then, Aristotle distinguishes two types of teleological explanations under (A) and (B). He is well aware that explanations of type (A) rest on taking as given the defining characteristics of the species. This is his conscious procedure both here in *PA* i 1, and in the earlier treatise on method: *An. Post.* He does not succeed so well in analysing all the patterns underlying explanations of type (B). But in some such explanations, it was suggested, he may make unconscious use of a teleological rule. In either case, the aim is to present the explanandum as expectable or unsurprising.[12]

I had better introduce some numbers alongside the letters (A) and (B) which have been used to mark Aristotle's first two types of explanation. The numbers, one and two, can mark the two patterns which I have distinguished in the course of analysing (A) and (B), The *first* pattern starts from defining characteristics, as do *all* explanations of type (A), the *second* from a teleological rule, as do *some* explanations of type (B).

I now turn to Aristotle's type (C), which concerns the explanation not of *parts*, but of *processes*. The illustration which he gives (*PA* i 1, 640a19–26), just before the passage we started with, is that we should explain the process by which the backbone gets articulated in the womb by referring to the kind of thing a fully developed man is. The human way of life requires that a man should be able to bend, and so, once the existence of humans is taken as given, together with their essential characteristics, it is only to be expected that the backbone should

---

[12] Unsurprisingness is sometimes what is established by explanations of type (A). Thus the camel's lack of horns is unsurprising, given its other defining characteristics. For its great size is defence enough without horns (*PA* 663a1–6). Thus its existence and its other defining characteristics do not lead us to expect horns, or warrant our being surprised at their absence.

develop with articulations rather than as a rigid unit. Empedocles got things the wrong way round when he tried to explain our having an articulated backbone by reference to the accident of the backbone being broken up as the foetus gets contorted in the womb. So far type (C) sounds merely like an extension of type (A).

But at this point Aristotle injects a new element into the explanation. For instead of appealing merely to the *final* cause or goal, the existence or welfare of the species, he refers in addition to an *efficient* cause. He points out that the *father* already possesses the human form, and that his *seed* contains a *dunamis* – a term which for the moment I shall leave untranslated. And these are all presumably *efficient* causes of the backbone's developing in the way it does. I shall call this appeal to an efficient cause the *third* pattern of explanation.

This last pattern raises peculiar difficulties of its own, and so I shall postpone discussion of it. What I want to emphasise at present is the *variety* of explanations. Of course, Aristotle does not recognise all the variety I have alluded to, since he does not acknowledge what I have called the second pattern. Moreover, he would see types (A), (B) and (C) as all having something in common: they all appeal at some stage, he would think, to the defining characteristics of the species as a given. None the less, within this unity, Aristotle recognises diversity. The same form of words ('this biological arrangement is present in order to . . .') conceals a variety of types and patterns. Aristotle diverges here from a common present day tendency, which is to look for a *single* pattern underlying explanations which state the function of a natural arrangement.[13] Indeed, it is often supposed that the single pattern of explanation must be that suggested by Carl Hempel, in other words, that it must present the thing to be explained as an instance of law.[14] Aristotle's awareness of diversity amidst unity is, of course, already exemplified in his recognition of the four causes within the system of syllogistic explanation. In types (A), (B) and (C), he recognises still further diversity within just one of the four causes.

Present day biologists still favour teleological explanations.[15] But their practice introduces yet a *fourth* pattern of explanation, and, incidentally, since 1958, some have preferred to call it 'teleonomic' rather than 'teleological' explanation. In that year, C. S. Pittendrigh intro-

---

[13] E.g. R. B. Braithwaite (20.2) 1953, ch. 10, esp. 333–5; C. G. Hempel (20.3) 1959, esp. 282–7.

[14] For this view, see not only Hempel, op. cit., but also E. Nagel (20.4) 1961, 401–28; Charles Taylor (20.5) 1964, ch. 1; and in connexion with the goals of behaviour, rather than the functions of parts, Jonathan Bennett (20.7) 1976, ch. 2. An honourable exception is Larry Wright (20.8) 1976, who gives his grounds for dissenting from Hempel's view.

[15] Jacques Monod thinks teleology, or teleonomy, essential to the very definition of living beings (21.1), translated 1972 from the French of 1970, Fontana edition 1974, 20 and 24. His only complaint against thinkers like Aristotle (whom he does not mention by name) is that they bring in teleology at the wrong point, 32–3.

duced the new term, in order to distinguish his own form of teleology from what he called 'Aristotelian teleology as an efficient causal principle'.[16] We have seen that in fact only the third of Aristotle's patterns of explanation relies on efficient causation; so that Pittendrigh was really at most dissociating himself from one strand in Aristotle's thought.

Present day teleological (or teleonomic) explanations in biology typically appeal to natural selection and evolutionary theory. A good example is provided by the work of the Nobel-prize-winning biochemist, Jacques Monod, mentioned in Chapter Two.[17] According to Monod, once species have got going, they would reproduce themselves with mechanical precision (he has been accused here of oversimplification),[18] and there would be no need thereafter to appeal to teleology, but for the interference of chance mutations which threaten the stability of the species. This threat is largely counteracted in its turn by a process of natural selection which discards most of the mutations. But natural selection preserves those few mutations which improve the ability to replicate, and thus brings about an evolution towards forms more capable of replication than their predecessors.[19] It is at the stage of natural selection that teleology comes in, or teleonomy as he calls it in Wainhouse's translation. For Monod sees replicative ability as a sort of goal which is protected by the natural discarding of unfavourable mutations, and positively promoted by the natural selection of the few favourable ones. Moreover if replicative ability is, as it were, an *ultimate* goal, we can distinguish certain *intermediate* goals. The mutations which produced extra stomachs in the camel served the intermediate goal of facilitating digestion, and the ultimate goal of providing a greater chance of successfully rearing offspring, i.e. of replicating.

Explanation in Monod takes the following form: we can explain why some mutation became the norm, by showing how it improved the chance of replication, and so was first promoted and then protected by natural selection. The explanation is teleological because of its appeal to goals.[20]

[16] C. S. Pittendrigh, in *Behaviour and Evolution*, ed. A. Roe and G. G. Simpson, New Haven Connecticut 1958, 394.

[17] Jacques Monod, op. cit.

[18] Monod is criticised in (21.2) 1974. See especially the papers of the biologists C. H. Waddington and R. E. Monro. One over-simplification pointed out by his critics is that a new choice of habitat can create new selective pressures which favour a different strain. This interjection of *choice* into the story interferes with the picture of mechanical precision disturbed only by mutation.

[19] Richard Dawkins makes things very clear in (21.3) 1976, ch. 2. In the case of a molecule, what constitutes replicative ability is its longevity, the rate at which it replicates, and the fidelity with which it does so. I shall not enter into the central contention of his book, which is that it is molecular shapes, not individual animals, nor groups of animals, which are selected by natural selection. But clearly, if we consider an animal as opposed to a molecule, its replicative ability will depend partly on its ability to *rear* its young.

[20] Monod's pattern of teleological explanation differs from the first one, the one concern-

This constitutes a fourth pattern of teleological explanation. The different patterns can be variously related to each other. The second pattern of explanation, for example, invoked a *rule* that physiological arrangements usually do some *good*. The fourth pattern, with its appeal to natural selection, could be used for explaining why such a rule obtains. But the different patterns of explanation need not in this way come in at *different* levels; they can provide alternative explanations at the *same* level to a question which has the same verbal form, e.g. why the camel has extra stomachs.

Compatibility with necessitating causes and with explanation by reference to necessitating causes

With four patterns of teleological explanation now distinguished, I can return to the question raised by the last chapter, whether Aristotle's teleological explanations are compatible with the existence of necessitating causes. I maintained that Aristotle thought teleological explanations were compatible with the *existence* of such causes, but that he wavered on the question of whether they were compatible with their having *explanatory value*. And I suggested that they should in fact be regarded as compatible with both.

The conviction that teleological and causal explanations must be incompatible is widespread, and so strong that the physicist Niels Bohr, followed by other scientists, were led to an elaborate solution. Teleological and causal explanations in biology are indeed incompatible, he suggested, but we avoid a head-on collision between them, because they are, in a special sense, *complementary*. That is to say, the conditions in which one kind of explanation can be investigated preclude the fruitful investigation of the other.[21] Probing the micro-structure of the organism for causal explanations must inevitably destroy the teleological organisation.

ing the camel's stomachs, in the goals which it postulates. For Aristotle, the goal is the existence of particular forms of life; for Monod it is the replication of living organisms in a succession of *different* forms. The two theories also differ in what they seek to explain. Aristotle is trying to account for why certain parts and processes are found in the species. Monod wants to explain, not indeed why the parts or processes first arose, but why, having arisen by chance mutation, they become the norm. And his explanation appeals to something which Aristotle rejects, natural selection.

[21] Niels Bohr's idea of complementarity arose out of considering the relations between the wave-treatment and the particle-treatment of light. It was extended by Bohr to the case of teleological and causal explanation in biology in *Atomic Theory and the Description of Nature*, Cambridge 1934, Introductory Survey, 22–4; and ch. 4, p. 118 (translated from the Danish of 1929); 'Light and life', *Nature* 1933, 458; *Dialectica* 2, 1948, 318. The suggestion was taken up by Walter Elsasser, in *The Physical Foundation of Biology*, London 1958. The idea of complementarity is further explained by P. K. Feyerabend and D. M. Mackay in *Proceedings of the Aristotelian Society*, supplementary volume 32, 1958, and by A. Grünbaum, in 'Complementarity in quantum physics and its philosophical generalization', *Journal of Philosophy* 54, 1957.

No such solution is needed. If we postpone discussion of the third pattern, which needs further consideration, none of the other patterns of teleological explanation would clash with an explanation by reference to ordinary efficient causes, and necessitating causes at that. The first two imply nothing one way or the other about the existence or explanatory value of such causes. Monod's pattern positively implies their existence and explanatory value. Indeed, he calls his book *Chance and Necessity*, because he thinks of the initial mutation as occurring by chance,[22] but he thinks of the process of natural selection by which a favourable mutation becomes the norm as depending on necessitating causes.[23]

Jonathan Barnes has improved on many authors by offering a *reason* for thinking that teleological explanation should rule out explanation by reference to necessitating causes. It would do so, if the teleological goal has to serve as a necessary prerequisite of the thing explained.[24] But in none of the four patterns distinguished above does the goal play this part.

Modern criticisms of teleological explanation

I have argued that teleological explanations in nature do not exclude explanations by reference to ordinary necessitating causes. And this nearly completes my answers to the question left unanswered in the previous chapter. It only remains to examine further the third of Aristotle's patterns of explanation. But before I do that, I want to broaden the discussion. For the supposed exclusion of explanation by reference to necessitating causes has, in modern times, been made a basis for *criticising* teleological explanation. Moreover, this has been only one of many criticisms. I propose next to consider these criticisms, because a large part of the necessary work has already been done. In order to assess the criticisms, we need to see exactly how teleological explanations work, and in some cases a criticism that holds against one pattern of explanation will not hold against another. So I shall be exploiting the distinctions that have already been made.

If we count (1) the supposed exclusion of explanation in terms of necessitating causes as a first criticism of teleological explanations, we

---

[22] He explains that chance mutations can be of two kinds, op. cit. 111–12: either an undetermined quantum event, or a rearrangement of molecules which results in chance collocations comparable to the kind of coincidence studied by Aristotle. The possibilities are still more lucidly described by Dawkins op. cit., ch. 3. Some shuffling occurs with each new generation because each individual animal will pass on only half its father's genes and half its mother's to each offspring. Further shuffling arises when a gene is broken up, or suffers an undetermined mutation at some point.

[23] This may be disputed by those critics of Monod who insist that a *choice*, e.g. of habitat, can enter into the story.

[24] Jonathan Barnes (27.4) 22.

can distinguish as a second criticism (2) the idea that they are not genuinely explanatory.[25] Except for the third pattern, which remains to be discussed, I have already done my best to show why I think the other patterns can be explanatory, at least given a suitable context.

A third objection (3) rests on the supposition that a teleological explanation must invoke a conscious agent at work. It should be clear that this is not true of any of the patterns I have so far distinguished. Of course, the same form of words, 'the camel has extra stomachs in order to cope with its thorny diet', *could* conceal yet a *fifth* pattern of explanation. The speaker *might* be intending to appeal to a deity who had arranged the stomachs to benefit the camel. There is, however, no need for a teleological explanation to invoke the work of a conscious agent in this way.

There are some who believe that Aristotle's teleological explanations do depend on attributing desires to all natural objects.[26] But in fact Aristotle draws some sharp distinctions: the motion of the *stars* does involve desire, at least at some stages of his thought.[27] But in the world below, only animals have desire, plants do not, and the four elements do not even have a soul. The denial of consciousness and desire to plants is not a casual step, but a *correction* of his predecessors.[28] Those, then, who see Aristotle's teleological explanations as invoking desire must clutch at stray analogies which he lets drop, most of them conscious echoes from the phrases of his predecessors, rather than independent formulations of his own viewpoint: matter desires form (in reference to Plato); if creatures can be generated in mud this shows that *in a way* all things are full of soul (in reference to Thales); the eye desires sight, the body health (in reference to Plato); motion is *like* life for natural bodies.[29]

(4) A further major suspicion is that teleological explanations are all very well, but only because they are reducible to something else. More than one doubt can be distinguished here.[30] First, it may be wondered

---

[25] So C. G. Hempel, op. cit.; C. J. Ducasse, 'Explanation, mechanism and teleology', *Journal of Philosophy* 1926, 150–5 (reprinted in *Readings in Philosophical Analysis*, ed. H. Feigl and W. Sellars, 1949).

[26] John M. Rist gives the fullest defence in 'Aristotelian teleology', *Transactions and Proceedings of the American Philological Association* 96, 1965, 337–49. See also E. Zeller, translated as *Aristotle and the Earlier Peripatetics* vol. 1, London 1897, 459–61; R. G. Collingwood, *The Idea of Nature*, Oxford 1945, 83–5; Max Hocutt (7.3) 1974, 398. Hocutt relies on one of the passages (*Phys.* ii 8, 199b15) to be explained below in which Aristotle treats *nature* as an efficient cause.

[27] For the development of his views, see W. K. C. Guthrie's introduction to the Loeb edition of *Cael.* (*On the Heavens*). In his final statement at *Metaph.* xii 7, 1072b3, where God moves *as* a beloved object moves, it may be debated how close the analogy is meant to be.

[28] This is most fully explained by Friedrich Solmsen, 'Antecedents of Aristotle's psychology and scale of beings', *American Journal of Philology* 76, 1955, 148–64. See also Sorabji, 'Body and soul in Aristotle', *Philosophy* 49, 1974, esp. 65–7.

[29] *Phys.* i 9, 192a16–25; *GA* iii 11, 762a18–21; *EE* 1218a24–33; *Phys.* viii 1, 250b14.

[30] See E. Nagel, loc. cit., and replies by Charles Taylor, loc. cit., J. L. Mackie (20.6) ch. 11.

whether a teleological explanation of why an organ is present is merely a disguised causal explanation. We have seen that Monod's explanations are exactly that, but that explanations of the first two patterns are not.

(5) A distinct doubt is whether anything distinctively teleological actually plays a role in explaining the presence of an organ. The answer to this is that in all the patterns considered there must be reference to the thing which is regarded as a goal, whether it be replication, or the existence of a species, or its welfare, or such intermediate goals as digestion. But another question would be whether we need to describe these goals in teleological language, in order to make the explanation work. The answer to this will differ from one pattern to another. Certain patterns depended on showing that there was no breach of a rule, and that rule was itself teleologically framed. There was a rule that organs usually do some *good*. To establish that such a rule has not been breached, we must employ teleological notions, and show that the organs in question do serve a goal. With other patterns of explanation, however, the goal can often be described in non-teleological terms. Whether we use teleological language can depend on quite extraneous factors. If there is a mechanism which keeps our body temperature strictly to 98.6°, we are likely to describe the intermediate goal in these mathematical terms, in explaining the mechanism's presence. But if the mechanism allows a great variety of temperatures, depending on what *suits* the organism's current *needs*, it will often be more convenient to describe its activity in these terms, which are *teleological* ones.

(6) A final suspicion is that teleological explanations are only second best, that they are rendered otiose by purely causal explanations with no teleological element. This is surely not so. In many contexts, and for many purposes, we shall always want teleological explanations. If we want to know why a certain species of animal shivers in the cold, we may or may not feel that knowledge of the causal mechanism of shivering gives us a more satisfying explanation than knowledge that shivering raises the animal's temperature. This will depend on our purposes. To take a very simple example, if someone is concerned about the welfare of his own particular pet, and whether it is suffering something untoward, he will be more interested in the teleological explanation. That explanation has an added advantage, as others have pointed out,[31] in that it can perform extra duties. It can explain not only the shivering, but also the increased pulse rate, the fluffing out of fur, the cowering, huddling, or

---

This question is different from the one discussed in Sorabji (20.9). I was there considering the meaning of our ordinary talk about the function of an organ. And I argued that it is not reducible to non-teleological language, because it contains an irreducibly evaluative element. But the present question concerns not the *meaning* of a function statement, but the way in which it *explains* the presence of an organ.

[31] This sort of point is made by Charles Taylor, 'Teleological explanation – a reply to Denis Noble', *Analysis* xxvii, 1966–7, 141–3, and J. L. Mackie, loc. cit.

burrowing, or going to sit by the fire. Different causal mechanisms are required to explain these various bits of behaviour, but one and the same teleological explanation (the adjustment of temperature) can cover them all, and relate them to each other. We can see why they should coexist in the animal. Further, a different teleological explanation, which takes into account the animal's *other* characteristics, can help us to see why it should have one rather than another of the possible defences against cold. This is a typically Aristotelian use of teleological explanation.

Nature, soul and dunamis *as efficient causes of achieving the goal*

We can defend teleological explanations, then, against the commonest criticisms, once we see in detail the various ways in which they work. But the defence may not cover all patterns of teleological explanation equally; and in particular it may not cover the third pattern, in which Aristotle appeals to a special kind of efficient cause as well as to a goal. Let us now examine how this pattern works.

Aristotle tells us that the *nature* of an animal can act either as a final cause or as an efficient cause.[32] In explaining the camel's extra stomachs, the *nature* of the camel featured only as a final cause, or goal. The stomachs served the goal of ensuring that animals with that nature should exist. Nature would enter quite differently into the explanation, if it were acting as an *efficient* cause.

In the case of an animal, we are further told, its nature is a certain part of its soul,[33] and of the soul too it is said that it can act not only as final, but also as efficient, cause.[34] It is, for example, the efficient cause of orderly growth and of perceiving.

So far nature and soul have been associated as efficient causes, but there is also a third term to be taken into account, *dunamis*, which often means capacity, ability, or power. *DA* II 3 opens by listing the *dunameis* of the soul as the nutritive, desiderative, perceptive, locomotive, and ratiocinative (414a29–32). The chapter closes by saying that the most appropriate account of the soul will be an account of each of these (415a12–13). This remark is immediately pursued in the next chapter (II 4, 415a14–22), and sets the programme for what follows. Already it suggests the thought that perhaps the soul just *is* this set of *dunameis*.

This thought is confirmed elsewhere; for we find the nutritive, perceptive and ratiocinative described as *parts* of the soul (*DA* 413b7, b27 – 32; *Mem.* 450a17), as if the soul consisted of these *dunameis*. Moreover, at *GA* II 4, 740b29–37 the nutritive *dunamis* seems to be equated with the nutritive *soul*.

---

[32] *PA* I 1, 641a25–8.
[33] *PA* I 1, 641a28, b9–10; *GA* II 4, 740b29 – 741a2.
[34] *DA* II 4, 415b8–12, b21–8, 416a8–9, b21–2.

We see, then, that nature, soul and *dunamis* are associated with each other, and we may expect that they can *all* act as efficient causes. Certainly, in other contexts, *dunameis* play this role.[35]

The idea of *nature* is defined in *Phys.* II 1 as an internal origin of change or stability.[36] Artifacts are subject to change by *external* influences; but natural objects, including the stuffs of which artifacts are made, have an internal origin of change, which is their nature. The nature of the element, earth, is a *dunamis* for downward motion. The nature of a plant is a *dunamis* for assimilating nutriment, and using it to grow to the pattern of the species, to maintain itself there, and to produce seed. A plant's nature is already a kind of soul; the nature or soul of an animal includes this nutritive *dunamis* along with the *dunamis* for perceiving.

Occasionally, Aristotle personifies nature and talks of it as doing this or that. But this talk of nature can always be understood in terms of the natures of things.

In *GA* Aristotle brings all the foregoing ideas together.[37] He speaks of the soul, or rather of one of the *dunameis* that go to make up the soul, the nutritive *dunamis*. He says that this part of the soul is transmitted in the father's seed. He equates it with the nature, or part of the nature, of the father. And he seems to treat all of these as *efficient* causes of the embryo's development.[38]

His account is as follows. It is not enough to say that heat and cold make the parts of the embryo hard, soft, tough and brittle. This is true, but we need some *other* cause to explain how the right *ratio* is obtained for making flesh or bone. We may compare how heat and cold soften or

[35] *Dunamis* is defined in *Metaph.* V 12 and IX 1 as a certain source of change. That expression leaves it open which of the four causes is intended. But the *dunamis* of sculpting is explicitly said to be an *efficient* cause of the statue (*Phys.* II 3, 195a5–8), and this will presumably apply too to the *dunamis* of building and of healing (*Metaph.* V 12, 1019a16–17; *Phys.* II 3, 195b23–4).

[36] *Phys.* II 1, 192b21–3.

[37] Many of the following points are incorporated in *GA* II 4, 740b25 – 741a3. 'Now the products of a craft are produced through instruments, or it would be truer to say through the movement of the instruments. This movement is the actualisation of the craft, while the craft is the form of the products residing not in them but in something else [sc. the mind of the craftsman]. In the same way, the *dunamis* of the nutritive soul uses heat and cold as instruments, for its movement resides in heat and cold, and each product is produced according to a certain ratio. At a later stage, in the resultant animals and plants, this *dunamis* produces growth out of the nourishment supplied, but at the beginning in just the very same way, it consolidates the thing which is being produced by nature. For it is the same matter by which it gets its growth and out of which it is consolidated in the first place. Hence the creative *dunamis* is the same. Now if this *dunamis* is the nutritive soul, then the nutritive soul is what generates. And this soul is what the *nature* of each thing is, being present in all plants and animals alike, whereas the other parts of the soul belong to some living things and not to others.'

[38] See the analogies between nature and craft in *GA* II 1, 4 and 6, esp. II 4, 740b25 – 741a2 and II 6, 743a34. For a *dunamis* as a source of change in this context, see also *GA* I 19, 726b18–21; I 21, 729b27; II 4, 739a17; *PA* I 1, 640a23.

harden the iron, but some further cause is responsible for making the sword.[39] This further cause turns out, in the case of the embryo, to be nature, which is here identified with a certain part of the soul, namely, the nutritive *dunamis*.[40] And these causes use heat and cold merely as instruments.[41]

Similar points are made elsewhere: Empedocles failed to explain how the right *ratio* for bone is obtained.[42] It is not enough to invoke heat or coldness, as the pre-Socratics did.[43]

Sometimes instead of invoking a *dunamis*, Aristotle invokes a *kinēsis* (or *change*), which resides in the seed, or in the heat of the seed, and which is transmitted to the matter supplied in the female's womb.[44] But this makes little difference, because a *dunamis* is defined as an origin of *change*, and, as he reminds us, it is actualised by a process of change.[45] So in explaining the development of the embryo, he can refer indifferently to the *dunamis*, or to the change which originates from it: both are responsible for the embryo's development.

The foregoing explanation can be thought of as teleological, because a *dunamis* is a *dunamis* for achieving some result, and in the present case the result can be thought of as a *goal*, the completion of the animal with all the right ratios. But the teleological explanation follows a pattern different from the first four we considered, because the *dunamis* is acting as an *efficient* cause. We must see whether that exposes the explanation to any of the standard modern criticisms.

One criticism can be set aside at once, because it rests on a simple misunderstanding. When Aristotle claims that the nature which directs embryological development is a part of the *soul*, this might be taken (wrongly) to mean that he is postulating a *conscious* agency.[46] But, the assumption that the soul has to do only with *consciousness* is a legacy from Descartes. Descartes deliberately rejected the Aristotelian conception, when he returned to the Platonic conception of the soul as coextensive with *consciousness*.[47] Aristotle made the soul coextensive not with consciousness but with life. The soul is the set of *dunameis* which distinguishes living from non-living things, so that even a plant can be

[39] *GA* ii 1, 734b20 – 735a4.
[40] *GA* ii 4, 740b25 – 741a2; ii 6, 743a34.
[41] *GA* ii 4, 740b31; ii 6, 743a36.
[42] *GC* ii 6, 333b7–22; *DA* i 4, 408a21; ii 4, 416a9–19.
[43] *Phys.* ii 8, 198b12–14; *PA* i 1, 640b4–11.
[44] *GA* ii 1, 734b9 – 735a4; ii 3, 737a18–22; ii 4, 738b9–15; ii 6, 743a28.
[45] *Dunamis* is defined in *Metaph.* v 12 and ix 1 as a certain origin of change. Aristotle reminds us here that the movement (*kinēsis*) of the craftsman's tools is the actualisation (*energeia*) of the craftsman's *dunamis* (*GA* ii 4, 740b27–8), and similarly the movement (*kinēsis*) which resides in the heat of the seed is an actualisation (*energeia*, ii 6, 743a28).
[46] This is how R. G. Collingwood argues in *The Idea of Nature*, Oxford 1945, 85.
[47] Descartes, *Reply to Objections brought against the 2nd Meditation*, § 4 in the 5th *Objections*, translated by Haldane and Ross, vol. 2, Cambridge 1931, 210. The point is explained in Sorabji, 'Body and soul in Aristotle', 65.

said to have a soul. The plant's soul is not concerned with consciousness, but is merely the *dunamis* in virtue of which the plant takes in nourishment, and uses it for growing, maintaining its distinctive structure and producing seed. It is this same merely *nutritive dunamis* to which Aristotle appeals when he makes part of the soul responsible for the embryo's development.

A second criticism is that Aristotle has left no room for a *physiological* explanation of embryological development. There would be no room, for example, for the modern explanation by reference to DNA structure, since the place of this structure has been usurped by appeal to the *dunamis*.

I am not convinced that this criticism captures Aristotle's intentions. For he is very interested in finding a physiological cause of embryological development, and makes a series of attempts. According to the last of his suggestions,[48] there is in seed a stuff called *pneuma* which is endowed with a special kind of heat. This heat is compared with the stuff of which the stars are made. *Pneuma* and heat can vary in value, and it is only the most valuable kind of heat that we find here. He goes so far as to say that this heat 'generates animals'.[49]

In *GA* v 8, Aristotle is prepared to allow that, in some of its roles,[50] *pneuma* (789b8) *necessitates* the outcome (789b4). He only insists that it should be viewed as a material cause, and therefore as an instrument or tool (*organon*, 789b7–9), which answers the question 'how?' rather than 'why?'. It is not 'through' the *pneuma* that the outcome occurs (not *dia*, 789b6).

This last passage brings out the truth and the falsity in the second criticism of Aristotle. It is false that he leaves no room for necessitating physiological causes. What is true is that he does not always consider them the real *explanation*, at least in cases where a purposive explanation is available. I say 'not always', because, as will be seen in more detail below, he is not consistent on the question, but frequently allows such ideas as that horns are shed of necessity 'through' their weight, as well as for a purpose (*PA* iii 2, 663b14). I say 'where purposive explana-

---

[48] *GA* ii 3, 736b29 – 737a7. That Aristotle's thought develops, and culminates in this passage, is shown by Friedrich Solmsen, 'The vital heat, the inborn pneuma, and the aether', *Journal of Hellenic Studies* 77, 1959, 119–23.

[49] It is only a minor difference from modern theory that Aristotle denies the male seed has to *enter* the embryonic material (*GA* i 21–2). This would preclude modern appeals to the idea of genetic material acting as a *template*. The *dunamis* and heat (i 21, 729b27) acts differently.

[50] *Heat* and *pneuma* play a role in connexion with other functions of the soul: sense perception and motivation. For heat and the central sense of touch, see *DA* ii 11, 423b27 – 424a10, and the interpretation offered in 'Body and soul in Aristotle', 75–6, slightly expanded in *Articles on Aristotle*, vol. 4. For *pneuma* and sense perception, see *GA* 744a2, 781a23. For heat and *pneuma* in connexion with motivation, see *Mot.* 6–10. According to *PA* ii 7, 652b9–11, hot stuff is the most serviceable for the functions of the soul: nutrition and locomotion.

tion is available', because *GA* v 8 itself allows that, where it is not available, things do happen 'through' the material cause (789b20).

An interesting attempt has been made to discount some of the evidence for Aristotle's interest in physiological necessitation. Allan Gotthelf takes up Aristotle's reference to the *purity* of heat in man (*GA* II 6, 744a29), and suggests that purity is not a physiological concept in quite the way one would expect.[51] For the property would need to be specified as a *dunamis* for producing an organism of a certain sort, and could not be given a purely physical definition. There is no sign of this in the text however, and Aristotle would need to make it explicit, since he is borrowing his terminology in this passage from medical writers who took themselves to be talking in physical terms. The nearest thing I can find in Aristotle to Gotthelf's idea is his view that blood, flesh, and bone are defined as performing certain vital functions, and so, when dead, are not blood, flesh and bone in the same sense of the word.[52] I doubt if this is close enough, however, to support Gotthelf's argument.

I believe, then, that the second criticism does not do justice to the facts. Aristotle has not excluded necessitating physiological causes, even if he does not always regard them as explanatory. But there is a third and last criticism which is more difficult to set aside. We need to ask about Aristotle's *dunameis* whether their character is in principle specifiable otherwise than by reference to the effects which they are invoked to explain. If they are not specifiable except as the capacities to produce those effects we may well doubt whether they are sufficiently independent of those effects to provide genuine explanations of them. We may compare the appeals made by modern vitalists to an *entelechy* or *conatus* in living things, a *nisus*, a *hormē*, a drive, or striving.[53] No objection ought to be raised to the idea that a capacity can be explanatory. It is easy to understand Aristotle's idea that the capacity for desire explains animal movement. What is hard to understand is the idea that the capacity for desire explains *desire itself*, and, in general, that a capacity for F explains F.

[51] Allan Gotthelf (18.3) 1976. See his note 32.
[52] *GA* 726b22–4, 734b25–7, 735a8; *Metaph.* 1035b16–17, b24–5, 1036b30–2; *DA* 412b20–5; *PA* 640b34 – 641a7; *Meteor.* 389b31 – 390b2; *Pol.* 1253a20–2.
[53] The term entelechy was used by H. Driesch in *The Science and Philosophy of the Organism*, London 1908 (see e.g. vol. 2, 135–51). For the term *hormē*, see the report in W. McDougall, *An Outline of Psychology*, London 1923, 72-3. The other terms are all used by E. S. Russell, *The Directiveness of Organic Activies*, Cambridge 1946 (143–4, 178, 190–1), whose book is a mine of information about the undoubtedly teleological processes in nature, but still treats teleological explanation as a rival to causal explanation (140, 144, 157–8, 172, 183–4). The term *conatus* is derived from Spinoza and Leibniz. (For Spinoza, see *Ethics*, 1677, part III, proposition VII. For Leibniz, see the *Specimen Dynamicum*, 1695, translated by L. E. Loemker in *Leibniz, Philosophical Papers and Letters*, 2nd ed., Dordrecht, 1969, 435–53, and by G. Langley, in the appendix to his translation of Leibniz's *New Essays Concerning Human Understanding*, Chicago 1916, 670–92.) R. G. Collingwood attributes belief in a *nisus* to Aristotle, with approval, but he also conflates a *nisus* with a want (*The Idea of Nature*, 83–5).

Aristotle could avoid this last objection, if the appeal to a *dunamis* of the soul were meant to be a disguised appeal to the physiological basis, as yet undiscovered, of that *dunamis*, and if the physiological basis were meant to provide the real explanation. But this cannot be his view. Among other objections is the fact that, however closely a *dunamis* is related to its physiological basis (and the relation is probably not very close),[54] Aristotle would not think that the physiological basis was the real source of explanation. If this had been his idea in appealing to *dunameis* for explanations, he could not, even momentarily, have been attracted by the view we have just seen expressed in *GA* v 8, 789b2–20. The claim of that passage is that where purposive explanations are available (as they are when a *dunamis* of the soul is at work), the necessitating physiological causes merely show us how, not why, the outcome occurs.

At this stage, the third pattern of purposive explanation may appear highly vulnerable. But we need to consider an illuminating interpretation by Allan Gotthelf, who has explicitly defended Aristotle against the charge of vitalism at this point.[55]

Gotthelf's interpretation

Gotthelf's idea is as follows. Some behaviour is explained by appealing to a *dunamis* of the whole organism, while some is explained by appealing to the *dunameis* of the materials which compose the organism, and these two kinds of *dunamis* are defined by reference to quite different goals. An appeal to the first, for example, an appeal to the animal's nature or soul, excludes appeal to the second, for example, to the heat or cold of its tissues. The appeal explains by a process of *identification*:[56] we show *which* of the possible *dunameis* is the one at work. Appeal to a *dunamis* is fundamental, for Aristotle, in the way that appeal to a law of nature is taken to be fundamental by modern philosophers of science such as Carl Hempel.[57] All changes are due to the operation of *dunameis* whose existence in the universe cannot be further explained any more than can that of Hempelian laws. Explanation merely takes the form of selecting among the *dunameis*, and revealing which one is operating in the present case.

[54] Admittedly, a *pathos* (passion) of the soul is very closely related to its physiological basis. Aristotle says of anger, and of all other *pathē of the soul, that in some sense each 'is' a physiological process*. (See *DA* i 1, 403a25 – b9, and the interpretation offered in 'Body and soul in Aristotle', 77–8.) But in *Nicomachean Ethics*, he distinguishes *dunameis* and *hexeis* (dispositions) of the soul from *pathē* (ii 5), and says of *hexeis* at least that they have less to do with the body (iv 9, 1128b14–5). We may also recall Plato's point about *dunameis* in the *Republic* (477c–d), that a *dunamis* can be defined *only* by reference to the objects on which it is directed, and to what it brings about, and *cannot* be defined in terms of colour, or shape, or any such property.
[55] Gotthelf, op. cit. 253.   [56] Gotthelf, op. cit. 234.   [57] Gotthelf, op. cit. 232, 234.

Such is Gotthelf's interpretation: does it answer the charge that Aristotle's account is incapable in principle of explaining? Of course, we do not believe that his method of explanation has in fact proved successful; what I am asking is whether, as the present objection alleges, it was logically debarred from succeeding.

Certainly, Aristotle's account is not empty, but on the contrary, bold and informative, for it claims to be able to *rule out* explanation by reference to such things as heating and cooling. Admittedly, ruling out, though informative, need not be explanatory. The girl in the song who says 'It's not because I wouldn't; it's not because I shouldn't; and you all know it's not because I couldn't' has not yet reached her explanation ('It's just because I'm the laziest girl in town'). But Aristotle goes beyond ruling out, and tells us what to look to. We are to take it as *basic* that all living things have the power to grow to the pattern of their species and to maintain themselves there, and that this power can be transmitted to the embryo in the father's seed.

Perhaps it will be objected that this is only to say that there is *no* further explanation of embryos developing. At this point, we might go beyond Gotthelf, and compare the centuries of attempts to explain why a javelin continues to move, after it has left the thrower's hand. Newton declared that javelins are not propelled by angels nor by anything else; it must just be taken as a *basic* fact that any body persists in the same state of motion or rest, unless a force acts on it to the contrary. Somebody might complain that Newton has only said that there is *no* further explanation of a javelin's continuing to move, and in a sense he has said this. And yet there is a sense in which he has explained why javelins continue to move by giving their continued motion a place in a much wider scheme. Aristotle has attempted something similar: he shows us how to think of the development of embryos by placing it in a scheme: the power of all living things to grow to the pattern of the species and maintain themselves there is basic in this scheme; powers of heating and cooling come in merely as prerequisites. Aristotle has done something else too. We are not left to think that the power to grow to a pattern springs up in each embryo from nowhere. Rather, it has always existed and is transmitted in the father's seed.

Not everybody will be satisfied. But I think that Gotthelf's account, as thus elaborated, does the best that can be done to enable us to see Aristotle's view as logically capable of explaining. Having said that, I must distinguish three points on which I would not agree with Gotthelf's interpretation.

First, it does seem to me misleading of Aristotle to pick out the nutritive *dunamis* and call that the explanation, and indeed the efficient cause, of embryological development. For if anything explains, it is rather the whole *complex* of facts into which the nutritive *dunamis* fits. This makes the explanation here unlike even its closest analogue:

the explanation of works of art. In their case too, Aristotle picks out a *dunamis*, the builder's technical ability, as the efficient cause of the house. But he is prepared to identify that ability with the form of a house existing in the builder's mind. We can therefore think of the *dunamis* as a state of mind in the builder, and it is not difficult to see how a state of mind can explain, and be the efficient cause of, a house. But the nutritive *dunamis* of the soul is not in this way made into a detachable factor in the explanation. As remarked, it is part of a whole story which explains, and this is not brought out in Gotthelf's account.[57a]

Secondly, if anyone is dissatisfied with the present pattern of explanation, I would urge that it is only one of three which I have distinguished in Aristotle, and that the other patterns are not objectionable in the same way. But on this Gotthelf disagrees; for he considers that all other patterns are definable in terms of this one. He holds that in the end Aristotle would appeal to this pattern, not only in explaining developmental *processes*, but also in explaining why man has the *parts* he has.[58] This seems to me to *reverse* Aristotle's order of priorities. In the passage with which this chapter starts (*PA* i 1, 640a10 – b4), reference to a *dunamis* occurs only in explaining *processes*, and the passage in question makes the explanation of processes *subordinate* to the explanation of why man has the parts he has.

Finally, something must be said about the sense in which Aristotle rules out the properties of materials, for example, the powers of heating and cooling. It is not that these powers are not exercised; indeed, they are needed as prerequisites. Gotthelf takes Aristotle to mean that embryological development cannot be 'the result of' the properties of materials, if it is to be explained by the nature, soul, or *dunamis* of the parent. At least, it cannot be the result of the properties of materials, so long as the identification of those properties includes no mention of the form of the mature organism.[59] Moreover, he generalises the point: its not being the result of such properties is 'the core of Aristotle's conception of final causality', and lies 'at the root of the distinction between explanation in terms of material-efficient causes and explanation in terms of final-formal causes'.[60] This does not seem to me possible, because of the cases in which Aristotle says that something happens *both* of necessity *and* for an end. Of the many examples in the preceding chapter, one has already been recalled: the shedding of horns happens *both* for the sake of an end *and* of necessity through sheer weight.

[57a] The importance of stressing the whole story was made clearer to me by David Hamlyn.
[58] Gotthelf, op. cit., note 19.
[59] In making this qualification, Gotthelf does not intend merely to be referring to Aristotle's doctrine, mentioned above, that flesh and bone are defined by reference to a certain function, in such a way that dead flesh or bone, which cannot perform this function, is not flesh or bone in the same sense of the word.
[60] Gotthelf, op. cit. 236, 243; cf. note 19.

Recognising this, Gotthelf suggests that at least the *goal achieved* (in this example, the greater lightness which ensues on the shedding) is not produced of necessity, even if the phenomenon itself (the shedding) is.[61] But this does not seem plausible in connexion with the present example (surely, the lightness is produced of necessity), and in any case it would not suffice to make the absence of such causes the core of Aristotle's conception of final causality.

What Gotthelf could legitimately say is that necessitating physiological causes, though present, are not considered explanatory, when purposive explanation is available. This certainly is the view we found expressed in *GA* v 8, 789b2–20. Even so, it is not sufficiently close to the heart of Aristotle's conception of final causality for him to remain consistent about it. The word 'through' (*dia*), which is said to be inappropriate at 789b6, is cheerfully used when it is said that animals shed their horns in season for the purpose of gaining lightness, but also of necessity 'through' the sheer weight of the horns (*ex anankēs de dia to baros*, *PA* iii 2, 663b14). Indeed, Aristotle uses a tattoo of words implying that the necessitating causes which he cites for biological arrangements really do explain them. For he talks in terms of 'through', 'explanation', 'which is why', 'for', 'therefore', 'because', 'so that' (*dia, aition, aitia, diho, dihoper, gar, men oun, dihoti, hoti, hōste*). And he talks this way not only in connexion with bile, eye colour and types of hair, which he regards as serving no purpose,[62] but also in connexion with purposive arrangements.[63]

[61] Gotthelf, op. cit., note 32.

[62] *PA* 677a18; *GA* 778a35 – b1, b14, b18; 782a20 – 783b8; 789b20.

[63] *PA* 658b2–5, 663b14, 677b25–30, 679a28, 694b6; *GA* 738a33–4, 743b7–18, 755a21–4, 766a16–30, 767b10–23, 776a25 – b3, 788b33 – 789a4, 789a12–14.

CHAPTER ELEVEN

Ancient and Modern Theories of Natural Selection: their relation to purpose

In the last chapter, I interpreted the notion of teleological explanation so broadly that it covered modern evolutionary explanations of animal organs. In this, I was merely following the lead of many modern biologists who are prepared to talk of teleonomy, even if not of teleology. But it may be objected that I must have been distorting Aristotle's intentions. For Empedocles, like modern evolutionary biologists, had a theory of natural selection. Yet Aristotle regarded Empedocles' theory as the very antithesis of a teleological one. Does this not show that Aristotle included more restrictions in the idea of teleological explanation than I have yet allowed?

I believe the answer to this challenge will reveal something of independent interest, namely, just how far Empedocles' theory of natural selection fell short of modern theories. It fell sufficiently far short for its unteleological character to establish nothing about the character of modern theories. None the less, I ought also to acknowledge that some aspects of modern evolutionary theory might have struck Aristotle as contrary to the spirit of final cause explanation.

For one thing, modern theory appeals to chance mutations, and chance, for Aristotle, excludes final cause.[1] But he might have been reassured to notice that chance is largely confined by modern theory to the original isolated mutation. The mutation's subsequent selection is not to the same extent due to chance. Another idea that would have struck Aristotle as anti-teleological is the great wastage involved in the discarding of unfavourable mutations. This would have seemed to go

[1] Aristotle does give chance an *indirect* link with final causes (196b17 – 197a6). For on the whole, we do not call some thing *lucky* unless we think it is the kind of thing that someone *might well* have wanted; and we seldom are interested enough in a situation to pick it out as *chance*, unless we think of it as something that someone *might well* have wanted to happen or not to happen. In the same way, Aristotle insists that we do not talk of chance or spontaneity (*tuchē, to automaton*), unless we are talking of something which *might well have* been brought about on purpose or by nature, and hence for the sake of an end (196b22, b34, 197a35, 198a6). At the same time, he insists that chance events are *not in fact* brought about for the sake of an end (197a35, b18–19, 198b29). And so he treats chance as *opposed* to final cause (e.g. 199a3–5).

against his principle that 'nature does nothing in vain'. Again, he might have been reassured, however, by an argument of Monod's that this wastage is actually the most efficient means of attaining the goal.[2] Of course, Aristotle did not foresee the discovery of DNA molecular structure. But, unlike Gotthelf, I do not think that the very idea of final causation rules out embryological development being the result of such a thing.

Let us now see what Empedocles' theory was. Empedocles suggested that there were four stages in zoogony, the development of animals on the earth.[3] First, individual organs arose out of the earth, heads without necks, arms bereft of shoulders, eyes in want of foreheads.[4] Secondly, the members coalesced into monstrous unions, shambling creatures with countless hands, man-fronted ox-types, ox-headed man-types, part male, part female.[5] Thirdly, in a single long night, primitive creatures sprang up out of the earth complete, first trees,[6] then primitive humans.[7] As these developed, fruit and seed were formed, and eventually the humans mated, producing the fourth and current stage of zoogony, in which there is sexual reproduction.[8]

It is in connexion with Empedocles' second and fourth stages that Aristotle mentions natural selection (*Phys.* ii 8, 198b23–32).

So what prevents natural parts from being like this, for example, teeth from springing up of necessity with the front ones sharp and suitable for slicing the food, the molars broad and useful for grinding it, since it did not happen for the sake of this end, but was a coincidence? And the same goes for the other parts in which things have seemed to be for the sake of an end. Thus where everything came about accidentally as if it were coming into being for the sake of an end, those things survived, having come together in a fitting way spontaneously. Whatever was not like this perished, and still does perish, as Empedocles says of his man-fronted ox-types.

It is obvious how natural selection might apply to the second stage, that of the monstrous conglomerates. But how does it apply to the fourth and present stage? Aristotle implies that it does when he says that monstrosities still do perish, and the ancient commentator Simplicius repeats this, saying 'nowadays too everything happens in the same way'.[9] The reference is to Empedocles' theory of embryology. An embryo

[2] The process of chance mutation, wastage, and natural selection is vital, according to Monod, if there is to be improvement of replicative ability. In the special case of forming antibodies against bacteria and viruses, he argues that it is more efficient that our cells should randomly produce antibodies of many different kinds, most of which will be wasted, because only so will our bodies be able to repel attack in whatever shape it comes (119–20).

[3] Aëtius v 19 5. = Plutarch v 19 = A72 under 'Empedocles' in Diels, *Die Fragmente der Vorsokratiker*.   [4] Fragment 75 in Diels.

[5] Fragments 60, 61.   [6] Aëtius v 26 4 = A70 in Diels.

[7] Fragment 62; cf. Aëtius v 18 1 = Diels A75.   [8] Aëtius v 19 5, as above.

[9] This is the final sentence in Simplicius' account, *in Phys. CIAG* 371, omitted by Diels from his preface to fragment 61.

is formed, in his view, through tiny members being drawn from all over the parents' bodies in the excitement of union, and assembled in the form of seed in the womb of the mother.[10] The embryos are nourished through blood and air being delivered in four tubes.[11] The whole process provides opportunities for monstrosities to be formed once again, and Empedocles describes five distinct ways in which this can happen.[12] On the other hand, things are not quite so haphazard as at the second stage of zoogony. For Empedocles does try to formulate some rules governing the development of embryos.[13]

Such is Empedocles' theory. I now want to pick out some of the differences from modern theory which prevent it from supplying teleological explanations. The first difference is that natural selection plays quite a different role: it is not used in explaining why certain organs and arrangements are present. In modern theory, natural selection both imports the teleological element, and contributes to explaining the presence of parts.

In order to see how differently natural selection is used by Empedocles, let us first consider the second stage of zoogony. Natural selection is invoked here, not in order to explain why the conglomerates have the characteristics they do have, but only to explain why certain of them, having acquired these characteristics by chance conglomeration, managed to survive (*esōthē*, 198b30), for a while. It would only be if these lucky conglomerates had *descendants*, that we could explain characteristics by reference to natural selection. The characteristics of the *descendants* might then be explained by the natural selection exercised upon their *ancestors*. But did any of the original conglomerates have descendants?

It would seem impossible that they did, on the view which has prevailed over the last hundred years, and which was endorsed by Zeller and Burnet. For on this view, the conglomerates were all swept away. They belonged to a different stage of the cosmic cycle, a stage at which there was a different world from ours. According to Zeller and Burnet, two separate worlds are successively created and destroyed in the course of one of Empedocles' cosmic cycles. During the 1960s, this idea of two separate worlds per cycle was challenged by Bollack and others.[14] But even so, it is difficult to think that we are descended from the conglomerates. For Empedocles speaks as if our ancestors sprang fresh out of the earth at the third stage of zoogony.

[10] *GA* I 18, 722b17–30.   [11] Soranus, quoted by Diels A79.

[12] Aëtius v 8 1. = Diels A81: excess of seed, or deficiency of it, or disturbance of the movements, or too much dividing up, or bending.

[13] See the quotations collected by Diels under A81, 83 and 84. There are rules governing the sex of embryos, their resemblances to relatives, the speed of development, its order, and the period required for the articulation of parts.

[14] For the details, see A. A. Long, 'Empedocles' cosmic cycle in the 'sixties', in *The Pre-Socratics*, ed. A. P. D. Mourelatos, Garden City New York 1974.

As for our ancestors at this third stage, there is no mention of them being subjected to natural selection at all. Natural selection next comes in with the embryology of the fourth stage. But here it has a very negative role. It is used to explain why monstrosities disappear, but not to explain why normal embryos develop with the parts they do have. This question indeed is scarcely answered. At the third stage, it is left unexplained why so many creatures should spring out of the earth, equipped with similar parts, at the same time. At the fourth stage, all we are told is that the embryo's tiny parts are drawn from the limbs of the parents, but why the parental limbs should contain these parts we are not told. Certainly, natural selection is not offered as part of the answer.

This, then, is the first relevant difference from modern theory: the lack of interest in why we have the parts we have. The next difference is that chance, which is opposed to teleology, is not confined to isolated mutations, but applied to widespread phenomena. At least Aristotle makes this complaint in *Phys.* ii 8.[15] The example he gives is that front teeth grow sharp and suitable for tearing the food, back teeth broad and suitable for grinding. This is allegedly ascribed by Empedocles to chance. And Aristotle's complaint is that it is a self-contradiction to ascribe a widespread phenomenon to chance, since chance events are by definition exceptional. Modern theory would escape this criticism, since it ascribes to chance only the original isolated mutation.

Is Aristotle's criticism of Empedocles fair? There is certainly room for ascribing widespread phenomena to chance at the third stage of zoogony. For all we have been told is that earth, air, fire and water are moving around under the influence of Love, or, on the interpretation of Zeller and Burnet, under the influence of Strife. Why then should this mingling produce so many creatures with similar parts in one long night?

We are given many further examples of Empedocles' appeals to chance, and it is sometimes hard to know with which stage of zoogony we should connect them. Aristotle complains at *Phys.* ii 4, 196a24, that Empedocles says most animal parts are created by chance, and Simplicius illustrates this with quotations from Empedocles,[16] some of which are listed by Diels as fragments 75, 85, and 98. Fragment 98 tells us that blood and flesh arose, when earth, anchoring in the perfect harbours of Aphrodite, chanced upon (*sunekurse*) equal quantities of air, fire and water. According to fragment 75, animals with an internal skeleton chanced upon (*tuchonta*) pliable exteriors at the hands of the Cyprian goddess of love. Fragment 85 tells us that, in forming another part (the eye?) fire chanced upon (*tuche*) a very small quantity of earth. Aristotle

[15] *Phys.* ii 8, 198b23 – 199a5.
[16] Simplicius, *in Phys. CIAG* 331. Some of the quotations recur elsewhere in Simplicius (*in Phys.* 32, *in Cael.* 530).

further complains that Empedocles fails to explain how we get exactly the right *ratio* of ingredients for bone, and that his appeal to the *mingling* of elements is in effect an appeal to chance.[17] Empedocles is also said to suggest that the articulated backbone is due to the accident (*sumbēnai*; *sunebē*) of the spine getting broken into segments, as the animal gets contorted in the process of development.[18]

Some of these quotations can only refer to the third or fourth stages of zoogony,[19] while others may well refer both to these later stages and to earlier ones, since in many ways the stages are analogous.[20] Blood, flesh and bone, for example, must have been a component of the solitary limbs at stage one, of the whole-natured forms at stage three, and, as we are told, of the seed at stage four;[21] while blood continues to be fed into the developing embryo.[22] If the exact ratio of ingredients has been left to chance, this will be true at all these stages. And this tends to confirm Aristotle's complaint, that widespread phenomena have been left to chance, and to establish the second contrast with modern evolutionary theory.

A third and last contrast with modern theory is that the role given to natural selection is the merely negative one of discarding unsatisfactory products. There is nothing corresponding to the positive search, postulated by modern theory, for ever greater replicative ability.

In all three ways, Empedocles' theory differs from modern quite enough to account for Aristotle's complaint that it does not offer a teleological explanation of animal parts.

But two possible objections must be considered. First, it has been disputed that the conglomerate animals of stage two had no descendants. Jean Bollack, in the most extensive commentary on Empedocles, makes use of a passage in which Simplicius comments on Aristotle's report.[23] The passage reveals that in some cases the conglomerates were not monstrosities, but reasonably like ourselves. The organs which amalgamated with each other 'fulfilled each other's needs, the teeth cutting and grinding the food, the belly digesting it, and the liver making blood'. There might be a *human* head joined to a *human* trunk, and in these favourable cases, the organism survived.

---

[17] *GC* II 6, 333b7–22; cf. *DA* I 4, 408a21.   [18] *PA* I 1, 640a19–26.

[19] This would apply to the backbone being broken in the womb and to the pliable exteriors. Aëtius' report is headed, 'from what elements each of the parts *in us* is made', which might suggest the fourth stage, though he also describes the bones as being mixed 'within the earth', which suggests the third (v 22 1 = Diels *Doxographici Graeci* p. 434 = Diels A78 under 'Empedocles' in *Die Fragmente der Vorsokratiker*, although this last excludes the heading).

[20] For some analogies, see *GA* I 18, 722b8–30; and Aëtius v 7 1 with *GA* 764a1 (both in Diels A81).

[21] *GA* I 18, 722b30 – 723a9, 723a21–3.   [22] Soranus, Diels A79.

[23] Simplicius *in Phys. CIAG* 371. This appears as no. 506 with French translation in Jean Bollack (21.5), vol. 2, 1969, and, without the final sentence, in Diels, in preface to fragment 61. I am grateful to A. A. Long for drawing my attention to this passage.

Bollack's speculation is that some of these organisms survived long enough to reach the third stage and to mate in the fourth. There is no actual mention of this having happened, however. If it did happen, then at the third stage the surviving conglomerates would have to have lived alongside the organisms which sprang fresh out of the earth, which is what Bollack suggests. In that case, we would have a double ancestry, and to the extent that we were descended from conglomerates which had been favoured by natural selection, the characteristics we inherit would be explicable by reference to natural selection, in something approaching the modern manner. However, to the extent that we were descended from the organisms which sprang fresh out of the earth at stage three, our characteristics would not be explicable by reference to natural selection. Bollack's suggestion, then, even if accepted on such a slender basis, would still give us only a watered down version of modern theory.

The other objection arises from John Burnet's treatment of Empedocles' view about backbones.[24] He takes it that the snapping of a backbone to which Empedocles refers was an *isolated* event befalling one *individual* ancestor. It would then be comparable to those *isolated* favourable mutations which modern theory postulates; and from that point on, Empedocles' theory might have continued along the same lines as modern theory.

The context, however, suggests that Aristotle is not talking of an *isolated* snapping, in his discussion of Empedocles, but of what *regularly* happens in the process of development. The point he is making is that processes of development should be explained by reference to the final state of the animal, not the final state by reference to the processes. He describes Empedocles' view as being that many properties belong to animals because of things having happened that way during development. It is natural to take it that he means during the development of those same animals, not of some solitary ancestor. He then gives the example: they have a backbone like that because it happened to get broken, as the animal got twisted. Admittedly the aorist tense of 'it happened', and the singular number of 'the animal', might suggest reference to some *one* solitary ancestor. But in the absence of any corroborative evidence, it is simpler to suppose that Aristotle is here referring to the development of *each* individual specimen.

I conclude that Aristotle has every reason for refusing to see teleology in the particular use to which *Empedocles* put natural selection. He rightly points out that Empedocles brings in teleology at a different point; and his complaint is that Empedocles does not in the end make sufficient or proper use of the teleological principle.[25] He postulates Love as a guiding force which forms structures by combining the ele-

[24] John Burnet, in his classic work *Early Greek Philosophy*, London 1892, is commenting on *PA* ɪ 1, 640a19–22.
[25] *Phys.* ɪɪ 8, 198b14–16; *Metaph.* ɪ 4, 985a10–23.

ments, while Strife separates them. Taking the idea further, Empedocles speaks of the elements, earth, air, fire and water, as *'desiring'* to join their likes.[26] The teleology which Empedocles resorts to here is unlike Aristotle's, and would be more open to some of the strictures which have wrongly been directed against Aristotle.

[26] Fragment 62; cf. fragments 22, 110.

PART IV

NECESSITY AND THE ESSENCES OF KINDS

CHAPTER TWELVE

Analytic or *de re*?

We have encountered a good many kinds of necessity. Before summarising them, it will be as well to take into account some further distinctions. They do not have a direct bearing on determinism. But they are important for understanding Aristotle's view of necessity, and they are intimately bound up with some of the liveliest debates going on in current philosophy.

In the *Posterior Analytics* Aristotle discusses statements giving the essences of kinds. He attributes necessity to such statements, and this attribution relates to two controversies, which will be the subject of the present chapter and the next. A number of continental scholars have thought that Aristotle treated these necessities as analytic, while Quine in America has repeatedly associated Aristotle's name with a non-analytic, *de re* necessity.[1] Admittedly, Quine was discussing statements ascribing an essence to an *individual*. But might not Aristotle have attributed the same kind of necessity to statements giving the essence of a *kind*? The two questions to be considered in this chapter, then, are whether Aristotle treats these statements as analytic, and, if not, whether he treats them as necessary *de re*.

Aristotle has been castigated from both sides, both by Quine for believing in *de re* necessity, and by Lukasiewicz for basing science on analytic truths. I must first explain the terms involved in the discussion, and I shall start with analyticity.

The analytic versus what is knowable only a posteriori

A typical example of an analytic judgment would be the judgment that bachelors are unmarried. It was Kant who made the notion of analyticity central to modern philosophy. Here is one of his accounts of analytic judgments.

---

[1] See note 7.

All analytic judgments depend wholly on the law of contradiction, and are in their nature *a priori* cognitions, whether the concepts that supply them with matter be empirical or not. For the predicate of an affirmative analytic judgment is already contained in the concept of the subject, of which it cannot be denied without contradiction ... For this very reason all analytic judgments are *a priori* even when the concepts are empirical, as, for example,'Gold is a yellow metal'; for to know this I require no experience beyond my concept of gold as a yellow metal. It is, in fact, the very concept, and I need only analyse it without looking beyond it.[2]

The point that will chiefly prove relevant is that analytic judgments can be known *a priori*. That is, their truth (not their necessity) can be known not on the basis of experience beyond that involved in having the concept. For someone who has the concept of gold, it is suggested, needs no *further* experience to know that it is yellow.[3]

The notion of analyticity stems ultimately from the practices of Greek geometry,[4] and the notion of knowledge *a priori* from discussions like that in Aristotle's *Topics* vi 4, of defining by reference to what is prior, though less accessible to sense experience. It is equally true of the next distinction that its remote origins lie in Greek thought. William Kneale finds the first explicit formulation of the distinction between *de dicto* and *de re* modality in Abelard, although, as he points out, the idea derives ultimately from something in Aristotle.[5]

De re *necessity*

In *SE* 4, 166a23–31, Aristotle distinguishes between saying that it is possible for a sitting man to walk and saying that it is possible for a man to walk-while-sitting. In the second, the walking and sitting are combined into a *compound*, and it would be a 'fallacy of composition' to infer the compound formula from the 'divided', or non-compound.

Abelard's point is that a modal word, such as 'possible' or 'necessary', sometimes qualifies the *whole* of a proposition or *dictum* (what is said). After Abelard, a modality of this kind was sometimes called *de dicto*, and sometimes described in Aristotle's terms as involving the whole *compound* of subject and predicate. But the modal word may instead qualify the *predicate* part of the proposition on its own, i.e. the predicate as 'divided' from the subject; and then the modality is called in Abelardian terms *de re*. For it will tell us something about the subject, which is

[2] Immanuel Kant, *Prolegomena to any Future Metaphysics* (1783), Preamble, Section 2b.

[3] For clarification of what Kant counts as being based on experience, see the *Introduction* to his *Critique of Pure Reason*, edition A (1781), edition B (1787).

[4] See Jaakko Hintikka (25.1) 1974, esp. chs 6 and 9; (25.2) 1965.

[5] William Kneale (24.1) 1962. Kneale cites Abelard's commentary on Aristotle's *Int.* (*Abaelardiana Inedita*, ed. L. Minio Paluello, 13 ff.); *Dialectica* (ed. De Rijk, pp. 195, 204–6).

a *res* or thing. For example, if we say that necessarily every bachelor is unmarried, our claim will be true, provided it is read strictly about the whole *dictum* that every bachelor is unmarried. But suppose that the 'necessarily' is read as qualifying the 'unmarried', and that we are making a claim about bachelors – that every one is such as to be necessarily-unmarried: then our claim will be false. For in most cases, bachelors have not encountered insuperable barriers to marriage.

In recent logic, several tests have been used for distinguishing between necessity *de dicto* and *de re*, and I shall concentrate on two. The first is obviously related to Abelard's. Consider the sentence 'Necessarily the number nine is greater than seven'. One test is whether the sentence is best read by making the modal word 'necessarily' govern the whole sentence 'the number nine is greater than seven', or best read by making the modal word govern just the predicate 'greater than seven', so that we obtain a new, hyphenated predicate 'necessarily-greater-than-seven'.[6] The new predicate would be understood as introducing a single unit of meaning. In the former case, we can think of ourselves as talking about the *dictum* or proposition that nine is greater than seven and as saying that it is necessary; in the latter case as talking about the *res* nine and as saying that it is necessarily-greater-than-seven.

The first test concerns the scope of the word 'necessarily'. There is another test in modern logic which concerns the scope of the words 'all' and 'some' in their interaction with 'necessarily'. But although this test is more widely used nowadays, I want to set it aside, because its relation to the original distinction is much more indirect.

Instead, I shall pick out a different test as the second one for consideration. Suppose we replace the subject term 'the number nine' by another designation of the same subject, such as 'the number of the planets', thus obtaining the sentence: 'necessarily *the number of the planets* is greater than seven'. Can such a replacement alter the truth-value of the sentence from truth to falsehood? If it can, the necessity will be *de dicto* by the second test.[7]

I have picked out this second test, because it has been much discussed in connexion with Aristotle, and because it is closely related to the first. For if we are not talking about the number nine *however described*, this provides a sense in which we are not talking about the *res* nine at all; and conversely if we are talking about the *dictum* that nine is greater than seven, we cannot safely substitute an alternative subject term and expect still to be talking about the same *dictum*. Again, if the 'necessar-

[6] See David Wiggins (24.4) 1974, (24.5) 1976 with appendix by C. Peacocke.

[7] See W. V. Quine, 'Three grades of modal involvement', and 'Reply to Professor Marcus', in *The Ways of Paradox*, New York 1966, 173–82; 'Reference and modality' in *From a Logical Point of View*, 2nd ed., Cambridge Mass. 1961, 139–59; *Word and Object* New York 1960, 195–200. The point is well explained by Kirwan in (24.3) 1970–1. Quine comes closer to Wiggins' approach in his latest contribution: (24.2) 1977.

ily' in some sentence governs only the predicate, and the subject stands *outside* its scope, then the presence of the word 'necessarily' ought not to interfere with our varying the designation of the subject.

The two tests can be applied to a sentence with a singular subject and a predicate, whether the subject term refers to an individual or to a kind. Both tests might also be applied to a universal sentence, such as 'all humans are necessarily rational'. But the application of the substitution test would involve a certain extension. We should have to ask whether or not the sentence was being used in such a way as to license the inference with regard to any particular individual (say, Socrates) who is known to be human that *he* is, however described, necessarily rational. The *de re* interpretation of universal, necessary sentences in Aristotle would take them as licensing this inference; the analytic interpretation would not. Again, the *de re* interpretation would take the universal sentences to be best read in terms of the hyphenated predicate 'necessarily-rational', while the analytic interpretation would take them to be best read by making the modal word govern the whole sentence 'all humans are rational'.

Necessity associated in An. Post. *I 4 to 6 with definitional connexion*

Aristotle discusses statements giving the essences of kinds in *An. Post.* I 4–6, and it is here that he says most about the necessity which he has in mind. He lays down a very strict requirement for a predicate's attaching *necessarily* to a subject: it must belong to the subject *in itself* (*kath' hauto*).[8] This means that subject and predicate must be definitionally connected in one or other of two ways. For subject and predicate are said to have an 'in itself' relation, if either belongs in the definition which says what the other is (*ti esti*). Clearly, the definitional connexion can run in either direction, and the examples with which Aristotle illustrates the two possibilities are probably meant to run: 'a triangle is an arrangment of lines' and 'numbers are odd or even'. In the first, a triangle (the subject) is definable by reference to lines; in the second, oddness or eveness (the predicate) by reference to numbers.

Aristotle has a vision of how a scientific text book should ideally be set out. His scheme is in some ways like, though in other ways unlike, that adopted by Euclid a generation later. The scientist would start with definitions of his key terms,[9] and use them as premises. Then with the aid of further premises, he would deduce and explain the further characteristics of the thing defined.[10] A favourite example of such a further

---

[8] *An. Post.* I 6, 74b12, 75a20–2, a31.

[9] For the role of definitions as first premises, see *An. Post.* I 2, 72a14–31; I 3, 72b18–25; I 8, 75b31; I 33, 89a18; II 3, 90b24; II 13, 96b23; II 17, 99a22; *DA* I 1, 402b16–26; *NE* VI 8, 1142a26; VI 11, 1143b2; *Metaph.* VII 9, 1034a30–2; XIII 4, 1078b23; *Top.* VIII 3.

[10] That the premises should explain the conclusion is required in *An. Post.* I 2, 71b29 – 72a5. The broad outlines of the programme are given in *An. Post.* I 1 to 8.

characteristic is the equality of the interior angles of a triangle to two right angles.

Aristotle insists, in *An. Post.* I 2, 4 and 6, that the predicates should attach necessarily to their subjects in the premises and conclusion of a scientific syllogism. It may well be wondered how, on his own terms, this requirement can be met. For in the conclusion that a triangle has interior angles equal to two right angles, the predicate does not enter into the definition of the subject. Nor can he have required the predicate to enter into the definition of the subject in *all* scientific premises. None the less, he claims that an 'in itself' relation exists between subject and predicate in premises and conclusion.[11] And he cites as an illustration of this the conclusion that a triangle has its interior angles equal to two right angles.[12] How can this be? He must think that the conclusions and the remaining premises involve a definitional connexion running in the opposite direction. Indeed, he cites examples of such connexions alongside the example of a triangle having its interior angles equal to two right angles.[13] It is doubtful whether he is right, however, that a triangle would enter into the definition of this kind of equality.[14]

The insistence that necessity is confined to definitional connexions is more restrictive than Aristotle's normal practice. For he allows elsewhere that an *idion*, i.e. a predicate which belongs to all and only the members of a species, but which does not enter into the species' definition, belongs to that species necessarily. An example is that man is capable of learning grammar.[15] Again, a predicate that belongs everlastingly to an everlasting subject, as motion belongs to the sun, attaches necessarily to its subject.[16] Yet there is said to be no definitional connexion here.[17] Yet again, Aristotle elsewhere allows that having milk in the breasts is a necessary sign of having conceived,[18] yet one of his remarks here may be intended precisely to rule that out.[19]

Do Aristotle's necessary predications concern kinds or their numbers?

When Aristotle talks of predicates attaching necessarily to their subjects, provided they attach definitionally, it is natural to suppose that

[11] *An. Post.* I 4, 73b32–3, 73b39 – 74a2; I 6, 75a29–30. Cf. the passages where the predicates of the conclusions are paradoxically described as *in-itself* accidents (I 6, 75a18; I 7, 75b2).

[12] *An. Post.* I 4, 73b28–32, 73b39 – 74a2.   [13] *An. Post.* I 4, 73b28–32.

[14] Besides the two 'in itself' relationships already illustrated, Aristotle mentions two others which are not definitional connexions *An. Post.* I 4, 73b5–16. But this will not help, because in one of the passages where he says that only 'in itself' relationships are necessary, he makes clear that he is thinking of the first two 'in itself' relationships, the definitional connexions (*An. Post.* I 6, 74b5–12).

[15] *Top.* I 5, 102a18–30.   [16] *Cael.* I 12, 281b3–25.

[17] *Metaph.* VII 15, 1040a27–33.   [18] *An. Pr.* II 27; *Rhet.* I 2, II 25.

[19] *An. Post.* I 6, 75a31–4.

the subjects he has in mind are *kinds* like triangle or man, not the *members* of a kind. For only *kinds* have definitions; individuals do not.[20]

Now one cannot infer, without more ado, that if the *kind*, man, is necessarily rational, then all *individual* men are necessarily rational. There are at least two obstacles to such an inference. One is the question whether Socrates is necessarily a man, or whether he could, for example, be reincarnated as a bird. We know from other works that Aristotle would think this impossible. But until it is ruled out, we cannot infer from the necessity of *man* being rational to the necessity of each *individual* man, e.g. Socrates, being rational.

The other obstacle to inference can be brought out by asking which of two things is implied by the claim that the kind is necessarily rational. Is it implied that every man is rational, or only that every *normal* man is rational? In the latter case, there would be a second obstacle to inference; for the species could survive the existence of some non-rational specimens, provided that they remained exceptional. The *Topics* goes some way towards recognising this obstacle, if, as I believe, it allows that not every specimen need possess the defining characteristics of the species.[21] But the *Posterior Analytics* seems to disagree, when it declares that definitions hold true universally.[22] At most, it mentions belatedly the possibility of degenerate, non-necessary premises in which predicates attach to their subjects only for the most part.[23]

In spite of these obstacles to inference, Aristotle introduces, at I 4, 73a28–34, the idea of belonging to every instance (*kata pantos*) an idea which he contrasts here with belonging to some instances and not to others (*epi tinos men, tinos de mē*, I 4, 73a28–9) and elsewhere with belonging to *no* instance (*kata mēdenos*, e.g. *An. Pr.* I 1, 24b28–30; I 4, 25b37 – 26a1). He introduces predication *kata pantos* as a characteristic which must belong to the first premises of scientific demonstrations (I 4, 73a24–5). And, indeed, his examples of scientific premises are typically given in the form 'A belongs (of necessity) to every B', where 'every B' is contrasted with 'no B' and 'some B'. Evidently, then, the subject of predication is here conceived as the *members* of the kind. Aristotle simply does not trouble to explain what justifies his moving from necessary truths about the kind to necessary truths about its members.[24]

The need to distinguish these two kinds of truth is made particularly clear by the example of reincarnation; for this would make it possible that *no* individual man should be necessarily rational, in spite of the

---

[20] *Metaph.* VII 12.

[21] *Top.* v 5, 134a10–17, b6–8: not every man has two feet. Yet (*Top.* v 3, 132a1–4; cf. v 4, 133a1–5; VI 6, 143b1, 144b12–30) this does not prevent biped from being a defining characteristic of man.

[22] *An. Post.* I 14, 79a28.   [23] *An. Post.* I 30, 87b19–27; II 12, 96a8–19.

[24] I am grateful to Jonathan Barnes for drawing my attention to this oscillation.

necessary rationality of the kind. Aristotle might well be able to justify his move from one kind of truth to the other; but what is striking is that he makes no comment on it. And the move will be all the more surprising, if it is right to interpret *Metaph.* vii 15, as I shall interpret it in Chapter Thirteen, as implying that there are no necessary truths about perishable individuals.

Aristotle's conception of essence

I have said that subject and predicate have an 'in itself' relation, if either belongs in the definition which says what the other is (*ti esti*). English translators commonly put the point in terms of *essence*: an 'in itself' relation is called an essential one, and what something is (*ti esti*) is called its essence. One could give a partial summary of what a statement of essence is by saying that it tells us what something is.

But Aristotle has a large number of ways of expressing the idea of essence.[25] One is the phrase *to einai autōi* (the for so-and-so to be). Another is the still stranger expression *to ti ēn einai autōi* (the what it was for so-and-so to be). Perhaps the second phrase expands the first, and means: the thing it was agreed was the answer to the question what it is for so-and-so to be. The essence is further said to be identical with the form or formal cause of a thing (*eidos*).[26]

Both kinds and individuals can be said to have a form or essence; but whereas the essence of a kind consists of its *defining* characteristics, individuals do not have definitions. According to one Aristotelian view, the essence of an individual is simply the essence of the kind under which it falls.[27] Thus *rational animal* might be the essence both of Socrates and of the kind man. But whereas *rational animal* gives the *definition* of man, it does not give a *definition* of Socrates, partly because it does not have to apply to him uniquely (*Metaph.* vii 15, 1040a33 − b1). None the less, it tells us in some sense what Socrates is, as well as telling us what the kind man is. Moreover, it is equally true of Socrates and of the kind man that they could not survive the loss of this predicate (see *Metaph.* vii 15, 1040a29–33 for kinds and, e.g., *GC* i 4 for individuals).

In what follows, I shall be concerned primarily with the essences of *kinds*. Aristotle often implies that the essence of a species is made up of the *genus* under which it falls and the *differentia* which differentiates it

[25] Yet other expressions are discussed by G. E. M. Anscombe in G. E. M. Anscombe and P. T. Geach, *Three Philosophers*, Oxford 1961, 24–6, 34–8.

[26] *Metaph.* i 3, 983a26–b3; vii 7, 1032b1–2; vii 8, 1033b5–7; vii 10, 1035b16, b32; viii 4, 1044a36; *Phys.* ii 2, 194a21; ii 3, 194b26–7, 195a20 − 1 (= *Metaph.* v 2, 1013a26–7, b22–3).

[27] I shall not try to discuss the evidence for a more individualised sort of essence in Aristotle. On this, see Rogers Albritton, 'Forms of particular substances in Aristotle's *Metaphysics*', *Journal of Philosophy* 54, 1957, 699–708.

from other species of the same genus.[28] But sometimes he stresses the differentia only, and equates it with the form or essence.[29]

English philosophers may be confused by the fact that Locke introduced two kinds of essence into the tradition, real and nominal. I should say straight away that Aristotle's essence is closer to Locke's *real* essence. Indeed, nominal essence was introduced in order to get an alternative to Aristotelian essences.[30] Locke felt that the real essences of stuffs could never be known. The nominal essence would at least be known to ordinary speakers, being a boundary constructed in their minds for demarcating each sort of species.[31] In the nominal essence of gold many ideas are combined, different ones for different people: yellowness, weight, fusibility, malleability, solubility in aqua regia, ductility, or fixedness.[32]

Aristotle's essences are very different, and it may help, if I give some examples. The essence of *lunar eclipse*, for Aristotle, is loss of light by the moon due to the interposition of the earth between sun and moon.[33] The essence of *thunder* is noise produced by the quenching of fire in the clouds or whatever the right cause is. Aristotle was aware of several theories, and chose as an illustration Anaxagoras' theory of the cause rather than his own.[34] *Consonance* in music was the ability of two notes to blend, if played simultaneously, and to sound pleasant to the ear. It

---

[28] This is made clear for *to ti ēn einai* at *Top*. vii 3, 153a14–19. *An. Post* ii 6 is probably disagreeing with this passage, but it does not question the claim that the essence consists of genus and differentiae. Indeed, this claim is assumed in the discussion at *An. Post*. ii 13, of how to reach the essence of triad and other essences by the process of division, and again at *An. Post*. i 22, 82b37 – 83a1, 83a39 – b3; ii 8, 93a21–33.

[29] Thus according to *Metaph*. vii 17, 1041a20–32, the essence of thunder is simply the cause of there being a noise in the clouds. According to vii 12, 1038a25–6, the last differentia reached in the process of division will be the form (i.e. the essence) of the thing. This is reflected in Aristotle's willingness sometimes to define thunder or lunar eclipse by the briefer formula, quenching of fire in cloud or interposition of the earth (*An. Post*. ii 8, 93b7–8), deciduousness simply as the coagulation of sap where the seed joins on (*An. Post*. ii 17, 99a28–9), squaring the rectangle simply as the discovery of a mean proportional (*DA* ii 2, 413a13–20. This second approach is connected with a desire to downgrade the genus, in order to represent definition as a unitary thing, in which genus and differentia do not form two separate components. One method of downgrading the genus is to argue that the differentia (biped) entails the genus (animal), which therefore requires no separate mention (*Top*. vi 6, 144b16, b27; cf. *Metaph*. vii 12). The other is to argue that the genus is to be compared with matter, rather than form, in that it is a mere potentiality, imposing no distinctive characteristics of its own (*Metaph*. v 28, 1024b8–9; vii 12, 1038a5–9; viii 6, 1045a14–31; x 8). But contrast *Top*. iv 6, 128a20–9: the genus reveals *ti estin*, what a thing is, better than the differentia.

[30] John Locke, *Essay Concerning Human Understanding* (1690) 3 3 17, 3 8 2, 4 6 8.

[31] Ibid. 3 3 13, 3 6 2, 3 6 26, 3 6 36–7.

[32] Ibid. 3 2 3, 3 3 18, 3 6 2, 3 6 6, 3 6 31, 3 9 13, 4 6 8.

[33] For lunar eclipse, see *An. Post*. ii 2, 90a15; ii 8, 93a 30–3, b6–7; *Metaph*. 1044b12–15. Aristotle knew the right theory, that lunar eclipse, unlike solar, involves a shadow on the eclipsed object.

[34] For thunder see *An. Post*. ii 8, 93b7–14; ii 10, 94a5. This theory is ascribed to Anaxagoras and contrasted with his own in *Meteor*. ii 9.

had been discovered that the two strings required to produce a pair of consonant notes differed in length from each other by certain very simple mathematical ratios (2:1, 4:3, 3:2, 3:1, 4:1). Dissonant pairs had complex string-length ratios, involving larger numbers. Thus Aristotle gives the essence of consonance as an uncomplicated ratio between a high and a low note.[35] *Particular hues*, such as yellowness, are assigned an essence on the basis of an analogous theory. The essence is a ratio between the dark and bright ingredients of the coloured body.[36] The essence of *heat* is the power to conglomerate things of the same kind, while that of *cold* is the power to conglomerate both things that are like each other and things that are unlike.[37] The essence of *deciduousness* is the coagulation of sap at the point where the seed joins on, if this causes the fall of leaves.[38] In connexion with *animal species,* Aristotle eventually decides that it is no good looking for a single differentia by which to define them. Each needs to be defined by several differentiae, and the differentiae which he considers in *HA* include four distinct kinds: (i) parts of the body and their shapes, (ii) activities, including bodily functions, (iii) the way of life, e.g. feeding habits, and (iv) psychological character.[39]

One salient point about these essences is that they are features which would not all be known to ordinary speakers of the language, in which case they could not be used by them for drawing a boundary round the sort. The causes of thunder and lunar eclipse were not universally known in Aristotle's time, but were still a matter for debate. Elsewhere, in *Top.* vi 4, Aristotle explains that a definition which states the essence may have to refer to things that are quite unfamiliar to us. The penalty if we insist on mentioning only what is familiar to people is precisely the one Locke specifies in connexion with his nominal essence: we shall have to give different definitions for different speakers.[40]

The examples should also help to make intelligible Aristotle's idea that scientific definitions, coupled with extra premises, can be used to explain further facts about the thing defined. Indeed, one can refute a proposed definition (*horismos*), by showing that it is not explanatory in this way (*DA* i 5, 409b13–18). The definition of lunar eclipse might, with extra premises, explain such further properties as the periodicity of eclipses, their short duration, and the shape of the dark patch. Simi-

[35] *An.Post.* ii 2, 90a18–19. I have written more about this in 'Aristotle, mathematics and colour', *Classical Quarterly* 22, 1972, 293–308. Cf. *Phys.* ii 3, 194b28; *Metaph.* v 2, 1013a28. The form and cause of consonant pairs an octave apart is the ratio 2:1.
[36] *Sens.* 3, 439b25 – 440a6.   [37] *GC* ii 2, 329b26–9.   [38] *An. Post.* ii 17, 99a28–9.
[39] *HA* i 1, 487a11 and *PA* i 2–4. For this subject see David Balme's notes on *PA* i 2–4, in (1.6) 1972, and his 'Aristotle's use of differentiae in his zoology' in *Aristote et les Problèmes de Méthode*, Proceedings of the 2nd Symposium Aristotelicum, ed. S. Mansion, Louvain and Paris 1961, revised in *Articles on Aristotle*, vol. 1. The need for many differentiae was at one stage denied by Aristotle (*Metaph.* vii 12).
[40] *Top.* vi 4.

larly, the conglomerative power of heat and cold can be used in *Meteor.* iv to explain some of their distinctive actions. In the ideal text book, these further facts would be syllogistically deduced and explained by reference to the essence. Some attack this whole project of syllogistically deducing and explaining the properties of things. Probably the single most useful point for avoiding misunderstanding is the one established by Jonathan Barnes, that Aristotle does not for one moment think of his syllogisms in the *Posterior Analytics* as providing a method for making scientific discoveries. They provide a method for expounding results already discovered.[41]

Aristotle would go further; not only can *further* properties of the thing be explained, but, in many cases, the essence is, or includes, in a way, a cause or explanation of the thing *itself*. Thus the interposition of the earth causes the moon's loss of light, and the quenching of fire causes the noise. The simplicity of the ratio explains the blending and pleasantness in consonance, and the proportion of dark to bright explains the hue, while the coagulation of sap explains the fall of leaves.

Aristotle's essences are also supposed to possess a certain unity.[42] This remains true even in the case of animal species. For when Aristotle gives a list of differentiae, he is interested in why the differentiae go together in some combinations and not in others.[43] They form mutually supportive and coherent combinations, so that the presence of one can be explained by its coherence with the others.

Not only does an Aristotelian essence *possess* unity; it also *confers* unity.[44] Heat might seem to involve a plethora of different dispositions and abilities, but these are unified when they are all related to a central conglomerative ability which constitutes its essence.[45] This unifying function of the essence is related to its *explanatory* function.

One objection sometimes made to the idea of essence is that there may be no essence, since there may be no property common to all the instances and peculiar to them. Wittgenstein has argued that games have no common essence, but only a family resemblance. As an objection to Aristotle, however, this would be misplaced. He, more than almost any philosopher, insisted that a single word can be applied to very different kinds of case, so that there is no feature common and peculiar to all the cases, but only at most a variety of complex inter-relationships between the different applications of the word.[46] In any event, he had no

---

[41] Jonathan Barnes (27.1) 1969. Further E. Kapp (27.2) 1931, distinguishes between the relevance of the syllogism to dialectic, to scientific research, and to the teaching of science. In the first two cases, one *starts* with knowledge of the conclusion, and only *subsequently* looks for premises.

[42] *Metaph.* vii 12, viii 6.   [43] *HA* i 7, 491a10–11.

[44] See *Metaph.* x 1, 1052a33, for its conferring unity on *individual* substances.

[45] *GC* ii 2.

[46] *Metaphysics* book v, for example, Aristotle's dictionary, is devoted to distinguishing and interrelating different applications of each of thirty key terms.

belief that essences were to be found everywhere. In the strictest sense, he held, only substances have them; thunder and eclipse have them only in a secondary sense.[47]

Definitions which allude to, and definitions which specify, the essence

I have now explained the terms involved in the discussion; and I can come to a point which bears directly on whether statements assigning an essence to a kind are, for Aristotle, analytic. The point is that essence can enter into a definition in two radically different ways. It may simply be *alluded* to, or it may be fully *specified*. Sometimes *part* of the essence (the genus) will be specified, while there is only an allusion to the differentia.

Hilary Putnam has repeatedly suggested over the years that by our words for such natural kinds as gold, water thunder, or multiple sclerosis, we mean something like this: that kind whose members have the same cause, structure, or other uniting property, whatever it may be, as belongs to all or most of the individual samples that we have hitherto called by the name 'gold', 'water', 'thunder', or 'multiple sclerosis'.[48] A similar view, that our words for natural kinds may refer to an unspecified uniting property or essence, was taken by Locke and Leibniz, and has been endorsed by Saul Kripke.[49] In an earlier paper, I drew attention to the relevance of this view to Aristotle.[50] He often suggests that we know what a thing is when we know its cause.[51] This idea makes sense when we are dealing with a kind like thunder, if its name means something like this: a noise in the clouds with the same cause, or other uniting property, as belongs to most of the agreed instances of thunder. If this is what we mean by 'thunder', it can throw a flood of light on what thunder is, when we discover what the cause, or other uniting property, actually is. This cause, or other uniting property, is the differentia, and hence part of the essence, of thunder.

I also argued that Aristotle did not insist on *analytic* definitions, which list logically necessary and sufficient conditions known to ordinary speakers. And I suggested, as one of several reasons for this, that many of the kinds he investigated were like thunder, in that the crucial uniting property was not yet known.

In an illuminating article, with which, however, I agree only par-

[47] *Metaph.* vii 4.
[48] Hilary Putnam (22.3) 1962, (22.4) 1965, (22.6) 1975.
[49] For Locke, see *Essay Concerning Human Understanding* 2 31 6, 3 6 44–51, 3 10 17–20. For Leibniz, see the references in H. Ishiguro (22.7) 1972, ch. 4; for Kripke, see (22.1) 1971 and (22.2) 1972.
[50] Richard Sorabji (23.1) 1969.
[51] *An. Post.* i 2, 71b9–12; ii 2; ii 8; ii 10; ii 11, 94a20–1; *Phys.* i 1, 184a12–14; ii 2, 194b18–19; *Metaph.* i 3, 983a25–6; viii 4, 1044b13. See (23.1), esp 130–2.

tially, Robert Bolton has taken the discussion further.[52] He suggests that an account of natural kinds very like that of Putnam and Kripke can be found in *An. Post.* II 7 – 10. Here Aristotle distinguishes between a definition which tells us part of the essence (*ti estin*) and a fully scientific definition of thunder (II 8, 93a21–30). The partial definition would be: 'a certain sort (*tis*) of noise in the clouds' (93a22–3). It is arguable that Aristotle would classify this definition as being an 'account of what the name "thunder" signifies' (*logos tou ti sēmainei to onoma*).[53] At any rate, he says of these accounts (*logoi*) of what the name signifies, when they are genuine definitions (*horismoi*) – and I take it not all of them are[54] – that they are accounts of the *ti esti* (II 10, 93b29), and that they differ from the full scientific definition in that they do not display the differentiating cause of thunder (II 10, 93b38 – 94a1). And both these features exactly fit the definition, 'a certain sort of noise in the clouds'. For when we possess this, we are said to be in relation to the *ti estin* (*pros*, II 8, 93a26, a29), and to have part of it (II 8, 93a22, a29). Moreover, the definition differs from the full scientific definition precisely in not displaying the differentiating cause of the noise: quenching of fire in the clouds.

Bolton argues that the word *tis* (a certain sort) is important in this account of thunder. For without this warning that thunder is only *one* sort of noise in the clouds, Aristotle could hardly claim to be telling us what the name 'thunder' signifies. But what is equally important is that the sort is merely *alluded* to, not *specified*. Indeed, at II 10, 93b38 – 94a1, as Bolton interprets it, Aristotle actually says that his account of what the name signifies 'signifies, but does not display' the differentiating cause of thunder. In other words, it *specifies* the genus 'noise in the clouds', but only *alludes* to the differentia, and therefore does not 'display' the complete essence. This interpretation will be controversial;[55] but the case need not rest on it. For the word *tis* makes it clear that the differentia is alluded to, but not specified.

Bolton suggests a further resemblance to Putnam and Kripke, which cannot, I think, be endorsed as it stands. The sort which is left unspecified is, at the pre-scientific stage, understood in terms of what is familiar to us from perceived specimens of thunder. On this interpreta-

---

[52] Robert Bolton (23.2) 1976.

[53] In this I agree with Bolton and with W. D. Ross (634–5 of *Aristotle's Prior and Posterior Analytics*, Oxford 1949) as against Jonathan Barnes (209 and 213 of (7.1)).

[54] For example, I take it that there could be (*pace* Bolton) an account of what the name 'goat-stag' signifies (II 7, 92b5–8), but that, since there are no goat-stags, it would not be a genuine definition (*horismos*), i.e. an account of the *ti esti*. See further note 59.

[55] The translation 'displays' requires us to associate the word *deiknusi* in 94a1, with the verb *dēlōn* (showing) in the previous line, rather than with the noun *apodeixis* (proof) in the following line. The whole passage reads: 'Another definition will be the account *showing* why the thing exists..So the former definition signifies but does not *deiknusi*, while the latter will clearly resemble a *proof* of the *ti esti*, though it will differ from a *proof* in having the terms differently arranged.'

tion, the allusive expression 'a certain sort' is to be understood as: 'a sort having that differentiating feature, whatever it may be, which attaches to familiar *samples* of thunder'. One good reason for rejecting this interpretation is that Aristotle denies that a definition implies the existence of instances (ɪ 2, 72a18–24; echoed at ɪ 10, 76a32–6).[56]

What is true is that the scientist discovers the differentiating cause of thunder or lunar eclipse, by examining perceived instances (see *An. Post.* ɪ 31, ɪ 34, ɪɪ 19; *Metaph.* ɪ 1; *Phys.* ɪ 1). Moreover, even before he knows the differentiating cause, a person who has the definition 'a certain noise in the clouds' or 'a certain loss of light in the moon', knows that thunder or lunar eclipse exists, and this not merely in an accidental way (ɪɪ 8, 93a21–9; cf. 93b2–3), even though 93a29–33 reveals that he may know it only in rather a weak way. Perhaps[57] he knows that noises occur in the clouds, without yet knowing that noises *due to quenching of fire* occur in the clouds, or even that the noises form a scientifically viable kind with a uniting cause. Some commentators would object[58] that in ɪɪ 10, 93b29–35, the man who merely possesses an account of what a name signifies is implied, after all, to have merely accidental knowledge that instances exist. But if I was right to argue that this passage in chapter 10 is interested in definitions like 'a certain noise in the clouds', it would be a mistake to construe it as saying something which flatly contradicts what was said in chapter 8 about such definitions. For it can instead be interpreted quite smoothly as saying exactly the same thing, namely, that those who possess such definitions are to be *contrasted* with (not assimilated to) people who have merely accidental knowledge that instances of thunder exist.[59] There is, then, this

[56] Bolton seeks to reinterpret the second passage in his note 15, but does not take account of the first.

[57] This is suggested by J. L. Ackrill's contribution to (27.6); I am grateful to him for discussion.

[58] Such is the interpretation of Jonathan Barnes (209; 213 of (7.1)) and of J. L. Ackrill in (27.6).

[59] I have profited here from discussion with Dr Raaron Gillon, although I do not know whether he agrees with the interpretation. I would construe ɪɪ 10, 93b32–5 as follows. The man who possesses an account of what the name signifies which is also a genuine definition (*horismos*) of the *ti esti*, and who (sc. therefore) knows that the thing defined exists, can go on to seek its *cause*. He is to be contrasted with (d', 93b33), not assimilated to, the man who does not know that it exists (sc. except accidentally). The latter will find it hard to grasp in the causal way (*houtōs labein*) the thing whose existence he knows at best accidentally. And the reason for the difficulty, as has been said (sc. in ɪɪ 8, 93a21–9) is precisely that his knowledge of existence is at best accidental.

Those who construe the passage differently have various ways of trying to avoid a contradiction between chapters 8 and 10. Jonathan Barnes, for example, p. 209 of (7.1), does not accept the view that the two passages are interested in the same kind of definition. But my argument for this view is given in the main text above. Bolton would avoid a contradiction by saying that the passage in chapter 10, 93b29–35, is interested *not only* in definitions like 'a certain noise in the clouds', *but also* in merely *accidental* descriptions of thunder or lunar eclipse, like 'the moon's inability to cast shadows, though there is no obstacle between her and us'. We are meant to understand (without warning) (a) that Aristotle is talking about people who possess *only* this description; (b) that they

resemblance to Putnam and Kripke, that possession of either kind of account of thunder, of the one with or the one without the differentiating cause specified, involves *knowledge* that there are instances, even though the account itself does not imply the existence of instances.

To summarise the relation between definition and existence, as I see it, an account of what the name 'goat-stag' signifies does not qualify for the honorific title of *horismos* (definition), and does not amount to an account of *ti esti*, because goat-stags do not exist (ii 7, 92b5–8). None the less, there are accounts of what a name signifies which do qualify as *horismoi* and as accounts of *ti esti* (ii 10, 93b29–30), and an example would be the account of thunder as a certain noise in the clouds. These accounts *qualify* as accounts of *ti esti* only so long as instances of the thing defined exist (ii 7, 92b5–8), and a man will be said to *possess* one of these accounts only so long as he *knows* in some sense that instances exist (ii 8, 93a20–9, in agreement with ii 10, 93b32). This is perfectly compatible with Aristotle's denial (i 2, 72a18–24; i 10, 76a32–6) that the defining formula itself carries an implication of existence.

There is one more point of resemblance to Putnam and Kripke, this one not noticed by Bolton.[60] Aristotle recognises, in *Phys.* i 1, 184b12–14, that the refinement of concepts may involve us in revising our opinion about what to count as genuine samples. As the child refines his concept of *father*, he comes to recognise that he should not have called *all* men 'father'.

Starting from the preliminary definition of thunder, the scientist goes on to discover the full definition, which specifies the previously undiscovered differentia. On one theory, thunder is a noise *produced by quenching of fire* in the clouds. In referring to the quenching of fire (if that is the correct theory), the scientific definition is going beyond what is known to ordinary speakers. After all, it was only one theory, and not a theory Aristotle himself accepted, that the differentia in question was quenching.[61]

---

are a subgroup of those introduced at 93b29–32 as having an account of what the name signifies, which is at the same time a genuine definition and an account of *ti esti*; (c) that Aristotle's lament, 93b32–5, that certain people have only *accidental* knowledge of existence, applies *only* to this *subgroup*, not to the others whom he has introduced for discussion. My difficulty with (a) and (b) is that I wonder whether a man who possessed *only* an accidental description would be said (93b29) to have a genuine definition, and account of the *ti esti*. My difficulty with (a), (b) and (c) is that we have not been prepared to expect them. The passage ii 8, 93a37 – b3 has not prepared us, for it is concerned with a *different* group of people, namely, people who *know* (93b3) that lunar eclipse exists, presumably (so J. L. Ackrill has pointed out to me) because they possess *not only* the description 'the moon's inability (etc.)', *but also* the description 'a certain loss of light'.

[60] Indeed, Bolton takes the passage differently as implying that the child is progressing towards a concept of *man*, rather than refining his concept of *father* by coming to realise that fathers are differentiated from other men.

[61] *Meteor.* ii 9.

Aristotle's necessities of essence are not all analytic, because essences are not all knowable a priori

I can now discuss the question of analyticity. Jan Lukasiewicz has maintained that Aristotle treats his scientific definitions as analytic.[62] His reason seems to be that Aristotle treats them as *necessary*, and Lukasiewicz thought of analytic truths as the only necessary ones. He considered Aristotle's idea to have been 'disastrous for philosophy'. 'If we want to know what the "essence" of man is – if there is such a thing as "essence" at all – we cannot rely on the meanings of words but must investigate human individuals themselves.'

Lukasiewicz's criticism turns on the point that analytic judgments are knowable *a priori*, and that *a priori* investigation is quite inappropriate here. The reason why analytic judgments are knowable *a priori*, it will be recalled, is that the predicate cannot be contained analytically within the concept of the subject, if someone who possessed that concept would need *further* experience, in order to know that the predicate applied.

Three French writers have taken the same view as Lukasiewicz, and maintained that Aristotle treated his scientific definitions as analytic, though two of the three have added that Aristotle tended to confuse analytic necessity, which holds between concepts, with a real necessity which attaches to things themselves.[63]

The most careful proponent of the analytic interpretation is Suzanne Mansion, who discusses the question in the course of her important and illuminating book on Aristotle's philosophy of science. Her main evidence is that Aristotle is talking of a relationship in which one term belongs to another, and she cites *An. Post.* I 4, 73a34 – b24.[64] But this is not quite enough to establish that Aristotle views the statements in question as analytic. We must consider, for one thing, whether he thinks them knowable *a priori*. In her own discussion, Mansion recognises that we do not have analyticity here in quite the same sense as Kant's.[65] But the reason she gives is merely that subject and predicate each refer to an essence. What needs to be added is that in giving the definition of thunder, the speaker merely *alludes* to the differentia without specifying it, when he uses the subject term 'thunder', but in attaching the predicate, he *specifies* the differentia. Someone who knows what the name 'thunder' signifies therefore needs *further* experience to know the

[62] J. Lukasiewicz, *Aristotle's Syllogistic from the Standpoint of Modern Formal Logic*, Oxford 1st edition 1951, 2nd ed. 1957, 205–6, and 'The principle of individuation', *Proceedings of the Aristotelian Society*, supp. vol. 27, 1953, 74–6.

[63] J. M. Le Blond, *Logique et Méthode chez Aristote*, Paris 1939, 92. J. Chevalier, *La Notion du Nécessaire chez Aristote et chez ses Prédécesseurs, particulièrement chez Platon*, Paris 1915. S. Mansion (27.3) 1946, 2nd ed. 1976, ch. 4. The confusion is detected by Chevalier and Mansion.

[64] S. Mansion, op. cit. 71.   [65] S. Mansion, note 14.

complete essence. In her second edition, Mansion quite rightly adds that because Aristotle's definitions state essences, we must turn to reality, rather than just to the meanings of words, in order to discover them.[66] But once this much is acknowledged, it would seem that Aristotle's definitional truths, not being knowable *a priori*, should no longer be viewed as analytic in anything like Kant's sense.

I think this point is on its own sufficient to make the case. Admittedly, it may have been analytic that thunder was a noise but it cannot have been analytic that it was due to the quenching of fire, because this was not something that could be known *a priori*, that is, without further experience, by those who possessed the ordinary concept of thunder from which Aristotle started. The same applies to Aristotle's example of lunar eclipse. The ordinary concept from which Aristotle started may have implied that it was a loss of light by the moon, but it would have taken further experience to know the differentia – the mechanism that produced this loss of light. Even nowadays many people are unaware (though Aristotle was not) that lunar eclipse involves a different mechanism from solar: the casting of a shadow on the eclipsed object.

The need for further experience may well be the reason why Aristotle tells us that we cannot know *what* a thing is until we know *that* it is (*An. Post.* II 1, 89b34; II 2, 89b38 – 90a1, 90a22–3; II 7, 92b4–8; II 8, 93a20, a26–7, 93b33–5). Although we can know what a *name* like 'goat-stag' signifies, he says, we cannot know what a goat-stag actually *is*. The reason is presumably that to discover the full essence of a natural kind takes empirical investigation. Aristotle advocates the very thing which Lukasiewicz supposed he overlooked. To discover the essence of man, he would think we had to investigate human individuals.

The examples of thunder and lunar eclipse are not exceptional. Many of the essences I have mentioned could not be known in full *a priori*. This would be true, for example, for the essences of animal species, of consonance, of colours, of deciduousness, and of heat and cold. The passage in *Top.* VI 4 explicitly warned us that we should not expect defining characteristics to be features known to ordinary speakers.

I must now consider an objection from those who think that for Aristotle all statements giving the essence of a kind are analytic. The claim that thunder is a noise in the clouds due to the quenching of fire will have a different status, according to whether the speaker is employing Aristotle's pre-scientific concept or his scientific concept, when he talks of thunder. As Aristotle's scientific concept began to replace the pre-scientific one, the claim that thunder was a noise in the clouds due to the quenching of fire would become analytic; for it would merely spell out what was contained in the scientific concept, without exploiting empirical information beyond that contained in the concept.

[66] S. Mansion, new note 17, on p. 319.

To this objection I would reply, first, that we are not, concerned with the status which Aristotle's definitions might eventually acquire, but with the status they have originally. Secondly, Aristotle would be advised not to cut himself off altogether from the pre-scientific concept of thunder. He would need that concept not only for first formulating his discovery of the differentia, but also for imparting that discovery as a discovery to the uninstructed. If, moreover, he were to abandon the pre-scientific concept altogether, he could not claim to be concerned with thunder in the same sense as those who had embedded rival theories in their scientific concepts; and, in the event of his finding that there was after all no quenching of fire in the clouds, he would have to admit that thunder, as he had been using the term, did not even exist.

A variant of the present suggestion would be that, for the limited purposes of his ideal text book on meteorology, Aristotle might wish to *stipulate* that 'thunder' should be taken to mean the same as 'noise in the clouds due to the quenching of fire'. It would then become analytic within the system of that text book that thunder was such a noise. This would be a possible course for Aristotle to take: but I do not see any reason why he need take it, or any very clear evidence that he does. Both variants of the present suggestion, in any case, fall a long way short of supporting Lukasiewicz's charge of *a priorism*. For the process of making the scientific definition analytic, whether by stipulation or by gradual evolution, would depend on Aristotle's first discovering, and his hearers accepting, that the definition could safely be accepted as a *non*-analytic proposition.

I conclude that it is not true that for Aristotle all statements giving the essence of a kind are analytic. No doubt, some are, but there are many scientific definitions which at least do not start off as analytic.

If Aristotle's scientific definitions are not all analytic, this leaves us free to ask whether they are in some cases necessary *de re*. I shall cite three pieces of evidence. The first two will concern statements about *individuals*, and will suggest that Aristotle committed himself in some instances to a necessity which we can classify as *de re*. The third goes further: it concerns statements about *kinds*, and suggests that Aristotle himself drew a distinction which corresponds to that between a *de re* and a *de dicto* statement of essence.

Is there evidence that some necessities of essence are de re?

The most discussed passage is *An. Pr.* I 9, 30a15–23. Here Aristotle permits inference to a modal conclusion, when the minor premise is not modal. To supply an illustration where Aristotle's text has none: 'Every human is *necessarily* rational. Every animal in this room is human (no modal word). Therefore every animal in this room is *necessarily* rational.'

It is hard to make sense of this inference, unless we take the modal word as going closely with the predicate 'rational', to form a complex predicate 'necessarily-rational'. It will be implied that anything which is human, or which is an animal in this room, has the property of being necessarily-rational. If so, the necessity will be *de re* by one of our tests.

It will also be *de re* by the other. For if we took some particular animal in the room, Aristotle would presumably allow us to call it necessarily rational *regardless* of how we described it. He could hardly suppose that the necessity of its being rational depended on the description 'animal in this room'.

There is a second piece of evidence that some of Aristotle's necessities are *de re*. He discusses premises of the form 'Some A is necessarily B'. An example that occurs twice is '*Some white things are necessarily animals*'.[67] Others are that some white things are necessarily not animals, some men are necessarily white, some necessarily not, some lifeless things are necessarily white, some necessarily not.[68]

Again, it is hard to make sense of any of these examples, unless we take the modal word closely with the predicate. It will not be true that some white things are necessarily animals, unless there is something which is white and which is necessarily-an-animal. Moreover, if we take one of the individual white things which is necessarily an animal, the necessity of its being an animal can hardly depend on its being described as white.

The *de re* implications of *An. Pr.* ɪ 9 were already discussed by the mediaevals,[69] and were picked out again by A. Becker.[70] But Becker argued that Aristotle's practice cannot be viewed as consistent, if we consider his rules for the conversion of modal premises in *An. Pr.* ɪ 3.[71] Here, at 25a27–36, Aristotle allows us to infer that if necessarily A belongs to all or to some B, then necessarily B belongs to some A. Supplying an example, we can make sense of this contention, if we take Aristotle to mean that if it is necessary that there are losers some or all of whom are competitors, then it is necessary that there are competitors some of whom are losers. The necessities here must be taken as *de dicto*. We cannot understand Aristotle's view as relating to *de re* necessities. For no one would want to argue that if some or all losers are born competitors, it follows that some competitors are born losers.

I now turn to the third piece of evidence, which bears on statements ascribing an essence to *kinds*, and this one, unlike the others, I have not seen discussed. The relevant lines, *PA* ɪɪ 2, 649a13–24 and ɪɪ 3, 649b20–7, read as follows.

---

[67] *An. Pr.* ɪ 9, 30b5–6; ɪ 16, 36b12–18. These examples are recorded by Joan Kung, 'Aristotle on essence and explanation', *Philosophical Studies* 31, 1977, 361–83.

[68] *An. Pr.* ɪ 16, 36b12–18.   [69] See W. Kneale (24.1).

[70] A. Becker (28.1) 1933, 39.   [71] A. Becker, op. cit. 42.

Some things of this sort cannot even be called hot or not hot without qualification. For whatever the substratum happens to be is not hot, but when coupled (*sunduazomenon*) is hot. It is as if a special name were given to hot water or to hot iron. This is the way in which blood is hot; and these cases in which the substratum is hot because something has been done to it (*kata pathos*) make it clear that cold is not just a privation but something with a nature of its own. Possibly even fire may be a thing of this kind. For perhaps its substratum is either smoke or charcoal, of which the former is always hot, because smoke is an exhalation, but charcoal, once quenched, is cold . . .

With these distinctions made, it is clear that in this way blood is hot. For it is spoken of in the same way as we should speak of boiling water, if we marked it with a special name. The substratum and that whose existence constitutes blood is not hot; and in one way blood is in itself (*kath' hauto*) hot, in another not. For heat will be in its definition (*logos*), in the way that pale is in the definition of pale man. But insofar as the substratum is hot through having something done to it (*kata pathos*), blood is not in itself hot.

In these lines Aristotle considers whether blood is *in itself* (*kath' hauto*) hot, and declares that in one sense it is, and in one sense it is not. What interests me is the sense in which it is *not*, for here, I suspect, the in-itself relationship may be *de re*.

First, however, what is the sense in which blood *is* in itself hot? Aristotle makes a comparison. Suppose we gave a special name to boiling water, 'H': then in a sense H would be in itself hot; for heat would enter into its definition. In the same way, pale enters into the definition of pale man. None the less, the water which we called by the name 'H' would not be hot, except in virtue of having something done to it (*kata pathos*), and by being coupled with heat (*sunduazomenon*). Similarly, the subject to which we give the name 'blood' is not hot, except in virtue of having something done to it. Moreover, blood is in itself hot only through having heat in its definition, as H would. It is not in itself hot in the other way.

What is the other way? It seems to me significant that Aristotle says of *one and the same* subject, blood, that in a way it is in itself hot and in a way it is not. He is not merely talking of two *different* subjects. This suggests the following interpretation: neither blood, nor any sample of blood, can be described by the complex predicate 'in itself hot'. We can only take the whole sentence 'Blood is hot', and say that it expresses an in itself proposition. Alternatively, we cannot say of blood, nor of any sample of blood, that, however described, it is in itself hot. The in itself relationship which is here said to be missing appears to be *de re*. If so, the implication is that there will be *other* cases, unlike the case of blood, in which there *is* a *de re* relationship.

On the other side, it may be thought that some passages tell against the idea that the modal word can ever govern the predicate. Thus Aristotle defines the *terms* (*horoi*) of a syllogism as being subject and predicate, for example, 'human' and 'rational', with the proviso that the connecting verb 'to be' does not form part of either.[72] And in *An. Pr.* I 8, 29b36 – 30a2 he may appear to associate the modal word neither with the whole sentence 'every human is rational', nor with the predicate 'rational', but simply with the connecting verb 'is'. At any rate, he says there is little difference between syllogisms from necessary premises and syllogisms from premises which merely assert. The terms may be exactly the same, and the difference will be that the connective added to the terms is 'belongs of necessity' rather than just 'belongs'. So far as I can see, however, one would not be justified in reading into this claim a denial that the modal word can govern the predicate 'rational'. No particular doctrine on this question seems to be intended.

There is one other idea which has been thought to imply that all modal statements are *de dicto*. In *Int.* 12, 21b29 and 22a8–9, Aristotle suggests that we might think of 'is' in 'A man *is* white' as a sort of subject (*hupokeimenon*) to which 'it is possible' and 'it is not possible' are additions (*prostheseis*). Whether the resulting modal statement is affirmative or negative depends on the quality of the *addition*, *not* on the quality of the 'is' with which we started. Another passage, *An. Pr.* I 3, 25b19–25, agrees in doctrine. W. Kneale takes this as evidence that the modal word is treated in a *de dicto* way as saying something about the whole proposition that a man is white.[73] But Aristotle's point is very limited, and would apply equally to *de re* possibility. In the *de re* modal statement that Socrates is not capable of being white, the quality (affirmative or negative) of the whole statement depends on the quality of the modal term, not on the quality of 'being'.

I conclude that this is not counter evidence to the claim that Aristotle is willing to treat modalities as *de re*, by one or other of the tests described above. We have seen reason to think that he sometimes does so, both in connexion with statements giving the essence of a kind, and in connexion with statements giving the essence of an individual.

A major attack on *de re* interpretations has been launched by Nicholas White. His argument is restricted to the essences of particular individuals for he thinks that Aristotle very likely treats the essences of kinds differently. His article is full of interest, but on the central issue I find myself in disagreement. White is talking of singular propositions whose necessity is *de re* by the criterion that the designation of the subject can be varied. He holds that it would be a philosophical mistake to treat statements of essence as necessary *de re*, and in arguing that Aristotle does not do so, he views himself as defending Aristotle from Quine's charge.[74]

---

[72] *An. Pr.* I 1, 24b16–18.
[73] W. Kneale (24.1) 622–3.
[74] Nicholas White, 'Origins of Aristotle's essentialism', *Review of Metaphysics* 26, 1972–3, 57–85.

A large part of his argument is that Aristotle cannot be proved to be thinking in terms of *de re* necessity in many of the places where he has been thought to be doing so. This argument is good, as far as it goes, but White does not consider any of the evidence discussed above.

The most extensive remaining line of argument is that Aristotle did not have the equipment for formulating the idea of *de re* necessity in the way that certain people do nowadays. Some of this argument, incidentally, ought to apply as much to the essences of kinds as to the essences of individuals. In neither case, however, is it enough to answer the view that Aristotle commits himself to *de re* necessity, whether he formulates the idea or not.

I am not in any case convinced that Aristotle would have lacked the equipment for formulating the distinction. For one thing, I think it is debatable whether Aristotle was as confused about the placing of modal operators as White argues.[75] Further, he seems to have been clear-headed, when in *SE* he drew the distinction between compounded and divided possibilities. And this is the very distinction that was used in the mediaeval period for separating *de dicto* from *de re*. He expresses the distinction by contrasting two Greek locutions: *echei dunamin tou mē graphōn graphein* and *echei dunamin hote ou graphei tou graphein* (166a28–30). The Greek uses a battery of distinguishing devices, one of which is the placing of the word *tou*. The nearest English equivalent might be the placing of 'of' in the two expressions 'He has the power of not writing while writing' and 'He has the power when he is not writing of writing'. Finally, there is more than one way of trying to separate *de dicto* from *de re*, and the one that White himself actually relies on turns on alternative designations of the subject in a singular proposition. We saw Aristotle coming close to *this* formulation in his discussion of water and *hot* water in *PA*. And in general, he shows some awareness of the question of when we can interchange designations *salva veritate*. Two other instances play a role in this book. At *NE* v 8, 1135a28–30 and *EE* ii 9, 1225b3–6, he points out that the same action can be one of voluntarily and knowingly striking a man, and of involuntarily and unknowingly striking one's father. At *Phys.* ii 3, 195a27 – b30, he explains with regard

[75] Storrs McCall congratulates Aristotle on his placing of modal operators in *Int.* (op. cit. 36). On the other side, White offers three pieces of evidence for the charge of confusion: first, that of Becker, which was described above. Secondly, Gunther Patzig points out an oversight on Aristotle's part. Aristotle thinks of the necessity of a conclusion as *relative* to the truth of the premises, but does not see that there is an *absolute* necessity which attaches to the conditional which has as its *antecedent* the conjunction of the premises, and as its *consequent* the conclusion. I am not clear, however, that this *oversight* amounts to a *confusion* about the placing of modal operators. Finally, G. E. M. Anscombe has a hypothesis that Aristotle is unsure about the placing of modal operators, and for that reason switches in *Metaph.* iv 4, 1007a20 from discussing the law of contradiction, 'Necessarily (if *p*, then not-not-*p*)' to discussing the idea that an *in-itself* predication yields a necessary proposition. This passage is differently interpreted, however, by R. M. Dancy, *Sense and Contradiction* Dordrecht 1975, ch. 5.

to Polyclitus, the sculptor, that Polyclitus is an accidental cause, the sculptor a non-accidental cause, of a statue. I have mentioned other instances elsewhere.[76]

Plato's treatment of necessities of nature

Plato's treatment of necessity has been the subject of some analogous controversy. In the *Phaedo* (103c – 107a), he discusses sentences like 'fire is hot' (103c–d) and 'Fire imparts heat' (105b–d), and he seems to think of them as expressing necessities. The talk of necessity is explicit at 104d.

If there is any kind of necessity here at all, I would expect it to be a *causal* one.[77] I doubt if there is any *logical* necessity that fire is hot or imparts heat. Certainly, there is not, if we take a logically necessary truth as one which is forced on us by the meanings of the logical particles alone ('not', 'if', 'then', 'and', etc.). But even if we take logical necessity more loosely as any kind of conceptual necessity, it would be hard to show that there was one here. No doubt, in order to make sure, we should have to inspect the idea of heat as well as that of fire, to rule out any analytic connexion between them, and to rule out the possibility that thought experiments, of the kind to be discussed in the next chapter, might show that both were associated with some one and the same essence, such as molecular motion.[78]

Plato's view, however, according to Gregory Vlastos, is that the necessities here are *logical*. Vlastos further argues that Plato thinks any causal necessities there may be in the picture are *grounded on* and *reducible to* logical ones.[79] These two claims need to be distinguished, since the second is very much more startling than the first. It is not particularly surprising if people think that 'Fire is hot' and 'Fire imparts heat' are analytic. This is to think that we would not count some imaginary stuff as fire, if it was not hot, or did not impart heat. This view may be mistaken, as I believe, but it involves no commitment to the

[76] See *SE* 179a26 – b6 on objects of knowledge; *Poet.* ch. 4 on enjoying a picture *qua* splash of colour, while not enjoying it *qua* representation; *Phys.* 202a19–20, b10–16 on the same road being uphill and downhill. These instances are collected in 'Body and soul in Aristotle', *Philosophy* 49, 1974, footnote 37.

[77] The same goes for 'Snow is cold' (103c-d), and 'Heat melts snow', if that is in view at 103d; 106a. On the other hand 'Fever imparts sickness' (105c) could be an analytic statement, seeing that Aristotle defines fever as a *species* of sickness (*Top.* 123b35–6), and Plato seems to treat it the same way at *Timaeus* 86a. Vlastos objects against this last that we would not have an example of Plato's so-called 'clever', i.e. informative, explanation of someone's sickness, if fever were being viewed as a *species* of sickness. But why would not this explanation be informative? See footnote 72 of Gregory Vlastos (17.4) 1969.

[78] Aristotle also discusses the status of the claim that fire is essentially hot, and treats it somewhat like the claim discussed earlier, that blood is essentially hot (*PA* ii 2, 649a20–3). Fire is essentially hot in one sense, but insofar as the matter of fire is powdered charcoal, it is *not* essentially hot.

[79] Vlastos, op. cit.; see 320–1, 325 for this conclusion.

much more extreme view that any causal necessities in the picture can be *reduced* to logical ones. On the contrary, the believer in analyticity is free to hold that there is some causal necessity which makes heat and imparting of heat accompany the other characteristics of fire. If there is any grounding in either direction, it may be this causal necessity that persuaded him to build the ideas of heat and of imparting heat analytically into the meaning of the word 'fire'.

What then is the basis of Vlastos' interpretation? The main evidence is that (a) fire is said to be hot and to impart heat because of relations of entailment between Forms. And relations between Forms are (b) immutable, and (c) knowable *a priori*.[80] The claim in (a) has been disputed.[81] If it is accepted, however, then without dwelling on other complications,[82] we can agree that Plato is treating 'Fire is hot' and 'Fire imparts heat' as analytic, though that would not be his way of putting the matter, and hence as (in a broad sense) *logically* necessary.

But need Plato also have taken the more extreme view that any causal necessities involved are *reducible* to logical ones? May he not simply be *ignoring* the status of causal necessities for the time being? He does reach the subject of the causal necessities involved much later in the *Timaeus*. There at 61D – 62A, he explains why fire is hot by reference to the rending, cutting, cleaving and mincing effect of its small, angular corpuscles. And he is prepared to talk of necessity in this sort of connexion: things are moved by others and *of necessity* set yet others in motion (46E 1–2). But so far from *reducing* this necessity, which we should class as causal, to logical necessity, he distinguishes it even more sharply than a modern philosopher would. He associates it with the 'wandering' cause, which produces chance results without order (46E, 48A). Admittedly, I agree with Glen Morrow, against some others, that he allows quite a lot of *regularity* to these causal necessities,[83] and he also allows that God can have a kind of knowledge of such things (68D 6). True knowledge, however, cannot be had of fire corpuscles, but only of the *Form* of fire and other Forms (51B – 52B). And physical bodies are incapable of perfectly regular behaviour (*Republic* 529D, 530A–B;

---

[80] Vlastos 320.

[81] Concerning (a), there is a rival interpretation, according to which it is not the *Form* fire that is said to bring on the Form heat, but common or garden fire in the grate, and the bringing on is not a logical relation like entailment. See the full explanation of 103C – 107A by D. Gallop, *Plato: Phaedo*, Clarendon Plato Series, Oxford 1975.

[82] A modern philosopher, told that he was dealing with an immutable relation, would not necessarily rule out its being a merely causal one. For there is a sense in which causal relations can be regarded as immutable: circumstances that would alter a universal accident would not alter a causal law. None the less, if our philosopher was further told that the relation was knowable *a priori*, he would conclude that the relation, even if a causal one like fire's imparting heat, must have been built analytically into the meaning of the word 'fire', so that one who had the relevant concept of fire would need no *further* experience to know that fire imparted heat.

[83] Glenn R. Morrow (17.2) 1965, esp. 428.

Statesman 269D–E). All this would have to represent a change of mind, if he had performed a *reduction* in the *Phaedo* of causal to logical necessity. But I doubt if he there did more than treat certain causal relations as if they were analytically built into the meaning of the word 'fire'.

CHAPTER THIRTEEN

Why Necessary rather than Contingent?

A new question now becomes acute. Aristotle escapes Lukasiewicz's criticism, if his scientific definitions are in some cases not analytic. But will he not run into the objections of Quine, who denies that there are any *de re* necessities,[1] and of J. J. C. Smart and others who have maintained that many scientific definitions are contingent rather than necessary?[2] Examples of definitions described in the literature as contingent are the propositions that heat is molecular motion, water is H_2O, and gold the element with atomic number 79 (i.e. 79 protons in the nucleus of each atom). Why does not Aristotle accept that some scientific definitions are contingent?

When I ask why Aristotle views his scientific definitions as necessary, rather than contingent, it may be thought that the answer is obvious. Scientific definitions are, for Aristotle, statements which assign an *essence* to a kind, and it is just part of his *concept* of essence that a statement of essence is a necessary truth. This answer, however, does not get to the root of my question. I am, in effect, asking *why* Aristotle should make it part of his concept of essence that a statement of essence is necessary. After all, one way in which Aristotle refers to essences is by the phrase *ti estin*: what the thing is. A statement of a thing's essence, then, has to tell us what it is. No doubt, it has to do this in a special way, giving the genus and differentia, revealing the unity in a large collection of specimens, and providing the means for explaining superficial features. But why should it combine these roles with also being a necessary truth?

When I return to Aristotle's concept of essence below, it will become apparent that the account of essence just sketched is oversimplified, and

---

[1] For Quine, see Chapter Twelve, note 7.

[2] The most influential articles have been those of U. T. Place, 'Is consciousness a brain process?' *British Journal of Psychology* 47, 1956, 44–50; H. Feigl, 'The "Mental" and the "Physical" ', in H. Feigl, M. Scriven, G. Maxwell (eds), *Minnesota Studies in the Philosophy of Science* vol. 2, Minneapolis 1958; and J. J. C. Smart, 'Sensations and brain processes', *Philosophical Review* 68, 1959, 141–56. The articles by Place and Smart are reprinted, along with some of the literature to which they gave rise, in C. V. Borst (ed.), *The Mind-Brain Identity Theory*, London 1970; and John O'Connor (ed.), *Modern Materialism: Readings on mind-body identity*, New York 1969.

that there is more to being an essence than I have yet said. But at this point, a contemporary reader may be struck by the resemblance between Aristotle's views and those recently put forward by Saul Kripke.[3] For Kripke maintains that statements giving the essences of what he calls natural kinds do indeed involve a non-analytic, *de re* necessity. If their conclusions are so similar, it may be wondered whether their reasons are similar as well. In the end, I shall answer this question negatively. But first let me emphasise the points of resemblance between Aristotle and Kripke.

Kripke

One point of resemblance, noticed in the last chapter, was that Kripke and Aristotle, along with Locke, Leibniz and Putnam, agree that our words for kinds often contain an allusion to an essence or differentia whose exact character is not specified. There was the difference, however, that Aristotle did not share Kripke's view that the allusion is made *via* familiar samples.

The claim that a correct specification of the essence will have some kind of necessity is a further step. But here too, as we have seen, Aristotle and Kripke would agree, and so would Leibniz and Putnam.[4] Kripke explains that the necessity of which he is talking is necessity 'in the highest degree'.[5]

Aristotle and Kripke are further agreed that the truth of their necessary propositions is, in many cases, knowable only *a posteriori*. In this, their view differs from that of Kant, who held that necessary truths are all knowable *a priori*.[6]

Insofar as the definitions which concern Aristotle and Kripke are knowable only *a posteriori*, they are not *analytic*. This gives them still more in common. Someone who was looking for an *analytic* definition of lunar eclipse would think that a differentia like *interposition of the earth between sun and moon* was too narrow. It would cover all *actual* examples of lunar eclipse, but would not, on such a view, be wide enough to cover all conceptually possible examples. The definer would need to *stretch* his differentia, with a view to covering non-actual instances. Kripke, like Aristotle, shows no such concern. The scientist who discovers what gold is *actually* identical with has *thereby* discovered what it is *necessarily* identical with, on Kripke's view, and need not *stretch* his definition.

The comparison goes further still. Just as Aristotle treats the neces-

---

[3] For Kripke, see (22.1) 1971 and (22.2) 1972.

[4] For Leibniz's view, see the excellent discussion in Hidé Ishiguro (22.7) 1972, ch. 4. For Putnam, see (22.6) 1975. Locke's views are qualified: individuals have a real essence attaching necessarily to them, only in so far as they are described as falling under a certain sort (3 6 6); kinds only probably have a real essence (3 6 36).

[5] Kripke (22.2) 1972, 304, 769.   [6] Kant, *Critique of Pure Reason*, B 4.

sity, at least in certain instances, as *de re*, so also does Kripke, although his account of the *de re* is not quite the same as any of those given in the last chapter.

Surprisingly, in spite of all this similarity, Kripke does not mention Aristotle as an ally. On the contrary, he speaks as if anyone who believes in defining by genus and differentia must have a view radically opposed to his own. He connects such a belief with an idea he rejects, that a definition will give the *connotation* of a word.[7] Such definitions would be analytic. We have seen, however, that it is a mistake to suppose that Aristotle's scientific definitions of thunder and lunar eclipse are like this.

Lunar eclipse and thunder

My question, why Aristotle should view scientific definitions as necessary, will seem to have no bite to those who consider this the natural view to take. Let me therefore consider two kinds which are favourite examples for Aristotle: lunar eclipse and thunder. Is it simply obvious, on reflection, that proper definitions of these will be necessary truths? In considering whether a case can be made for saying so, I shall make use of Kripke's techniques alongside others, and particularly of his technique of thought experiment. But I cannot hope here to do justice to his rich discussion. I believe he does enable us to see that there is necessity in many places where we might have supposed that there was contingency. But I doubt if he could succeed in doing so with all examples, and in particular with some of the examples which interest Aristotle most.

Let us start with the genera of thunder and lunar eclipse, and suppose that they are, as Aristotle says, noise in the clouds and loss of light by the moon. Anyone who thinks it *necessary* that the genera are what they are might think it easiest to argue for an *analytic* necessity. But even this would be quite difficult to establish. We know now, for example, that there are such things as radio eclipses, and Aristotle would have known that many of his fellow Greeks, unlike himself, believed in bolts from the blue, i.e. in thunder without clouds,[8] though doubtless not in thunder without noise. Of course, we accept that all lunar eclipse does *in fact* involve loss of light, and all thunder cloud; but is this truth analytic?

What happens when we turn to the differentiae? Let these be, for example, quenching of fire in the clouds and interposition of the earth between sun and moon. Here Aristotle speaks of a necessity which we

---

[7] Kripke (22.2) 327. On connoting and denoting, see John Stuart Mill, *A System of Logic*, London 1846, book i, ch. ii § 5.

[8] See Xenophon *Hellenica* 7 1 31; Cratinus, fragment 53, ed. Koch; Homer *Odyssey* xx 113.

should classify as causal, although that is not one of his categories. Quenching necessitates noise, and is therefore *sufficient* to produce the noise we call thunder,[9] but it is much harder to see why it should be *necessary*. Why should not something *else* have produced the noise or loss of light, in which case the differentiae would have been different from what they are?

Would an appeal to thought experiments help? We may find that we cannot coherently imagine an *individual* lunar eclipse having a different cause from the one it in fact has and still retaining its identity. One strategy would be to try and argue from the inconceivability of the *individual* eclipse having a different cause to the inconceivability of the *kind* having a different cause. This would seem a very appropriate strategy, given the view taken by Kripke (but not, we have seen, by Aristotle), that the kind is conceived by reference to instances: it has the same essence as belongs to certain familiar samples.

Even so, may not the kind admit of more variation than an individual before it loses its identity? Perhaps the *individual* lunar eclipse could not have had a different cause and retained its identity. Yet the *kind* lunar eclipse might have admitted of *extra* instances involving a different sort of causal mechanism from any that is actually found. We already recognise a difference of mechanism as between lunar eclipse, which involves a shadow, and solar, which does not. Admittedly, this treatment of imaginary situations implies a modification of the idea that by lunar eclipse the layman means lunar loss of light whose instances have the same cause as belongs (sc. in the *actual* situation) to all or most of the *actual* instances which we have called lunar eclipse. For in the imaginary situation envisaged, there are two mechanisms by which lunar eclipse occurs, only *one* of them being the mechanism actually attaching to actual instances. But the concept of lunar eclipse surely admits this degree of flexibility.

Perhaps lunar eclipse will be considered a special case: it is because eclipses in general (lunar and non-lunar) exhibit more than one mechanism that we are prepared to imagine more than one mechanism for *lunar* eclipse. Perhaps too someone might prefer to start by defining eclipses in general, and, when asked to define lunar eclipse, would differentiate it merely as eclipse befalling the moon. But if so, he could not hope to elucidate Aristotle's procedure, which is different. Moreover, such a treatment of lunar eclipses could not be extended to thunder.

My conclusion is that the question posed still needs an answer. It is not obvious simply from reflection on lunar eclipse and thunder why their definitions should be *necessary* truths. In order to see why Aristotle believes that they are, I think we shall need to go into very different kinds of consideration from any advanced so far.

---

[9] See *An. Post.* ii 8, 93b7–14, if this has in mind the premise that noise belongs necessarily to the quenching of fire, and more explicitly ii 11, 94b32–3.

Aristotle's reasons

The first point to be made is that I have so far underplayed the metaphysical element in Aristotle's conception of essence. It is true that he sometimes refers to essence *via* the neutral phrase *ti estin*: what a thing is. But he also uses expressions which are metaphysically more charged, particularly the notion of *being*. Thus at *At. Post.* I 4, 73a35–7, in explaining the notion of 'in itself', he says that line belongs in the *ti estin* of triangle, and point in the *ti estin* of line, 'for their *ousia* (*being*, i.e. essence) is made up of these, and they occur in the account which tells *ti estin* (what they are)'. The notion of *being* occurs again in some of Aristotle's other expressions for essence: *to einai autōi* (roughly, the *being* of the thing), and *to ti ēn einai autōi* (what was [agreed to be?] the *being* of the thing). Indeed, the Latin word *essentia*, from which '*essence*' comes, is a coinage formed from the Latin verb 'esse', to *be*. If we connect being with existence, these ways of referring to essence suggest that a thing's essence is not merely what it is, but something on which it depends for its very *existence*, something, in other words, which it is of *necessity*.

This is not yet, however, an answer to the question raised. Rather, it invites us to put the question again in a new form: why should the essential characteristics of lunar eclipse, the genus and differentia which tell us what it is (*ti estin*), be characteristics on which lunar eclipse depends for its *existence*? Why should not lunar eclipse have existed with a somewhat different differentia? At this point, Friedrich Solmsen, in his masterly study of the *Posterior Analytics*, refers to the influence of Plato.[10] Aristotle's essence is the successor to Plato's Forms, and Plato's Forms were supposed to combine two roles: they were sources not only of intelligibility, but also of *existence* (e.g. *Republic* 508D – 509B, *Phaedo* 101B-C). In the same way, Aristotle's essence plays two roles: not only does it answer the question what a thing is, but it provides a thing with its very existence.

So long as we are relying on the influence of Plato for an answer, we can make a further point. Plato expected his philosophers to come, through dialectical training, to understand the answers to such questions as 'What is largeness?', 'What is smallness?' (*Republic* 524C), and ultimately 'What is goodness?' (*Republic* 504B – 541B). And he surely thought that the answers to these questions were necessary truths.

There is another point: it is a very natural view that the truths of mathematics are necessary, and Plato seems to have assumed it (e.g. *Republic* 458D; *Theaetetus* 162E). Now Aristotle draws his examples of 'in itself' predications in *An. Post.* I 4–6 from the field of mathematics. Indeed, Solmsen has argued that *An. Post.* I is mainly concerned with

---

[10] Friedrich Solmsen (27.8) 83.

the methodology of mathematics.[11] It is not surprising if Aristotle does not think of questioning the assumption, which is both natural and Platonic, that the truths of mathematics, definitions included, are necessary. Indeed, on a natural interpretation, he echoes the assumption at *An. Post.* I 2, 71b9–12. For he there presents it as something we all think (*oiometha*) that the kind of scientific understanding (*epistasthai*), which has just been illustrated by *mathematical* examples involves knowing that things cannot be otherwise.

So far, the two main suggestions have been that Aristotle simply *inherited* certain assumptions from Plato, and that at the opening of *An. Post.* I, he had his eyes chiefly on *mathematics*. But are there not elements in his own thought which would in any case have commended to him the assumption that scientific definitions will be necessary truths? One such element that may spring to mind is this. He believes that the kinds studied by scientists are everlasting, and we saw in Chapter Eight that he believes that what is everlastingly the case about an everlasting subject is *necessarily* the case about it. Moreover, he produces a fallacious argument for this conclusion *Cael.* I 12, 281b3–25. Is this argument not enough to convince him that scientific definitions will be necessary truths? The suggestion may seem to be confirmed, when we notice that the premises of his scientific syllogisms must everlastingly be the case,[12] and must have subjects which exist everlastingly.[13]

Curiously enough, however, in *An. Post.* I 4 to 6, Aristotle takes a much stricter line than in *Cael.* I 12. If predications are necessary, then, as we have seen, the subject must be *definable* in terms of the predicate or vice versa. Evidently, everlastingness is not *on its own* the source of necessity.

From this it would seem that the definitional connexion is (part of) the reason for the necessity. But we should notice that in the statement that all lines are straight or bent, the predicate (straight or bent) is not actually being *defined* in terms of the subject (lines). Aristotle's point is merely that it is so *definable*. Does this mean that the mere *definability* of subject in terms of predicate or vice versa helps to generate necessity? This suggestion may seem to be made explicit by the word 'for' at *An. Post.* I 6 74b7:

What belongs to a thing *in itself* is necessary to that thing; *for* some such predicates belong in the essence (*ti estin*) of the thing, while others are predicates in whose essence (*ti estin*) the thing itself belongs, and here it is necessary for one of the two opposite predicates [e.g. straight and bent] to belong.

The quotation, however, does not make it quite certain that Aristotle regards the mere possibility of defining predicate in terms of subject as

[11] Solmsen, op. cit. 92–107.
[12] *An. Pr.* I 15, 34b7–18; *An. Post.* I 4, 73a28–34; I 8; I 31, 87b30–3; II 12, 96a9–19.
[13] *An. Post.* I 8.

helping to generate necessity in the statement that all lines are straight or bent. And the idea would be very hard to understand. For although we may agree that the statement is necessary, we cannot easily feel that the mere possibility of a definition helps to supply the *reason* for the necessity. If Aristotle thinks that it does, then I believe that he is simply mistaken.

There is another place where we might look for an explanation of why scientific definitions are to be viewed as necessary. In *An. Post.* ɪ 2, ɪ 4 and ɪ 6, Aristotle explains why science requires *necessary* propositions. Most of the passages do not bear directly on the question raised here. They are concerned to show that science requires necessary propositions, but not primarily to show why statements of essence meet this requirement.[14] However, in ɪ 6, we come to a set of four arguments designed to show that scientific understanding (*epistēmē*) of a thing, gained by presenting it as the conclusion of a demonstrative syllogism, must start from necessary premises. The first two arguments (74b13–18, b18–21) are not relevant to our purpose, but the third one is. For in 74b26–32 and again in 75a12–17, a31–5, Aristotle has an argument turning on the concept of *explanation*. If the thing to be explained is a necessary truth, then it can only be explained by reference to necessary truths. This is relevant to the concept of *essence*; for it is part of that concept that if something is to constitute the *essence* of lunar eclipse it must be capable of playing an *explanatory* role, and of *explaining* the superficial features of lunar eclipses: their periodicity, and so on. From the present argument it appears that, if it is a necessary truth that lunar eclipses are periodic, then the periodicity can only be explained by reference to a necessary truth. The statement of essence will then have to be necessary.

The fourth argument turns on the concept of knowledge (*eidenai*, 74b32–9): the propositions which constitute the knower's reasons must be incapable of ceasing to be true. This point about knowledge is not immediately connected with the concepts of essence and definition. But we will find some such connexion, if we turn to the discussion in *Metaph.* vɪɪ 15. For there Aristotle emphasises the role of definition as a source of *knowledge* and *certainty*. There cannot be a definition in which the subject defined might cease to exist (1039b27 – 1040a7), or in which it

---

[14] Thus *An. Post.* ɪ 2, 71b9–16, lays down two attributes which scientific understanding (*epistēmē*) must possess. The scientist must know both the explanation and the necessity of a thing, in order to have scientific understanding of it. These two requirements concerning explanation and necessity are at first treated as separate; and from the second of them, the necessity, Aristotle infers in ɪ 4, 73a21–4 (cf. ɪ 6, 75a14, a34), that where a thing is made scientifically intelligible by presenting it as the conclusion of a demonstrative syllogism, that syllogism must have necessary premises, in order that the conclusion may be exhibited as necessary.

He next maintains, but without further explanation, that premises will have the requisite necessity, only if the subject is definable in terms of the predicate or vice versa, ɪ 6, 74b5–12 (cf. 75a28–37). He then moves on to the four arguments cited in the text.

might still exist while the predicate ceased to hold true of it (1040a29–33). The reason for the first of these two requirements (1039b31 – 1040a7) is that definition is not like mere opinion (*doxa*) which can be about contingent matters (*to endechomenon allōs echein* 1040a1), and can be first true and then false. Rather, definition is connected with *epistēmē*, where this is to be contrasted with opinion, and thought of as scientific *knowledge*. Now if a formula in your mind constitutes definitional knowledge at one time, it cannot fail to do so at another. And yet this is what would happen, if one could define things that might cease to exist. For as soon as they were out of sight, they would no longer be apparent (*adēla*), and so (presumably) one would lack the requisite certainty that the subjects still existed for the formulae to hold true of. Aristotle is assuming that the formulae could not hold true, if the subjects were non-existent.

Extrapolating, we might say that a definition is supposed to give us *knowledge* of what the kind is, and it was a common Greek presupposition that only *necessary* truths could be objects of knowledge, because any others were liable to change from being true to being false.[15] It is assumed that the latter could happen either through the subject's ceasing to exist, or through its continuing to exist while the predicate ceased to apply.

The two passages just considered, then, *An. Post.* I 6 and *Metaph.* VII 15, seem to yield two reasons why definitions might be thought of as necessary. One turns on the *explanatory* role of definitions, and one on their role as sources of *knowledge*. We have now surveyed some of the most substantial influences which led Aristotle to think of scientific definitions as necessary. But there are undoubtedly additional sources of influence. First, many definitions are arguably analytic, unlike the ones we have been discussing, and are necessary for that reason. We must, however, be cautious here: I earlier discussed a suggestion that *all* Aristotle's definitions might eventually be made analytic, either by stipulation or through the gradual evolution of concepts. Even if this suggestion were correct, which I doubted, the *eventual* analyticity would not account for the necessity of these definitions. For Aristotle clearly thinks, in *An. Post.* I 6, that they are necessary from the start, and *not* because of some subsequent stipulation or evolution of concepts.

[15] This is a confusion; for one thing, the tenseless proposition that Julius Caesar is [tenseless] assassinated in 44 B.C., though once capable of either truth value, was never capable of *changing* its truth value, yet, for all that, was not necessary, at least not before 44 B.C., For another, what knowledge requires is that the risk of error be negligible, and the satisfaction of this requirement turns not merely on the character of the proposition known, but also partly on the status of the knower. A correct hunch about a necessary truth is not risk-free; a correct conclusion about a contingent truth may be. None the less, it has been shown, notably by Jaakko Hintikka, how widely this view of knowledge was held ('Time, truth and knowledge in ancient Greek philosophy', *American Philosophical Quarterly* 4, 1967, 1–14, revised as ch. 4 of (1.3) 1973).

A second additional source of influence is that Aristotle did not distinguish as sharply as we should like between the plausible statement that every *individual* lunar eclipse is necessarily a loss of light due to the interposition of the earth and the less plausible definitional statement that the *kind* lunar eclipse is necessarily such a loss of light. Thirdly, Aristotle sometimes appeals to a kind of necessity which we should classify in our terms as *causal*. In connexion with biological species, he eventually comes to think that a large number of differentiae is needed for distinguishing the species, although this view is not yet fully apparent in *An. Post.*[16] Ideally, he would like to show that each differentia is necessary for the species, because it is required by the other differentiae.[17] The necessity is, in our terms, a causal one. In Aristotle's terms, the necessity of one differentia given the others is so far only a relative one. To exhibit it as an absolute (i.e. non-relative) necessity, he would have to fall back on his view that the presence of the other differentiae is (absolutely) necessary.

A final source of influence on Aristotle is more complex. It has been argued by G. E. L. Owen and others that Aristotle sometimes thinks of statements which give the essence of a thing, or part of its essence, as *identity* statements.[18] This interpretation is based on his saying that it is by being something *other* than a pale thing (viz. a man) that a man is pale, but it is not by being something *other* than an animal that he is an animal.[19] Again, pale is predicated of an individual man as one thing of *another*, whereas man is not predicated of him as one thing of *another*.[20] Owen construes these denials of *otherness* as implying the view that when one calls something a man or an animal, one is making an *identity* statement.

A more restricted claim is made elsewhere.[21] At least where a subject is not a *compound* involving *matter* as well as form (*suneilēmmenon tēi hulēi*), it will be identical with its essence.

Now Plato held that one could not be mistaken about certain identity statements. No one, mad or sane, has ever said to himself that a horse was an ox.[22] There are various interesting hypotheses about why Plato held this.[23] What I have not seen remarked is that Aristotle appears to hold a similar view, at least when the identity statements concern those

[16] See Chapter Twelve, note 39.   [17] *PA* i 1, 640a33 – b1.
[18] G. E. L. Owen, 'The Platonism of Aristotle', *Proceedings of the British Academy* 50, 1965, 125–50, esp. 136–9, reprinted *Articles on Aristotle* vol. 1; Christopher Kirwan, *Aristotle's Metaphysics Books Γ, Δ and E*, Clarendon Aristotle Series, Oxford 1971, 100.
[19] *Heteron ti on*: *An. Post.* i 4, 73b5–10; i 22, 83a32; *Phys.* i 4, 188a8; *Metaph.* xiv 1, 1087a35, 1088a28.
[20] *Allo kat' allou*: *Metaph.* vii 4, 1030a2–6; 10–14.
[21] *Metaph.* vii 11, 1037a33 – b7.
[22] Plato *Theaetetus* 190b-c; cf. 188b and *Phaedo* 74c 1–2.
[23] See John McDowell, 'Identity mistakes: Plato and the logical atomists', *Proceedings of the Aristotelian Society* 70, 1969–70, 181–96. An even more persuasive answer is due to be published by Myles Burnyeat.

218 *Necessity and the Essences of Kinds*

incomposite subjects which do not involve matter as well as form. The reason why this is not immediately obvious is that the passage is usually interpreted differently.[24]

In *Metaph*. ix 10, 1051b27–1052a4 and *DA* iii 6, 430b26–31, Aristotle discusses incomposite entities (*asuntheta* 1051b17, *adiaireta* 430a26). I believe he is discussing definitions of incomposite subjects which state what their essence is (*ti esti* 1051b26, b32; *ti esti kata to ti ēn einai* 430b28). It may be thought that this cannot be his meaning, for he says that he is discussing neither predicating something of something (*ti kata tinos* 430b28–9), nor assertion (*kataphasis* 1051b24). This might be taken to mean that his subject is not propositional thought, but contemplation of concepts taken singly. However, it is an embarrassment for this interpretation that we should expect there to be *neither* truth *nor* falsehood, unless in *some* sense we are combining concepts, and indeed Aristotle himself sometimes expresses this view;[25] yet in the present case he thinks truth attainable (430b28, 1051b24). It is easier to suppose that the reason why he says there is no predication or assertion in the present case is that he thinks of the statement of essence as an *identity* statement. One is not predicating one thing of another, but identifying something with itself. This interpretation has more than one advantage.[26]

But why should Aristotle say, as he does, that falsehood is not possible in these cases? His claim is that one cannot be mistaken, but only touch or not touch (1051b24–33). Could the rationale be that if you try to state the essence of an incomposite subject and fail, you are not in error, because you have not succeeded in talking about the subject at all? The contact metaphor is more useful than the seeing metaphor here, because there are degrees of clarity in seeing, but contact is an all-or-nothing affair. Plato uses the metaphor of grasping in the corresponding passage (*Theaetetus* 190c 6). The idea will be that if you try to take an incomposite subject and assign it an essence which does not belong, you will not have made contact with the subject at all.

[24] See, for example, A. C. Lloyd, 'Non-discursive thought – an enigma of Greek Philosophy', *Proceedings of the Aristotelian Society* 70, 1969–70, 261–74; and for a survey of interpretations, see the helpful paper by E. Berti, in *Aristotle on Mind and the Senses*, *Proceedings of the Seventh Symposium Aristotelicum*, Cambridge 1978, ed. G. E. L. Owen and G. E. R. Lloyd, 'The intellection of indivisibles according to Aristotle, *De Anima* iii 6'. Berti expresses agreement with my interpretation.

[25] *DA* iii 6, 430a27 – b6; *Cat*. 4, 2a7–10; *Int*. 1, 16a9–18.

[26] A further advantage of this interpretation is that it helps better to explain something to which Berti draws attention, namely, that the kind of thinking which is described here seems to be identical with that in which God engages, and to which philosophers attain in their happiest moments (*Metaph*. xii 7, 1072b14–26; *NE* x 8). This, at any rate, is suggested by the fact that both kinds of thinking are compared to touching (*Metaph*. xii 7, 1072b21). Now it is much easier with regard to definitional propositions than with regard to isolated concepts to see why apprehending them should be thought so important and rare an attainment.

If this is how Aristotle thinks, could it help to explain why he should hold that a statement giving us the essence, or part of the essence, of an incomposite subject is *necessary*? If you try to think it possible that that subject might have had a wholly or partly different essence, you will not have succeeded in making contact with the subject at all. Hence it is not a possible thought that its essence might have been different.

To make this explanation more general, we should have to suppose that at some time Aristotle was tempted, as Plato was, to treat a wide range of identity statements in the same way, and not just ones with incomposite subjects. Even then we would only have an explanation, and not a *justification*, for his thinking that all statements of essence are necessary. For his own perceptive treatment of such concepts as thunder or lunar eclipse should make it clear that the point about making contact is quite inapplicable here. There is a pre-scientific concept of thunder or lunar eclipse as a certain noise or loss of light. This prescientific concept will enable us to make 'contact' with thunder and lunar eclipse all right, while we speculate how to complete the statement of essence. Aristotle's own insights about this kind of case should deter him from arguing that in general one cannot entertain falsehoods about the essence of a subject, but only miss the subject altogether.

The diversity of kinds

Earlier in the chapter, I concentrated on Aristotle's examples of thunder and lunar eclipse. But these are not examples chosen by Kripke. If we had selected some of the many kinds which are discussed by Aristotle and Kripke in common, might it not have seemed more obvious why correct definitions should be treated as necessary?

I believe the answer to this is that kinds are far more varied than appears at first sight, and that one cannot make any general statement about whether correct definitions of them will be necessary, but must proceed case by case. To illustrate, biological species are subject to evolution (although Aristotle did not recognise this), metals are not. Again, yellowness is normally detected simply by a visual sensation, whereas heat is detected in a great variety of ways, tactual sensation being only one. Although Kripke tends to give a somewhat similar treatment to these kinds, I believe the differences between them can make a difference to our verdict on necessity. So also can our choice of candidate for what constitutes the essence. Let us take a quick glance at these four examples in turn.

(i) In connexion with biological species, it is not *analytic*, even though it is often true, that they have the features which Aristotle assigns them as differentiae. For his list of differentiae cannot be known *a priori*.

Possibly, thought experiments might be useful in connexion with the list taken as a whole . For it is very comprehensive, and hence, if we try to imagine that camels might have existed with *none* of their many differentiae, we may find we lose our grip on what species it is about which we are trying to imagine this.

On the other hand, if we take the differentiae singly, thought experiments seem unlikely to help. An appeal to the necessity of *individual* specimens having a given differentia runs into the difficulty that an *individual* specimen may be deformed. As for the species, since this is subject to evolution, it may come to admit of all sorts of variation. This makes it dangerous to insist on the necessity of any one differentia for the species. And this is all the more true of families, like the rose, which contain many species.

There are, of course, other suggestions about what defines biological species or families. But I doubt if the difficulty concerning evolutionary variation would be overcome by Putnam's suggestion that the essence may be a DNA molecular structure.[27] Another suggestion, made about the species within a family, is that these may be united by having the right relation to certain paradigm species, perhaps the relation of being crossable with the paradigms.[28] But it is, of course, contingent what species are available to serve as paradigms.

(ii) Yellowness is a property on which Aristotle and Kripke agree: its essence is an inner structure. Aristotle makes it a certain *ratio* between the dark and bright ingredients of the coloured body.[29] But, as Kripke recognises, the standard test for whether things are yellow is whether they give us the appropriate visual sensation. Because this is the only everyday test, it has assumed enormous importance, and it is plausible to hold that it is analytic that yellowness gives us this sensation. Suppose a change in our sense-organs brought it about that a new group

---

[27] Hilary Putnam (22.6) 1975, and (22.5) 1970. But DNA structures are also subject to evolution. Long ones (that is, ones of great *physical* length) are likely to get broken up within a few generations, while very short ones may be so long-lived as to appear in remote ancestors, cousins and descendants of the species or family (see Richard Dawkins (21.3) 1976, ch. 3). It may be wiser, then, to view it as *contingent* what molecular structure, if any, will prove in the end to be common to past and future members of a species or family. Doubt has also been cast on how efficient DNA structure is *on its own* as a means of distinguishing one species from another. Chimpanzees prove to be much closer to humans in molecular structure than their gross morphology would lead one to expect (M. Cherry, S. M. Case and A. C. Wilson, 'Frog perspective on the morphological difference between humans and chimpanzees', *Science*, 14 April 1978, vol. 200, p. 209). If a certain molecular structure succeeds in differentiating, it may be wiser to regard this too as contingent.

[28] This is Douglas Gasking's revision of a suggestion made by William Whewell about the family of roses. Whewell suggested defining the family by taking a paradigm species or 'Type', and making membership of the family depend on resemblance to the paradigm species in respect of at least two important independent functions, say, the nutritive and reproductive organs (William Whewell (22.9) 1840; Douglas Gasking (22.10) 1960).

[29] Kripke (22.2) notes 66 and 71. For Aristotle's theory, see *Sens* 3, and Sorabji, 'Aristotle, mathematics and colour', *Classical Quarterly* 22, 1972, 293–308.

of objects, with a different physical structure, looked yellow. Provided the change was permanent and universal, ought we not to say that the new objects actually *were* not merely that they *looked*, yellow? If so, it must be contingent what structure yellow things have. Again, recent experiments have cast some doubt on whether there is a unitary physical basis for the things we call yellow: if there is one, it appears not to be a function of wavelength.[30] But should we allow this sort of consideration to jeopardise our former ascriptions of yellowness? Ought we not rather to stick to them, and maintain that it is contingent whether there is a unitary physical basis?

The view I am suggesting is in effect that of John Locke, who said that colours were nothing but powers to produce sensations in us. For a very able defence, I would refer to the work of Jonathan Bennett.[31]

(iii) Heat differs from yellowness. It is true that, as Kripke insists, we can easily imagine it existing without the sensation of heat, or the sensation existing without it. But the important question is whether we can imagine heat sometimes or always existing apart from its *full range* of manifestations, or the full range sometimes or always existing apart from heat. I think we cannot imagine all these things. For, as Aristotle stresses, heat manifests itself not only in sensation, but also in melting, igniting, consuming, solidifying, boiling, vaporising and expanding.[32] He does not even think the sensation a very important manifestation.[33] If heat and this *full range* of manifestations cannot be imagined as existing separately, what are we to say of the *essence* of heat, which for

[30] The belief that hue is a function of wavelength has been called into question above all by the experiments of Edwin H. Land, inventor of polaroid lenses and of the Polaroid camera. Land has shown that he can produce almost all the colours of the garden on a screen, using only two wavelengths of light, both taken from the so-called yellow waveband, and two black-and-white photographic transparencies containing no colour. Many years of further research have suggested to him that there *is* a unitary physical basis for hues, but that it is a function not of wavelength, but of reflectance, i.e. of the efficiency with which a given area reflects light. Unfortunately, the following two articles expounding this theory say how it accounts for *some* of the earlier experiments, but not how it accounts for the one involving the yellow waveband: 'Lightness and retinex theory' (with John J. McCann), *Journal of the Optical Society of America* 61, 1971, 1–11: and 'The retinex theory of colour vision', *Scientific American*, December 1977. The original experiments are described in 'Experiments in color vision', *Scientific American*, May 1959, repr. as *Scientific American* offprint no. 223.

[31] See Locke, *Essay Concerning Human Understanding* 2 8 8–26; and Jonathan Bennett in 'Substance, reality and primary qualities', *American Philosophical Quarterly* 2, 1965, 1–17, and again in *Locke, Berkeley, Hume: Central Themes*, Oxford 1971, ch. 4.

[32] *PA* ii 2, 648a36 – ii 3, 650a2, and (assuming that Aristotle is the author) *Meteor.* iv.

[33] In the *PA* passage he points out that other criteria can conflict with the criterion of sensation, and he puts no premium on the test of sensation. Indeed, he warns that it is positively unreliable, because the sense-organs may be at fault (648b15–17). Further, as Balme points out (1.6) 1972, 148, Aristotle believes that heat is present in cases where it would be very hard to detect it by sensation. Wine contains more heat than water, and what has once been formed by heat, concocted, or burnt still contains heat (*Meteor.* iv 11; *PA* ii 2, 649a24).

Aristotle is the ability to conglomerate certain kinds of thing[34] and for Kripke is molecular motion?

If we are to represent the essence of heat as *necessarily* related to heat, the safest line would be to argue that the essence is necessarily related to the *manifestations*. And this is a harder task than the one Kripke sets himself, although it is a task that Aristotle would probably want to undertake. At least, if he is the author of *Meteor.* iv, he appeals back to the essential conglomerative ability to *explain* why heat is an active, not a passive, property, and then goes on to describe the many ways in which it is active (boiling, melting, vaporising, etc.).[35]

(iv) Our last example is that of metals. Kripke treats gold as having its essence reside in a certain atomic structure. This suggests a fresh problem: if, in some imaginary situation, a metal has the same structure as our samples of gold actually have, is that *sufficient* to make it gold? What if we imagine (supposing we can imagine this) that all the samples that ever have that structure, through a difference in causal laws, have a quite different superficial appearance, and resemble junket? Would they, as Kripke holds, still be gold? This problem is less likely to arise for Aristotle, because he makes the essence of a metal to be one of its powers or liabilities, its rigidity, for example.[36] Such an essence might prove incompatible with junket-like behaviour.

I believe that Kripke's ideas are of great interest; they help with some examples, and they enable us to approach Aristotle's thought with fresh interest. But I have also been arguing that Kripke's work does not show Aristotle's belief in necessity to be a natural view in all cases, and that Aristotle's motivations are in fact very different from Kripke's.

Appendix: Kinds of necessity in Aristotle

Now we have taken into account Aristotle's treatment of necessity in the *Posterior Analytics*, we are ready to take stock of the many kinds of necessity he recognises. Modern philosophers have tended to be very parsimonious in their recognition of distinct kinds. Lukasiewicz, as we saw, recognised only *analytic* truths as necessary. Quine has been reluctant to admit *any* necessity, and has denied that there are analytic truths.[37] We saw in Chapter Two that it is disputed whether there is such a thing as *causal* necessity. Very recently logicians have begun to readmit other categories. Some have recognised Aristotle's necessity of

---

[34] *GC* ii 2, 329b26–32. A very different account of Aristotle is given by Christopher Taylor in 'Forms as causes in the *Phaedo*', *Mind* 78, 1969, 57–8.

[35] *Meteor.* iv 1, 378b14–26. For other places where *Meteor.* iv presupposes the definitions of hot, cold, fluid and dry in *GC* ii 2, see iv 4, 381b29 – 382a2, 382a10; iv 5, 382a22–7; iv 9, 387a11–12.

[36] *Meteor.* iv 12, esp. 390a17–18. Examples of powers which define kinds of stuff are tension, elasticity, fragmentability, hardness and softness.

[37] W. V. Quine (25.3) 1953.

the past, as was noted in Chapter Five, and we have just seen Kripke and Putnam allowing a *de re* necessity 'in the highest degree'.

In contrast with this parsimony, Aristotle recognises a rich collection of cases. Moreover, his system of classification is refreshing to study, precisely because it does not mesh with ours. In particular, we have noted repeatedly, and I have argued elsewhere,[38] that he does not recognise a distinction between causal necessity and necessity which is (in a broad sense) logical, i.e. conceptual. Let us recall some of the distinctions we have encountered.

(i) First, we saw Aristotle talking of blood being in itself hot not in the sense that it could not go cold, but only in the sense that it could not go cold and still be called 'blood'.[39]

(ii) Then, we saw him distinguishing the non-existent possibility of the *compound* walking-while-sitting from the possibility for a seated man of the *divided* walking.[40] Both distinctions so far are related to, and the second actually inspired, that between *de re* and *de dicto* modality.

(iii) One example of an impossible compound would be the truth of the premises and the falsity of the conclusion in a valid syllogism. Aristotle further classifies this case by saying that the conclusion has a relative necessity, given the premises.[41]

(iv) This relative necessity needs to be distinguished from the hypothetical necessity of certain conditions, if a certain goal is to be realised.[42]

(v) Necessity in the sense of irrevocability is ascribed to the present or past.[43]

(vi) What we should think of as the causal necessity of events is split by Aristotle between two of his major classes:[44] cases where the necessity is natural, as when a stone falls down, and

(vii) cases where it is unnatural, as when a stone is thrown up.

This split is not the only evidence of Aristotle's ignoring our distinction between causal and conceptual necessity. Once the causal necessity of bile, given the presence of a liver, is assimilated to the relative necessity (which we would count as conceptual) of a conclusion, given the premises.[45] A further analogy between what we call causal and conceptual necessity is this: just as the necessity of necessary premises is transferred to the conclusion, so, if necessitating causes possess the irrevocability of the past, this is transferred to the effect.[46]

[38] Richard Sorabji (23.1) 1969.
[39] *PA* ii 2 and 3, 649a13–24, b20–7 (Chapter Twelve).
[40] *SE* 4, 166a23–31; cf. *Cael.* i 12, 281b3–25 (Chapters Seven, Eight, Twelve).
[41] *An. Pr.* i 10, 30b31–40; *An. Post.* ii 5, 91b14–17; ii 11, 94a21–2 (Chapter One).
[42] *Phys.* ii 9; *GC* ii 11; *PA* i 1 (Chapter One).
[43] *Cael.* i 12, 283b12–14; *NE* vi 2, 1139b7–9; *Rhet.* iii 17, 1418a3–5; *Metaph.* vi 3, 1027b1–9; xi 8, 1065a19; arguably *Int.* 9, 19a23–4 (Chapters One, Five and Six).
[44] *An. Post.* ii 11, 94b37 – 95a3; *Rhet.* i 10, 1368b35 (Chapters Three and Nine).
[45] *PA* iv 2, 677a17 (Chapter Nine).   [46] *Metaph.* vi 3 (Chapter One).

(viii) Some have equated the necessity of what is *always* the case about *everlastingly* existing subjects with the causal necessity of laws of nature.[47] But this seems a mistake, because various conceptual necessities could presumably fit under this heading alongside the causal ones.

We noticed that in general Aristotle was not very inclined to connect what we should call causal necessity with what is *always* the case. For a stone may fall by natural necessity, or rise, when thrown, by unnatural necessity; and Aristotle characterises the difference between these two possibilities by saying that the first happens *either* always *or* for the most part, the second *neither* always *nor* for the most part. In neither case does he think that the necessity implies that something happens *always*.[48]

(ix) We saw that in *An. Post.* I 4–6 Aristotle did not derive the necessity of essential predications simply from the necessity of what is always the case about an everlasting subject. Rather, he required an essential (i.e. definitional) connexion between subject and predicate.[49]

The category of necessity contrary to nature (vii) is often called force (*bia*),[50] and we shall find that it plays an important role in evaluating human conduct as voluntary or involuntary. Force is defined as an external cause to which the agent contributes nothing, or which acts contrary to the tendencies within him. Mere threats, Aristotle explains, do not constitute force.[51]

(x) None the less, he sometimes speaks of actions as being necessitated when they are performed under threat.[52] So this can be recorded as a distinct, though closely related, kind of necessity.

This list covers most of the Aristotelian kinds of necessity to be encountered in this book, but for other purposes one could draw attention to other Aristotelian distinctions. Hintikka, for example, has a quite different classification of kinds of possibility recognised by Aristotle.[53] Aristotle has his own lists of kinds of necessity and possibility in his dictionary, *Metaphysics* v (chs 5 and 12), but he never assembles in one place the ten kinds catalogued here.

[47] For the necessity associated with *always*, see *GC* II 11; *Cael.* I 12, 281b3–25 and Chapter Eight. For the view that it is a kind of causal necessity: Richard Taylor, 'The problem of future contingencies', *Philosophical Review* 66, 1957, 1–28; Colin Strang, 'Aristotle and the Sea Battle', *Mind* 69, 1960, 447–65.

[48] Chapter Three, and for nature associated with what happens for the most part, see: *GA* 727b29, 770b9–13, 772a35, 777a19–21; *PA* 663b28; *An. Pr.* 25b14, 32b4–13.

[49] *An. Post.* I 4–6 (Chapter Twelve).

[50] *Metaph.* v 5, 1015a26; vi 2, 1026b28; xi 8, 1064b33; xii 7, 1072b12; *An. Post.* II 11, 95a1; *Rhet.* I 10, 1368b35 (Chapters Fourteen, Sixteen, Seventeen).

[51] *NE* III 1, 1110a15–17. This interpretation will be defended in Chapters Sixteen and Seventeen.

[52] *NE* III 1, 1110a26, 28, 32, b1; III 8, 1116a30, 33, b2; x 9, 1180a4; *EE* II 8, 1225a17.

[53] J. Hintikka (1.4) 79–88.

PART V

NECESSITY AND BLAME

CHAPTER FOURTEEN

Cause and Necessity in Human Action
(*Int.* 9, *Phys.* VIII, *NE* III 1–5)

In connexion with coincidences (Chapter One), I have represented Aristotle as denying necessity and causation. In connexion with tomorrow's sea battle or the future cutting up of a cloak (Chapters Five and Eight), I have represented him as denying necessity, but not as denying causation. Yet W. D. Ross has lumped together these two ideas of necessity and causation, as we saw in Chapter Two (notes 1 and 2). His description of Aristotle as postulating 'fresh starts' strongly suggests a denial of causation as well as of necessity, and he finds 'fresh starts' postulated especially in connexion with human action, though he also finds them in Aristotle's philosophy of nature. In both regards, he has been followed by some of the ablest recent commentators, by David Furley in relation to human action, and by David Balme in relation to the philosophy of nature.

I believe that in both spheres, Aristotle denied necessity at certain points, without thinking of this as committing him to a denial of causation. Having considered nature in Chapter Nine, I shall now take up the sphere of human action, and the passages that have been taken to imply a denial of causation.

Does action involve a break in causation?

Ross detects 'fresh starts' in *Int.* 9, in the middle part of the chapter which I have not yet discussed (18b26 – 19a22). Here Aristotle is arguing that there must be something wrong with the determinist's conclusion because of the strange consequences it would have *inter alia* for deliberation and action. Aristotle objects that if the determinist were right that everything happens of necessity, the deliberations and actions of the generals could not be an origin (*archē*, 19a7) of the sea battle. For this objection he probably has a double reason. First, deliberation could not even occur, if the determinist were right, judging from Aristotle's view that we do not deliberate about what is necessary. We do not deliberate, for example, about the past, nor about celestial motions or mathematical truths,[1] and the reason (*NE* 1139b7–9) why we

[1] *EE* III 3, 1112a21 – 6; VI 1, 1139a13; VI 2, 1139b7–9; VI 5, 1140a31 – b1; VI 7, 1141b10–11; III 3, 1112a30–1; with III 5, 1113b7–8; *EE* II 10, 1226a20–30; *Rhet.* I 2, 1357a8.

do not is that such things are necessary. By ruling out deliberation, the determinist would also rule out deliberate action (*praxis*), the kind of action that distinguishes adult humans from children and animals, for this is produced by deliberation (*NE* vi 2, 1139a31–3).[2] But Aristotle would probably also say that even if deliberation and action occurred, they could not act as origins (*archai*)of events in the world. For he has just told us (18b31–3) that if the determinist were right, there would be no need to deliberate or to take trouble, thinking that if we do this, that will happen, but if we do not, it will not.

Neither ground is satisfactory: Aristotle ought not to say that we do not deliberate about what is necessary, but rather that we do not deliberate whether to *Φ* or not to *Φ*, if we *believe* that one of the two is necessary, and if we *believe* we know which. He never weakens his requirement in this way, however, although there is a slightly different acknowledgment at *EE* ii 10, 1226a26. Against Aristotle's second ground, which was subsequently revived and known as the Lazy Argument, the Stoic Chrysippus was later to make a just objection. Action and its outcome might be fated not independently of each other, but conjointly as *confatalia* (Cicero *De Fato* xii 28 – xiii 30). When Aristotle entertains the determinist's hypothesis that the sea battle is necessary, he is not free to ask himself what would happen if the generals omitted their deliberation and their order for battle. For the determinist never declared the sea battle to be necessary independently of what the generals did.

Our present interest, however, is not in the correctness of Aristotle's view, but in whether Ross is right to say that Aristotle here sees a 'fresh start' in human deliberation and action. We should notice that the word '*archē*' (origin) proves nothing, for although it can be translated 'beginning', Aristotle makes no attempt to reserve it for the very first member of a chain. Thus according to *NE* vi 2, deliberation and desire are the *archē* of deliberate choice (*prohaeresis* 1139a32–3), while deliberate choice is the *archē* of deliberate action (1139a31; cf. b5); and the present passage in *Int.* 9 adds that deliberate action is in its turn an *archē* of events like sea battles. There are other examples too of Aristotle applying the word '*archē*' to several members of a chain, without reserving it for the first member.[3] I believe that here, in calling deliberation and deliberate action an *archē*, Aristotle is simply claiming that they influence events. There is no sign that he thinks they are 'fresh starts', if that means that they are uncaused. Admittedly, he cannot allow that when

---

[2] By this criterion the action of a weak-willed man is not a full-scale *praxis*, for such a man does not act in accordance with his deliberation. Even so, Aristotle would presumably think that, if determinism excludes deliberation, it also excludes a great many weak-willed actions. For the kind of weak-willed man to whom he devotes most attention (see vii 7, 1150b19–22; vii 10, 1152a18–19) has engaged in deliberation, and his weakness consists precisely in going against his deliberation.

[3] E.g. *DA* iii 9, 433a16–17; *Mot.* 698a7–9; cf. *NE* vi 3, 1139b28–30.

the deliberation starts, the conditions are already such as to *necessitate* the action that follows. The action may eventually be necessitated, but it must not be necessitated by earlier conditions which are in their turn necessitated by earlier ones, in such a way that the chain stretches back to conditions that were all satisfied when the deliberation started. If there are any chains of necessitation, then, they must be broken somewhere. But this does not logically commit Aristotle (so it was argued in Chapter Two) to postulating uncaused events, and he shows no awareness of being so committed.

Seekers after 'fresh starts' may take comfort in a different passage which has been perceptively analysed by David Furley.[4] In *Phys.* VIII, Aristotle speaks of animals as self-movers, while saying (VIII 5, esp. 258a1–2) that a self-mover must contain an unmoved component. This unmoved component may sound like a source of 'fresh starts'. But no such conclusion can be drawn, because in VIII 6, 258b12, 20, 32, Aristotle does not endorse the idea that animals contain an unmoved component, while in VIII 2, 253a7–20 and VIII 6, 259b1–20 he actually denies it. In these last two passages, he attributes animal motion to external influences in the environment, presumably because he wants to reserve for God the title of *unmoved* mover. This may leave one puzzled, as Furley brings out, why he ever allowed that animals were self-movers in the first place. But I suggest the answer may be that this is the ordinary way of looking at them; it is something that 'we say' (*phamen*, VIII 2, 253a14). And Aristotle is happy to speak in the ordinary way, while taking his analysis to show that animals are not self-movers strictly speaking (not *kuriōs*, VIII 6, 259b7).

The most difficult passage, and the most persuasive evidence for a belief in 'fresh starts' in human conduct, comes from the end of *Nicomachean Ethics* III 5 (1114b3–25). This passage is taken as clear evidence by Furley. Hardie also thinks that Aristotle may mean a person is the uncaused cause of his actions, and Ross considers it the place where Aristotle comes closest, though he does not go all the way, towards postulating free will.[5]

Aristotle is here considering an opponent who argues, not that all actions are involuntary, but that all *wicked* actions are involuntary. The last in a series of arguments which this opponent offers is that wicked actions are involuntary because they are due to our ideals, while our ideals depend on our character (1114a31 – b1). Aristotle replies with a dilemma: either we acquire a fixed character by the actions we per-

---

[4] David Furley, 'Self-movers', in *Aristotle on Mind and the Senses*, *Proceedings of the 7th Symposium Aristotelicum*, ed. G. E. R. Lloyd and G. E. L. Owen, Cambridge 1978.

[5] W. D. Ross, *Aristotle*, London 1923, ch. 7 (Meridian Books edition, 1959, 196). W. F. R. Hardie, *Aristotle's Ethical Theory*, Oxford 1968, 178. David Furley (29.2) 1967, 193–4; cf. 220, 227, 232 of the original. Tony Long agrees with Furley that determinism is at issue in the passage (A. A. Long (31.7) 1971, 194).

form before it is fixed, and so we are in a way responsible (*pōs aitios*) for the form our character eventually takes, and hence for our ideals (1114b1–3; this is Aristotle's own theory: 1114a4–21, b22–4). Or we are simply born with a certain character and ideals already fixed; but that would prove too much for the comfort of the opponent, because it would make virtue as involuntary as vice (1114b3–16), which he never intended (1113b7–17; 1114b22).

Now why should this make virtue and vice alike involuntary? Is it because if character and ideals are fixed at birth, this rules out the possibility of their being created by what Ross calls 'fresh starts'? This is how Furley takes the passage, in his thoughtful account of Aristotle (which was originally designed only to throw light on Epicurus). His view depends on a certain interpretation of Aristotle's talk of internal and external origins (*archai*). If wicked character or conduct is to be voluntary, it must have an internal origin, Aristotle tells us. And Furley takes an internal origin to be a cause internal to the agent, which cannot in its turn be traced to still earlier causes lying outside the agent, perhaps in his parents before he was born. It is an uncaused cause, and Furley takes Aristotle's view to be that the actions which establish a man's character cannot have their origin traced back to anything beyond the man himself. On this view, the reason why Aristotle's opponent will have prevented a man's character from being voluntary is that he will have ascribed it to an *external* origin, the man's parents, from whom his character was inherited. And in case it be protested that the man's *actions* (as opposed to his character) could still have an internal origin, so long as they were due to such internal things as his ideals and character, the reply would be that in Furley's sense they would not have an internal origin. For the causal history of the actions could still be traced back ultimately, *via* the man's ideals and his character, to his parents.

One disadvantage of this interpretation is that it saddles Aristotle with a needlessly unsatisfactory argument. Indeed its unsatisfactoriness has been remarked by Furley, Hardie and others.[6] The voluntariness of later actions will be made to depend on the voluntariness of acquired character, and the voluntariness of acquired character on the voluntariness of earlier actions, which will in turn be due to a break in the causal chain at the stage of those earlier actions. But Aristotle will not have explained why it is easier to break the causal chain at that early stage than at a later one. The problem is merely shuffled back. A further difficulty is that the reference to parents, on which this interpretation rests, is not explicit in the text. Aristotle talks of a man's charac-

---

[6] Furley, op. cit. 235 and note 12; Hardie, op. cit. 175; Reginald Jackson, 'Rationalism and intellectualism in the ethics of Aristotle', *Mind* 1942, 349. Compare also R. A. Gauthier, commentary on *NE* 1114b1–3, in (29.4).

ter at birth, but does not draw attention to the external source of that character.

There is another way of looking at the argument. If the thesis of inborn character which Aristotle offers to his opponent would make everything involuntary, this need not be the result of its postulating unbroken chains of causation. In the first place, Aristotle need not think that unbroken chains of causation would make things involuntary, so long as they do not imply unbroken chains of necessitation. Admittedly, he thinks that there is an internal origin of voluntary conduct, but an internal origin may be a member of a chain which stretches back ultimately to external factors. We have already seen in this chapter that the notion of an origin need not imply the very first member of a chain, and we shall see later in the chapter that the notion of an internal origin need not exclude external co-operating influences. Why need it then exclude external antecedents? In the second place, the thesis of inborn character would not commit Aristotle's opponent to unbroken chains, either of causation, or of necessitation. The thesis, as stated, simply does not specify whether the inborn character is caused, or necessitated, by what went before. Rather, the reason why the thesis of inborn character rules out voluntariness may be that it treats character as fully formed at birth, and so provides no stage at which it was up to a man (*ep' autōi*) what character he had. Aristotle's rival view is that a man cannot be called good or wicked until his character and ideals are firmly fixed,[7] and these do not become firmly fixed, except by his first performing many actions (NE III 5, 1114a4–31, b1–3, b21–5; cf. II 1–4).[8] In this way, it comes to depend to some extent on the man himself what character he acquires. The thesis of inborn character prevents character from being voluntary, not necessarily by removing its contingency (which it need not do), nor by letting the causal chain stretch back into the remote past (which will not matter, if it is done), but by not allowing a man's character to depend in any way on the man himself. This is enough to prevent it being 'up to the man' what character he has, and so to prevent his character from being voluntarily acquired.

I am suggesting then that, contrary to a common view, Aristotle's strategy here does not commit him to rupturing any causal chain. It may be objected that if he is to preserve voluntariness, he must deny that it has all along been necessary what character a man would have, or how he would act. But I have argued earlier that it would be quite possible for Aristotle to deny this without denying causation, so long as he gives up

[7] This is very clear in the case of good character, II 4, 1105a31–3. But most wickedness also involves deliberate choice (see note 34 in ch. Sixteen), and deliberate choice presupposes a fixed character (VI 2, 1139a33–4). On self-indulgence, see 1150a21–2, b29–32; 1151a13–20.

[8] Our natural make-up at birth exerts some influence on how we develop, but does not fix the character of a normal man, *NE* VI 13, 1144b3; VII 5, 1148b18; VII 8, 1151a18; x 9, 1179b4–31; *Pol.* VII 13, 1332a40 – b11; VII 15, 1334b6.

the uncharacteristic thesis of *Metaph.* vi 3 that what is caused is necessitated. A child may take another child's attractive toy, in spite of remembering that he is supposed to get permission. In taking the toy, the child is responding to one set of feelings rather than another – the action is not uncaused. But neither these feelings nor anything else need necessitate the action. As to how an action can be caused without being necessitated, I must refer to Chapter Two.[9]

I am not suggesting that Aristotle had worked all this out. He did not devise an example, and decide at what point to postulate an unnecessitated effect. It is merely that he has committed himself to denying necessitation at some point, without recognising any commitment to denying causation. The child's action, as just described, is ideally suited to supply what he wants. It is caused, without being necessitated. The cause is an internal one (the child's feelings), though the causal antecedents can stretch back indefinitely far. Moreover, the child's action can play the required role in character formation. His taking the toy, or not taking it, will strengthen the corresponding tendencies in him. And so he contributes to the firm character which he will eventually acquire.

This interpretation gives Aristotle a much more defensible position. He is quite right to reject the view that a man's eventual character is not influenced by his earlier actions. Further, there is a genuine point in considering the man's earlier actions rather than his later ones; he is not merely shuffling the problem back. He would presumably allow that even at the later stage there is some choice about what a man does. But his character may by then be so ingrained that he cannot get rid of it (*NE* iii 5, 1114a13–21), and he may merely be choosing between different wicked actions, and different ways of fulfilling his wicked goals.[10] If we want to know what makes his later wrongdoing voluntary, the best direction in which to look is towards the voluntary acquisition of his character through earlier acts of wrongdoing. At that earlier stage his character was not firm, and it was just about as easy to refrain from wrongdoing as to indulge in it.

[9] In the very same circumstances, the child could have acted in the other way. Yet his action has an explanation and a cause, namely, that set of incentives which favoured taking the toy. (Perhaps he misses a similar toy of his own which was lost.) This will explain his action, for example, to someone who has seen the case on the other side (the child wants to obey his parents), but has not seen what is so attractive about this toy (the child has plenty of his own). Admittedly, there is no answer available for someone who already knows both sets of incentives in full and wants to be told why the child acted on the one set rather than the other. But then a call for explanation need not presuppose this particular question, so it was argued in Chapter Two. See the rather similar examples there.

[10] Compare how the man with a wicked inborn character could still choose the means for fulfilling his wicked goals (*NE* iii 5, 1114b18, b21). Aristotle entertains the idea of using this fact to establish voluntariness. But this is a manoeuvre he offers his opponent, rather than one he wants to pursue himself.

The 'fresh starts' reading of Aristotle may appear after all to gain support from his idea that 'we cannot refer our actions to origins other than those in us' (*NE* III 5, 1113b19–20).[11] But this need not mean that the internal origins (our desires, for example) are 'fresh starts' in the sense of lacking origins of their own external to us. Aristotle could mean either of two things: he could have in mind that in an extended causal chain the first member is not very naturally called the cause or origin of the last. It is more natural to think of members as being the cause or origin of their immediate or close successors.[12] On this reckoning, the origin of our actions would be our desires, rather than items further back in the causal chain. Alternatively, Aristotle could merely mean that we cannot refer our actions to origins other than those in us *instead of* to the ones in us. There would be two ways of trying to refer our actions to other origins instead. One would be to cite a causal chain which entirely bypassed the internal factors. Another would be to concede that the internal factors entered into the relevant causal chain, but to suppose that the *real* causes of the action were not these internal factors, but something further back in the causal chain instead. Aristotle would reject both these moves.

I have so far combatted the idea that Aristotle thinks of human action as involving a break in *causation*. I see no clear evidence of this. The other half of my claim, however, is that he does perceive a failure in necessitation. He does not regard our actions as having been necessary all along. To this half of my claim I shall now turn.

Action does involve a failure in necessitation

It is, first of all, clear enough for the case of fully adult human action (*praxis*), the kind that is based on deliberation, that Aristotle does not think that how we will act is already fixed at the time we engage in the deliberation (see notes 1 and 2). And if so, the same will go for all virtuous action, for Aristotle thinks that virtuous action must be based on deliberate choice (*prohaeresis*: NE II 4, 1105a31; VI 12, 1144a19), which is in turn based on deliberation. But this fully deliberate action is not the only kind of action there is. Voluntary action forms a wider class, as he explains in *NE* III 2, 1111b8 and *EE* II 10, 1226b30. And to show that he will not allow any of our voluntary actions to have been necessary all along, we need to consider the relation of voluntariness (*to hekousion*) to two other concepts: what is up to us (*to eph' hēmin*, often

[11] 1113b19–20: *ei . . . mē echomen eis allas archas anagagein para tas en hēmin*. Hardie is more impressed by the clause: 'something comes also from the man himself', 1114b17.

[12] Aristotle himself makes a point like this about chains of explanation: some members of the chain are too far back to be considered explanations of the last member (*An. Post.* I 13, 78b28–32; II 18). On the other hand, he sometimes speaks the opposite way, as if the very first member of a chain provides the best explanation of the last (*An. Post.* I 9, 76a18–22; I 24, 85b23 – 86a3; *Metaph.* II 2, 994a11–16; cf. *Phys.* II 3, 195b21–5).

translated as what is in our power), and internal origin (*archē en hēmin*).

Both concepts exclude the idea of necessity. Concerning the first, Aristotle says at *NE* III 5, 1113b7–8 that what it is up to us to do, it is equally up to us to refrain from doing (similarly *Phys.* VIII 4, 255a8–10). So here he sees the dual possibility of acting or not acting which is incompatible with necessity. This contingency is not the only element in the concept, however, as *EE* II 10, 1226a22–5 points out. Sometimes there is a dual possibility of something happening or not happening, but it has nothing to do with *us* whether it happens or not; rather, it depends on nature, or on something else other than ourselves. Such things are not up to us.

The concept of an action being up to us is connected in its turn with the concept of our being, or having within us, the 'origin' (*archē*) of the action. This again implies a dual possibility in the case of humans: whenever we are, or have within us, the origin, then it is up to us to perform the action (III 5, 1113b20–1, 1114a18–19), or to refrain (III 1, 1110a17; *EE* II 6, 1223a2–7), and the action cannot be necessary (*NE* VI 4, 1140a10–16). But the point about refraining applies only to humans, not to God. For we can call God an origin, even though whatever he does, he does necessarily. Indeed, this entitles him even more than men to be called an origin (*EE* II 6, 1222b22–3, 1223a1–2).

Actions, then, are capable of being left undone, so long as they are 'up to us', or so long as we are, or have within us, the 'origin'. But before taking this conclusion as firm, I had better say that Richard Loening has once again applied his special interpretation to what Aristotle says.[13] He suggests that the dual possibility of being done or left undone attaches only to *classes* of action. Aristotle's point, he thinks, is that men do not always steal, so that *in abstracto* there is a possibility of stealing or not stealing; but for a given individual on a given occasion, it is causally determined whether he will steal. When Aristotle talks of its being up to a particular man on a particular occasion to perform a particular action or to leave it undone, according to Loening, he has in mind that that man plays some part in the causal sequence, and that there is a possibility *in abstracto* of acting either way, but not that it is undetermined whether he will steal. It must be conceded to Loening that Aristotle's arguments sometimes seem to prove no more than this.[14]

[13] Richard Loening, op. cit., ch. 18.

[14] When Aristotle maintains, for example, that good and bad conduct are up to us because we are influenced by punishment and honours (1113b21–30), he proves only that our conduct is in some way dependent on us (otherwise our mentors would not direct their actions towards us), and that there is a possibility *in abstracto* of acting either way. He does not prove that an individual on a particular occasion is capable of acting either way. (The individual's conduct might be determined by the honours or punishments.) But if Aristotle omits to consider this, I do not believe that this is due to his having no objection to a deterministic position. I shall offer a different explanation of his silence in Chapter Fifteen.

None the less, Loening's interpretation is hard to square, for example, with *NE* III 5, 1114a13–21, where Aristotle says it is no longer possible (*esti, exesti, dunaton*) for the man of ingrained character not to be wicked, but that it was once possible for him not to become so, and for certain sick men not to be sick. Loening wishes to see all references to possibility in this context as references to a possibility *in abstracto*. But Aristotle is unlikely to mean merely that there was once a possibility *in abstracto* of not becoming wicked or sick. For it is unclear why a merely abstract possibility should have ceased to exist. As noted in Chapter Eight, Loening himself stops short in the end from ascribing to Aristotle the view that it has *all along* been causally determined how a man will act.

If the concepts of being up to us and of having an internal origin both exclude necessity, what does this prove concerning Aristotle's view of voluntary action?[15] It will follow that voluntary actions cannot all along have been necessary, just so long as Aristotle thinks of voluntary actions as being up to us and having an internal origin. And does he think this? The clearest affirmative statements come in *NE* v 8, 1135a24, where a man's voluntary actions are defined as being 'up to him', and in the *Eudemian Ethics* book II, where voluntary action is defined in terms of its being 'up to one' to *refrain* (II 9, 1225b8; cf. II 10, 1226b31–3). Consequently, according to these chapters, a voluntary action enjoys the dual possibility of being performed or left unperformed, and so cannot all along have been necessary, even if it is eventually necessitated. The view taken in *NE* III is less clear; we might infer that here too it is thought to be 'up to us' to perform or refrain from, any voluntary action. For an action is said to be 'up to us', whenever its 'origin' is within us (III 1, 1110a17; III 5, 1113b21, 1114a18–19), and according to III 1, 1111a23, its origin is within us, whenever it is voluntary. In the end, I think, it is true that *NE* III agrees that it is up to us to perform, or refrain from, any voluntary action. But there are complications, which obscure Aristotle's intention in *NE* III, and one is that the notion of the 'origin being within' appears to change its meaning.

The meaning appears to change in two respects. First, in III 1 one source of involuntariness is force (*bia*), conceived as an external origin (*archē*) to which the agent contributes nothing, such as a wind which blows him off course. The storm is not inside him, but external, and the agent does not contribute to getting himself off course. The important qualification about the agent contributing nothing is repeated in each of the three places where Aristotle characterises this source of involuntar-

---

[15] It establishes once again, if we need it establishing, that the kind of action that we base on deliberation has not, in Aristotle's view, been necessary all along. For this fully deliberate action is said to be up to us and to involve an internal origin (*NE* III 2, 1111b30; III 3, 1112a31, 31, 1113a5–6, a10–11; VI 2, 1139a31, b5; *EE* II 10, 1225b36 – 1226a2, a19–32, b17).

iness (III 1, 1110a2, b2, b16). It leads us to expect that correspondingly a voluntary action can be subject to external influence, so long as the agent contributes something. But curiously the reference to the agent contributing something gets left out, when Aristotle switches from talking about the involuntary to talking about the voluntary, and he speaks simply of the origin being internal.[16] This may give rise to the impression that he shifts to thinking of what is voluntary as being *altogether* free of external influence, and sometimes this is taken to be his view.[17] But I do not think that this is his intention. For one thing, in arguing for the voluntariness of vice and virtue, he claims only that we contribute in a way to causing (*sunaitioi pōs*, 1114b23; cf. b2–3) our dispositions. He does not deny that external influences also contribute. Moreover, it is clear from elsewhere that he would not deny that such external factors as our ancestry, the training we receive from parents, and the constraints of the law play their part as well. Again, he is willing to say even of the man who jettisons his cargo to save his life in a storm (III 1, 1110a15) that the origin is internal, though he evidently finds this easier to say of the origin of his moving his limbs than of the origin of his jettisoning the cargo. In spite, then, of insisting on an internal origin, rather than simply on a contribution from the agent, Aristotle does not seem to be ruling out external influence; so the shift in his terminology does not here involve an important shift of doctrine.

The second apparent change in meaning arises because the existence of an internal origin is in III 1 only one of two preconditions for an action's being voluntary. The other requirement is that it should not be performed on account of non-culpable ignorance (1109b35 – 1110a1; 1110b18 – 1111a21), ignorance, that is, of the relevant factual circumstances (ignorance of right and wrong is no excuse, III 1, 1110b30 – 1111a1). These two requirements appear to be treated as separate at 1111a22–4. And if Aristotle sometimes speaks as if an internal origin guaranteed voluntariness, this is normally because the context makes clear that the other condition concerning ignorance is assumed to be satisfied (1110a15–18, b4–5; cf. 1114a18–19). But in III 5, at 1113b20–1, Aristotle speaks again of an internal origin guaranteeing voluntariness, without the context supplying any indication that we can assume the satisfaction of the condition concerning ignorance. Does this mean that the concept of an internal origin has been altered in such a way as to *include* the requirement that the cause of action should not be non-culpable ignorance? (There is a similar lack of clarity about whether the

[16] *NE* III 1, 1110a15, a17, b4, 1111a23; III 3, 1112b28, b32, 1113a5–6; III 5, 1113b18, b20, b21, b32; 1114a19; cf. VI 2, 1139a31, a32, b5.

[17] A. A. Long (31.7) 1971, 188, but on the basis of a different passage – the one that says we cannot refer our actions to origins other than those in us, *NE* III 5, 1113b19–20. I have already interpreted this passage differently above.

requirement of an action's being 'up to us' incorporates, or is separate from, the condition concerning ignorance.)[18]

Fortunately neither of these two apparent shifts in the notion of an internal origin affects our inference that *NE* III agrees with the other two books that our voluntary actions are such as it is in our power to do or refrain from doing. But a third complication arises from Aristotle's concession (*NE* III 5, 1114a13–21) that it may no longer be possible (*esti, exesti, dunaton*) for the wicked man to refrain from being wicked, and hence, presumably, from doing some wicked things or other, because his character has become too ingrained. He is able to refrain from one wicked action and to prefer another,[19] but not to refrain from wicked actions altogether. In spite of this concession, Aristotle still holds that wicked character and, presumably, the performing of some wicked actions or other, is voluntary (*NE* III 5, 1113b16; 1114a22, b20, b24; cf. III 1, 1110b32) and up to the agent (1114a31). Consequently, we learn from *NE* III 5 something that we do not learn from *EE* II and *NE* V 8, namely, that the voluntariness of wicked character is compatible with there no longer being a possibility of avoiding that character. And presumably the voluntariness with which a man performs some wicked actions or other will be compatible with there no longer being a possibility of his refraining from performing some wicked actions or other. None the less, Aristotle still maintains that there must have been a possibility once. So we can still conclude that voluntary bad character, and the voluntary doing of some wicked deed or other, cannot *all along* have been necessary.[20]

I have been arguing, in connexion with human voluntary action, that

---

[18] On the one hand, in *EE* II 9, 1225b8–10, Aristotle seems to speak as if the two requirements were separate. On the other hand, this is not conclusive, because although the two requirements are *mentioned* separately, it could still be that the one concerning ignorance is implied by the requirement that it be up to us to refrain. And indeed it would seem rather unnatural to say that it was 'up to' a man to refrain from administering poison in a case where he could not know that the stuff was poison. Further, there are places where Aristotle seems to speak as if an action's being up to us entailed its being voluntary (*NE* III 1, 1110a18), or was equivalent to it (III 5, 1114a18, a22, a31, b13), in which case again the condition concerning ignorance would be already implied by the notion of 'up to us'. None the less, these passages are not conclusive: it may be because ignorance is not in question here that being up to us is treated as a sure sign of voluntariness.

[19] This much freedom of choice would be allowed by Aristotle even to a man, if there were one, who had been born with his wicked character fully formed, *NE* III 5, 1114b18, b21.

[20] It may help the reader to follow what has just been said, if I recapitulate the relations between the key terms which have been used. If an action of ours is voluntary (*hekousion*), this entails both that its origin (*archē*) is in us, and that it is up to us (*eph' hēmin*) whether we do it or not, so that it cannot all along have been necessary. Conversely, Aristotle sometimes suggests that if the origin is in us, then the action is up to us, and that if either of these conditions is met, the action is voluntary. But here Aristotle's intention is less clear, because it is a prerequisite of voluntariness that we should not be acting because of ignorance of the relevant circumstances; and this requirement is not included in the notion of an internal origin, as he first presents it, and is possibly not included in the notion of an action's being up to us either.

Aristotle would deny it has all along been necessary. (The case of God's action or of the movement of the stars is a separate question.)[21] None the less, I have found no trace of a denial of causation in human action. Although accidental conjunctions are uncaused, that fact is not especially connected with human conduct. If causation can occur without necessitation, Aristotle must have quietly forgotten the unfortunate principle of *Metaph.* VI 3, that what is caused is necessitated.

The objection that Aristotle's account of action is necessitarian

I must now prepare to meet the objection that Aristotle's account of action is full of references to necessity, and repeatedly betrays a deterministic way of thinking. It may be wondered whether his way of talking elsewhere is consistent with his denial that voluntary action has all along been necessary. We have already noticed that Aristotle thinks some character so ingrained that it cannot be changed (*NE* 1114a13–21, 1150a21, b32, 1151a14). He also thinks that some actions are necessitated (*NE* 1147a27, a30; *Metaph.* IX 5, 1048a14; *Mot.* 9, 702b24; *Poet.* 1450b27–31, 1451a12–15, a38, b9, b35, 1452a20, 1454a33–6). And everything is necessary once it is present or past (*Cael.* 283b12–14, *NE* 1139b7–9, *Rhet.* 1418a3–5, *Int.* 9, 19a23–4). There is a very mechanistic account of animal movement in *De Motu Animalium* 6–10, and another in an earlier work, *Phys.* VIII, where he denies that animals can originate movement *de novo*, because he wants to make way for the influence of God, the unmoved mover (VIII 3, 253a7–20; VIII 6, 259b1–20). Action is due to desire, desire to the perceiving or conceiving of the object desired, and this, judging from the *Physics* account, is due to influences in the environment, which seem to be viewed here as efficient, rather than final, causes. Sometimes the *strength* of the desire is treated as causally relevant to the outcome (*NE* 1110a23–6, 1150b6–16, 1151a2, 1148a17–22; cf. 1147b14–17 with 1145b31 – 1146a7), although Aristotle does not, like Thomas Hobbes, think this explains what goes on in deliberation. Aristotle further speaks as if children, and many adults, simply follow, or are led by, their passions (*NE* 1095a4–9, 1150b21–2, 1156a32–3, 1179b7–16), and we may add the strong influence that he assigns to upbringing.

Not all of these points, however, bear on necessity. Let us examine the four which do. One context is the discussion of self-control and its

---

[21] Aristotle regarded the movement of the stars as voluntary in a very early work, the *De Philosophia*, as recorded by Cicero (*voluntarius*, Cicero, *De Natura Deorum* 2 16 44 = fragment 21 in W. D. Ross' Oxford translation of the fragments). And this might seem to fit with his view in a relatively late work, *Metaph.* XII 7 (1072b3), where he explains stellar motion by saying that God, the prime mover, moves the spheres which carry the stars in the way that the beloved moves the lover. But if so, the definition of voluntariness would need to be changed, because the stars move always, and hence, in Aristotle's view, necessarily.

absence. This means that the kind of action which Aristotle is discussing constitutes a special case. The uncontrolled man whom he has in mind has deliberated and based a choice (*prohaeresis*) on his deliberation, yet acts against it.[22] He has chosen the policy about diet which is mentioned in one of the major premises. We should therefore assume that the controlled man who is contrasted with him has also deliberated and made a deliberate choice. In Aristotle's example, he has chosen a sweet diet. I assume it is because of his careful deliberation and choice that, when certain further conditions are met, it becomes *necessary* for this man to act and to take sweet food (*NE* 1147a25–31). Some commentators suppose that in these lines Aristotle is describing voluntary action in general, and one interpreter accordingly infers that all voluntary action is necessitated.[23] I think this overlooks the evidence that Aristotle is confining himself to action based on a deliberate choice of policy.

A second context also involves a special case. In *Metaph.* IX 5, 1048a14, Aristotle is discussing a man who possesses a rational skill like medicine. Under certain conditions, the exercise of such a rational skill becomes necessary, but this is not a remark about all actions. There are claims made earlier in Aristotle's chapter which I considered in Chapter Three to see whether they carried deterministic implications about all events whatever. But insofar as Aristotle is concentrating on actions, he is discussing a special class.

The *De Motu Animalium* is the most far-reaching passage and someone who took it as representative would get a misleading impression. Because of a sequence of physiological changes, initiated by perception and desire, motion takes place in animals *of necessity* (9, 702b24). When the active and passive elements in this causal chain are assembled, and no essential aspect of them is missing, they interact *straightaway*, so that the agent goes, *unless there is an obstacle* (8, 702a10–17). I think the special context of animal motion has made Aristotle think of rather simple examples. The Chapter 9 passage explicitly confines itself to the motion of *animals*, and even though human action is illustrated elsewhere, there are no examples in which there are rival desires (assuming the words 'unless there is an obstacle' are not intended to allude to the possibility of rival desires). Aristotle's current interest has made him simply overlook such cases as that of the child with the toy. It would be rash to assume that if he had had his attention directed

[22] *NE* 1145b11, 1148a9, 1150b19–22, b30–1, 1151a2, a7, a26, a30–5, b26, 1152a17, a18–19, a26, a28. The other kind of uncontrolled person, who does whatever comes into his head without having deliberated at all (*NE* 1095a4–9, 1111b6–10, 1150b19–22, 1151a1–3, 1152a19, a27–8, 1156a32–3, 1179b13–16) is not illustrated in our chapter: *NE* VII 3.

[23] J. A. Stewart, *Notes on the Nicomachean Ethics of Aristotle*, Oxford 1892, vol. 2 156; Sanford G. Etheridge, 'Aristotle's practical syllogism and necessity', *Philologus* 112, 1968, 20–42, esp. 37–41. It is Etheridge who draws the inference about necessity.

to it he would have been happy to affirm that the child's action is necessitated.

The fourth and last passage, the *Poetics*, creates no difficulty at all. Aristotle requires that events in a tragedy, including the actions, should be *either* the necessary *or* the probable outcome of what precedes. But at the same time, the beginning should not be the necessary outcome of some antecedent, and the end should not have a necessary or usual sequel. There is clearly no implication here that *all* actions are necessitated.

The strongest suggestion that all actions are necessitated comes from those passages which seem to imply that *all* effects are necessitated, without paying particular attention to *actions*. These passages were discussed in Chapter Three, but it was argued that there was only one unequivocal one, namely *Metaph*. vi 3, where it is implied that whatever is caused is necessitated. We have seen that this view is contradicted elsewhere. And my suggestion has been that in the passages which concern us, such as *NE* iii 5, it is quietly forgotten. Here Aristotle denies that actions have all along been necessary, without thinking of this as committing him to denying causation.

If we turn from those passages which talk of necessity to those which treat the *strength* of desire as explaining the outcome, we will see that Aristotle clearly thinks of these actions as exceptional. Indeed, he thinks that pardon will be in order in some of these cases (*NE* 1110a24, 1146a2, 1150b8). And he contrasts those who give in to overwhelming desires with those who give in to slight ones (1148a17).

Physiology plays an extra role when we act against a deliberate choice through passion. For the physiological processes connected with the passion can impair our knowledge of what we are doing (*NE* vii 3, 1147b6–8). But this too is clearly a special case.

Some of the evidence cited for a necessitarian view of action in Aristotle does not bear on necessity at all, but only on causation. In *Phys*. viii, for example, Aristotle wants God to be the only original cause of motion, and for this reason denies that animals can be original causes of it. It is also a point about causation, with no commitments about necessity, when Aristotle describes many people as being led by passion. As for the influence of upbringing, this does not make any particular action inevitable; it is not even clear that it makes any particular character inevitable.

We ought now to recall some of the evidence on the other side. We have seen that voluntary action cannot, for Aristotle, have been necessary all along. We know that he thinks it is not fixed at first what character a man will have, and that, at the time of deliberation, it is not yet fixed what he will conclude or what he will do. Even when he decides what to do on the basis of deliberation and makes a deliberate choice (*prohaeresis*), we have seen that he can act against it, although here, admittedly, the strength of the rival desire may be relevant. Most important, we have seen that his remarks about necessity and strength do not seem to be generalised to all cases of action. This leaves it open to Aristotle to say, what I believe *NE* III 5 requires if it is to allow responsibility for character, that some actions are not necessitated at all.

Physiological processes as unexplanatory prerequisites

Necessitation is not the only thing that would impair responsibility, and it may be felt that Aristotle's references to physiology pose a threat to responsibility of a different kind. For even with regard to unnecessitated actions, could not a man shrug off responsibility by saying that physiological factors explained his acting on a given desire?

The first major discussion of this kind of issue is put into the mouth of Socrates in Plato's *Phaedo* (98c – 99b). If Socrates continues to sit in prison, awaiting execution, when he was given every opportunity to escape to Megara or Boeotia, it would be absurd to say that the explanation is his anatomical arrangement. This is a *necessary prerequisite* of his sitting, but the *explanation* of his sitting is that he decided it was better to sit there and undergo the penalty prescribed.

Aristotle takes up the discussion. He thinks that desire involves a physiological process, but that this process is only a necessary prerequisite of the desire. At least, he compares the relation of the physiological process to desire with that of the bricks to a house (*DA* I 1, 403a25 – b9), a relationship which he elsewhere describes (*Phys.* II 9) as being that of a necessary prerequisite. Admittedly, a bad state of the body can encourage desires to form (*DA* I 1, 403a19–22), as Plato agrees (*Timaeus* 86b – 87b). Admittedly, too, the physiological embodiment of desire leads by physiological processes to limb movements, in the manner described in *Mot.* 6–10: the heating and cooling expands and contracts the *pneuma*, and this moves the limbs. But Aristotle insists repeatedly that the *pneuma* is only an *organon*, that is, an instrument or tool (*Mot.* 10, 703a20; *DA* III 10, 433b19; *GA* v 8, 789b9). And in the last cited passage he goes on to say that to cite the *pneuma* as the *explanation* of what happens is like citing the lancet as the explanation of fluid being drawn off the patient.

To find a justification for the last part of what Aristotle says, I think we should have to go a little further than he does, and draw a sharp distinction between the action performed and the limb movements involved in its performance. I find it hard to believe that the physiological embodiment of desire could not explain the *limb movements*. What is plausible is that it will not explain the *action*. Let us apply this to the case of the child who takes the forbidden toy when nothing necessitates his doing so. I shall assume for present purposes that the internal heating and expanding does not necessitate his taking the toy – it could have been inhibited up to the moment of action. If we may now add that it also does not *explain* his taking the toy, but explains only the limb movements he performed in taking it, then it is no wonder that he cannot escape responsibility by appealing to physiology.

Retrospect

In this chapter, I have concluded my case against *deterministic* interpretations, by denying that Aristotle's treatment of action is wholly deterministic. The remainder of my case was summarised at the end of Chapter Eight.

My case against the more radical *indeterministic* interpretations was made in Chapters Nine to Eleven, where I denied that Aristotle virtually excluded causal necessitation from natural processes.[24] An accompanying view, that he denied causation in connexion with natural processes[25] and with action,[26] has been considered and opposed in the present chapter and in Chapter Nine. My general conclusion is that Aristotle is an indeterminist in the sense defined in the Introduction, but not in the more radical sense suggested by others.

[24] Ross, Balme, Preus, Weiss, Wieland, Sambursky, Düring, Kullmann.
[25] Ross, Balme.
[26] Ross, Furley, Hardie.

CHAPTER FIFTEEN

The Relation of Determinism to Involuntariness: Aristotle's alleged nescience

The standard account of Aristotle's view

I come now to the question of how determinism is related to involuntariness. Many commentators nowadays hold one or more parts of the following view.[1] Determinism creates a problem for belief in the voluntariness of actions. Regrettably, but inevitably, Aristotle was unaware of this problem, and so failed to cope with it. Indeed, the problem was not discovered until Hellenistic times, perhaps by Epicurus, who was over forty years junior to Aristotle, and who reached Athens just too late to hear his lectures. In Aristotle's time no one had yet propounded a universal determinism, so that he knew of no such theory. His inevitable failure to see the threat to voluntariness is all the more regrettable in that he himself entertained a deterministic account of actions, which exacerbated the problem of how any could be voluntary. I shall argue that this account misrepresents the situation.

First, Aristotle is aware of the idea that everything is determined, whether causally or non-causally.[2] He considers a non-causal determinism in *Int.* 9, and a causal determinism not only in *Metaph.* VI 3, but also in *Phys.* II 4, where he remarks that some people had denied that there was such a thing as chance,[3] on the grounds that a cause could always be found for everything (195b36 – 196a11). Admittedly, he takes the falsity of determinism as fairly obvious in *Metaph.* VI 3, and feels little need to

---

[1] Although one or more parts of this view can be found in each of the following authors, I must in fairness emphasise that the view is a composite one and probably none of the authors holds it in its entirety. W. D. Ross, *Aristotle*, ch. 7, Meridian edition 1959, 196; R. A. Gauthier (29.4) 1970, vol. 2, 168–9, 217–20; Pamela Huby (29.3) 1967; David Furley (29.2) 1967, 184–95; A. W. H. Adkins (32.1) 1960, 324; E. R. Dodds (36.2) 1966, 42; D. J. Allan, *The Philosophy of Aristotle*, Oxford 1952, ch. 13, 175; and 'The practical syllogism', in *Autour d'Aristote* (essays presented to A. Mansion) Louvain 1955, 333; P. Tannery, 'Des principes de la science de la nature chez Aristote', *Mémoires Scientifiques*, vol. 7, n.20 § 12, p. 306, 1900; K. J. Dover (33.9) 1973, 60; M. Pohlenz (3.2) 1940, p. 105; J. B. Gould, *The Philosophy of Chrysippus*, Leiden 1970, 152; R. Loening (1.2) 1903, ch. 18.

[2] Admittedly in mythology we find only the restricted idea that certain selected outcomes are fated. This is well explained by R. B. Onians in (33.1) 1954, part III, ch. 7. But the evidence to be cited shows that Aristotle knew of a more radical thesis.

[3] *Tuchē* and *to automaton*, two species of accidental conjunction.

discuss it in *NE* III, or in *GC* II 11. Indeed, in the last passage he asks not whether all coming to be is necessary, but whether any is. None the less, he does sometimes produce arguments against determinism (*Int.* 9, 18b26 – 19a22; *Phys.* II 5, 196b14; *GC* II 11, 337b3–7). And he also thinks that in the light of its falsity, he needs to do some explaining, and to show how there can be events without a cause (accidental conjunctions, *Metaph.* VI 3), or how some predictions can avoid being already true (*Int.* 9, 19a22 – b4, on the traditional interpretation).

What Aristotle failed to discuss was not determinism, but something that William James was later to call 'hard' determinism,[4] the view that not only is determinism true, but that also, because of it, there is no such thing as moral responsibility or voluntary action. The commentators mentioned above are right insofar as they only want to say this. But what is debatable is whether we should see Aristotle's silence about 'hard' determinism as simply a failure to see a problem, and how far the subsequent Hellenistic period differed from Aristotle in their readiness to discuss 'hard' determinism. Determinists in antiquity did not make it a triumphant conclusion that all actions are involuntary. Rather, they would have thought it an objection to their view, if they had to banish voluntariness. There is a whole battery of arguments, which turn up in treatise after treatise, urging against determinism, that it would do away with many of our conceptions about conduct and morality. In the *De Fato* of Alexander of Aphrodisias (*fl. c.* A.D. 200), where many of these arguments are used, it becomes clear that the Stoics, against whom they were directed, replied not by conceding the point, but by urging that fate did not exclude the standard moral concepts (chs 13–14, 33, 35–8). Occasionally, they seem to have gone over to the offensive, and argued, like certain modern philosophers,[5] that the standard moral concepts actually presuppose determinism (chs 35–7). But, as we saw in Chapter Four, they felt little attraction towards 'hard' determinism, even if their founder Zeno (*fl. c.* 300 B.C.) deployed an argument in an *ad hominem* way which is used also by hard determinists, that our moral practices are inevitable, whether justifiable, or not (Diogenes Laertius 7 1 23).[6] Most ancients would have said, and so would Aristotle, that, if there is a genuine incompatibility between determinism and voluntariness, this is so much the worse for determinism, not for voluntariness; and even in modern times, 'hard' determinism is much rarer than 'soft'.[6a]

---

[4] William James, 'The dilemma of determinism', *Unitarian Review* 1884, reprinted in *The Will to Believe and Other Essays*, London 1897.

[5] E.g. R. E. Hobart (30.3) 1934, Schlick (30.2) 1939.

[6] The other references for this argument were: Epicurus, *On Nature,* ed. Arrighetti, 2nd edition, 34. 27; Eusebius, (*c.* A.D. 260–340) *Praeparatio Evangelica* VI 6 15 244A; Manilius (first century A.D.), *Astronomicon* IV 106–18; Galen (*c.* A.D. 129–99) *Quod Animi Mores* 11 init.; cf. Aeschylus *Choephoroe* 909–11.

[6a] For another pointer, we may recall the fact recorded in Chapter Seven, that many preferred to ask how the gods could have foreknowledge given that we were free, rather than to ask how we could be free given that the gods had foreknowledge.

Aristotle himself, so far from failing to observe any incompatibility between determinism and our ordinary ways of thinking about conduct, actually tended to see such incompatibilities too readily. Moreover, so far from his successors starting a new tradition, they are often simply echoing Aristotle's own comments, when they argue that there is an incompatibility, and that it counts against determinism. We have seen that Aristotle thinks voluntariness incompatible with an action's having all along been necessary, and further that he goes so far as to argue (wrongly) against determinism that it is incompatible with the efficacy of effort or deliberation (*Int.* 9, 18b31–3, 19a7–8). This latter was echoed in one of the famous named arguments of antiquity, the Lazy Argument, according to which belief in determinism would make us lazy.[7] A related argument, which we have already noticed, appears in *NE* III 5 (1113b21–30), where Aristotle claims (again wrongly) that since punishment and honours influence conduct, good and bad conduct must be up to us. Aristotle may here have been ignoring, rather than answering, the idea that wicked conduct is determined, and may have been concentrating instead on the point that our conduct is in some way dependent on us. But his successors used arguments like this one in order to attack determinism,[8] and he too might have been willing to use the argument against a determinist, if he had felt himself to be confronted by one. Aristotle often repeats that we do not deliberate about what is necessary (*NE* III 3, 1112a21–6; VI 1, 1139a13; VI 2, 1139b7–9; VI 5, 1140a 31–b1; VI 7, 1141b10–11; III 3, 1112a30–1 with III 5, 1113b7–8; *EE* II 10, 1226a20–30; *Rhet.* I 2, 1357a8), and only once comes at all close to adding the desirable qualification 'unless we do not realise that such and such a course is necessary'.[9] If determinism is incompatible with deliberation, it will also be incompatible with *praxis*, the distinctively human kind of action, and with moral virtue, both of which presuppose deliberation. Similar views on the relation of deliberation to determinism reappeared among Aristotle's ancient and modern successors.[10] And

[7] Cicero *De Fato* XII 28 – XIII 30; Ps-Plutarch *De Fato* 574E; Aulus Gellius *Attic Nights* VII 2 4–5; Alexander of Aphrodisias *De Fato* 16, Origen *Against Celsus* II 20; Eusebius *Praeparatio Evangelica* VI 6 243B, VI 8 265D; Iulius Firmicus Maternus *Mathesis* I 2 6–8; John Chrysostom *Homilies of first letter to Timotheos* I 3 (= *Patrologia Graeca*, ed. Migne, vol. 62, 507–8); *Homily in Church of St. Paul* 6; (= *Patrologia Graeca*, vol. 63, 509–10); *On Fate and Providence* V (= *Patrologia Graeca*, vol. 50, 765–8); Servius on Vergil *Aeneid* IV 696. Many of these texts are collected by David Amand in *Fatalisme et Liberté dans l'Antiquité Grecque*, Louvain 1945. Others can be found in H. von Arnim, *Stoicorum Veterum Fragmenta*.

[8] Epicurus *On Nature* 31 27 3–9 (Arrighetti); Alexander of Aphrodisias *De Fato* 16; Eusebius *Praeparatio Evangelica* VI 6 12–16 244A; Iulius Firmicus Maternus *Mathesis* 1 2 7; John Chrysostom *Homily in Church of St. Paul* 6; *On Fate and Providence* V; Nemesius *On the Nature of Man* 39.

[9] What he actually says at *EE* II 10, 1226a26, is, 'unless we do not realise that it depends on nature or on other causes, rather than on us'.

[10] Alexander of Aphrodisias *De Fato* 11; Nemesius *On the Nature of Man* 39, 42. Thomas Reid claimed that the facts of deliberation and choice threw the onus of proof on those who

they also turned against determinism the comment, which Aristotle makes in another context, that we cannot bestow praise and blame for what happens of necessity (*NE* III 5, 1114a23–9; *EE* II 6, 1223a10; II 11, 1228a5), although we can bestow honour, e.g. on the gods (*NE* I 12, 1101b10 – 1102a4).[11]

Those who think that determinism endangers voluntariness have every right to disagree with Aristotle's view that our ways of thinking about conduct endanger determinism. But they should recognise it as an alternative view. It misrepresents the situation to suggest that Aristotle was merely not yet in a position to appreciate the problem; he would not have agreed that the problem was one for believers in voluntariness. And the succeeding age would have supported him.

Aristotle would have been all the more confident about where the onus of proof lay because of his whole method of doing philosophy, which was a dialectical one. He defines dialectic as reasoning that starts from what people have *accepted* (*endoxa, Top.* I 1, 100a29 – b23), and he thinks that a view that has been accepted by *everyone* is unchallengeable (*NE* x 2, 1172b35 – 1173a2; cf. *Phys.* II 5, 196b14). The belief in the voluntariness of some actions was such a view, and he would therefore not expect it to be controverted. Admittedly, it would be wrong to suggest that the accepted opinions from which Aristotle starts are always popular ones; he is willing to start from the opinions of philosophers, especially of Plato's Academy.[12] It would also be wrong to suggest that he leaves accepted opinions to stand as they are; his recommendation is rather to start by assembling what has been accepted, to raise difficulties for it, to dissolve the difficulties as far as possible, and to retain all that survives of the accepted opinions (*NE* VII 1–2, 1145b2–7, 1146b6–8). But an opinion as widely held as the voluntariness of some actions would have for him a special status.[13] It is an instance of this dialectical approach when Aristotle argues in *Int.* 9 that the efficacy of deliberation and action show that there is something wrong with the determinist's argument somewhere, as also does the fact that a particular cloak may be cut up or not. These are things which are

believed in determinism (*Essays on the Active Powers of Man*, 1788, Essay IV, ch. 6). And Hobbes seems to have seen significance in deliberation, since he gave a special analysis of it as an alternate succession of competing desires, in order to represent it as compatible with determinism (*Leviathan*, 1651, part I, ch. 6).

[11] Alexander of Aphrodisias *De Fata* 16, 20, 27, 32, 34, 36; Philo *De Providentia* I 82; Eusebius *Praeparatio Evangelica* VI 6 5–6; John Chrysostom *On Fate and Providence* V; Nemesius *On the Nature of Man* 35. I am grateful to Robert Sharples for drawing my attention to the argument about honouring the gods.

[12] Examples are the way in which he reaches his definition of the happy life in *NE* I 7, 1097b22 – 1098a18, or of moral virtue in *NE* II 5 and 6. But even here he is anxious to show that the definition conforms to more popular opinions.

[13] The subject is admirably explained by G. E. L. Owen, 'Τιθέναι τὰ Φαινόμενα', in S. Mansion (ed.), *Aristote et les Problèmes de Méthode*, Louvain and Paris 1961 (reprinted in *Articles on Aristotle* vol. 1) See further J. Donald Monan, *Moral Knowledge and its Methodology in Aristotle*, Oxford 1968, 96–104.

'clear' (19a12), and which 'we see' (a7). Similarly in *GC* ɪɪ 11, Aristotle cites facts of ordinary language as reminders that it is 'clear' that some things at least do not come about of necessity (337b3–7). Its now being true to say that something is about to (*mellei*) happen, unlike its now being true to say that it will (*estai*) happen, is compatible with its not happening after all. Once again, the fact that chance exists is made apparent by the fact that everyone ascribes certain things to chance (*Phys.* ɪɪ 5, 196b14).

We can now understand better why Aristotle does not consider a 'hard' determinist in *NE* ɪɪɪ 5. A 'hard' determinist would want to protest when Aristotle argues that the efficacy of reward and punishment shows that our conduct is up to us (1113b21–30), and again he would not accept Aristotle's final proof (1114b3–25) that wickedness is voluntary. But if Aristotle does not consider his view, this is not due to a failure to see a problem, but to his having a different opinion about who is threatened by the problems that there are.

The impression that Aristotle is insufficiently alive to problems is fostered by the common interpretation of the concluding argument in *NE* ɪɪɪ 5 (1114b3–25). If Aristotle wants to prevent us from tracing the causal history of an action back to the agent's ancestry, he has not appreciated that it is no easier to find a break in the causal chain at an earlier stage in the man's development than at a later stage. But I have suggested that Aristotle would not need to break any chains of causation, only of necessitation (if anyone tried to forge them) and that this is a defensible position.

But is there no truth, it may be asked, in the common view that a new development took place in the Hellenistic period after Aristotle? The answer is that there was a new development, but that it was not the invention of determinism, nor the realisation that determinism clashed with ethical presuppositions. The new development was that Diodorus and the Stoics persisted in endorsing determinism in a context where many people, Aristotle included, had already become aware of the clash. This made the subject of determinism a central preoccupation, and led to two new moves. First, there was the argument, known to Epicurus and Zeno, and shared by 'hard' determinists, that punishment and admonition are inevitable, whether justifiable or not. Secondly, there was the 'soft' determinism argued by Chrysippus and others, according to which ethical presuppositions are compatible with determinism. But these new moves should be seen for what they are, that is as new moves in a subject which had already been advanced by Aristotle.

There are, admittedly, some things to be regretted about Aristotle's handling of the question. One is that, as was argued in Chapter Three, he never manages to make clear to himself the principle that his argument needs, that what is caused need not be necessitated; indeed, in one place he denies it. Nor does he try to locate, in connexion with human action, the exact point at which necessitation fails. The example of the child with the toy had to be supplied, since no example was offered by Aristotle. The argument against causal determinism in *Metaph.* vi 3 picks out *accidents* as the unnecessitated events, but that does not help with the present problem. That determinism is wrong he thinks sufficiently established, by reference to action among other things; but as to just where necessitation is missing in this context, he has not said enough. In spite of this, he is not in a radically different position from Epicurus and other successors, who were equally convinced that human action shows determinism wrong, but who often had less satisfactory suggestions about just where it breaks down.

We can also understand better now a fact to which Gauthier has drawn attention in his commentary on the *Nicomachean Ethics*, that the theses which Aristotle discusses in *NE* iii are quite different from determinism. People would not have chosen the field of ethics and action as one in which to argue for determinism, except perhaps those few bold Stoics of a later date who argued that moral concepts actually presuppose determinism. In Aristotle's time, the arguments for involuntariness that had been put forward did not concern *all* actions (but only wicked ones or certain passionate ones), and they did not on the whole operate via the concept of *necessity* (only one of those considered by Aristotle seems to me clearly to do so: *NE* iii 1, 1110b10).[14]

The remaining suggestion in the composite view I described at the beginning of this chapter is that, by his own concessions to determinism, Aristotle has unwittingly debarred himself from regarding any actions as voluntary. I have already discussed this suggestion in Chapter Fourteen, and I there concluded that the only concession that really mattered was the idea entertained in *Metaph.* vi 3 that what is caused is necessitated. I took it that this idea was quietly forgotten in the ethical discussions. None of Aristotle's other concessions would imply that our actions had been necessary well in advance. The child in our fictitious example who takes the toy he knows to be forbidden need not do so of necessity. Admittedly, Aristotle is not alive to all the threats to voluntariness that

---

[14] Thus in *NE* iii 5, Aristotle is attacking not the thesis that all actions are necessary, but the more limited thesis, derived from Socrates, that *wicked* actions are involuntary (1113b7–17). This is why Aristotle's opponent is crushed when it is pointed out that his final argument would make *all* actions involuntary, even virtuous ones (1114b12–13). Clearly he never wanted this result, as is confirmed in the summary at 1114b22, when it is said to be agreed that *virtuous* actions are voluntary. The position is similar in iii 1, where again Aristotle considers only a limited view, suggested, for example, in some of Euripides' tragedies, or in Gorgias' specimen legal defence of Helen of Troy, that pleasant things force us to act, because they are external causes which necessitate action. Again the thesis is crushed, as soon as it is pointed out that it would make *all* actions into forced ones. Evidently, this was not intended, as is confirmed when Aristotle reveals that the opponent did not wish to ascribe *virtuous* actions to an external cause (1110b14–15). A rather similar treatment is given later in the chapter to the thesis that acts performed through anger or appetite are involuntary (1111a24–9). It is not expected that anyone will want to say this of *virtuous* acts.

there are, and I shall discuss some of those threats in Chapter Sixteen. But they do not come (if we ignore the unfortunate concession in *Metaph.* VI 3) from the direction of determinism.

J. L. Austin's account

What has been said enables us to assess another view of Aristotle's treatment of determinism and voluntariness. J. L. Austin made Aristotle's treatment of voluntariness popular in the 1950s by the praise he lavished on it in his presidential address to the Aristotelian Society.[15] He approved of Aristotle's defining voluntariness negatively in terms of the absence of certain excuses, and said:

In examining all the ways in which each action may not be 'free', i.e. the cases in which it will not do to say simply 'X did A', we may hope to dispose of the problem of Freedom. Aristotle has often been chidden for talking about excuses or pleas and overlooking 'the real problem': in my own case, it was when I began to see the injustice of this charge that I first became interested in excuses.

The problem of freedom is presumably the problem of whether, in the light of determinism, men can be considered free. What Austin says may give the impression that Aristotle thought that to establish freedom it would not be necessary to consider determinism. We need only observe that in ordinary language we call ourselves free when we are not the victims of ignorance, of external force, or of other excusing conditions. This way of putting things seems to me to obscure the situation in several ways. First, it does not bring out that Aristotle thought there would be a real incompatibility between determinism and our ordinary thought about conduct. Voluntariness involves not only the absence of certain excusing factors, but also its being *up to us* to act or refrain. This fact is mentioned in *NE* III, and actually put into the definition of voluntarinesss in *NE* V 8, and *EE* II 9. If Aristotle felt no need to discuss determinism in *NE* III, this was only because he thought the incompatibility counted against *determinism*, not because he was content with ordinary language. Secondly, Aristotle thought it necessary elsewhere to attack the reasons that made determinism seem plausible. And in order to attack those reasons, he put forward a theory about truth values, which by no means respected ordinary language, and another theory about the character of accidents.

Yet a third thing needs to be said: in *NE* III, Aristotle is not in any case discussing when people are *free*, but when their action is *voluntary*, which is different. We cannot infer from *NE* III alone what he would say about freedom. One difference between freedom, as it features in the problem of freedom, and voluntariness is that lack of freedom is by

---

[15] J. L. Austin (29.5) 1956–7.

definition a *detrimental thing*. Voluntariness, however, is closely linked to moral and legal responsibility by the opening of *NE* iii 1, and by the legal context of *NE* v 8 and *Rhet.* i 13. And these two, voluntariness and responsibility, are not things whose absence is by definition detrimental. This is only one of many differences between freedom on the one hand and voluntariness or responsibility on the other.[16]

Aristotle on freedom

Aristotle does discuss freedom elsewhere, but freedom in a different sense, the political freedom which is opposed to slavery. None the less, what he has to say is of interest. Once he draws an analogy which shows how differently he views political freedom from voluntariness. For he does not regard political freedom as being *opposed* to necessity. On the contrary, he compares the stars, which always and *necessarily* move in the same way, to the *free* men (*eleutheroi*) in a household, to whom it is least permitted (*exestin*) to do whatever may chance (*ho ti etuche*), and for whom nearly everything is laid down (*tetaktai*), whereas the animals and slaves do whatever may chance for much of the time (*Metaph.* xii 10, 1075a19–23).[17]

Although the passage is referring to political freedom, it enables us to guess what Aristotle might have said if he had discussed freedom of the kind that features in the problem of freedom. It looks as if this kind of freedom too would not have been opposed by him to necessity. For the passage reveals that he has a view, which we would not necessarily share, that necessity is in some way more *desirable* than contingency. Or at least, necessity is more desirable, if it guarantees that one comes closer to the ideal state which is enjoyed by God.[18] This implies that as our conduct approximated to the necessary behaviour of God or the

---

[16] It is not easy to make a clear contrast between 'free' and 'responsible', because there are so many uses of these words, and this remains true, even when I say that by 'responsible' I mean something like: liable to justified praise or blame. None the less, besides the contrast mentioned in the text, (i) that absence of freedom is a detrimental state, while absence of responsibility is not necessarily so, it may be worth mentioning the following further points of contrast. (ii) Because of its connexion with praise and blame, responsibility, unlike freedom, has a special link with morally good or bad acts. (iii) Responsibility for one's acts seems to imply the presence of other people, in a way that freedom does not. (iv) One can be responsible not only for becoming blind drunk or incurably lazy by free choices, but also for the acts one performs in this state, even if one no longer performs them freely. (v) Certain uses of 'free' actually conflict with certain uses of 'responsible': a man may be treated as responsible, and praised or blamed, according as he sticks to the narrow path of duty or diverges from it. Yet we may think, when praising him, that in one sense his obligations were so numerous as to restrict his 'freedom', or when blaming him, that in another sense he was not 'free' to act as he did.

[17] We may compare a passage already encountered, *EE* ii 6, 1222b22, where Aristotle says that God deserves to be called an origin, *archē*, of motion more fully than man does, because the motions he causes are necessary ones.

[18] This last qualification suggests the possibility of a position intermediate between the view that necessity always excludes freedom and the view that it never does. The inter-

stars, Aristotle would not think this constituted a loss of freedom, in the relevant sense. For he would not think such an approximation a *bad* thing, whereas loss of freedom is meant to be something *detrimental*.

Arguments for the compatibility of determinism with responsibility

It will now be as well if I make my own position clear about the relation of determinism to ethical matters. But I shall not try to prove that that position is right, since I do not know how to do so. All I shall undertake is to summarise some of the main attempts, starting with the Stoics, to show that it is *wrong*, and to indicate briefly why I do not find them convincing. This in itself may be a useful thing to do, since the standard objections are seldom assembled together. Meanwhile, I do not think that any of my main theses depends on my being right. It is rather that it will supply some orientation to reveal what my belief is, and how it compares with Aristotle's. And it will bring out part of my reason for attaching importance to the question of determinism: naturally I do, if I think that it would rule out responsibility.

If it had all along been necessary that a person should act as he did, this would be incompatible, I believe, with an important part of our thinking about conduct and morality. It would not exclude it all: I have already said that I do not accept Aristotle's view that deliberation would be inefficacious or impossible. It could survive even our *recognition* of determinism, so long as we did not know *which* outcome was necessary. Other things too could survive that recognition: people could still be admired or despised; there could still be relief, regret, respect and worship. But other attitudes might not fare so well. An important group has been studied by P. F. Strawson:[19] could we still feel compunction, remorse, guilt, obligation, indignation, or resentment? Could we engage in self-criticism, repentance, or forgiveness? Or could these attitudes survive only as a sort of illusion? For once we recognised the truth of determinism and its implications, we should have to view people in a more impersonal way. And there are other things which might not survive even the truth of determinism, let alone its recognition. Could it still be the case that we *ought* to have done what we failed to do, seeing that some people think (not quite accurately, as we shall see) that 'ought to have' implies 'could have'? But I shall confine myself to one question, the one closest to Aristotle's interests: could we still be *responsible*, that is, deserving of praise or blame? I believe we could not, if it had all along been necessary that we should act as we did. And if not, the example is

---

mediate position would be that necessity does not exclude freedom for a being like God who of necessity achieves the best state, but would exclude freedom for a being who of necessity fared badly.

[19] P. F. Strawson (30.10) 1962. Strawson's eventual conclusion, however, is quite different from the one I shall be advocating.

important that was given in Chapter Fourteen of the child who takes the toy he knows to be forbidden, even though nothing makes it necessary that he will respond to one set of feelings rather than another. The existence of this case and others like it makes responsibility possible.

Some thinkers would not mind our being unable to blame people, or to hold them responsible.[20] They believe that we should in any case concentrate on reforming rather than on assigning responsibility. But this view can have harsh consequences, as will become clear in Chapter Eighteen when we come to discuss Plato's *Laws*. For some blameless offenders may be reformable only through very severe treatment. Once again, the view would require us to treat people in a very impersonal way.

What precedes is simply a statement of belief. Only in connexion with objections to that belief, do I reach the stage of argument. Some of those who object that determinism is after all compatible with all our ethical attitudes do not mean what I mean by *determinism*, and so are not in disagreement with me in respect of their conclusion. Moritz Schlick, for example, in one of the most influential modern pleas for compatibility,[21] thinks of determinism as involving not necessity, but only exceptionless regularities. He models himself on Hume, who held that there was no necessity in nature, only constant conjunction. Similarly, as was seen in Chapter Four, some Stoics sought to preserve our ethical attitudes by disclaiming belief in necessity. This is not the position I am opposing, although some of Schlick's arguments have been used in support of such a position. What I am opposing is the idea that responsibility is compatible with the truth of determinism in my sense, that is, with the truth of the thesis that whatever happens has all along been necessary. This is the idea I shall be referring to when I talk of 'compatibilism'. When compatibilism is combined with the belief that such determinism is true, the combination is called 'soft determinism'.

Some Stoics, as we saw, did argue for such a compatibility, and we can distinguish theirs as the first of many arguments.

(i) They held that in spite of an action being necessary all along, it can still be *up to us* (*eph' hēmin*), in which case we will be responsible for it. The action will be up to us, so long as it is in accordance with our nature (*phusis*), that is, with impulse (*hormē*), and occurs *through* us (*di' hēmōn*).[22]

(ii) In modern times, Moritz Schlick has offered a different, but equally unsatisfying, account of some of the key terms.[23] A man is *free*, he suggests, so long as he does not act under *compulsion*; and compul-

[20] E.g. Moritz Schlick (30.2) 1939. [21] Schlick, loc. cit.
[22] Nemesius *On the Nature of Man* 35; Alexander *De Fato* 13–14 (repeated 33, 36, 38); Alexander? *De Anima Libri Mantissa CIAG* 172 8.
[23] Schlick, loc. cit.

sion is defined, in Stoic fashion, as the hindrance of natural desires by external factors or by unnatural internal ones.

(iii) Further, Schlick connects responsibility with educability. If one can achieve reform of a man, or deterrence of others, or spur a man on by punishing or rewarding him for an act, then he is responsible.

These special definitions of 'up to us', 'free', 'responsible', could be used (though that is not Schlick's own procedure), in an effort to show that responsibility is compatible with the action's having been necessary all along. What I cannot bring myself to believe is that these definitions come anywhere near to capturing the meanings of the terms.

Another expression which has been the subject of special definitions is 'He could have done otherwise'. And these definitions constitute a second group of arguments. Those who accept determinism in the sense I am discussing, which involves *necessity*, thereby accept that in *some* sense a man *could not* have acted otherwise than he did. But in order to make room for responsibility, they sometimes argue that there is more than one sense of 'could have done otherwise', and that the sense relevant to assigning responsibility is a different one.

(iv) One such argument maintains that 'He can act otherwise' can be taken as meaning no more than 'He will act otherwise, if he wants', or something like that. Versions of this analysis have been very popular during the present century.[24] And they have historical interest, because one version was already given by Aristotle in *Metaph*. ix 5, as was seen in Chapter Eight, although Aristotle's purpose was not to defend compatibilism. Such adequate rebuttals of the proposed definition have been offered in the literature, that I can simply refer to some of the most outstanding replies.[25] I need only say that, if the definition had supplied a possible sense in which someone could have acted otherwise, that sense would not have justified our holding him responsible, unless it could also be shown that he could have *wanted* otherwise.

(v) The proposal is similar to, though different from, another, according to which 'could have done otherwise' is elliptical for something like 'could have done otherwise, if he had wanted to do otherwise'.[26] To this proposal some of the same objections will apply.

(vi) A different treatment of the expression 'could have done otherwise' points to the many different uses of 'can' and of 'possible' that exist in ordinary language. Anthony Kenny distinguishes ten in a recent

[24] For examples, see: G. E. Moore, *Ethics*, Oxford 1912; C. L. Stevenson, *Ethics and Language*, Newhaven Conn. 1944; P. H. Nowell-Smith (30.4) 1954.

[25] J. L. Austin (30.6) 1956 (reprinted in his *Philosophical Papers*); Roderick M. Chisholm (30.7) 1964, both reprinted in (30.1); K. Lehrer (30.8) 1966; G. E. M. Anscombe (30.9).

[26] Proposals of this kind are to be found in A. Kaufman, 'Moral responsibility and the use of "could have" ', *Philosophical Quarterly* 12, 1962, 120–8; James W. Lamb, 'On a proof of incompatibilism', *Philosophical Review* 86, 1977, 20–35; and, along with the preceding one, in Moore and Nowell-Smith.

book.[27] We noticed earlier that in *Metaph*. ɪx 1–5 Aristotle was not discussing possibility in general, but only the capacities or abilities of things, and he distinguished several kinds of these. It is on this sort of distinction that soft determinism sometimes trades. Admittedly, it is said, determinism implies it was all along impossible that a man should do otherwise, but this need not be for want of ability (in the sense of skill), or opportunity (as that term is usually understood). We can express his possession of skill or opportunity by saying that it was possible for him, or he was able, to do otherwise. This account of possibility is reminiscent of Philo's suggestion, recorded in Chapter Four, that it is possible for a log at the bottom of the ocean to be burnt, in virtue of bare *fitness* for burning, even though external obstacles prevent its being burnt. Such a sense of 'possible' seems to me not to help. It does not make a difference to our assessment of a man's responsibility to hear that what made it all along impossible, even before his birth, that he should do otherwise was not a shortage of skill, or a lack of opportunity in the conventional sense.

A third group of arguments looks for examples in which we think it right to blame someone for not doing something, or to say that he ought to have done it, even though we accept that it was impossible for him to act in the required way.

(vii) One such argument points out that, if a man stays in a room because he wants to, he can still be blamed, if staying was a bad thing to do, even if it transpires that there was no possibility of his leaving. Perhaps, without knowing it, he lacked the opportunity (the door handle had jammed), or the ability (his hand would have been too weak to turn it). Here the impossibility of doing otherwise does not remove responsibility; so why should it do so in the case of determinism?[28]

One answer is that the factors which make it impossible for the man to leave in this story are not the ones which *explain* his staying, and this is why he can still be blamed. On the thesis of causal determinism, however, the causal antecedents which made it impossible for a man to do otherwise would also *explain* his doing what he did, and therefore he ought to escape blame.

This answer would suggest that at least *causal* determinism is incompatible with moral responsibility. But what about other kinds of determinism, for example, determinism based on God's infallible foreknowledge, as discussed in Chapter Six? Here it may look as if the infallible foreknowledge is like the jammed door handle, in that it makes it impossible for a man to act otherwise, but is not what *explains* his acting as he does. Ought not this kind of determinism, then, to be compatible

---

[27] A. J. P. Kenny (30.5) 1976, ch. 7. Cf. M. R. Ayers, *The Refutation of Determinism*, London 1968.

[28] Such arguments, and first reply, though not the second, are very well discussed by Harry Frankfurt (30.11) 1969.

with moral responsiblity? In fact, it is rather obscure what makes it impossible for the man to act otherwise, and what explains his acting as he does, so long as it remains obscure why the predictor is infallible. But in any case, a separate reply can be offered: the man in the locked room was at least able to *try* and leave, and can be blamed because he did not try. But on any deterministic thesis, a man who does not try is *unable* to try, and so can hardly be blamed (while if he does try and fails, again he has an excuse).

(viii) There are further examples in which we think it just to blame someone, although he could not act otherwise. These are cases in which he would once have been in a position to act otherwise, but surrendered this possibility through his own conduct. Clearly, however, determinism in the sense under discussion does not make room for blame through this channel. For the deterministic thesis is that all along, even before his birth, it was not open to him to act differently.

(ix) A third argument in this group criticises the idea that 'ought' implies 'can'. To put it another way, 'could not have done otherwise' does not exclude 'ought to have done otherwise'. For example, I ought to be at the dying man's bedside. Even if I am prevented by a wholly unforeseeable hijacking of my aeroplane, it remains true that I ought to have been there, and it would be reasonable for me to feel very badly about failing to be there. None the less, this argument fails to show that determinism would leave room for blameworthiness. For the hijacking does exonerate me from blame, even though it does not prevent it from being true that I ought to have been there. In other words, 'ought to have' admittedly does not imply 'could have', but then neither does it imply 'can fairly be blamed for not'.

(x) A final argument belongs to a different category. It has been said that the only attractive form of determinism nowadays is a restricted one which says that every *physical* state (but not every state whatever) has all along been necessary.[29] And such a restricted determinism, it is said, would be compatible with moral responsibility. I think this suggestion very hard to assess, because, as explained in Chapter Two, I am not clear how to define the idea of 'every physical state'. But at any rate, the view is not relevant to my present purposes, for by my definition it is describing an *indeterministic* position, since it does not postulate the necessity of every state whatever. It belongs then with those arguments of the Stoics and of Moritz Schlick, which I excluded from the present discussion, because they were not concerned with belief in necessity.

Further prerequisites for responsibility

I have been claiming that the falsity of determinism is a necessary prerequisite for moral responsibility. What I should now add is that it is

[29] See A. J. P. Kenny, op. cit., chs 6–8.

very far from being sufficient. Aristotle himself makes the point that not everything that is contingent is up to us (*EE* II 10, 1226a22–5). One important prerequisite for responsibility is consciousness. A mere tree might grow in undetermined directions, but it would not be morally responsible if it grew in such a way as to remove my sunlight. For moral responsibility we need consciousness, an understanding of one's situation, and preferences about it, and we need these to be influential on conduct. When we have such an agent, and Aristotle presupposes that we have, many further conditions must be met before he will be responsible. The internal causes just mentioned must be working, he points out, and certain kinds of ignorance or duress must be absent. Aristotle's list of conditions goes a long way towards showing us what responsibility is. But I do not believe that there could be such a thing as a complete list of conditions. I shall not be able to do more than indicate some of those which Aristotle noticed, and some which he did not. As an example of the latter, I shall ask in the next chapter whether the child who acts against good precepts is not responsible to a greater degree for acquiring a bad character than the child who acts in accordance with the evil precepts of those who have reared him.

CHAPTER SIXTEEN

Involuntariness and Equity: Aristotle's alleged parsimony

Aristotle has been praised for defining voluntariness negatively.[1] He did not connect it with the occurrence of some mental act, in the way that the Stoics were to define 'up to us' (*eph' hēmin*) in terms of an act of 'assent' (*sunkatathesis*),[2] or later ages were to postulate acts of will or volitions. One negative requirement for voluntariness has already been discussed: determinism must be false, for it must be 'up to' the agent whether he acts or refrains. But the negative requirements which have attracted most attention are Aristotle's excusing factors. For an act to be voluntary, certain excusing factors must be absent.

Admiration may turn to disappointment, however, when we count up how many excusing factors Aristotle recognises as rendering an action involuntary.[3] I shall argue that in *NE* III 1, the passage most commonly discussed, he recognises only two, one concerning force (*bia*), and one concerning ignorance. Is this not excessively parsimonious? I shall argue that it is not quite as parsimonious as it seems. But first let us get a quick idea of how he defines the voluntary and involuntary (*hekousion* and *akousion*). There are three passages involved, the first, as I shall maintain, being rather different from the other two.

In *NE* III 1, Aristotle says (1109b35 – 1110a3):

Those things are thought to be involuntary which occur by force (*bia*) or through ignorance, and something is forced, if its origin is from outside, being an origin to which the one who acts or is acted on contributes nothing, as e.g. if a wind carried him somewhere, or men who had him in their power.

Aristotle goes on to explain that the ignorance must be ignorance of the particular circumstances of what he is doing, not ignorance of right and

---

[1] J. L. Austin (29.5) 1956–7; A. J. P. Kenny, 'Freedom, spontaneity and indifference', in *Essays on Freedom of Action*, ed. T. Honderich, London 1973, 91. Cf. H. L. A. Hart, 'The ascription of responsibility and rights', *Proceedings of the Aristotelian Society* 49, 1949, 171–94.

[2] For the Stoic view, see Cicero *Academica* II 37–9. The sceptic Arcesilaus replied that action was compatible with the sceptic practice of *withholding* assent, and that it required only sensory appearances (*phantasia*) and impulse (*hormē*): Plutarch *Adversus Colotem*, 1122B-D.

[3] So Kenny, loc. cit.

wrong. For example, he mistakes someone for an enemy. Moreover, the thing must be done not merely *in* ignorance (*agnoōn*), but *through* ignorance (*di' agnoian*). In other words, the ignorance must be genuinely responsible for what happens, and not, for example, the drunkenness or rage which led to ignorance. Finally, it is important whether the man experiences regret: if he does not, then, even though he has acted through ignorance, the act is better called neither voluntary nor involuntary, but rather non-voluntary.

The account in *EE* II 9 is somewhat different. First, Aristotle elaborates the point about ignorance: it matters whether one has non-accidental knowledge (this is often mistranslated). For example, it matters whether one knows not merely that he is offering a drink, but also that he is offering poison. He then says (1225b6–16):

What is done through ignorance of what one is doing, with what instrument, or to whom, is involuntary. So the opposite is voluntary. Hence that which a man does, when it is up to him not to do it, and does not in ignorance, but does through himself, must be voluntary, and the voluntary is this. But what he does in ignorance and through ignorance, he does involuntarily.

But since understanding and knowing is of two kinds, viz. possessing and using knowledge, the man who possesses it without using it can in one case rightly be called ignorant, but in another case not, for example, if he did not use his knowledge through carelessness. Similarly, one who did not possess knowledge would also be blamed, if what he lacks is easily had or necessary, and he lacks it through carelessness or pain. So these points must be added to the definition.

Force (*bia*) is not explicitly mentioned here, as it is in *NE* III, but this is presumably because it had been the subject of the previous chapter, and is here covered by the clause, 'when it is up to him not to do it', perhaps supported by the phrase 'through himself'.

Finally, I shall argue, the definition in *NE* v 8 (1135a23–33) harks back to that in *EE* II:

I call that voluntary, as was said before, which it is up to one to do, and which one does knowingly and not in ignorance of the person to whom one does it, or with what instrument, or with what effect (e.g. whom one is hitting, or with what, or with what effect) it being understood that one knows each of these things non-accidentally. Moreover, one does not act by force (*bia*); e.g., if someone took one's hand and struck another, one would not strike voluntarily, for it would not be up to oneself. Now it is possible for the man struck to be one's father, and for one to know that it is a man, or one of the people present, but not to know that it is one's father. And a similar point must be put in the definition as regards the effect of one's act, and concerning the whole action. It follows that what is done in ignorance, or, though not done in ignorance, is not up to one, or is done by force, is involuntary.

These are Aristole's three attempts at defining the voluntary. In all three, at least two excusing factors are recognised, one connected with force and one with ignorance. But if not more than two are recognised, can anything be said to meet the charge that Aristotle has been parsimonious? I shall be making at least two points. First, I shall argue that *EE* II and *NE* v 8 express a different view from *NE* III, and recognise more sources of involuntariness. Secondly, I shall maintain that among actions which are not formally recognised as involuntary, Aristotle is prepared, on the basis of what he calls *equity*, to recognise a certain number as pardonable, or at least as less culpable than others. To understand this, we shall have to take into account the extent to which the written law, in Aristotle's time, left areas of discretion to the judges.

If Aristotle is parsimonious, it is particularly in two areas that this becomes very noticeable; mental abnormality and disadvantaged upbringing. But I shall first consider two areas in which Aristotle has not been as parsimonious as may appear at first sight, fear and passion.

Fear

In *NE* III 1, I have said, Aristotle seems to recognise only two excuses as rendering an action involuntary. Either the action must be due to force (*bia*), i.e. to an external origin (*archē*) to which the agent contributes nothing, or it must be due to ignorance of his particular circumstances. An example of the first would be a man's sailing to the wrong place because a storm carried him off. A storm, unlike his desires, is not inside him. An example of the second would be his shooting at a friend in battle in mistake for an enemy.

In the other two places, I believe, Aristotle recognises a third class of actions as involuntary, besides those due to force or ignorance. Thus in *NE* v 8, 1135b4, he speaks as if some actions (not all) performed from fear are involuntary (the agent is *akōn*). It is clear that he means these actions to be thought of as involuntary in the strict sense, and not merely in the sense of reluctantly performed, as some translations suggest. For the point he is making is that a man who from fear does something which happens to be just or unjust is not thereby committing an injustice, nor being just. And earlier in the chapter, it was said that the distinction between merely doing what happens to be unjust and actually committing an injustice turns on whether the action is voluntary or involuntary in the carefully defined sense of those terms (1135a15–33). The same verdict seems to be given in the *Eudemian Ethics*, for at *EE* II 8, 1225a19, Aristotle appears to treat some actions which are performed from fear of a greater evil as involuntary (the agent acts *akōn*; cf. a25–6: what is up to him depends on what his nature can bear). In that case, he is at least prepared to think of these actions from fear as constituting a third category of involuntary action, for they are not performed in ignorance, and he will not definitely plump for

saying that they are due to force (*bia*); he may well be denying it.[4] If he is
at least prepared to count them as a third category, this will in turn help
to explain why the definition of the voluntary at *EE* II 9, 1225b8, does not
use the notion of force (*bia*), even though that notion had been carefully
defined in the preceding chapter, but instead uses the notion, discussed
above in our Chapter Fourteen, of its being up to oneself (*eph' heautōi*) to
refrain, and the notion of acting through oneself (*di' hauton*). Presumably, one advantage of using the term 'up to oneself' is that it will
exclude certain cases of duress, as well as straightforward cases of force,
from the category of the voluntary. Indeed, it is made clear at II 8,
1225a11, a25–6 that it will exclude extreme duress. *NE* v 8 follows *EE* II
9 in using the phrase *eph' heautōi* in its definition (1135a23–33).

In *NE* III 1, I believe, the situation is quite different. Aristotle discusses certain cases of acting from fear in 1110a4 – b9. He gives as examples
the tyrant who has your children or parents in his power, and orders you
to do something wrong, if you want their lives spared, or the captain who
jettisons the cargo, to save the ship in a storm. Some commentators
think that Aristotle classes these acts as both voluntary and involuntary, because he calls them 'mixed' (1110a11).[5] But it would be suprising
if he called them involuntary, since this would violate the account of the
involuntary which he gives immediately before, during and after this
passage (1109b35, 1111a22, 1113b19–25), and in which he recognises
only two grounds for calling something involuntary, with no mention of
a third way. The cases of acting from fear fit neither criterion, since the
actions are not performed on account of ignorance of one's circum-

[4] Thus actions from fear are *not* due to force without qualification (1225 a12). But could
someone plead, as one possible interpretation, that this means they *are* due to force, if we
add the qualification mentioned in a16, that we are thinking of actions done from fear of
a *greater* evil that would be incurred by refraining? The mss., however, make Aristotle
deny that these actions are due to force at a17 (*mē biāi*), while Bonitz' emendation (*ē biāi*)
makes him hedge: they are *either* due to force, *or at least* not to nature. This line at least
shows that Aristotle has not fully decided to count them as due to force. Nothing conclusive emerges from the talk of force at a23, since this is a report on ordinary language,
which is not necessarily endorsed in its every aspect. On the other side, it is also not quite
decisive when Aristotle defines force (II 8, 1224a22, b7–8) as something from outside the
man acting contrary to the tendency (*hormē*) within him, although it would be hard to
apply this definition to cases of duress, seeing that it is explicitly argued not to apply to
cases of resisting, or succumbing to, temptation.

[5] I have heard two interesting papers in the last year which interpreted Aristotle as
meaning that mixed acts were both voluntary and involuntary. One singled out Aristotle's
mixed acts as a star example of the coexistence of opposites. But if one wants to find
anything in Aristotle like a recognition that an act may be both voluntary and involuntary, it would be better to cite *NE* v 8, 1135a28–30 and *EE* II 9, 1225b3–5 which suggest the
idea that in voluntarily striking a *man*, one may involuntarily be striking one's *father*, if
one does not realise that the man is one's father. Here the description of the action
changes. On the other hand, the *Eudemian Ethics* is emphatic that an action cannot be
both voluntary and involuntary at the same time, and in respect of the same aspect of itself
(II 7, 1223b11, b17, b25; cf. the mutilated sentence at 1225a35). The possibility mentioned
at II 8, 1224b38, of being simultaneously voluntary and involuntary had been ruled out by
1224b5–16, b27–9.

stances, and just in case someone supposes that the origin is external, Aristotle explains that it is not (1110a15–18), for the man's own desires move his limbs. Moreover, acting from fear does not meet the very strong requirement that the agent contributes nothing, a requirement which is repeated three times, immediately before, during, and almost immediately after the passage on acting from fear (1110a2, b2, b16).

But if actions performed from fear are not involuntary, why does Aristotle call them mixed? The answer is that he does not say they are involuntary, but that they are in the absence of qualification (*haplōs* 1110a18) or in themselves (*kath' hauta* 1110b3, b5) involuntary. This makes all the difference. The relevant qualification is specified in 1110a10: no one voluntarily throws away his goods in the absence of qualification, but any man of sense does so, given the qualification that it will save him and the others. Thus to call the jettison *haplōs* involuntary is not to call it involuntary, it is rather to say that it is involuntary, if taken in abstraction from the qualification that the man acted to save himself. But lines 1110a12–15 explain that this abstraction is illegitimate, because whether an action is involuntary must be decided by reference to the circumstances actually prevailing at the time of the action. Hence the final verdict is that the jettison does not merely 'look more like' the voluntary (1110a12), but actually *is* voluntary (1110a18).

My first point, then, is that Aristotle's three accounts of voluntariness do not all say the same thing about fear, and that if *NE* III is parsimonious about it, *EE* II 9 and *NE* v 8 are not. But now I must raise a question about whether *NE* III is parsimonious after all. I believe it is significant that in *NE* III 1, 1110a24, Aristotle is prepared to allow that some actions performed in fear are pardonable. Why, then, does he not treat these actions as involuntary? I would hazard the following guess. He wants to supply fairly hard and fast criteria of involuntariness, because this will help makers of *written* law, which he declares to be one of his aims in III 1, 1109b30–5. The pardonable cases of acting from fear do not answer to any neat formula. For whether they are pardonable depends on such imponderables as whether the circumstances 'overstrained human nature' (1110a25), on how great was the good gained (1110a21), and how great the evil accepted (1110a26). Aristotle twice says that it is hard to judge or state (1110a29; b7) what should be endured in return for what, for particular cases differ. The decision not to make acting from fear involuntary does not commit Aristotle to refusing pardon, however, because there is such a thing as equity, which is defined in *NE* v 10 and *Rhet.* I 13. Equity arises because the written formulae of the law are too general to fit all the variations of particular circumstances, and so a judge is given discretion, whereby he can extend pardon to cases which the generalisations of the written law do not fit. This corresponds to contemporary Athenian practice, which allowed enormous discretion to judges.[6] For this the judge needs a certain kind of perceptiveness (*NE* vi 11), to see where pardon is called for. And if certain actions from fear are pardoned, it should be on this basis, because the pardonable ones cannot be isolated by any verbal formula, but must be judged by the perceptiveness of the man of equity. We shall see that in book vii, as well as here, Aristotle feels free to extend pardon to *some* voluntary actions.

It is true that the references to equity or pardon, other than iii 1, 1110a24, come from the middle books, v, vi and vii, which I shall later argue to belong in whole or part, to the *Eudemian Ethics*, and to be, in whole or part, earlier than book iii of the *Nicomachean*. But this does not mean that Aristotle had come to discard all the views he expresses in them. I shall consider more closely in the next chapter which ones he had come to discard.[7]

A last factor to consider in evaluating whether Aristotle has been parsimonious in *NE* iii is the state of contemporary Athenian law on fear. Compared with this, Aristotle's treatment may seem not harsh, but, if anything, progressive. For the written law paid comparatively little attention to fear as a motive. Attention was paid in the case of *wills and testaments* which were by Solon's law invalid, if made under duress.[8] But it is doubtful that the law recognised duress as invalidating contracts.[9] Plato may well have been innovating when he recommended this in *Laws* 920D. Rather than appealing to a written law in this area, orators may have appealed to the equity of the judges who might well be sympathetic to a plea that the contract was made under duress.[10] As for jettison of cargo, Demosthenes against Lakritos expects the case to turn on the wording of the particular written contract that was entered into. There is no mention of a law saying that storms in general provide an excuse. The contract in this particular instance was fairly stern: in order to excuse non-repayment of loan, the shippers would have to show that

[6] See, e.g., Paul Vinogradoff (32.13) 1922, vol. 2, 68–9.

[7] The only variation which has much relevance at present is that in *NE* v 8, having extended the category of the involuntary to cover all cases of ignorance of what one is doing, even negligence and unnatural passion, he compensatingly regards the involuntary as admitting degrees of culpability. In *NE* iii, where he has more interest in helping makers of written law, he keeps the category of involuntariness narrower, and would probably prefer it to provide an automatic pardon.

[8] Demosthenes 46 14, Hypereides *Against Athenogenes* 17.

[9] For Hypereides loc. cit. is not able to cite such a law, when it would have suited him, but can only cite the law about wills. Evidence on the other side is that the laws are sometimes said to regard contracts as valid provided they were made voluntarily (Demosthenes 56 2, Plato *Symposium* 196c, and for a similar phrase, without mention of the law, Demosthenes 48 54). But the expression meaning voluntary is not the same in each of these citations, and the authors may have been generalising from laws about a few specific kinds of contract, to give the impression that the law dealt with all contracts in the same way. It is also not clear whether duress would establish involuntariness. So R. Maschke (32.12) 1926, L. Gernet (32.7) 1956, and article in *Archives d'histoire du droit orientale* i 1937. (On the other side, J. Demeyère, in the same journal, when it became amalgamated with *Revue Internationale des Droits de l'Antiquité*, and renumbered, vol. 1 1952.)

all passengers agreed to the jettison (§11), and the cargo jettisoned must be the one specified in the contract (§32). The second provision is similar to one in English law, judging from Stroud's judicial dictionary (4th edition, London 1973). Given this background, Aristotle is not departing far from current law, in declining to treat actions done from fear as involuntary, and in expecting them to be pardoned, if at all, on the basis of equity instead.

To complete the picture, I ought to add that Aristotle brackets with bad actions performed under extreme threat those which are performed for the sake of a great and noble end (1110a4–5, a20–2).

Passion

Somewhat similar to his treatment of fear is Aristotle's treatment of anger and lust. The plays of Euripides about Medea, Phaedra and Helen, and the model speech by Gorgias in defence of Helen, had exhibited people pleading passion as an excuse, though admittedly Euripides does not always represent the plea as successful. Aristotle firmly resists the idea that actions due to anger or lust are involuntary.[11] None the less as with cases of extreme duress, he says we sometimes pardon passionate actions, if people give in after resisting extreme temptation which few could withstand (*NE* vii 2, 1146a2; vii 6, 1149b4; vii 7, 1150b8).

Aristotle further distinguishes different degrees of culpability. It is less disgraceful to give in to anger than to lust (*NE* vii 6),[12] partly because we excuse more readily the more natural and common desires (1149b4; cf. *Rhet.* 1373a27, 1374b10, 1375a6). All succumbing against one's better judgment, whether to anger or to lust, is less serious than having a wicked character (vii 8, and vii 10, 1152a15–19). An injury inflicted knowingly is less serious if it springs from anger or other natural passions than if it is based on deliberation and choice (v 8, 1135b20 – 1136a3).

In treating some passionate acts with leniency, while refusing to count them as involuntary, Aristotle is in line with the legal practice of the time. Orators might plead passion in appealing to the equity of the judges,[13] but it was not recognised by written law as a source of involuntariness. At most there is some evidence, which will be discussed further in Chapter Eighteen, that the written law distinguished between volun-

[10] That popular sentiment would be favourable to such appeals is suggested by Plato *Crito* 52ᴇ and Aristotle *Rhetoric* i 15, 1376b22–3.

[11] *NE* iii 1, 1110b9–15, 1111a24 – b3; cf. at least for cases where the man knows what he is doing, v 8, esp. 1135b20; and for cases where he gives in against his better judgment, vii 10, 1152a15–16; *EE* ii 8, 1224b26–36.

[12] Has there, however, been a change of mind in *NE* ii 3, 1105a7–9, where it is said to be harder to fight against pleasure than against anger?

[13] E.g. Demosthenes *Against Meidias* 41 and 73–5.

tary injuries that involved forethought or a plot to kill and voluntary injuries that occurred on the spur of the moment, for example, in the heat of a fight.[14] The law was not more lenient than Aristotle. If anyone had gone further than he it was Plato, who, as I interpret him, classed certain angry actions as *neither* voluntary *nor* involuntary (*Laws* IX 866D – 867D).[15]

Aristotle has, then, been no more parsimonious about anger and lust than about fear. His refusal to count the resulting acts as involuntary leaves him free to recognise gradations of culpability, and occasionally even to extend pardon.

Mental abnormality

When it comes to mental abnormality, however, Aristotle does begin to seem more parsimonious, and with less justification, since Plato had recognised insanity as an exculpating circumstance in *Laws* 864D-E and 881B. At the end of *NE* v 8 (1136a5–9), Aristotle envisages someone who acts on account of unnatural passion. Examples supplied in book VII, chapter 5, include the female who ripped open pregnant women to devour the embryos, people who ate each other's children, the man who sacrificed and ate his mother, or ate the liver of his fellow slave, practising homosexuals, and victims of abnormal fears. Some of these abnormalities arise from habit, some from natural constitution at birth, some from imperfect development, some from attacks of disease or madness. In v 8, Aristotle considers a man who acts in ignorance of what he is doing, but not on account of (*dia*) ignorance, rather on account of unnatural passion. By the criteria of book III, actions performed merely *in* ignorance of what one was doing would be classed as voluntary; in v 8, however, as I shall argue in Chapter Seventeen, he is prepared to class all actions in which the agent is ignorant of what he is doing as involuntary. But in case it be thought he is thereby being lenient, he explicitly says that the actions in question are not excusable (1136a9). This stern verdict may be connected with his remark elsewhere (VII 6, 1149b4–6; cf. *Rhet.* 1373a27, 1374b10, 1375a6) that we pardon people more readily for following natural human desires, because these are more common.

Aristotle would not have been any more lenient if he had considered a case in which the man's ignorance was not ignorance of what he was doing, but ignorance of its wrongness. Ignorance of right and wrong, he says in *NE* III 1, does not excuse, but is the cause of wickedness (1110b30–3); not that he thinks it right to classify these abnormal cases

[14] Aristotle *EE* II 10, 1226b36 (cf. *NE* v 8, 1135b25–7, b33); Lysias III 42.
[15] I am here disagreeing with the version of A. E. Taylor and with the very helpful Penguin translation of Trevor Saunders. I believe that 867B means 'class these as copies of the voluntary or involuntary', not, 'class these under the voluntary or involuntary, which they copy'.

as ones of wickedness in the ordinary sense of the word (vii 5, 1148b31 – 1149a20, 1149b30). They are merely analogous, he says.

Against this severe view, there is little of a more lenient character to be found. In *EE* ii 8, 1225a27–30, he recognises that when people are inspired and utter prophecies, we do not think that what they say and do is up to them. In *NE* iii 5, 1114a21–31, he points out that we do not blame people for *physical* defects, such as ugliness, weakness, deformity, or blindness, if these are due to natural constitution, or disease, or an accident. And he goes on to acknowledge (1114b3–25) that, if we were endowed with our ideals by nature, which we are not, then virtue and vice might be involuntary, though even then it could be argued that the choice of means for achieving those ideals was voluntary. Very little is conceded here. The remark at *NE* iii 1, 1111a7, that only a madman would be ignorant of all the circumstances of his action is not accompanied by any acknowledgment that such a madman would be excused; the passage cited from v 8 suggests the opposite.

Aristotle's failure to regard madness as an exculpating circumstance is not, however, surprising if we consider the attitude of his time. I do not know of any written Athenian law which recognised madness as an excuse, although there was a law of Solon, already mentioned in connexion with duress, which treated it as invalidating wills (references in note 8). And I would note the story that Solon gained impunity by feigning madness before he broke a law forbidding mention of Athenian hopes of recovering the island of Salamis.[16] Greek attitudes to madness have been very well studied by E. R. Dodds and more recently by K. J. Dover,[17] whom I shall follow in the remainder of this paragraph. As they point out, the treatment of madness in literature is complicated, because it is often considered to be sent by the gods, but even so, it only sometimes exculpates,[18] and more often does not.[19] Epileptics felt ashamed,[20] and when Plato speaks of the blessings of madness in the *Phaedrus*, and pleads on etymological grounds that once people did not think madness a matter for shame and reproach, he reveals that in his time people did think of it that way.[21] Mad people were shunned; one threw stones at them, or spat.[22] In the law courts, where it was more important than in English courts to speak for the character of oneself or one's client, people might well hesitate to plead madness. Nor, as K. J. Dover remarks, would it necessarily help to plead that the madness was sent by the gods. That would make you a dangerous person to associate with, and anyhow the gods might have their reasons.

---

[16] Plutarch *Solon* 8.
[17] E. R. Dodds (32.5) 1963, ch. 3, and K. J. Dover (32.6) 1974.
[18] Euripides *Troades* 408–10.
[19] Homer Iliad ix 119, 376; xix 137; Euripides *Bacchae* 997–1000.
[20] Hippocratic Corpus *On the Sacred Disease* 12.
[21] Plato *Phaedrus* 244B.
[22] Aristophanes *Birds* 524, Theophrastus *Characters* 16.

The conclusion to be drawn is that if Aristotle seems to us not to give due weight to the plea of madness, he was reflecting the view of his time; it was Plato whose view was exceptional. It should be added that we are hardly in a position to express surprise, when we recall the history of the M'Naghten Rules of Homicide, which prevailed in England up to 1957. These recognised madness as an excuse only if it removed knowledge of the nature or illegality of the act, not if it impaired self-control; and they offered as the reward for a successful plea indefinite detention in Broadmoor Criminal Lunatic Asylum.[23]

Upbringing

A question about Aristotle's parsimony is raised by David Furley:[24]

It is odd that Aristotle never (to my knowledge) asks himself why the discipline of parents and teachers is not to be taken as an external cause of man's dispositions. Our own experience of 'juvenile delinquency', and the generally held belief that young people's crimes may be due not to wickedness but to faulty environment, raise this question at once. But Aristotle seems never to have considered this point.

Rather similar complaints are made by A. A. Long and R. A. Gauthier.[25]

I think Furley's question of why parental discipline is not taken as an external cause or origin can be answered, but that there is an asymmetry between good character and bad character, and that in relation to bad character, there is a further question, slightly different from Furley's, which Aristotle fails to consider.

First, we should notice the important role that Aristotle gives to habituation. In the old debate about whether men are made good by natural constitution, by instruction, or by habituation, Aristotle gives a role to all three.[26] But in *NE* II 1–3 he puts a particularly heavy stress on habituation. Moreover, he repeatedly warns us that bad habits will create bad character.[27] He adds that habits, once formed, are hard to change,[28] and he thinks of unjust and self-indulgent men as incurable.[29]

[23] See H. L. A. Hart (38.3) 1968, ch. 8.
[24] David Furley, op. cit., p. 194; similarly, p. 235.
[25] A. A. Long (31.7) 1971, 174 and 188; R. A. Gauthier, commenting on *NE* 1114b1–3 in (29.4).
[26] *NE* II 1, 1103a23–6; x 9, 1179b4–31; *Pol.* 1332a40 – b11, 1334b6, 1338b4.
[27] *NE* 1103b13–25, b30–1, 1104a20–5, 1114a7–10; cf. the case of the child subjected to paederasty, 1148b30–1.
[28] *NE* 1152a30–1.
[29] *NE* 1114a13–21, 1150a21, b32, 1151a4. This is inspite of the fact that habit is sometimes contrasted with nature as admitting of more exceptions, and being less difficult to change (*NE* 1152a29–33, *Rhet.* 1370a6–9, *Mem.* 452a30 – b3), and that some vice is curable (*NE* 1121b10, 1165b18; *Cat.* 13a23–31). One optimistic passage even says that men can act against habit *and* nature if reason persuades them that they ought (*Pol.* 1332b7).

In forming our initial habits, other people play an enormous role. The context of devising proposals for education leads Aristotle to utter dire warnings about the influence, for ill as well as for good, of those who rear children, or who legislate how they are to be reared.[30] In childhood, when habits are being formed, the intellect is still immature,[31] and children are naturally obedient.[32]

But in spite of all this, Aristotle is not obliged to treat the discipline of parents as an external origin in the sense which he had in mind in *NE* III 1. For one thing, as we saw, that was three times described as an external origin which operates *without the agent contributing anything*. In the present case, the child must contribute something. As a minimum, he contributes the will to comply or the refusal. This can be important; if we recall the case of the child attracted by a toy which he knows he is forbidden to take, it may be up to him which course he follows. And by taking one course rather than the other, he will strengthen the corresponding tendencies in himself, and so he will share responsibility for the firm character which he does not yet have, but which he will one day have as a result of these earlier incidents. The discipline of parents, then does not operate without a contribution from the child.

Aristotle goes much further than this, as regards virtue, because he includes a very large intellectual effort in the process of becoming a good man, as I have argued elsewhere.[33] Not only does the process of habituation involve reflective habits of looking at situations in a certain way, and asking oneself what virtue requires of one in each new situation; but also, before one can be fully virtuous, he must think out a synoptic conception of what is involved in the best life, and be able to see in each situation how to realise such a life. If becoming virtuous involves all this, clearly the credit cannot all go to the man's parents and teachers.

I think these considerations are sufficient to answer the particular problem raised by Furley: the discipline of parents is not an external cause in the sense of *NE* III 1, because it requires a contribution from the child. But a different problem arises from the fact that there is an asymmetry between virtue and vice. It is not only that Aristotle includes far less intellectual content in the process of becoming a bad man.[34] This would not matter in the case of a man who becomes bad

[30] *NE* 1180a33 – b7; *Pol.* 1334b12, 1336b3–36, 1337b8; 1338b12, b34, 1340b2.

[31] *Pol.* 1260a14.

[32] *NE* 1180b7.

[33] Richard Sorabji, 'Aristotle on the role of intellect in virtue', *Proceedings of the Aristotelian Society*, 74, 1973–4, 107–29.

[34] Wicked character does not, in Aristotle's view, require one to have a unified, synoptic view of how to live, which incorporates all the vices. Unlike the good man, who must have all the virtues (*NE* VI 13), the wicked man may have just a few of the vices. He is unlikely to possess them all, since many are opposites of each other. Admittedly, most forms of badnesss have some intellectual content, since they involve deliberating and choosing (*prohaireisthai*) the bad actions out of a settled conviction that this is the thing to do. (So

through ignoring his mentors, for at least he makes a contribution to his eventual character by ignoring them. The difficult case is that of the man, who becomes bad by *heeding* his mentors, when they give him evil instruction. He too makes a contribution, but one he can hardly be blamed for, when he abides by what he was taught. Though Aristotle argues that standing by bad principles does not deserve credit (*NE* vii 2, 1146a16–31, and vii 9), he cannot maintain that, in a case like this, it deserves blame. It is a pity that Aristotle does not consider more carefully whether a man can then be blamed for the eventual outcome: acquiring a bad character. The problem, however, is not one about there being an external origin, with him contributing nothing; for he does contribute something. The question is rather one about whether he ever had a fair opportunity.

Although it is a pity that Aristotle did not consider this problem, the omission was perhaps almost inevitable. In Athenian law courts, as already remarked, it was important to establish excellence of character.[35] And a speaker would be most unlikely to appeal to a bad background, with any hope of thereby gaining leniency. K. J. Dover has assembled a collection of appeals to character in the Greek orators, and has supplied an enlightening commentary. These appeals, he says, reflect the fact that a jury might forgive a man of good character, even if he had done what he was accused of.[36]

So far I have talked about those who are definitely good, or definitely bad, but the great majority of people, according to Aristotle, fall in between (*NE* x 9, 1179b10 – 1180a32). What they respond to is the fear of punishment (1179b12–14), which is described as a kind of necessity (1180a4–5). And Aristotle recommends a programme of state supervision, which though less complete than Plato's,[37] extends far into areas of life which we think of as private. This is perhaps inevitable when the proper aim of the lawgiver is taken to be making men virtuous (*NE* 1099b29, 1102a8, 1103b3; *Pol.* 1280b4, 1327b35, 1333a14, b8). If the

---

for self-indulgence: *NE* 1146b22–3, 1151a13–26, 1152a6; cf. 1148 a 17, 1150a20, b36, 1151a7. For cowardice and injustice: 1134a17–23, 1135b25, 1137a4–26, 1138a20. For lying: *Metaph.* 1025a2. For boastfulness: *NE* 1127b14. For softness: 1150a24. For wickedness in general: *NE* 1144a27, a35, 1152a24; *EE* 1223a18, 1228a4, 1234a25.) But William Fortenbaugh has pointed out to me that some few vices seem to be regarded as involving the absence of values, rather than the presence of the wrong ones (lack of ambition, 1125b10–11; lack of anger, 1126a3).

[35] I am grateful to Trevor Saunders for directing my attention to this.

[36] K. J. Dover, op. cit., 294–5. On the other hand, Dover warns that the appeals do not show the jury was uninterested in whether the accused was guilty. In the absence of a Criminal Investigation Department, and of a system of cross-examination, the character of a party might provide some of the best available evidence on whether he was likely to have done what he was charged with.

[37] It is controversial how far Aristotle goes along with Plato. A milder picture of Aristotle is presented by D. J. Allan (32.2) 1965, than by Ernest Barker, *The Politics of Aristotle*, Oxford 1946, l-lii, or Alexander Grant, in his commentary on *NE*, London 1885 *ad* v 1 13.

lawgiver fails to achieve this by early education, at least he will legislate about everything, and require people to perform the outward acts of
virtuous men for the common good (*NE* 1129b14–25).[38] And there are to
be laws to make adults, no less than children, practise the right pur-
suits, and follow the right habits (1180a1–5).

In spite of all this state supervision, and the accompanying legal
sanctions, however, it does not occur to Aristotle that the behaviour of
ordinary people will be involuntary; and why should it? After all, the
fear of punishment to which he refers is not like the kind of fear which
overstrains human nature, which he regards as making actions pardonable in *NE* iii 1 (1110a24–6), or the kind which overstrains the individual nature and prevents actions being up to us in *EE* ii 8 (1225a25–6).
Political freedom is certainly restricted, but voluntariness has not been
removed. Aristotle surprises us by going to the opposite extreme, and
citing the efficacy of punishment, not as a threat to voluntariness, but as
a proof that our conduct is up to us (*NE* iii 5, 1113b21–30). What he has
in mind, presumably, is that if our behaviour is changed by punishment
or honours, this shows that it is in some way dependent on us, and on our
wills.

Physiological defects

A final case which may cause discontent is that of actions which are due
to physiological disorders. Suppose someone damages my property by a
jerk, tic, or sneeze, or by vomiting. One thing that may seem worrying is
that the cause of damage is not external to the agent, at least in one
sense, for it is inside his body. Moreover, it cannot easily be said that he
contributed nothing. When Aristotle talks in *NE* iii 1 of external causes
to which the agent contributes nothing, he makes no effort to subsume
cases of this kind. Does this mean that the damage must be viewed as
voluntary?

Not necessarily, for Aristotle has more resources than may at first be
apparent.[39] The man may be able to plead non-culpable ignorance that
by standing where he did, and handling what he did, he would be
jeopardising my property. This plea would be parallel to that of the man
who said he did not know the catapult would go off (*NE* iii 1,
1111a10–11).

Pleas of ignorance will not be available for all physiological examples.
At *NE* iii 5, 1114a21–31, Aristotle discusses blindness and shameful
deformities due to nature, disease, or a blow. These are not due to

---

[38] There has, however, been much discussion, of the claim that existing law enjoins all
virtues and forbids all vices in *NE* v 1, 1129b14–25; v 2, 1130b22–4. D. J. Allan (op. cit.,
preceding note) argues that this does not imply as much scope for state interference as
might at first appear. See also the discussion by Christopher Rowe, 'A reply to John Cooper
on the *Magna Moralia*', *American Journal of Philology* 96, 1975.

[39] I am indebted here to a comment of Michael Leahy.

ignorance, nor always to the kind of external cause discussed in III 1. But Aristotle has another resource: he pleads, what he was unwilling to plead in the case of madness, that these physiological states and processes are not 'up to' the man (III 5, 1114a29).

If we criticise Aristotle's list of excuses, we must be clear about the exact nature of our disappointment. It is sometimes thought that the concept of an external cause to which the agent contributes nothing is made to do too much work. It would be, if it were stretched to cover physiological causes, but this does not seem to be Aristotle's intention in *NE* III 1, where the concept covers a fairly well-defined class of cases – the overwhelming storm and the tidal wave. If it is stretched at all, this will be in III 5, where I voiced a suspicion (Chapter Fourteen) that it might be being made to cover cases of ignorance as well. Apart from this suspicion, our complaint should not be with the criterion of external cause, which is a good one as far as it goes, but only with Aristotle's not adding more categories than he does. And this complaint applies with more force to *NE* III than to *NE* V.

General assessment

I have argued that the impression that Aristotle is parsimonious in recognising sources of involuntariness is only partly justified. The most obvious point is that where Aristotle is harsh by our standards, as he is over mental health and upbringing, we should also compare him with the standards of his time. But I have also made two less obvious points. First, some acts which are classified as voluntary by *NE* III can none the less be treated leniently on the basis of equity. Secondly, some are in any case recognised as involuntary by *EE* II and *NE* V.

Insofar as he has been parsimonious, we shall not be able to assess the full significance of this, until we consider what he took the purpose of punishment to be. We cannot conclude that he ought to have more lenient, until we consider whether, like Plato, he thought two major purposes of punishment to be reform of the criminal, and the removal of pollution. Someone with these purposes will not necessarily think it right to be gentle with the involuntary offender. I shall, however, argue in Chapter Eighteen that these were not major aims for Aristotle, and that on the contrary the achievement of fairness was.

Although I hope to have shown that Aristotle is not as parsimonious as at first appears, we must not swing to the opposite extreme. It cannot be denied that Aristotle's list of excusing conditions is shorter than we should like. Somewhat surprisingly, in view of his concern with reform and pollution, Plato provides the basis for a longer list in his *Laws*,[40] and

[40] Plato recognises as mitigating or excusing circumstances madness or disease (864 D–E; 881B), old age, youthfulness, and over-persuasion by other parties (864 D; 934A), duress (920D), overwhelming force (943E–944D), sudden anger without premeditation (866 D–

so does the law of Solon mentioned above, which recognised as invalidating wills: insanity, old age, drugs, disease, being beside oneself because of the persuasion of a woman, necessity, and bondage. For an excellent modern list, I may refer to the work of H. L. A. Hart and A. M. Honoré, *Causation in the Law*, Oxford 1959, pp. 126–70. Modern science has added new categories – we may think of Freud's work on the unconscious – and fresh understanding of old ones, particularly of mental abnormality and of social pressures, which Aristotle treated so lightly.

On the other side, it can be said that no list of excusing conditions can be complete, and further that Aristotle would not have wanted to extend his list at the cost of considering categories which apply only to very special situations, e.g. to the making of wills.

The aim of this chapter has been defensive: I have been seeking to blunt the force of a certain objection. The positive merits of Aristotle's discussion will become clearer in Chapter Eighteen, where I shall assess what his contribution was to legal theory. Before that, I must bring something else more fully into the open.

867c), and overriding legal obligations (920d), and he distinguishes offences which are involuntary (774a; 861e – 863a; 865a; 869e; 876e; 879b). He also distinguishes thefts where the amount taken is small (941c–d).

CHAPTER SEVENTEEN

Voluntariness, Temptation, Negligence: a succession of attempts at analysis

It has been becoming clear that Aristotle tries out different suggestions in different passages. I have just claimed that in some passages he allows extreme duress to make an action involuntary while in some he does not. I believe we can see him attempting different treatments of three major issues: voluntariness, temptation and negligence. I shall try to see whether we can trace how his thought developed.

The question is of philosophical interest, but it is also connected with two scholarly issues. First, what was the original home of the three books which are nowadays printed as the middle books of the *Nicomachean Ethics*: v, vi and vii? Were they originally written as part of the *Eudemian Ethics*? Secondly, is the *Eudemian* or the *Nicomachean Ethics* the later work? I shall be returning to these two issues.

Voluntariness

I shall start with voluntariness, and in particular with the relation of *ignorance* to voluntariness. Some of the key passages were translated in the previous chapter. The relation varies significantly from one chapter to another. In *EE* II 9, Aristotle first defines voluntariness as if the man who acts voluntarily always knows what he is doing (1225b8–10). But then, in what looks like an afterthought (b11–16), he adds that a man who possesses the requisite knowledge of his circumstances, but fails to use it through carelessness (*ameleia*) cannot plead that he acted in ignorance. Further, he could still be blamed even though he lacked knowledge altogether, if the knowledge was important or easy to come by and if the lack was due to carelessness, or to the distractions of pleasure and pain. Since these remarks are to be added to the definition (*prosdihoristeon*, b16) of voluntariness, I take it that these people are to be regarded as acting voluntarily, even though they lack, or else fail to use, knowledge of the circumstances in which they are acting. This qualification to the original definition of voluntariness had to some extent been prepared for by the fact that *in*voluntariness had been associated with acting not merely in, but on account of (*dia*), ignorance of one's circumstances (1225b6, b7, b10). None the less, this last distinction was not in the end exploited in the account of voluntariness.

The treatment in *NE* vii is different, perhaps because the interest in temptation in that chapter forces Aristotle to think further about the relation between voluntariness and ignorance. He seems eventually to decide that in order for his action to be voluntary a man must have knowledge at least 'in a way' (vii 10, 1152a15–16). The idea of having knowledge in a way is introduced in vii 3. At 1147a11–14, Aristotle already diverges from *EE* ii, by saying that in some cases where a man possesses knowledge which he fails to use, it is only in a way that he can be said to possess it. This is then applied to the man who gives in to temptation against his better judgment (1147a14–24). This man, I take Aristotle to say, is temporarily (1147b6–9) unable to appreciate the minor premise (1147a3, a7, b9–17), which tells him the observable circumstances in which he is acting (1147a7, b9–10, b17). He knows perhaps that sticky things are bad for him, but cannot appreciate the fact that the sweet thing which he is about to eat is sticky. Aristotle is tempted to describe this as a case of his not possessing the minor premise at all (1147a7, b10), or of his possessing it in a way which does not amount to knowing it (1147b11–12). But he prefers in the end to describe it as a case of possessing knowledge in a way, like the man who is asleep, mad, or drunk (1147a11–18, 1152a15). He prefers the latter description, which is missing from *EE* ii 9, because only so does he see how to justify calling the act voluntary (1152a15–16). He does not then follow the view of *EE* ii 9, 1225b14–16, that it can be called voluntary when knowledge is altogether lacking, provided the lack is due to the distractions of pleasure, and the knowledge is important or easy to come by.

In *NE* iii, Aristotle has a different way of representing blind actions as voluntary. He puts full weight on the distinction which is not systematically exploited in *EE* ii 9, between acting merely in ignorance and acting *on account of* ignorance (iii 1, 1110b24–7; cf. iii 5, 1113b32–3). The man who acts in anger which makes him ignorant is acting only in ignorance, not on account of ignorance; rather on account of the anger. And Aristotle now uses this as the criterion for classing his act as voluntary. He diverges from *NE* vii, where the test for voluntariness is the *degree* of ignorance; here it is the *causal role* played by the ignorance.

Finally, *NE* v 8 is different again. Aristotle defines voluntary actions as all being performed knowingly, and makes all actions performed in ignorance to be involuntary (1135a23–33). The definition of voluntariness is thus in effect like the preliminary definition of *EE* ii 9, and diverges only in not adding the qualifications that were appended there. There is no mention of the rider about careless ignorance not rendering involuntary, and there is no reference at this point in the chapter to the distinction between acting in ignorance and acting on account of ignorance. I conclude that he is here extending the category of the involuntary to cover *all* cases in which a man is ignorant of what he is doing. And this is confirmed at the end of the chapter (1136a5–9), where he belatedly introduces the distinction between acting in ignorance and acting on account of ignorance, but treats it quite differently, making *both* kinds of case involuntary. He makes both involuntary, even though the particular case of acting in ignorance which he describes is called unpardonable. Presumably, the ground for the ascription of involuntariness is simply the man's ignorance. In correlating ignorance with involuntariness, Aristotle may be influenced by the legal tradition which lies behind this chapter, and which distinguished mistakes from injustices as involuntary and due to ignorance.[1]

To compensate for the extension of involuntariness to all cases in which a man does not know what he is doing, Aristotle recognises some involuntary actions as being more culpable than others. In this *NE* v 8 differs again from *NE* III and *EE* II, which show no sign of regarding any involuntary actions as culpable.

These different attempts at stating the relation between voluntariness and *ignorance* give Aristotle correspondingly different methods of answering another question: how can a man who gives in to temptation be acting voluntarily, if he is blinded by passion, and so ignorant of what he is doing? If I am right in what I shall suggest below, *NE* v offers the best way of handling this question. For it denies the presupposition (so I shall suggest) that a man who gives in to temptation must fail to appreciate what he is doing. But although in this regard the discussion in *NE* v may be closest to the truth, it is hard to view it as Aristotle's final thought on the subject. For the recognition that one can give in to temptation knowingly is too casually presented in *NE* v for us to construe it as superseding the very full discussion in *NE* VII.

I have so far concentrated on the relation of voluntariness to *ignorance,* but there are other features of the treatment of voluntariness which undergo variation. One already noticed is that Aristotle treats certain cases of duress as rendering an action involuntary in *EE* II 8 and *NE* v 8, while refusing to do so in *NE* III 1. This difference may be partly explained by a further difference, namely, that one aim of the discussion in *NE* III is to help the makers of *written* law (1109b30–5), while this aim is omitted in *EE* II (II 7, 1223a21–3). The significance of this was discussed in Chapter Sixteen.

A related change befalls the notion of what is 'up to oneself' (*eph' heautōi*). Aristotle actually makes this part of the definition of voluntariness in *EE* II 9 and *NE* v 8, and this helps him to treat action under

[1] See Chapter Eighteen and Demosthenes *On the Crown* 274–5; *Against Timocrates* 49; Lysias 31 11; Hypereides *Against Demosthenes* 26; Ps-Aristotle *Rhetorica ad Alexandrum* 4, 1427a30 – b1.

extreme duress as involuntary, because it is not 'up to the man' how he acts. In *NE* III, the notion of 'up to oneself' does admittedly form an important part of the discussion, but it is not inserted into the very definition of voluntariness. The treatment of what is up to oneself differs also in another way. For in *NE* III, as was noted in Chapter Fourteen, Aristotle reveals something that is not apparent in *EE* II or *NE* V, namely, that a thing may be up to a person, even though he has lost the power he once had of refraining.

A final variation concerns the notions of force (*bia*) and external origin (*archē*). I shall argue below that the notion of external origin at *NE* V 8, 1135b19, is quite different from that which features in *NE* III 1. The external origin which renders an action involuntary in *NE* III 1 is one which operates without the agent contributing anything. It is illustrated by overwhelming forces like the wind which blows a man off course, and it is said in the *Eudemian Ethics* to act contrary to the tendency (*hormē*) within the agent (1224a22, b7–8; cf. *Metaph.* 1015a26, 1072b12). In *NE* V 8, however, questions of whether the origin of the cause is external are questions about where responsibility lies: does it lie in one's own negligence, for example, in not looking to see where the spectators are before one throws the javelin, or does it lie in external circumstances, such as the erratic behaviour of a spectator who wanders into the throwing area? This external circumstance is not at all like an overwhelming force, nor can it naturally be described as acting contrary to the tendency in the agent, or as obviating any contribution from him. It is linked, whereas the notion of external origin in *NE* III 1 is not,[2] to the idea that the agent is ignorant of what he is doing.

In *NE* V 8, force (*bia*) is mentioned (1135a27, a33), but it is not defined in the manner of *NE* III 1 in terms of an external origin, presumably because the latter idea is about to be used in a quite different way. Indeed, force is not defined at all, but it is illustrated, and the illustration is one given not in *NE* III, but in *EE* II 8 (1224b13): someone seizes your hand and hits another man with it.

Temptation

NE VII contains Aristotle's main account of temptation, and, with one exception,[3] recent commentators have taken it that Aristotle here

---

[2] Admittedly this last part of the contrast is blunted, because, as observed in Chapter Fourteen, a link of this kind may be being forged in *NE* III 5.

[3] A. J. P. Kenny (37.4) 1966, 163–84. Kenny construes the *teleutaia protasis* at 1147b9 not as the last (i.e. the minor) premise, but as the last proposition, i.e. the *conclusion* (e.g. 'Avoid this!'). In that case, the man who gives in to temptation after all has all the premises he needs, and fails only in appreciating the imperative *conclusion* which follows from them. He then acts with knowledge of the facts, just like the man in *NE* V. I doubt myself, however, whether *teleutaia protasis* can refer to the *conclusion*, which is elsewhere said to be an action, not a proposition, and which in any case is not a *perceptual* proposition, as the

rejects the possibility of giving in to temptation with full realisation of what one is doing. I agree with this interpretation of *NE* vii; but I want to suggest that in *NE* v Aristotle does after all allow giving in to temptation with full awareness.

In *NE* vii, Aristotle concedes to Socrates that it looks as if (*eoiken*) knowledge of how one ought to act cannot be blotted out by passion (vii3, 1147b13–17). But he does not allow that, once a man has such knowledge, he will act accordingly. For this would overlook the possibility that passion might obscure a man's awareness of just how he is acting. This possibility is developed in vii 3. First, we must distinguish the major premise which represents a man's deliberate policy decision about how he should act:[4] he should stay off sticky food, for example. This is the premise which will not be blotted out, so long as it represents real knowledge. But a weak man can still act against this knowledge. And this will be due to an imperfect grasp of the minor premise (1146b35 – 1147a10), which concerns matters of sense perception (1147b10, b17), for example, the premise 'this food is sticky'. Appetite for a particular piece of food might in a variety of ways impair the realisation that it was sticky. First, the man might possess the knowledge, but not use it (1146b31–5). Then he might possess it only in a way, as a man who is mad, asleep, or drunk might be said to possess knowledge (1147a10–18). This is the alternative which Aristotle favours in the end (1152a15–16), although not before trying out such other formulas as that the man does not possess the minor premise, or possesses it in a way that does not amount to knowing it (1147a7, 1147b10–11).

It is too simple to say that Aristotle here denies the possibility of giving in to temptation knowingly. After all, the person who gives in has full knowledge of what he ought to do, and in this Aristotle differs from Socrates. He also has knowledge 'in a way' that the food is sticky. But he has it only in a way, and this is the truth in the claim that Aristotle does not here recognise giving in to temptation with full knowledge.

What is interesting when we turn to *NE* v is that the man who gives in to temptation against his better judgment may here be thought of as doing so with knowledge. The most striking passage is *NE* v 9, 1136a31–4, where Aristotle seems to envisage that the weak man who

---

teleutaia protasis is meant to be (1147b10, b17). Moreover, an earlier passage had connected giving in to temptation with ignorance of the *minor* premise (1147a3, a7), and the present passage is introduced not as offering an *alternative* explanation, but as describing the same thing from a more physical point of view (1147a24).

[4] I take it that the major premise which prescribes a certain diet represents a deliberate decision (*prohaeresis*). For Aristotle says that there are two kinds of weak-willed man, one who does not deliberate at all, and one who deliberates and makes a deliberate choice, but acts *against* it (1150b19–22, 1151a2; 1152a18–19, a28). The latter kind of man gets mentioned more often (1145b11, 1148a9, 1150b30–1, 1151a7, a26; a30–5, b26, 1152a17, a26), and it is evidently he who is under discussion in *NE* vii 3. Acting against his deliberate choice involves acting against the policy enunciated in the major premise.

gives in to temptation, thereby harming himself, *knows* what he is doing. At any rate, he says,

If to treat someone unjustly is simply to injure him voluntarily, and to do it voluntarily is to do it knowing whom one is acting on, with what instrument and how, and if the weak man (*akratēs*) injures himself voluntarily, then he would suffer injustice voluntarily and one could treat oneself unjustly.

Although Aristotle goes on to reply that in injuring oneself (*blaptein*) knowingly, one is not treating oneself unjustly (*adikein*), he does not retract the suggestion that the weak man who gives in to temptation acts *knowingly*.

Elsewhere in *NE* v, Aristotle describes certain passionate actions as being performed knowingly. A man may inflict injury from passion, knowing what he is doing (*eidōs*, *NE* v 8, 1135b20), but not from deliberate choice, and a man may commit adultery with a woman, knowing (*eidōs*) who she is, again not through deliberate choice, but on account of passion (v 6, 1134a20). Aristotle will be contradicting book vii in describing such people as acting with knowledge, if he means to include among them those who are giving in to temptation against their better judgment. And does he mean to include these?

It may be thought that on the contrary, he signals his agreement with book vii, and excludes people who act against their better judgment from the group who act knowingly. For he insists that the actions performed knowingly are not preceded by deliberation (1135b20), which may seem to suggest that the agents have never thought out any better judgment, and so cannot be acting against it. But he may only mean that the injury they inflict is not the product of deliberation. Admittedly, we find that *some* of the people under discussion are not acting against their better judgment, for they are prepared to maintain that their action was justified (1135b27 – 1136a1), but there is no suggestion that this is true of the whole class.

On the other side, there is some reason to think that Aristotle really is contradicting book vii, and including people who act against their better judgment among those who act knowingly. For if such people do not act knowingly, their actions, according to the criteria of v 8, will be involuntary, contrary to what Aristotle says everywhere else (*NE* vii, 10, 1152a–15-16; iii 1, 1110b9–15, 1111a24–b3; *EE* 1224b26–36). This would not in itself be surprising, for we already know that in v 8 Aristotle includes more than usual under the heading of involuntary. But it has a further consequence. For it means that the man who acts from anger or lust against his better judgment does not commit an injustice (*adikēma*), and does not treat anyone unjustly (*adikein*), since Aristotle ties these concepts in this chapter to acting voluntarily (1135a15–23, b6–8, b19–24). At most, he will do something which happens to be unjust (1135a18–19, a22, b6–8). This would seem a surprisingly lenient description, and it may be easier to suppose that, in conflict with book vii, Aristotle regards the man who gives in to anger or lust against his better judgment as *knowing* what he is doing.

Further confirmation comes from elsewhere. For in *NE* vii 8, 1151a10, Aristotle says that those who give in to temptation do indeed commit an injustice, even though they are not unjust men (*adikoi men ouk eisin, adikēsousi de*). This would place them in the third category of offences in *NE* v 8 (1135b20) along with those who *knowingly* commit an injustice, but are not unjust.

Finally, there is the consideration that if men who give in to temptation are not to be placed in the third category along with those who know, it will be hard to place them anywhere else in the fourfold scheme of offences. They do not fit comfortably into the second category, for example, along with those who could reasonably have been expected to foresee what would happen.

Aristotle has been criticised for his failure in *NE* vii to accept that the man who gives in to temptation can act knowingly. This makes it the more interesting if he does accept that possibility in *NE* v. There has been much more discussion of whether Plato changes his view about temptation, but I shall reserve consideration of that for another occasion.

Negligence

In *Rhet.* i 13 (1374b4–10), Aristotle distinguishes three kinds of injury, and grades them in order of seriousness. In *NE* v 8, he converts the threefold scheme into a fourfold one, by splitting up the third and most serious category. It is commonly supposed, and correctly I believe, that the second of the four categories is a class of *negligent* injuries. I shall start with a translation of the passage (*NE* v 8, 1135b10–25).

There are three kinds of injury that arise in associations. Those accompanied by ignorance are mistakes, when one has no idea whom one is acting on, or what one is doing, or with what instrument, or with what effect. Thus the man thought that he was not hitting anyone, or not with this instrument, or not this person, or not with this effect, but it turned out with an unexpected result (e.g. he threw not in order to wound, but in order to prick, or not to hit this man, or with this instrument). So (1) when the injury occurs contrary to reasonable expectation (*paralogōs*), it is a mishap (*atuchēma*). But (2) when it is not contrary to reasonable expectation, but is still without bad character, it is a mistake. For one makes a mistake when the origin of the cause (*archē tēs aitias*) is in oneself, and one suffers a mishap, when it is from outside. (3) But when one acts knowingly, yet without prior deliberation, it is an injustice (*adikēma*), for example, what is done through anger and other passions which are necessary and natural to man. For in these cases men act injuriously and mistakenly, and thereby unjustly, and their acts are injustices; but they are not yet unjust men on that account or evil. For the injury is not due to wickedness. (4) But when a man does it from deliberate choice (*prohaeresis*), he is unjust and wicked (*adikos kai mochthēros*).

Aristotle starts by distinguishing two kinds of injury (*blabē*) inflicted in ignorance (and therefore involuntarily). The first is a mere mishap (*atuchēma*); the second is called a mistake (*hamartēma*). It turns out to be a culpable mistake, for it is distinguished by reference to two ideas. First, the injurious outcome is not contrary to reasonable expectation (not *paralogōs*, 1135b16–17), as it would have been in a mere mishap. Secondly, the origin of the cause (*archē tēs aitias*, 1135b18–19 – I do not think it necessary to emend the text) lies within the agent, not outside, as it would in a mere mishap. I believe these two ideas are not independent of each other. They may be easier to understand if we consider what may well have helped to inspire Aristotle's distinction, the second Tetralogy attributed (probably wrongly) to the orator Antiphon (*c.* 480–411 B.C.). This set of four model speeches for trainees in rhetoric discusses a javelin thrower who hits and kills a spectator while practising. It is agreed by both parties to the dispute that the killing was involuntary. But one party wants to argue further that the thrower was not even the cause of death. The cause lay rather in the victim himself, who walked into the throwing area. If Aristotle's two ideas were applied to this case, he would be asking: was it contrary to reasonable expectation that the spectator would be in the path of the javelin? And did the origin of the cause lie in the thrower (in his negligence, for example), or elsewhere, e.g. in the spectator? Thus interpreted, Aristotle's two ideas, of not being contrary to reasonable expectation and of not having an external cause, will apply to the same situations. And I think this is his intention, because he links the two ideas by the word 'for' (*gar* 1135b18). Further, if he had not meant the two ideas to apply to the same situations, his classification would needlessly be prevented from covering an important range of cases.[5]

Aristotle's remaining categories of injury are two kinds of injustice (*adikēma*). They are distinguished from the first two categories by the fact that the agent acts knowingly.

Description is all important to this classification of injuries. For the same action can belong to one category under one description, and to another under another. To take an example from earlier in the chapter (v 8, 1135a28–31), an example which will remind us of Oedipus, someone may knowingly strike a man in anger, not knowing it is his father. Striking the man would be a voluntary action, an injustice (*adikēma*), according to Aristotle's classification. But what about the further

---

[5] For if the killing of a spectator could be contrary to reasonable expectation, and yet the cause of death be within the thrower, the case would be neither a mishap (*atuchēma*), nor a mistake (*hamartēma*), but would escape classification.

charge, more serious in Greek eyes, that he struck his *father*? This will not have been an injustice, for he did not do it knowingly.

The importance of description is also apparent when we ask whether his striking his *father* was a mistake or a mishap. His striking a man was not in any sense contrary to reasonable expectation, but his striking his *father* may have been. Similarly, the cause of his striking a man was internal, for it lay in his anger. But the cause of its being his *father* that he struck may have been external. It may have lain not in his own negligence in failing to realise that the man who annoyed him might be his father, but rather in the external circumstance that his father happened to be passing just then.

Now I can concentrate on my immediate concern, the category of mistake (*hamartēma*). The reason why this is commonly regarded as a class of negligent injuries is that the injuries are inflicted unknowingly, but *not* contrary to *reasonable* expectation. This description certainly does cover negligent injuries, and it would include the javelin thrower who hits a spectator through not looking to see where the spectators are. It would also include cases which it is slightly less natural to call cases of negligence, such as the man who causes injury because he is drunk, provided that he acts in ignorance of what he is doing, and that his causing injury after drinking was not contrary to reasonable expectation. If the category is, however, at least roughly a category of negligent injuries, we can see that Aristotle's treatment of negligence here differs from that elsewhere. *EE* ii 9 (1225b13–16) and *NE* iii 5 (1113b23 – 1114a3) also refer to culpable ignorance due to carelessness (*ameleia*). But the treatment in *NE* iii differs in that it extends to ignorance of the law, as well as of the particular circumstances of the action. Moreover, neither *NE* iii nor *EE* ii invokes the scheme of the *Rhetoric*, or attempts to slot the class of negligent injuries into a system of classification.

David Daube has published a scintillating lecture which, if correct, would refute what I have just said, and much of what I shall say in the next chapter. He argues that Aristotle does not have the idea of negligence in mind at all, and indeed that Aristotle's second category is not confined to *culpable* injuries.[6] He argues that when the outcome of a mistake is said to be 'not *paralogōs*', this merely means 'not contrary to expectation'. It does not mean 'not contrary to *reasonable* expectation'. It is the translation 'reasonable' that smuggles in the notion of negligence. Against Daube, Malcolm Schofield has provided textual evidence, to my mind conclusive, in favour of the translation 'reasonable'.[7] None the less, at the end of his paper, he concedes to Daube, mistakenly I believe, that the idea of negligence plays no important role, and that the category of *hamartēma* (as opposed to *atuchēma*) includes a mixture of pardonable and unpardonable mistakes.[8] Daube can derive further com-

[6] David Daube (32.4) 1969.   [7] Malcolm Schofield, note 5 of (35.3) 1973.
[8] Malcolm Schofield, op. cit. 69–70. Some of his arguments for making these concessions

fort from P. van Braam, who maintained in a much earlier paper that these mistakes were not culpable.[9]

I believe that Daube cannot be right, for first, on his interpretation, there would be a straight self-contradiction in the account of a mistake (*hamartēma*). For it is performed in ignorance (*met' agnoias*), the agent having no conception (*mēte hupelabe, ou ōiēthē*) of what he is doing (1135b12–16), and yet, on Daube's view, it is for the agent not unexpected. How can this be? Daube only makes it appear possible by illegitimately shifting the description of the action in mid-discussion. Striking a *man* is not unexpected; striking his *father* is something the agent does in ignorance. A related difficulty for Daube is that it is hard to see how a mistake would escape being voluntary, if it were not unexpected, in which case it ought to be classed not as a mistake, but as an injustice (*adikēma*). And a third difficulty is that, if to occur *paralogōs* is merely to occur unexpectedly, it is no longer clear why what occurs *paralogōs* should have an external origin, as I have argued it does. Finally, Daube (and those who join him in denying that the category consists of culpable injuries) must discount the indication in *Rhet.* I 13, 1374b4, and the legal tradition, to be discussed in Chapter Eighteen, which both made mistakes more culpable than mishaps.

I have been stressing the variation in Aristotle's thought. We have seen him trying out different solutions of the same problem (the relation of ignorance to voluntariness), recognising the truth of a view which he elsewhere rejects (in connexion with temptation), and gradually elaborating a classificatory scheme (including negligent injuries). But can we draw any conclusions about how his thought developed, and which variations are significant? It is time to return to the two scholarly issues mentioned earlier.

The disputed books and the dates of composition

One dispute concerned the books which are nowadays printed as V, VI and VII of the *Nicomachean Ethics*, and whether their proper home was the *Eudemian Ethics*. The history of the textual transmission has been

---

rest on the assumption, which is a common one, but which I am here questioning, that Aristotle is using the same concepts in v 8 and III 1. His major argument, however, is that the notion of mistake (*hamartēma*) in 1135b18 cannot have much to do with negligence, for whereas negligence would not be pardonable, 1136a5–9 implies that any unintended injury is pardonable, unless it is due to unnatural passion. I do not myself take 1136a5–9 in this way. An alternative is to see it as making no claim at all about the notion of mistake (*hamartēma*) employed in 1135b18, because it is only interested in the two extreme cases, the case where the unintended injury is wholly pardonable (this is a mishap, *atuchēma*), and the case where it is wholly unpardonable (this is the case where it is due to unnatural passion). The mistake of 1135b18 is ignored because it falls under neither of these two extremes, but has an intermediate degree of culpability, as indeed *Rhet.* I 13, 1374b4, indicates.

[9] P. van Braam, 'Aristotle's use of ἁμαρτία,' *Classical Quarterly* 6, 1912, 266–72.

assembled and lucidly presented in a masterly paper by Dieter Harl-finger.[10] Already in the second century A.D., Aspasius, who included a commentary on the disputed books within his commentary on the *Nicomachean Ethics*, none the less thought that the books belonged by rights to the *Eudemian*. Of the mss. of the *Eudemian Ethics* which have survived to the present day, some include the three disputed books, while others omit them, and refer to the *Nicomachean Ethics* instead. In modern times, at least since Spengel in 1841, the majority view has been,[11] that the disputed books belong to the *Nicomachean Ethics*. According to one variant of this view, it is conceded that in their original form the three books were written for the *Eudemian Ethics*, but it is said that the version we now have was rewritten for the *Nicomachean*.[12]

I believe that the passages we have encountered from book v, chapter 8, of the *Nicomachean Ethics* favour the minority view, that this chapter at least belongs to the *Eudemian Ethics*. This was already argued by Henry Jackson, in connexion with *NE* v 8,[13] and has been dramatically confirmed by some computer studies to be published by Anthony Kenny.[14] I hope here to add some support to this view, but it is certainly not the usual one. Quite apart from the dominant belief about the disputed books in general, many authors connect this chapter in particular with *Nicomachean Ethics*.[15] Its definition of voluntariness is preceded by a reference back (1135a23), and this is commonly taken to be a reference back to *NE* III.

A second scholarly issue is whether the *Nicomachean Ethics* is earlier

[10] Dieter Harlfinger (34.1) 1971.

[11] As Artur von Fragstein says in (34.5) 1974, 396. However, the *Eudemian Ethics* is preferred not only by himself and by the five scholars he cites (P. von der Mühll, H. Margueritte, A.-J. Festugière, P. Gohlke, and G. Lieberg), but also, if we go back to Schleiermacher in 1817, by F. Schleiermacher, H. A. J. Munro, Alexander Grant, Henry Jackson, and St. G. Stock. It will also be preferred by A. J. P. Kenny, in a forthcoming book (34.7).

[12] See A. Mansion (34.2) 1927; R. A. Gauthier, in (34.3) 1958, vol. 1, Introduction, 43–7; F. Dirlmeier (34.4) 1962, 361–3. Surveys of modern hypotheses can be found in Gauthier 43–7, von Fragstein 396, Dirlmeier 361–5, A.-J. Festugière, *Aristote, le Plaisir*, Paris 1946, xxv-xliv, Henry Jackson (34.6) 1879, xxii-xxxii.

[13] Henry Jackson, op. cit.

[14] Anthony Kenny (34.7), forthcoming 1978. Kenny kindly showed me a draft summary of his computer results (subsequently delivered as a lecture at King's College), and drew my attention to the work of Harlfinger cited above.

[15] So W. D. Ross and H. Rackham in their translations, J. Y. Jolif, H. H. Joachim, John Burnet, and F. Dirlmeier in their commentaries (*ad* 1135a23). Also G. F. Else, *Aristotle's Poetics: The Argument*, Cambridge Mass. 1957, 381; David Daube (32.4) 1969; Max Hamburger, *Morals and Law: The Growth of Aristotle's Legal Theory*, Newhaven 1951; Malcolm Schofield (35.3) 1973. On the other side, the chapter is connected with the *Eudemian Ethics* instead of the *Nicomachean* by H. Jackson (op. cit.); Alexander Grant, *The Ethics of Aristotle*, London 1885; Artur von Fragstein, op. cit. 177–83; St. G. Stock, introduction to the Oxford translation of the *Magna Moralia*, Oxford 1930, xiii-xix; D. J. Allan, 'Quasi-mathematical method in the *Eudemian Ethics*', in *Aristote et les Problèmes de Méthode*, Proceedings of the 2nd Symposium Aristotelicum, ed. S. Mansion, Louvain and Paris 1961.

or later than the *Eudemian*. When the *Eudemian Ethics* was thought to be the work of Eudemus of Rhodes, it had to be regarded as later. Now that it is generally accepted as being Aristotle's own work, it is usually considered earlier. This time I am tentatively inclined to side with the majority opinion, but I have not seen Kenny's arguments in favour of the minority.[16]

NE V 8 *belongs with* EE II, *not with* NE III

I shall take first the problem of the disputed books. Since it is held by some people that the three disputed books do not all go together,[17] it will be wise to confine any conclusion to *NE* v 8. This chapter at least belongs to the *Eudemian Ethics*, as is shown by the respects in which *NE* v 8 and *EE* II are like each other, while both differ from *NE* III. Of these respects, some have been noted by Jackson or Stock, some not.[18] They can be listed as follows:

(i) *EE* II and *NE* v 8 recognise duress as sometimes a source of involuntariness.

(ii) They both define the voluntary in terms of what is up to us, and neither discusses the case in which we have lost the power we once had of refraining.

(iii) They give the same illustration of force (*bia*).

(iv) They both declare merely 'accidental' knowledge irrelevant in their definitions of the involuntary (*EE* II 9, 1225b3–5 and 6; *NE* v 8, 1135a26 and 28–31). If you know that you are striking a man, and, unknown to you, he happens to be your father, this does not mean that you are voluntarily striking your *father*.

(v) In *EE* II 10, 1226b36, Aristotle promises further discussion, 'in our examination of justice', of the relation between his own distinction of choice (*prohaeresis*) from voluntariness, and the legal distinction of forethought (*pronoia*) from voluntariness. The reference forward seems to be to *NE* v 8, 1135b26.

(vi) *EE* II and *NE* v 8 omit the idea of *NE* III (1110b18–24, 1111a20–1) that if an action is not regretted, it cannot be involuntary, but at most non-voluntary.

(vii) Neither *EE* II 9 nor *NE* v 8 is concerned with ignorance of the law, but only of *particular* facts.

[16] In (34.7), forthcoming. Two other supporters of this minority view are Donald Monan, *Moral Knowledge and its Methodology in Aristotle*, Oxford 1968, and D. J. Allan (op. cit. preceding note).

[17] On one view, the three extant books consist partly of material from an earlier period, partly of revisions that have been substituted for that earlier material.

[18] For Jackson and Stock, see notes 12 and 15 above. Jackson modestly refers to his examples as 'trifling instances of agreement and difference' (p. xxvi). He there notes (v), (vi) and (vii), while Stock notes (iii) and (v). I have omitted as inconclusive a couple of further points which they make.

(viii) Both books show an awareness that some natural processes are neither voluntary nor involuntary (*EE* II 8, 1224a18; *NE* v 8, 1135b1).

It may be objected that in the preceding pages we have encountered some respects in which *NE* v 8 is distinctive. Can it really, then, belong with *EE* II? First, it is unique in its treatment of negligence; secondly, it alone makes all acts involuntary in which the agent is ignorant of what he is doing, and compensatingly treats involuntariness as not always an excuse; thirdly, it alone seems to imply that a man can give in to temptation knowingly. These three distinctive features are important, but I believe they are compatible with *EE* II, *NE* v, and *NE* VII all forming part of the same work (the *Eudemian Ethics*). Each of the three books (*EE* II, *NE* v, *NE* VII) has special interests of its own, and has been elaborated at the points where those special interests arise. The special interest in *NE* v 8 is the fourfold classification, while that in *NE* VII is temptation. As each special interest was elaborated or dropped, the three passages may have got slightly out of line with each other. But the deviations are comparatively slight,[19] and they leave the three books looking far more closely united to each other than any is united to *NE* III. Possibly the three books started off closer to each other, but came to diverge a little more through subsequent additions.

Dating: the order Rhet. *I;* EE *II* + NE *V 8* + NE *VII 1–10;*
NE *III*

The remaining scholarly issue is the relative dates of the *Eudemian* and *Nicomachean Ethics*, and on this I am less confident. I shall again confine myself to the particular chapters that have been under discussion (*NE* III 1–5, *NE* v 8, *NE* VII 1–10, *EE* II 6–11), and simply draw attention to a few pointers which favour the latest date for *NE* III 1–5.

First, there are several points at which *NE* III seems superior in philosophical doctrine. One is its method of allowing that a man can act voluntarily, even though unaware of what he is doing. *NE* III, it will be recalled, makes the voluntariness depend on the *causal role* played by the man's ignorance (III 1, 1110b24–7; cf. III 5, 1113b32–3), and this seems to be on the right track.[20] *NE* VII, by contrast, makes it depend on

---

[19] On negligence, *NE* v 8 differs from *EE* II, but does not contradict it. On the question of whether the voluntary agent always knows what he is doing, *EE* II 9 does not differ from *NE* v 8 in its preliminary definition of voluntariness. It diverges only through its addition of a footnote (*prosdihoristeon*, 1225b16) to that original definition. It is *NE* VII that disagrees most flatly, presumably because the subject of giving in to temptation provokes more elaborate consideration of ignorance and knowledge. As for the view of *NE* v that one can give in to temptation knowingly, again it is *NE* VII that disagrees most clearly, and again this is probably because the more detailed treatment has led to different ideas. *EE* II does not commit itself on the issue.

[20] In a way, admittedly, *NE* v 8 is on an even better tack. For it recognises that the man who gives in to temptation need not be unaware of what he is doing, and so avoids the

the *degree* of knowledge or ignorance. It is because the man possesses knowledge 'in a way' (1147a11–18, 1152a15–16) that Aristotle argues his action can be counted voluntary. But the way is similar to the way in which a man who is asleep, mad, or drunk possesses knowledge (1147a11–18, 1152a15). And it is not clear why Aristotle should think *this* degree of awareness would transform his action into a voluntary one. Worse, Aristotle quietly forgets his more extreme suggestion that the man lacks the relevant premise altogether (1147a7, b10) or possesses it only in a way that does not amount to knowledge (b11–12).

NE III is superior also to *EE* II, for although *EE* II 9 toys with the idea that voluntariness in these cases depends on the causal role played by the unawareness (1225b6, b7, b10), it wavers, and does not exploit this solution decisively. Instead, it resorts to a postscript (1225b11–16), which is unsatisfactory. The postscript gives the impression that Aristotle, finding his initial definition of voluntariness does not cover all the cases he wants, has listed some extra examples, without having thought out a rationale for including them on the list.[21]

A second respect in which *NE* III is philosophically superior is that it clarifies the status of cases in which a man once had the power to refrain, but has lost it through drunkenness, or through allowing bad character to become ingrained. Admittedly, *EE* II 9, pays attention to some of the cases discussed in *NE* III 5. Both chapters consider carelessness (*ameleia* 1114a1–2, 1225b14–16), and both consider whether it was easy or important to have the knowledge which the careless man lacks (1113b34, 1225b15). But *NE* III 5 takes the discussion much further, extending it to drunkenness and to ingrained character, and making clear that the important thing to consider, in deciding whether something of this kind is voluntary or up to us, is whether we once had the power to refrain, and let it go (1113b30 – 1114a31).

A third way in which *NE* III is philosophically superior to *EE* II is that for the first time Aristotle's *negative* approach to the definition of voluntariness stands out clearly and cleanly. It is defined by the *absence* of certain excusing factors. This approach, though already present in *EE* II, is mixed up with an attempt at *positive* definition. *EE* II 7 starts with

---

question how to square his unawareness with voluntariness. None the less, *NE* v cannot be regarded as Aristotle's latest thought on the matter for a reason I have already given in the text: it cannot be thought of as superseding the fuller treatment in *NE* VII.

[21] Admittedly, there is some attempt on Aristotle's part to say that the first of the two extra examples of voluntary conduct is covered after all by the preliminary definition, which connects voluntariness with knowledge. For the man who fails to *use* his knowledge through carelessness at least *has* the knowledge, and so perhaps cannot deny that he is acting voluntarily by the original definition. But one then wonders why Aristotle does not allow that this is equally true of *all* those who fail to use their knowledge *whatever* the reason. In any case, the second extra example of voluntary conduct is not covered by the preliminary definition. For this is the case of a man who, because of carelessness or the distractions of pleasure or pain, does not even *possess* knowledge, so that by the preliminary definition he would not be acting voluntarily.

three rival characterisations of the voluntary, as that which is in accordance with desire, with deliberate choice, or with thought. There is a laborious argument by elimination in support of the third characterisation, but though it gets supported, it is not thereafter put to use. Instead, Aristotle switches at the last moment to the negative style of definition, which has been so much praised. We know that the positive definition 'that which is in accordance with thought' comes from the Platonic school, since it appears in the Platonic *Definitions* (415A2, 416 line 26). It looks as if discussions in Plato's Academy have imposed an alien approach on the *EE* II treatment, from which Aristotle finally shakes free in *NE* III.

Fourthly, the discussion in *EE* II is highly aporetic. It is sometimes so tentative that it is hard to see what view Aristotle is endorsing: does he allow in II 8, for example, that any cases of duress are cases of force (*bia*)? And his suggestions are qualified by afterthoughts and alternatives: witness the definition of voluntariness eventually offered in II 9. It may be protested that some of these features, and also the appeal to three alien definitions, are merely the natural outcome of his normal method of starting his discussion from accepted opinions (*endoxa*). It is partly because he is recording the fluctuations of ordinary language that he is so indecisive in II 8 about the treatment of force. This is all true, but it does not counteract the impression that the *EE* discussion is the less satisfactory. The treatment of *endoxa* has been allowed to absorb an enormous proportion of the space. The discussion of alien definitions dominates, and decisive proposals by Aristotle himself are less forthcoming, at least up to the beginning of the last little chapter (II 9).

Finally, it may be a sign of earliness in *NE* v 8 that, in discussing mistakes, Aristotle here correlates involuntariness neatly with ignorance. Mistakes, involuntariness and ignorance had been grouped together in the legal tradition before Aristotle (see note 1). In *EE* II 9, he makes a similar neat correlation between voluntariness and knowledge, and only moves away from this position through the addition of a postscript. In *NE* III, he has moved much more definitely away.

The discussion in *Rhetoric* i 10 and 13 is most naturally regarded as the earliest.[22] The dating of the *Rhetoric* is controversial, though Düring has made a good case for saying that it belongs as a whole to Aristotle's early period in Plato's Academy.[23] Certainly, the discussion of culpability appears very primitive in character. i 10 offers cursory definitions of some of the key terms, ignoring the distinctions made elsewhere, and when i 13 comes to the degrees of culpability, it distinguishes only the

[22] I am ignoring the *Rhetorica ad Alexandrum*, which has a similar classification, since I take it not to be by Aristotle.

[23] Ingemar Düring, *Aristoteles*, Heidelberg 1966, 118–24. Others, however, do not agree whether it is a patchwork or a relatively unified work, and if relatively unified, whether it is early or late.

three traditional categories,[24] ignoring *NE* v's innovation of creating a fourth; it has fewer, briefer, and vaguer criteria for distinguishing the categories, and uses terms in senses different from those supplied by the careful discussions in other works. Even within these chapters, the sense of terms seems to waver. Whatever may be said about the special purposes of the *Rhetoric*,[25] I find it impossible to believe that if Aristotle had already worked out the distinctions he makes in the *Eudemian* or *Nicomachean Ethics*, he could have brought himself to ride over them so roughshod.

I have argued that the disputed books of the *Ethics* are, at least in part, a *Eudemian* version, and probably earlier than *NE* iii. The books, as we have them, may have been revised by Aristotle from time to time, but the revision was never such as to harmonise books v and vii completely with the undisputed books of the *Nicomachean Ethics*.

[24] For evidence that three categories were traditional, four an innovation, see Chapter Eighteen.

[25] In this connexion, the plea might be made that Aristotle repeatedly warns us that for his present purposes exact definitions are not required (1359b2–8, 1360b7–8, b14–18, 1366a20–2, a32–5, a36 – b1, b23–4, 1369b31–2), and says that the premises of rhetorical reasoning, like those of dialectical reasoning, should be accepted (*endoxa*) ideas, since abstruse knowledge will not be persuasive (1355a14–18, a24–9, 1357a12–13, 1360b18, 1362b29, 1366a37). But this is scarcely enough to explain away all the points that have just been made about the *Rhetoric*. And in any case, the plea that Aristotle is simply trotting out what the common man will accept cannot be pressed very far. It has been pointed out, for one thing, that some of the definitions Aristotle offers are ones accepted not by the man in the street, but by members of Plato's Academy (John Burnet, *The Ethics of Aristotle*, London 1900, p. 1, note 1, and p. 3, note 3; A.-J. Festugière, op. cit. 1946, lxiii; G. Lieberg, *Die Lehre von der Lust in der Ethiken des Aristoteles*, Zetemata 19, Munich 1957, 23–7). It has also been pointed out that Aristotle does not content himself with simply repeating Academic definitions, but introduces improvements of his own (Lieberg, and W. Fortenbaugh, 'Aristotle's *Rhetoric* on emotions', *Archiv für Geschichte der Philosophie* 52, 1970, 40–70).

CHAPTER EIGHTEEN

Aristotle's Contribution to Legal Theory

In Chapter Sixteen, I postponed trying to say where Aristotle's main contribution to legal theory lay. In fact both Plato and Aristotle made major contributions, but of an entirely different character, because of their different views on the purpose of punishment.

Plato's contribution is most fully developed in book IX of the *Laws*, a brilliant work, often neglected and written off as a product of his old age. He there argues for the view already canvassed in several earlier works,[1] that apart from compensating the victim of crime, a large part of the purpose of punishment must be to *reform* the offender (862C – 863A; cf. 728C; 854D – 855A, 908B – 9A, 934A–B, 941D, 944D, 957E). Although reformative theories of punishment have many champions today, one of the most notable being Barbara Wootton,[2] Plato is sometimes clearer than modern proponents, in recognising the implications of such theories. They are benign in intent, but can be very harsh in their consequences, as we shall see.[3]

Plato's reason for advocating a reformative theory is the view that people are not voluntarily unjust (860C – 862B). Admittedly, they voluntarily injure others, but they do not voluntarily behave unjustly, presumably because they want to inflict the injury, but do not want to be unjust. If that is so, considerations of fairness might suggest that we should not punish them. But punishment can be justified partly on the basis of viewing it as a method of reform.

The harsh consequences of such a theory are brought out starkly in Plato's account. For in 862D – 863A, he envisages that the best treatments of the offender may be to bestow on him pleasures, honours, or gifts. On the other hand, reform may prove impossible, and in that case there is nothing left but execution (cf. 854D – 855A; 908B – 9A; 957E;

---

[1] The reformist view of punishment had already been put into the mouth of Protagoras in Plato's *Protagoras* 323C–324D, and had reappeared as Plato's own in the *Gorgias* (464B, 472E, 476A – 481B, 508B, 525B-E), *Republic* (380A-B, 409E – 410A, 591B) and *Sophist* (229A-C).

[2] Barbara Wootton, *Social Science and Social Pathology*, London 1959; *Crime and the Criminal Law*, London 1963. There are, naturally, many differences between Plato's version of the reformative view and hers.

[3] So H. L. A. Hart (38.3) 1968, esp. chs 7–8.

Gorgias 525B–E), which will at least have the advantage of deterring and protecting the rest of society, and which he claims (862E; 957E; cf. *Rep.* 410A) is best for the man himself. At 908B – 909A (cf. 856D), a still harsher view is taken; for the man described there has a naturally just character (908B), and his atheistic beliefs are presumably not voluntarily held. But if five years of confinement and tuition do not reform these beliefs, he will have to be executed, apparently to protect others, rather than to benefit him.

In spite of this, Plato does after all attach great importance to the question of whether offences are involuntary, and whether there is some excuse or mitigating factor.[4] On the whole, such cases receive a lighter treatment or none at all. It might seem that he thereby forgets his principle that all injustice is equally involuntary, and that the size of the punishment should depend on what will effect a cure. But in some of these cases he argues that cure is not needed (944D), or is easier to effect (941D). This is fair enough in connexion with some examples, but it seems harder to believe when the excuse is madness, disease, old age, or the smallness of the amount stolen. A reform theorist should be prepared to penalise the mad offender, if he thinks that will reform him. And the same applies to the offender with a disadvantaged background.

Another reason why Plato's theory implied penalties for the guiltless was that he shared the Athenian concern with pollution. Under Athenian law, a man whose homicidal act was proved involuntary would none the less have to pay heavy penalties, which, on the usual interpretation,[5] were intended to rid the state of pollution. This harsh system has its parallel in Greek tragedy: Oedipus is polluted by his parricide and incest, and must pay the price, even if he is not to blame. The idea retains its full force in Plato's *Laws* (865–74).

Aristotle's view of punishment seems very different. He shows little respect for considerations of pollution.[6] Admittedly, he mentions the reformative theory as a view of others (*NE* III 5, 1113b26; x 9, 1180a12), and sometimes pays lip service to it himself (*Rhet.* I 10, 1369b12; *EE* I 3, 1214b32, II 1, 1220a35; *NE* II 3, 1104b16).[7] But we have already seen that in many cases Aristotle is pessimistic about the chances of changing a man, once his habits are formed (*NE* 1114a13–21, 1150a21, b32, 1151a4, 1152a30–1).[8] Instead he concentrates on two other roles for

[4] See the long list of mitigating or excusing circumstances recognised by him: note 40 to Chapter Sixteen.
[5] D. M. MacDowell, however, has questioned the importance of pollution in (32.11) 1963.
[6] There is a reference to the practice of purifications (*lusis*) after murder of a close relative (*Pol.* II 4, 1262a32). And he has a conception of what it is not holy (*hosion*) to do, both here, and in connexion with aborting a foetus after it has acquired sense perception (*Pol.* VIII 16, 1335b25).
[7] At *Rhet.* I 13, 1374b31, however, it may be the victim, not the offender, who needs healing.
[8] But see note 29 to Chapter Sixteen for references of a more optimistic tendency.

punishment, one of which is achieving fairness. In *Rhet.* ɪ 13 (1374b4),
he insists that *equity* demands different penalties for the offences which
he arranges in order of seriousness, and this is the passage, as was
argued in Chapter Seventeen, on which *NE* v 8 is based. At *NE* v 11,
1138a12, the reason why the state punishes suicides, by dishonouring
their bodies, is said to be that they have wronged the state. At v 4,
1132a6–19, Aristotle represents the judge as trying to restore a sort of
equality. Not only in cases of fraud, but also in cases of adultery, assault,
or homicide, one party has got too much loss or gain compared with
another, and the judge tries to see that they get the same amount. At v 5,
1132b34, it is said that men think themselves slaves, if they cannot
return evil for evil and good for good. Throughout the discussion of
justice in *NE* v, then, he often thinks of punishment as a means of
securing fairness. Though the view of punishment as a means of securing fairness is rudely called by its opponents 'the retributive theory', it is
probably less harsh than a thoroughgoing reformative view.

The other main role of punishment, for Aristotle, cropped up earlier in
our discussion of his views on upbringing. It is to deter people from
wrongdoing. We found this role most fully discussed in *NE* x 9. It is
distinct from the Platonic concern with reform, for to be deterred, a
person need not yet have done anything wrong. The primary aim is to
instil good habits into the young, but if that fails, Aristotle hopes, as a
second best, to achieve a conformity for the common good (*NE* v 1,
1129b14–25; x 9, 1180a1–5).

Aristotle's concern with equity may have been in direct response to
Plato. In *Laws* 757ᴇ, Plato regards equity (*to epieikes*), in some sense of
the word, as being contrary to strict justice (*dikē*), and as being a
regrettable concession that has to be made. He may not be thinking of
quite the same sort of thing as Aristotle – the example is of giving
everyone an equal chance by means of a lottery. But, as von Fragstein
has argued,[9] Aristotle probably has Plato in mind, when he says that
equity is only contrary to the *written* law, not to justice, of which it is
indeed one kind (*to para ton gegrammenon nomon dikaion, Rhet.*
1374a27), and a superior kind at that (*Rhet.* 1375a29; *NE* 1137b8–11,
b24, b33–4). We can add a second point at which Aristotle seems to be
responding to Plato. Plato's answer in the *Statesman* (294ᴀ–ᴄ) to the
inflexibility of the written law is to have a man who rules without laws.
Aristotle responds by rejecting this solution to the problem (*Pol.* ɪɪɪ
15–16), and by regarding equity in judges as the right solution (*NE* v
10).

Aristotle's main contribution to legal theory, however, does not lie in
his avoiding the harsher aspects of Plato's view. Rather, I believe, it lies
in his whole enterprise of trying to classify the different kinds of excuse

---

[9] Artur von Fragstein (34.5) 1974, 211.

and of culpability. This important step drew attention to whole classes of case, not only to the general categories of voluntary and involuntary, but also to overwhelming external force, fear of a greater evil, nonculpable ignorance of what one is doing, culpable ignorance, negligence, acts due to natural passion, or to unnatural passion, acts due to deliberate choice. Not only were these classes isolated for examination, but some of them received definitions for the first time. Previously they had on the whole been treated only piecemeal.[10] Aristotle's new enterprise enabled him occasionally to lay down foundations for the later system of Roman law.

One example of this is provided by Aristotle's treatment of fear. There was no general law in Athens covering all cases of human threat, much less one that brought in cases of jettison as well. It was noted in Chapter Sixteen that duress was covered by law in the case of wills, but not in the case of contracts, and that protection in the case of jettison depended on the wording of the individual contract made. Aristotle's collection of the cases together was fruitful, and his discussion in *NE* iii 1 may have influenced the Roman concepts found in Justinian of *coactus volui* (I willed what I was compelled to do) and *timor maioris malitatis* (fear of a greater evil).[11]

Further examples are provided by Aristotle's classification of injuries in *NE* v 8. Admittedly, this was not a creation *ex nihilo*. J. M. Bremer has shown that for a long time contrasts had been drawn between mishaps and injustices, mistakes and injustices, mistakes and mishaps.[12] Even the threefold distinction between all three terms had appeared, and since it had appeared in Gorgias, as part of his instruction in rhetoric, it was likely to have been influential.[13] Indeed, Demosthenes who uses it twice, speaks of it as a distinction he has found used by others.[14] And various criteria are offered, though not very systematically, for making the distinction. Mere mistake is associated by Demosthenes with involuntariness (*akōn*), and contrasted with plotting (*epibouleuein*), while injustice is associated with voluntariness

[10] This is true even of Plato. Perhaps Plato comes closest to Aristotle's kind of enterprise in his treatment of anger, *Laws* ix, 866d – 9e, 878b – 9b.

[11] Justinian's *Digest* 4.2.5: not any fear excuses, but only fear of a greater evil. ('Fear of greater evils' is exactly Aristotle's phrase at *NE* iii 1, 1110a4). 4.2.21(5): though compelled by fear to enter upon an inheritance, a man does become heir, because he wills what he is compelled to do. See on the subject: Fritz Schulz, 'Die Lehre vom erzwungenen Rechtsgeschäft im antiken römischen Recht', *Zeitschrift der Savigny — Stiftung für Rechtsgeschichte* 43, 1922 (= vol. 56 of *Zeitschrift für Rechtsgeschichte*).

[12] J. M. Bremer (36.3) 1969, 39–51. For mishaps versus injustices see Antiphon vi 1, Menander 359 (Koerte). For mistakes versus injustices: Thucydides i 69 6, iii 45, iii 62 4; Euripides *Hippolytus* 614–15; Lysias 31 11; Aeschines *Against Ctesiphon* 20; *Hypereides Against Demosthenes* 26; cf. *Rhet.* iii 2, 1405a26–7. For mistakes versus mishaps: Demosthenes *On the Crown* 207–8.

[13] Gorgias *Helen* 15 and 19.

[14] Demosthenes, *On the Crown* 274–5; see also *Letters* 2 1.

(*hekōn*).[15] *The Rhetorica ad Alexandrum*, wrongly ascribed to Aristotle, was written after, perhaps well after, 341 B.C., and so probably after Aristotle's *Rhetoric*, but it may reflect an earlier tradition. It offers the following criteria: an injustice is committed with forethought (*ek pronoias*) and by men of bad character (*poneroi*), a mistake is committed through ignorance, and a mishap occurs not through oneself, but through other people, or through bad luck.[16] The association of mistake with ignorance and with involuntariness is found in other authors too.[17]

Aristotle then has plenty of material bequeathed to him, but he does two new things with it, in *Rhet.* I 13 and *NE* v 8. First, he introduces the criterion of what is not contrary to reasonable expectation, and so turns the category of mistakes into a category of negligence. Previously, the classification had not divided ignorance into the negligent and the blameless. Secondly, after initially repeating the threefold distinction (in the *Rhetoric*), he turns it into a fourfold distinction in *NE* v, by splitting the class of injustices into two. Let us consider just how far this was innovative.

There was little precedent for Aristotle's isolation of a class of negligent injuries. The history of the treatment of negligence has been well studied by R. Maschke, whom I shall here largely be following.[18] In the case of homicide, Athenians had comparatively little incentive for drawing distinctions among cases of involuntary homicide, since there was a penalty of exile for them, which, on the usual view, was connected with pollution, rather than with the degree of culpability, and mitigation of sentence was left to the relatives of the deceased, not to the legal authorities. None the less, in the second tetralogy attributed to Antiphon, there is, as we saw, a rather sophistic debate about a case of involuntary homicide, and there is a reference to negligence. The question is whether the man who threw the javelin in the arena was the cause of the spectator's death, or whether the spectator caused his own death by his negligence (*aphulaxia* 4.7) in wandering into the arena across the path of the javelin. If the spectator caused his own death, it was he who incurred the pollution, and in that case the pollution has already been cleansed, for the one who incurred it has paid for it.[19]

Aristotle may have been influenced by this tetralogy, when he introduced his new criterion for mistakes. But if so, he has transformed the discussion. First, all reference to pollution has gone. Then the allusion

[15] Demosthenes, *Against Timocrates* 49; *On the Crown* 274–5.

[16] Ps-Aristotle (Anaximenes?) *Rhetorica ad Alexandrum* 4, 1427a30 – b1. The date of 341 B.C., as a *terminus post quem*, is supplied by a reference to the expedition of the Corinthians under Timoleon to aid Syracuse against the Carthaginians.

[17] Lysias 31 11, Hypereides *Against Demosthenes* 26.

[18] R. Maschke (32.12) 1926.

[19] A somewhat similar javelin case is recorded by Plutarch (*Pericles* 36). Pericles is said to have spent a whole day discussing with Protagoras whether the thrower, or some other agency, was the cause of death, it being again granted that the action was involuntary.

to the spectator's negligence, which was originally introduced not as a category of offence, but as a way of avoiding a charge, has by Aristotle been turned into a category of offence. Plato had mentioned particular examples of negligence in connexion with bonfires, care of parents, detecting subversion and trusteeship.[20] And Aristotle refers to recognised legal penalties for culpable ignorance of certain laws, or ignorance due to drunkenness (*NE* III 5, 1113b30 – 1114a3). But Aristotle does not take the cases piecemeal, he creates a general category. And he slots it in to a pre-existing scheme, sandwiching it between a more culpable class (of injustices) and a less culpable class (of mishaps). He can thus claim, as none of his predecessors can, to have provided the basis for the threefold Roman scheme of *dolus* (criminal intent), *culpa* (negligence), and *casus* (accident). It was this last comparison of Maschke's which Daube was out to deny in the spirited lecture which was discussed above in Chapter Seventeen. Daube argued that the comparison was worthless on the grounds that Aristotle's category of *hamartēma* was not especially associated with negligence. The remarks offered above in reply will so far serve as a defence of Maschke's comparison.

Aristotle's treatment of negligence is in some ways more satisfactory than that of recent English law. For English law has been preoccupied with the idea that culpability is connected with *mens rea* (the guilty mind), and that in turn is commonly associated with knowledge or intent. Consequently, as A. D. Woozley has brought out,[21] English law has got into a muddle over negligence, in which the injury is not foreseen or intended. On the one hand, it was held, in D.P.P. v Smith (1961) A.C. 290, that (with certain qualifications) a man was to be deemed to have knowledge of his situation if a reasonable man would have had knowledge. In other words, knowledge had to be introduced artificially, in order to represent him as culpable. On the other hand, in Reg. v Morgan (1976) A.C. 182, it was held that a man could not be convicted of rape, so long as he believed, however unreasonably, that his victim was consenting. In other words, the absence of knowledge exonerated. Aristotle more reasonably treats the absence of knowledge as reducing, but not necessarily removing, culpability.

I now turn to Aristotle's other innovation: the division of the class of injustices. He divides them into ones that are merely voluntary, and ones that are in addition inflicted because of a deliberate choice (*prohaeresis*). Aristotle tells us that this had a prototype in the lawgiver's distinction between the voluntary (*hekousion*) and the action performed with forethought (*pronoia EE* II 10, 1226b36; cf. *NE* v 8, 1135b25-7). It is hard to know which lawgivers he has in mind. Superficially, it might

[20] Plato, *Laws* 843c-e, 856b-c, 928c, 932a.
[21] A. D. Woozley, 'Negligence and ignorance', *Philosophy* 53, 1978, 293–306. See also H. L. A. Hart (38.3) ch. 6. Hart proposes extending the concept of *mens rea*, to take negligence into account.

appear that Athenian law marked off forethought (*pronoia*), because this is the word often used to characterise the most serious class of homicide charges which came before the court of the Areopagus. But in fact, in this context, the term *pronoia* was often interchanged with *hekousion*, as if no distinction were intended.[22] Certainly, the later work, *Rhetorica ad Alexandrum*, still associates injustices with *pronoia*, without making any suggestion that injuries due to *pronoia* are a *subclass* of the voluntary ones. But the orator Lysias supports Aristotle by claiming (III 42) that legislators distinguished wounding in the course of a *plot* to kill from wounding by chance in a fight. Another model may possibly have been provided by Plato in the *Laws*, who is making a recommendation, not reporting practice, when he says that the angry man who kills on the spur of the moment, and is sorry afterwards, should receive a different penalty from the man who *plots* his vengeance over a period of time and is not sorry. If Aristotle is influenced by Plato, however, Plato's ideas have undergone a transformation. For first Aristotle's plotting man at *NE* v 8, 1135b33 is not an angry one,[23] and second Plato's distinction is embedded among considerations of what will reform the offender.

Whatever sources may have influenced Aristotle, he is going beyond them. Not only does he take care to use a different term (*prohaeresis*) from the legal one (*pronoia*), but in *EE* II 10, 1226b36 he says that lawgivers are not precise about the term, and only touch the truth in a way. He promises further discussion, and this comes in *NE* v 8, 1135b25–6, where again he uses the legal term *pronoia* only to compare it with his own. One way in which Aristotle makes his term more precise than the legal one is that he insists that deliberate choice (*prohaeresis*) involves prior deliberation, and gives an account of what deliberation is.[24] Another difference is that he makes *prohaeresis* a mark of character which shows a man to be just (*NE* v 8, 1136a3–5) or unjust (*NE* v 8, 1135b22 – 1136a3).[25] But more important than any particular changes he makes is the fact that Aristotle again and again returns to the task of *defining* his concept of deliberate choice (*EE* II 10–11, *NE* III 2–3, *NE* VI 2).

[22] This has been shown by D. M. MacDowell, op. cit. Evidence: the Draconian inscription *IG*² 115; Demosthenes *Against Aristocrates* 24, 72, 73, 77, 78, *Against Meidias* 42–4; Aristotle *Ath. Resp.* 57.3; *Pol.* 1300b26; Ps-Aristotle *Magna Moralia* 1188b29–38. It is also relevant that cases brought before the Areopagus need not have involved a prior plan (Demosthenes *Against Conon* 25 28, *Against Meidias* 71–5; Ps-Antiphon *Third Tetralogy*).

[23] Instead, the plotter is *contrasted* with the angry man, as part of Aristotle's justification of his refusal to count the man who acts from anger as wicked and unjust. A similar contrast between anger and plotting is to be found in *NE* VII 6, 1149b13–18.

[24] The main discussions are in *EE* II, 10–11 and *NE* III 2–3 and VI 2.

[25] It is indeed a defining mark of *prohaeresis* that it reflects character (*NE* VI 2, 1139a34). It is made a test of character also at EE II 11, 1228a2–5; *NE* III 1, 1110b31–2; III 2, 1111b6, 1112a1–2; VIII 13, 1163a22; IX 1, 1164b1–2. This is why the man who uncharacteristically

The moral I would draw is that Aristotle's main contribution lies in his enterprise of isolating and defining whole classes of case, with a view to promoting fairness. He is alive, as we saw in connexion with *EE* II 9 and *NE* v 8, to the importance of different descriptions of an action: striking a man versus striking one's father. His categories seem to have had a definite influence on Roman law, and at certain points compare favourably with those of English law. The contrast with Plato is interesting. Plato's was the more brilliantly imaginative theory, both in its general conception, and in its details. No one before, so far as I know, had suggested the use of incarceration, except as a way of detaining people before trial. Plato suggests its use not for this purpose, nor for the modern purpose of retribution, but as a way of trying to achieve moral reeducation. None the less, for all Plato's originality, the proposals of Aristotle are ones which we should probably find easier to accept.

Appendix: Tragic error

By way of appendix, I should like to consider Aristotle's treatment of tragic error in the *Poetics*. This is closely related to his classification of injuries in *NE* v 8.

In *Poet*. 13, Aristotle says that the tragic hero's downfall must be due to *hamartia*, as in the case of Oedipus. Only so will it arouse our pity, and thus lead to *catharsis*. A great controversy has raged around the subject of whether the *hamartia* is something culpable or not. Some writers have thought that it would help us to decide, if we considered the category of mistake (*hamartēma*) as opposed to mishap (*atuchēma*) in *NE* v 8.[26] And indeed it would seem surprising if *NE* v 8 should have nothing to do with tragic *hamartia*, in view of the fact that Oedipus answers so well to the description at *NE* v 8, 1135a28–30 of the person who strikes his father, knowing he is striking a man, but not knowing he is striking his father. None the less, I think that the nature of tragic *hamartia* must be decided on independent grounds; *NE* v 8 does not help in the end, but it needs to be seen why.

---

gives in to temptation is said not deliberately to *choose* (*prohaereisthai*) to act as he does (*NE* III 2, 1111b14; VII 4, 1148a6; a17), even though various passages allow that he may well have planned in advance how to act (*NE* VI 9, 1142b18; VII 6, 1149b13): the reason why his planning does not constitute deliberate choice is presumably that it does not reflect his normal settled character, but represents an aberration. It is a slight puzzle that Aristotle introduces the reference to character so late in *NE* v 8. At first, he defines deliberate choice as if it were equivalent to prior deliberation (*probouleusis* 1135b10–11, b20). Why does he not bother to say that he is thinking only of prior deliberation which reflects character? Perhaps the reason is that the uncharacteristic kind of deliberation arises in connexion with lust rather than anger (*NE* VII 6, 1149b13–20), whereas the present chapter (v 8) is more concerned with anger and fraud.

[26] P. van Braam, 'Aristotle's use of ἁμαρτία'; David Daube, op. cit.; Roger A. Pack, 'A passage in Alexander of Aphrodisias relating to the theory of tragedy', *American Journal of Philology* 58, 1937, 434.

The controversy has arisen, because it has seemed natural to critics of another era to think that a downfall should be preceded by some kind of weakness, usually conceived of as a flaw of character. But as we have seen, it was not always true in the Athenian law courts that a downfall was supposed to be preceded by guilt. The man who killed involuntarily might have to pay a heavy penalty, apparently to rid the state of pollution. The same applies to tragedy: as various writers have argued, Oedipus and Thyestes, who is mentioned along with him at *Poet.* 1453a11, were polluted each by unwitting incest, and one by the unwitting slaying of his father, the other by the unwitting slaying of his children.[27] Greek tragedies were not always portrayals of a weakness punished, but were sometimes studies of the sheer pity and horror of human situations.[28]

If tragic *hamartia* really corresponds to the category of mistake, (*hamartēma*), as opposed to mishap, it should be easy to decide what Aristotle has in mind. Given the interpretation of *hamartēma* supported by van Braam and Daube (two of those who have looked to this category in *NE* v 8 for the solution), tragic *hamartia* can involve a non-culpable error. Given my interpretation of *hamartēma*, however, as involving negligence and related faults, tragic *hamartia* would have to be something culpable.

But this last result goes against the weight of evidence which critics have assembled to show that tragic *hamartia* is not in every case culpable, even if it is sometimes.[29] Their case is certainly powerful, if we can assume that Aristotle is referring, as he does explicitly in the next chapter, to Sophocles' version of Oedipus (in particular to the *Oedipus Tyrannus*),[30] and if we may take it that Oedipus' parricide and incest are instances or manifestations,[31] of tragic *hamartia*. The latter assumption has been made all the more plausible by Dodds (note 27), who points out that Plato calls the incest of Oedipus and Thyestes a *hamartia* (*Laws* 838c); and I would add that Oedipus seems to be saying that his incest and parricide involved *hamartia* at *Oedipus Coloneus* 966–8 (*hēmartanon*, 968).[32] If Aristotle does have the incest and parricide in mind, and

---

[27] See the eloquent accounts of John Sheppard (36.1), 1920, ch. 2, and of E. R. Dodds (36.2) 1966.

[28] In this regard, however, Aeschylus was different from Sophocles. See the references in the select bibliography.

[29] I accept the argument of T. C. W. Stinton that tragic *hamartia* can include culpable acts, even though I disagree with his claim that it *cannot* include mishaps. See his valuable contribution to the subject: (36.4) 1975.

[30] There were Oedipus tragedies by at least twelve poets. Sophocles wrote two, the *Oedipus Tyrannus*, and some years later the *Oedipus Coloneus*.

[31] A manifestation, if *hamartia* is a disposition, rather than an action.

[32] I take Oedipus to be saying here that he committed a *hamartia* (*hēmartanon*, 968) against his father and mother and himself, but that this was not in return for any earlier *hamartia* (cf. 439: *hēmartēmenōn*). The assumption that Aristotle has in mind the incest and parricide has been challenged by P. van Braam (op. cit.), and by R. D. Dawe, in an

Sophocles' version of them, then the case is very strong for saying that tragic *hamartia* is not necessarily culpable. For it is Sophocles' message that Oedipus was not to blame for these.[33] It has been wondered whether Oedipus was not to some extent negligent. But he had every reason to believe that his parents were the people he had safely left behind in Corinth.[34] And the suggestion that he should have avoided killing any man older than himself hardly takes account of the military and political requirements of the time, or of the extent to which Oedipus killed Laius in self-defence.[35]

If we now compare this evidence with *NE* v 8, we seem to get a very paradoxical result: if Oedipus' parricide is to be fitted into one of the categories of *NE* v 8, it is not a *hamartēma* at all, but an *atuchēma*.[36] For it was contrary to reasonable expectation for Oedipus that he should be slaying his father. The cause of this lay not in his own negligence, but in the external fact that the passer-by happened to be his father. The verdict that the parricide was an *atuchēma* may be compared with the statement in the pseudo-Aristotelian *Magna Moralia* (1195a18), that the man who slays his father in mistake for an enemy is *atuchēs* (unlucky).

But has the discussion of *hamartēma* in *NE* v 8 nothing to do, then, with the *hamartia* of Oedipus? This paradox can be avoided, by noticing something which I have not previously mentioned, that the word *hamartēma* is once used in *NE* v 8 (at 1135b12) for the genus which includes both *atuchēma* and *hamartēma* in the specific sense.[37] It is in this generic sense that the *hamartēma* of *NE* v 8 is related to the

---

otherwise excellent and valuable articles, 'Some reflections on *atē* and *hamartia*', *Harvard Studies in Classical Philology*, 1967. Dawe surprisingly cites *Oedipus Coloneus* 966–8 as if it favoured his view. No alternative candidates for Oedipus' *hamartia* seem to me to have much plausibility: he was neither negligent in failing to identify his mother and father, nor over-zealous in trying to discover the murderer of Laius.

[33] No characters in the *Oedipus Tyrannus* blame Oedipus for the incest or parricide, whereas the suicide of Jocasta is sharply distinguished as voluntary (1230), and Oedipus' self-blinding is criticised (1367). In the *Oedipus Coloneus*, Oedipus is allowed to mount a complete defence of himself (281–4, 521–48, 963–1002), which is endorsed by Antigone (240) and the Chorus (1014–15).

[34] It was only a drunken man who had ever suggested to Oedipus that Polybus and Merope, who had brought him up, were not his real parents (*OT* 779). Polybus and Merope strenuously denied this (783). Nor did the oracle confirm it (788). The oracle merely warned Oedipus that he would kill his father and marry his mother, but Oedipus thought he could avoid this fate by leaving Polybus and Merope behind in Corinth, and he left them for this very purpose (793, 997). I am grateful to A. A. Long for drawing my attention to these passages.

[35] He was outnumbered, five to one (*OT* 752, 842), and had already been struck on the head by Laius with a two-pronged goad (*OT* 809). In the *Oedipus Coloneus*, he is allowed to plead outright that Laius would have killed him (270–4, 547, 993).

[36] I do not think Stinton has established (op. cit.) that a tragic *hamartia cannot* be a mishap.

[37] There is yet a third usage later in the chapter, as Stinton rightly insists (op. cit.). For the corresponding verb, *hamartanein* is applied to a different category again: the injuries inflicted knowingly through natural passion (1135b22).

hamartia of Oedipus. We can thus do justice both to the claim that there must be some relationship between the two discussions, and to the evidence that tragic *hamartia* is not necessarily culpable. This means, however, that *NE* v 8 contributes no evidence of its own to the controversy about the culpability of tragic *hamartia*, since we need independent evidence in order to decide which use of the word *hamartēma* in *NE* v 8 is relevant to the *Poetics*.

A last point to notice is that if Oedipus' mistake as regards his father was non-culpable, we must not infer that his action, however described, was non-culpable. For under the description 'killing a man', his act was neither a mistake nor a mishap, on Aristotle's classification. Insofar as he acted through anger (*di' orgēs*, *OT* 807) it will have been an injustice (*adikēma*, *NE* v 8, 1135b20).[38]

---

[38] Insofar as he acted in self-defence, and so from fear, the act could again be classified, though a little less naturally, under the same heading.

Bibliography

My aim is to select a few writings on each topic which I think will be of particular interest to readers. More extensive references will be found in the footnotes.

1. *Is Aristotle a determinist?*

Deterministic interpretations will be found in

1.1   Theodor Gomperz, *Greek Thinkers*, vol. 4, chs 10 and 16, translated London 1912, from the German of 1896.

1.2   Richard Loening, *Die Zurechnungslehre des Aristoteles*, ch. 18, Jena 1903, repr. Hildesheim 1967.

There is a modified deterministic treatment in

1.3   Jaakko Hintikka, *Time and Necessity*, Oxford 1973, chs 5, 8 and 9.

1.4   Jaakko Hintikka, with U. Remes and S. Knuuttila, *Aristotle on Modality and Determinism*, *Acta Philosophica Fennica* 29, Amsterdam 1977.

A radically indeterminist view is given by

1.5   S. Sambursky, 'On the possible and the probable in ancient Greece', *Osiris* 12, 1956, 35–48, esp. 46–8.

1.6   David Balme, *Aristotle's De Partibus Animalium I and De Generatione Animalium I*, Clarendon Aristotle Series, Oxford 1972, 76–84.

See also Furley, Huby, Gauthier, under 'Aristotle on the relation of determinism to voluntary action'.

2. *Causation*

There are historical treatments by

2.1   William Wallace, *Causality and Scientific Explanation*, vols 1 and 2. Ann Arbor 1972

2.2   Mario Bunge, *Causality: The Place of the Causal Principle in Modern Science*, Cambridge Mass. 1959.

Two major influences on modern views are

2.3   David Hume, *A Treatise of Human Nature*, London 1739, book I, part III, and

2.4   J. S. Mill, *A System of Logic*, London 1843, book III.

Modern controversy is judiciously expounded and criticised in

2.5   J. L. Mackie, *The Cement of the Universe*, Oxford 1974, and anthologised in

2.6   E. Sosa (ed.), *Causes and Conditionals*, Oxford 1975.

Two protagonists are

2.7 Donald Davidson, 'Causal relations', *Journal of Philosophy* 64, 1967, 691–703.
2.8 Donald Davidson, 'Mental events', in *Experience and Theory*, ed. L. Foster and J. W. Swanson, University of Massachusetts 1970.
2.9 G. E. M. Anscombe, 'Causality and extensionality', *Journal of Philosophy* 65, 1968, 152–9.
An important and unusual treatment is
2.10 H. L. A. Hart and A. M. Honoré, *Causation in the Law*, Oxford 1959.

3.   *The Stoics on cause*

3.1 O. Rieth, *Grundbegriffe der stoischen Ethik*, Berlin 1933, ch. 7.
3.2 M. Pohlenz, *Grundfragen der stoischen Philosophie, Abhandlungen der Gesellschaft der Wissenschaften zu Göttingen*, Phil-hist. Klasse 3, 26, 1940, 104–112.
3.3 M. Frede, forthcoming in *Doubt and Dogmatism: Studies in Hellenistic Epistemology*, Proceedings of a conference held in Oxford, 1978, ed. J. Barnes, M. Burnyeat, M. Schofield, Oxford University Press.

3a.   *The idea of laws of nature in antiquity*

3a. 1 Gregory Vlastos, *Plato's Universe*, Oxford 1975, ch. 1.
3a.2 Klaus Reich, 'Der historische Ursprung des Naturgesetzbegriffs', in *Festschrift,* Ernst Kapp, ed. H. Diller and H. Erbse, Hamburg 1958.
The classic work on the contrast between law and nature is
3a.3 F. Heinimann, *Nomos und Physis*, Basel 1945.

4.   *Causal determinism*

4.1 G. E. M. Anscombe, *Causality and Determination*, inaugural lecture, Cambridge 1971.
4.2 E. Nagel, *The Structure of Science*, London 1961.

5.   *Causal necessity*

5.1 William Kneale, 'Universality and necessity', *British Journal for the Philosophy of Science* xii, 1961, 89–102.
5.2 William Kneale, 'Natural laws and contrary to fact conditionals', *Analysis* 10, 1950, 121–5 repr. in M. MacDonald, ed., *Philosophy and Analysis*, Oxford 1954.
5.3 Karl Popper, *The Logic of Scientific Discovery*, second edition London 1960, new appendix *X, with new note on p. 441 of the 1968 edition.
5.4 Karl Popper, 'A revised definition of natural necessity', *British Journal for the Philosophy of Science* 18, 1967, 316–21.
5.5 G. C. Nerlich and W. A. Suchting, 'Popper on law and natural necessity', *British Journal for the Philosophy of Science* 18, 1967, 235–5.
5.6 W. A. Suchting, 'Popper's revised definition of natural necessity', *British Journal for the Philosophy of Science* 20, 1969, 349–52.

6. *Explanation*

6.1 C. G. Hempel, *Aspects of Scientific Explanation*, New York and London 1965.

6.2 M. Scriven, 'Explanations, predictions and laws', *Minnesota Studies in the Philosophy of Science*, vol. 3, ed. H. Feigl and G. Maxwell, Minneapolis 1962.

6.3 M. Scriven, review, in *Review of Metaphysics* 17, 1963–4, 403–24, of E. Nagel's, *The Structure of Science*.

7. *Cause and explanation in Aristotle's* Posterior Analytics

7.1 Jonathan Barnes, *Aristotle's Posterior Analytics*, Clarendon Aristotle Series, Oxford 1975.

7.2 Baruch Brody, 'Towards an Aristotelian theory of scientific explanation', *Philosophy of Science* 39, 1972, 20–31.

7.3 Max Hocutt, 'Aristotle's four becauses', *Philosophy* 49, 1974, 385–99.

7.4 Myles Burnyeat, 'Aristotle on understanding knowledge', in 27.6.

8. *Arguments for determinism based on prior truth (the Sea Battle)*

8.1 J. L. Ackrill, *Aristotle's Categories and De Interpretatione*, Clarendon Aristotle Series, Oxford 1963, provides the only accurate translation of *Int.* 9, coupled with a lucid exposition. He prefers what is sometimes (misleadingly) called the traditional interpretation, in contrast to that of

8.2 G. E. M. Anscombe, 'Aristotle and the Sea Battle', *Mind* 65, 1956, 1–15 (repr. with corrections in *Aristotle*, ed. J. Moravcsik, New York 1967). The 'traditional' solution of denying that all predictions need be true or false in advance, was taken up in three brilliant articles on determinism by

8.3 Jan Lukasiewicz (translated as chapters 1–3 of *Polish Logic 1920–39*, ed. Storrs McCall, Oxford 1967, and again on pp. 87, 110, 153 of *Jan Lukasiewicz, Selected Works*, ed. Borkowski, Amsterdam 1970). The same kind of solution is favoured in

8.4 A. Prior, 'Three-valued logic and future contingents', *Philosophical Quarterly 3*, 1953, 317–26.

8.5 Storrs McCall, 'Temporal flux', *American Philosophical Quarterly*, 3, 1966, 270–81. Others have preferred a solution which represents truth as timeless. See

8.6 M. Kneale, in W. and M. Kneale, *The Development of Logic*, Oxford 1962, 45–54.

8.7 A. J. Ayer, 'Fatalism', in *The Concept of a Person*, London 1963. A fuller bibliography of the colossal literature on the subject is given by

8.8 Richard Gale (ed.), *The Philosophy of Time: A Collection of Essays*, London 1968, 506–9

8.9 Jaakko Hintikka, *Time and Necessity*, Oxford 1973, ch. 8.

8.10 For later arguments from prior truth, see 31.1 and 31.2.

9.	*Is truth timeless?*

One issue is the nature of token-reflexives, on which see

9.1	Hans Reichenbach, *Elements of Symbolic Logic*, New York 1948, § 50–1
9.2	Richard Gale, *The Language of Time*, London 1968, esp. ch. 4
9.3	Jonathan Cohen, 'Tense usage and propositions', *Analysis* 11, 1950–51, 80–7
9.4	P. F. Strawson, *Individuals*, London 1959, ch. 1.
	The following are, in one way or another, sympathetic to the idea of timeless truth:
9.5	W. V. O. Quine, *Word and Object*, Cambridge Mass 1960, esp. 194
9.6	Nelson Goodman, *The Structure of Appearance*, Cambridge Mass 1951, ch. 11
9.7	D. C. Williams, 'The myth of passage', *Journal of Philosophy* 48, 1951, 457–72.
	On the other side, see
9.8	Storrs McCall, 'Temporal flux', *American Philosophical Quarterly* 3, 1966, 270–81.

10.	*The Master Argument of Diodorus Cronus*

For Diodorus' life and philosophy, see

10.1	David Sedley, 'Diodorus Chronus and Hellenistic Philosophy', *Proceedings of the Cambridge Philological Society* 203, 1977, 74–120.
	For one reconstruction, see
10.2	Arthur Prior, 'Diodoran modalities', *Philosophical Quarterly*, 5, 1955, 205–13, whose interpretation is endorsed and related to Aristotle by
10.3	O. Becker, 'Zur Rekonstruktion des "Kyrieuon Logos" des Diodoros Kronos', in *Erkenntnis und Verantwortung*, Festschrift für Theodor Litt, edd. J. Derbolav and F. Nicolin, Düsseldorf 1960, 250–63.
	For a rival interpretation, see
10.4	Jaakko Hintikka, *Time and Necessity*, Oxford 1973, ch. 9 (revised from an earlier version in *American Philosophical Quarterly*, 1964).
	Diodorus' link with determinism is denied by
10.5	Robert Blanché, 'Sur l'interpretation du κυριεύων λόγος', *Revue Philosophique de la France et de l'Étranger,* 155, 1965, 133–49.

11.	*Deterministic accounts of possibility*

11.1	Arthur O. Lovejoy, *The Great Chain of Being*, Cambridge Mass. 1936.
11.2	Jaakko Hintikka, *Time and Necessity*, Oxford 1973, chs 5, 8 and 9.
11.3	C. J. F. Williams, 'Aristotle and corruptibility', *Religious Studies* I, 1965, 95–107 and 203–13.
11.4	S. Sambursky, 'On the possible and probable in ancient Greece', *Osiris* 12, 1956, 35–48.

12.	*Arguments for determinism based on prior knowledge*

12.1	Robert Sharples, 'Alexander of Aphrodisias, *De Fato*: some parallels', *Classical Quarterly*, 28, 1978, 243–66.
12.2	P. T. M. Huber, *Die Vereinbarkeit von göttlicher Vorsehung und*

menschlicher Freiheit in der Consolatio Philosophiae des Boethius, diss. Zurich 1976.

12.3 H. R. Patch, 'Necessity in Boethius and the Neoplatonists', *Speculum* 10, 1935, 393–404.

12.4 Nelson Pike, 'Divine Omniscience', *Philosophical Review* 74, 1965, 27–46.

12.5 Nelson Pike, *God and Timelessness*, London 1970.

12.6 A. Prior, 'The formalities of omniscience', *Philosophy* 1962 (repr. in his *Papers on Time and Tense*, Oxford 1968, ch. 3).

12.7 Gary Iseminger, 'Foreknowledge and necessity: Summa Theologiae la, 14, 13, 2', in *Midwest Studies in Philosophy*, vol. 1 ed. Peter A. French, Theodore E. Uehling jr., and Howard K. Wettstein, Morris Minnesota 1976, 5–25. There are comments by Edward Langerak, George I. Mavrodes, David M. Rosenthal.

12.8 A. Kenny, 'Divine foreknowledge and human freedom', in A. Kenny (ed.), *Aquinas: a Collection of Critical Essays*, Garden City N.Y. 1969.

12.9 J. R. Lucas, *The Freedom of the Will*, Oxford 1970, ch. 14.

13. *Arguments for determinism based on the relativity of the past*

13.1 C. W. Rietdijk, 'A rigorous proof of determinism derived from the Special Theory of Relativity', *Philosophy of Science*, 33, 1966, 341–4.

13.2 Storrs McCall, 'Temporal flux', *American Philosophy Quarterly* 3, 1966, esp. 281.
      and five papers in the *Journal of Philosophy* 64, 65, 66, 67:

13.3 Hilary Putnam, 'Time and physical geometry', 1967, 240–7 (repr. in his *Philosophical Papers* I, Cambridge 1975).

13.4 Howard Stein, 'On Einstein-Minkowski space-time', 1968, 5–23.

13.5 Paul Fitzgerald, 'The truth about tomorrow's sea fight', 1969, 307–29.

13.6 John W. Lango, 'The logic of simultaneity', 1969, 340–50.

13.7 Howard Stein, 'A note on time and Relativity Theory', 1970, 289–94.

14. *Returning to the past*

14.1 Pierre Duhem, *Le Système du monde*, vol. 1 repr. Paris 1954, 65–85; 164–9; 275–96; vol. 2 repr. Paris 1974, 298–9; 447–53.

14.2 M. Capek, 'Eternal return', in P. Edwards (ed.) *Encyclopaedia of Philosophy*, New York 1967.

14.3 H. Reichenbach, *The Philosophy of Space and Time*, New York 1957, 139–43 (translated from the German of 1928).

14.4 H. Reichenbach, *The Direction of Time*, Berkeley and Los Angeles 1956, 36–40.

14.5 R. P. Feynman, 'The theory of Positrons', *Physical Review* 76, 1949, 749–59.

14.6 Kurt Gödel, 'A remark about the relationship between Relativity Theory and Idealistic philosophy', in P. A. Schilpp (ed.) *Albert Einstein, Philosopher-Scientist*, New York 1951, 555–62.

14.7 Hilary Putnam, 'It ain't necessarily so', *Journal of Philosophy* 59, 1962, 658–71 (repr. in his *Philosophical Papers* I, Cambridge 1975, 237–49).

14.8 John Earman, 'On going backwards in time', *Philosophy of Science* 34, 1967, 211–22.

14.9   Howard Stein, 'On the paradoxical time-structures of Gödel', *Philosophy of Science* 37, 1970, 589–601.

15.   *Arguments for indeterminism based on quantum theory*

15.1   A. H. Compton, *The Freedom of Man*, Terry Lectures, Newhaven Conn. 1935.
15.2   Richard Feynman, *The Character of Physical Law*, London 1965, ch. 6.
15.3   Jacques Monod, *Chance and Necessity*, translated London 1972, from the French of 1970.

16.   *Aristotle's treatment of necessity in nature*

16.1   David Balme, *Aristotle's De Partibus Animalium I and De Generatione Animalium* I, Clarendon Aristotle Series, Oxford 1972, 76–84.
16.2   W. Kullmann, *Wissenschaft und Methode*, Berlin 1974.

17.   *Necessity and chance in Aristotle's predecessors*

17.1   F. M. Cornford, *Plato's Cosmology*, London 1937, 161–77.
17.2   Glen Morrow, 'Necessity and persuasion in Plato's *Timaeus*', in R. E. Allen (ed.), *Studies in Plato's Metaphysics*, London 1965.
17.3   W. K. C. Guthrie, *A History of Greek Philosophy*, vol. 2, Cambridge 1969, 163–4; 414–19.
17.4   Gregory Vlastos, 'Reasons and causes in the *Phaedo*', *Philosophical Review* 78, 1969, 291–325 (repr. in his *Platonic Studies*, Princeton 1973).

18.   *Aristotle's treatment of purpose in nature*

18.1   David Balme, 'Aristotle's use of the teleological explanation', inaugural lecture, Queen Mary College, London 1965.
       Regrettably, this was not published, but printed versions exist in the libraries of King's College and University College, London. Otherwise a shorter treatment can be found in
18.2   David Balme, *Aristotle's De Partibus Animalium I and De Generatione Animalium I*, as above, 93–100
18.3   Allan Gotthelf, 'Aristotle's conception of final causality', *Review of Metaphysics* 30, 1976, 226–54.

19.   *Ancient treatments of purpose in nature*

19.1   A. S. Pease, 'Caeli enarrant', *Harvard Theological Review* 34, 1941, 163–200.
19.2   W. Theiler, *Zur Geschichte der teleologischen Naturbetrachtung bis auf Aristoteles*, 2nd ed., Berlin 1965.

20.   *Modern treatments of purpose in nature*

20.1   John V. Canfield (ed.), *Purpose in Nature*, Englewood Cliffs N. J. 1966, collects some of the most important papers including Braithwaite's, Nagel's, and a part of Hempel's.

20.2 R. B. Braithwaite, *Scientific Explanation*, Cambridge 1953, ch. 10.
20.3 C. G. Hempel, 'The logic of functional analysis', in *Symposium on Sociological Theory*, ed. Llewellyn Gross, New York 1959 (repr. in Hempel's *Aspects of Scientific Explanation*, London 1965).
20.4 E. Nagel, *The Structure of Science*, New York 1961, 401–28.
20.5 Charles Taylor, *The Explanation of Behaviour*, London 1964, ch. 1.
20.6 J. L. Mackie, *The Cement of the Universe*, Oxford 1974, ch. 11.
20.7 Jonathan Bennett, *Linguistic Structures*, Cambridge 1976, ch. 2.
20.8 Larry Wright, *Teleological Explanations*, Berkeley and Los Angeles, 1976.
20.9 Richard Sorabji, 'Function', *Philosophical Quarterly* 14, 1964, 289–302.

21. *Natural selection, purpose and necessity*

For recent expositions, see
21.1 Jacques Monod, *Chance and Necessity*, translated London 1972, who is criticised in
21.2 John Lewis (ed.), *Beyond Chance and Necessity*, London 1974
21.3 Richard Dawkins, *The Selfish Gene*, Oxford 1976.
For Empedocles' theory, see
21.4 John Burnet, *Early Greek Philosophy*, London 1892, ch. 5
21.5 Jean Bollack, *Empédocle*, Paris 1965–9, vols 1–3.

22. *Natural kinds, essence and necessity*

There are two papers by Kripke:
22.1 Saul Kripke, 'Identity and necessity', in Milton K. Munitz (ed.), *Identity and Individuation*, New York 1971, 135–164
22.2 Saul Kripke, 'Naming and necessity', three lectures in *Semantics of Natural Languages*, edd. G. Harman and D. Davidson, Dordrecht 1972, 253–355, with appendix 763–9.
Four papers by Putnam are reprinted in his *Philosophical Papers*, Cambridge 1975, vol. 2:
22.3 Hilary Putnam, 'Dreaming and depth grammar', in *Analytical Philosophy*, Series 1, ed. R. J. Butler, Oxford 1962
22.4 Hilary Putnam, 'Brains and behaviour', in *Analytical Philosophy*, Series 2, ed. R. J. Butler, Oxford 1965
22.5 Hilary Putnam, 'Is semantics possible?' in *Metaphilosophy* 1, 1970, 187–201
22.6 Hilary Putnam, 'The meaning of "meaning" ', in *Minnesota Studies in the Philosophy of Science* VII, ed. K. Gunderson, Minneapolis 1975
See further
22.7 Hidé Ishiguro, *Leibniz's Philosophy of Logic and Language*, London 1972, ch. 4
22.8 J. L. Mackie, *Problems in Locke*, Oxford 1976, ch. 3
22.9 W. Whewell, *Philosophy of the Inductive Sciences*, London 1840, 2nd edition 1847, esp. VIII.2.4–12; VIII.4.1–8; XIII.3.12–16
22.10 D. Gasking, 'Clusters', *Australasian Journal of Philosophy* 38, 1960, 1–36.

23.   *Aristotle's treatment of natural kinds*

23.1   Richard Sorabji, 'Aristotle and Oxford philosophy', *American Philosophical Quarterly* 6, 1969, 127–35.
23.2   Robert Bolton, 'Essentialism and semantic theory in Aristotle: *Posterior Analytics* II 7–10', *Philosophical Review* 85, 1976, 514–44.
23.3   J. L. Ackrill, 'Aristotle's theory of definition: some questions on *An. Post.* II 8–10', in 27.6.

24.   De re *necessity*

A historical explanation, with reference to Aristotle, is given by
24.1   W. Kneale, 'Modality *de dicto* and *de re*', in *Logic, Methodology and Philosophy of Science*, edd. E. Nagel, P. Suppes, A. Tarski, Stanford 1962.
The latest in a series of critical discussions by Quine is
24.2   W. V. Quine, 'Intensions revisited', *Midwest Studies in Philosophy* II, 1977, Morris Minnesota, 5–11.
A more favourable treatment is offered by
24.3   C. Kirwan, 'How strong are the objections to essence?', *Proceedings of the Aristotelian Society*, 71, 1970–1, 43–59
24.4   David Wiggins, 'Essentialism, continuity and identity', *Synthese* 23, 1974, 321–59
24.5   David Wiggins, 'The *de re* "must": a note on the logical form of essentialist claims', in G. Evans and J. McDowell (eds), *Truth and Meaning*, Oxford 1976
24.6   A Plantinga, *The Nature of Necessity*, Oxford 1974.

25.   *Analyticity*

A historical explanation is offered by
25.1   Jaakko Hintikka, *Logic, Language-Games, and Information*, Oxford 1974, esp. chs 6 and 9
25.2   Jaakko Hintikka, 'Are logical truths analytic?' *Philosophical Review* 74, 1965, 178–208.
For criticisms of the concept, see
25.3   W. V. Quine, 'Two dogmas of empiricism', in his *From a Logical Point of View*, Cambridge Mass. 1953 (revised from *Philosophical Review* 1951)
25.4   Hilary Putnam, 'The analytic and the synthetic', *Minnesota Studies in the Philosophy of Science* III, ed. H. Feigl and G. Maxwell, Minneapolis 1962 (reprinted in his *Philosophical Papers*, Cambridge 1975, vol. 2).

26.   A priori *and* a posteriori

The locus classicus is
26.1   Immanuel Kant, Introduction to *The Critique of Pure Reason*, Riga, edition A 1781, edition B 1787.

27.   *Aristotle's scientific programme in the* Posterior Analytics

27.1   Jonathan Barnes, 'Aristotle's theory of demonstration', *Phronesis* 14, 1969, 123–52.

27.2 E. Kapp, 'Syllogistik', in Pauly-Wissowa's *Real-Encyclopädie der klassischen Altertumswissenschaft*, IV A, 1931, cols. 1046–67.
Both appear, the first with revisions, the second in English translation and under the title 'Syllogistic', in *Articles on Aristotle*, edd. J. Barnes, M. Schofield, R. Sorabji, London 1975.

27.3 S. Mansion, *Le Jugement d'Existence chez Aristote*, Louvain 1946, 2nd edition 1976.

27.4 Jonathan Barnes, *Aristotle's Posterior Analytics*, Clarendon Aristotle Series, Oxford 1975.

27.5 Richard Sorabji, 'Aristotle and Oxford philosophy', American Philosophical Quarterly 6, 1969, 127–35.

27.6 The Proceedings of the Eighth Symposium Aristotelicum, held in Padua, September 1978, and devoted to Aristotle's *Posterior Analytics*, are to be edited by E. Berti and published at Padua, under the title, *Aristotle on Science: the 'Posterior Analytics'*.

27.7 Jonathan Barnes, 'Proof and the Syllogism', in 27.6.

27.8 Friedrich Solmsen, *Die Entwicklung der aristotelischen Logik und Rhetorik*, Berlin 1929.

28. Aristotle's modal syllogisms

28.1 A. Becker, *Die aristotelische Theorie der Möglichkeitsschlüsse*, Berlin 1933.

28.2 Storrs McCall, *Aristotle's Modal Syllogisms*, Amsterdam 1963.

28.3 N. Rescher, 'Aristotle's theory of modal syllogisms and its interpretation', in Mario Bunge (ed.), *The Critical Approach to Science and Philosophy*, Glencoe Illinois 1964.

29. Aristotle on the relation of determinism to voluntary action

29.1 Richard Loening, *Die Zurechnungslehre des Aristoteles*, ch. 18, Jena 1903, repr. Hildesheim 1967.

29.2 David Furley, *Two Studies in the Greek Atomists*, Princeton 1967, 184–95, 215–26, 235–7 (repr. in *Articles on Aristotle*, vol. 2, eds. J. Barnes, M. Schofield, R. Sorabji, London 1977).

29.3 Pamela Huby, 'The first discovery of the free will problem', *Philosophy* 42, 1967, 353–62.

29.4 R. A. Gauthier, in Gauthier and Jolif, *L'Éthique à Nicomaque* Louvain and Paris, 2nd edn 1970, vol. 2, 268–9, 217–20.

29.5 J. L. Austin, 'A plea for excuses', *Proceedings of the Aristotelian Society* 57, 1956–7, 1–30.

30. The alleged compatibility of determinism with moral responsibility

30.1 Bernard Berofsky (ed.), *Free Will and Determinism*, New York 1966, includes the papers by Schlick, Hobart, Austin and Chisholm, as well as other important ones.
For the compatibilist view, see e.g.:

30.2 Moritz Schlick, 'When is a man responsible?' in his *Problems of Ethics*, tr. by David Rynin, New York 1939

30.3 R. E. Hobart, 'Free will as involving determination and inconceivable without it', *Mind* 43, 1934, 1–27

30.4   P. H. Nowell-Smith, *Ethics*, Harmondsworth 1954
30.5   A. J. P. Kenny, *Will, Freedom and Power*, Oxford 1976.
       For criticism, see e.g.
30.6   J. L. Austin, 'Ifs and cans', *Proceedings of the British Academy* 42, 1956,
       109–32 (repr. in his *Philosophical Papers*)
30.7   Roderick M. Chisholm, 'J. L. Austin's philosophical papers', *Mind* 73,
       1964, 20–5
30.8   K. Lehrer, 'An empirical disproof of determinism', in *Freedom and
       Determinism*, ed. K. Lehrer, New York 1966 (repr. in G. Dworkin, ed.,
       Determinism, Free Will and Moral Responsibility, Englewood Cliffs
       N. J. 1970)
30.9   G. E. M. Anscombe, 'Soft determinism', in G. Ryle (ed.), *Contemporary
       Aspects of Philosophy*, Oriel Press 1976
30.10 P. F. Strawson, 'Freedom and resentment', *Proceedings of the British
       Academy* 48, 1962, 187–211, repr. in his book of the same title
30.11 H. Frankfurt, 'Alternate possibilities and moral responsibility', *Journal
       of Philosophy* 66, 1969, 829–39.
       On ancient anticipations of some of these arguments, see
30.12 Robert Sharples, 'Responsibility, chance and not-being', *Bulletin of the
       Institute of Classical Studies* 22, 1975, 37–63.

31.   *Aristotle's successors on determinism*

       Two major sources are
31.1   Cicero, *De Fato*, translated in the Loeb edition with *De Oratore*, book III,
       by H. Rackham, 1968
31.2   Alexander of Aphrodisias, *De Fato*, at present translated only in a post-
       humously published version, which needed revision, by Fitzgerald,
       Scholartis Press, 30 Museum Street, London 1931. Neither translation
       is wholly satisfactory, and the awaited edition of Alexander with trans-
       lation and commentary by Robert Sharples (Duckworth, London, in
       press) will fill a gap.
       Surveys of later thought are
31.3   George L. -Fonsegrive, *Essai sur le Libre Arbitre*, Paris 1887
31.4   David Amand (now called E. Amand de Mendieta), *Fatalisme et Liberté
       dans l'Antiquité Grecque*, Louvain 1945
31.5   W. Gundel, 'Heimarmene', in Pauly-Wissowa, *Real-Encyclopädie der
       klassischen Altertumswissenschaft*
31.6   W. C. Greene, *Moira*, Cambridge Mass. 1948, ch. 11.
       For more detailed studies, see above under *The Master Argument of
       Diodorus Cronus* (no. 10) and *Arguments for determinism based on
       prior knowledge* (no. 12) and see
31.7   A. A. Long, 'Freedom and determinism in the Stoic theory of human
       action', in his (ed.) *Problems in Stoicism*, London 1971
31.8   A. A. Long, 'Stoic determinism and Alexander of Aphrodisias *De Fato*
       (i–xiv)', *Archiv für Geschichte der Philosophie* 52, 1970, 247–68
31.9   A. A. Long, *Hellenistic Philosophy*, London 1974
31.10 A. A. Long, 'The early Stoic concept of moral choice', in *Images of Man*,
       Studies presented to G. Verbeke, ed. C. Laga, Louvain 1976
31.11 Robert Sharples, 'Aristotelian and Stoic conceptions of necessity in the
       De Fato of Alexander of Aphrodisias', *Phronesis* 20, 1975, 247–74

31.12 Robert Sharples, 'Responsibility, chance and not-being', *Bulletin of the Institute of Classical Studies* 22, 1975, 37–63
31.13 Robert Sharples, 'Alexander of Aphrodisias *De Fato*: some parallels', *Classical Quarterly*, 28, 1978, 243–66
31.14 P. L. Donini, 'Crisippo e la nozione del possibile', *Rivista di filologia* 101, 1973, 333–51
31.15 P. L. Donini, 'Fato e Voluntà umana in Crisippo', *Atti dell' Accademia delle Scienze di Torino* 109, 1974–5, 1–44
31.16 S. Sambursky, *Physics of the Stoics*, London 1959, esp. ch. 3
31.17 W. Theiler, 'Tacitus und die antike Schicksalslehre', in *Phyllobolia für P. von der Mühll*, Basel 1946, 35–90 (repr. in Theiler's *Forschungen zur Neuplatonismus*, Berlin 1966, 46–103)
31.18 J. den Boeft, *Calcidius on Fate* (translation and commentary) Leiden, 1970
31.19 David Furley, *Two Studies in the Greek Atomists*, Princeton 1967.
       Further, H. Cherniss has supplied very useful footnotes to the Loeb edition of Plutarch's *De Stoicorum Repugnantiis*:
31.20 *Plutarch's Moralia* vol. 13, part 2, Loeb edition, 1976, ed. with notes by H. Cherniss.
       Relevant treatments of Stoic logic are
31.21 M. Kneale in W. and M. Kneale, *The Development of Logic*, Oxford 1962, ch. 3
31.22 M. Frede, *Die Stoische Logik*, Göttingen 1974, 80–93; 107–17.

32.   *The social and legal background to Aristotle's treatment of voluntariness*

32.1   A. W. H. Adkins, *Merit and Responsibility*, Oxford 1960.
32.2   D. J. Allan, 'Individual and state in the *Ethics* and *Politics*', in Fondation Hardt, Entretiens XI, *La 'Politique' d'Aristote*, Geneva 1965.
32.3   J. M. Bremer, *Hamartia*, Amsterdam 1969, 39–51.
32.4   David Daube, 'Dolus, culpa and casus', in his *Roman Law: Linguistic, Social and Philosophical Aspects*, Edinburgh 1969.
32.5   E. R. Dodds, *The Greeks and the Irrational*, Berkeley and Los Angeles, 1963.
32.6   K. J. Dover, *Greek Popular Morality in the Time of Plato and Aristotle*, Oxford 1974.
32.7   L. Gernet, introduction to the Budé edition of Plato's *Laws*, Paris 1956.
32.8   Gustave Glotz, *La Solidarité de la famille dans le droit criminel en Grèce*, Paris 1904, esp. 413–19.
32.9   H. D. P. Lee, 'The legal background of two passages in the *Nicomachean Ethics*', *Classical Quarterly* 31, 1937, 129–40.
32.10 W. T. Loomis, 'The nature of premeditation in Athenian homicide law', *Journal of Hellenic Studies* 92, 1972, 86–95.
32.11 D. M. MacDowell, *Athenian Homicide Law in the Age of the Orators*, Manchester 1963.
32.12 R. Maschke, *Die Willenslehre im griechischen Recht*, Berlin 1926.
32.13 Paul Vinogradoff, *Outlines of Historical Jurisprudence*, Oxford 1922, vol. 2.

33.   *The literary background*

There is an interesting treatment of fate in
33.1   R. B. Onians, *The Origins of European Thought*, Cambridge, 2nd edition
1954, part III.
Other evidence is assembled by
33.2   W. C. Greene, *Moira*, Cambridge Mass. 1948.
On responsibility, see
33.3   A. W. H. Adkins, *Merit and Responsibility*, Oxford 1960
33.4   E. R. Dodds, *The Greeks and the Irrational*, Berkeley and Los Angeles
1963, esp. chs 1 and 2.
There are many interesting works on individual authors, e.g. on
Sophocles, see ch. 2 of
33.5   John Sheppard, *The Oedipus Tyrannus of Sophocles* Cambridge 1920.
33.6   E. R. Dodds, 'On misunderstanding the *Oedipus Rex*', *Greece and Rome*
13, 1966, 37–49, repr. in his *The Ancient Concept of Progress*, Oxford
1973.
There has been a useful series on Aeschylus in the *Journal of Hellenic
Studies* 85, 86, 93:
33.7   N. G. L. Hammond, 'Personal freedom and its limitations in the *Oresteia*',
1965, 42–55
33.8   Albin Lesky, 'Decision and responsibility in the tragedy of Aeschylus',
1966, 78–85
33.9   K. J. Dover, 'Some neglected aspects of Agamemnon's dilemma', 1973,
58–69
to which may be added
33.10 E. R. Dodds, 'Morals and politics in the *Oresteia*', *Proceedings of the
Cambridge Philological Society* vol. 186, pp. 19–31, 1960.

34.   *The order of Aristotle's ethical writings*

34.1   Dieter Harlfinger, 'Die Überlieferungsgeschichte der Eudemischen
Ethik', in *Untersuchungen zur Eudemischen Ethik* Akten des 5 Symposium Aristotelicum, edd. Paul Moraux and Dieter Harlfinger, Berlin
1971, explains the problem of the disputed books. He assigns them to
the *Nicomachean Ethics*, as do
34.2   A. Mansion, 'La Genèse de l'oeuvre d'Aristote d'après les travaux
récents', *Revue Néoscolastique de Philosophie* 29, 1927, 307–41 and
423–66
34.3   R. A. Gauthier, in Gauthier and Jolif, *L'Éthique à Nicomaque*, Louvain
and Paris, 1st edn. 1958, vol. 1, 43–7
34.4   F. Dirlmeier, *Aristoteles, Eudemische Ethik*, Berlin 1962, 361–3.
On the other side, see
34.5   Artur von Fragstein, *Studien zür Ethik des Aristoteles*, Amsterdam 1974
34.6   Henry Jackson, *The Fifth Book of the Nicomachean Ethics of Aristotle*,
Cambridge 1879, repr. Warminster 1973.
Further support for this view, and for a late date for *EE*, is expected
from
34.7   A. J. P. Kenny, *Aristotelian Ethics*, Oxford 1978.
Questions of dating are well handled in the synoptic work of
34.8   Ingemar Düring, *Aristoteles*, Heidelberg 1966.

35. *Aristotle's treatment of negligence*

35.1   R. Maschke, *Die Willenslehre im griechischen Recht*, Berlin 1926, gives the classic account.
       The lively challenge by

35.2   David Daube, 'Dolus, culpa and casus', in his *Roman Law: Linguistic, Social and Philosophical Aspects*, Edinburgh 1969
       is answered by

35.3   Malcolm Schofield, 'Aristotelian mistakes', *Proceedings of the Cambridge Philological Society* 19, 1973, 66–70.

35.4   Henry Jackson, *The Fifth Book of the Nicomachean Ethics of Aristotle*, Cambridge 1879, repr. Warminister 1973, provides the best English commentary on *NE* v 8.

36. *Aristotle's treatment of tragic error*

The error of Sophocles' Oedipus is very well discussed by

36.1   John Sheppard, *The Oedipus Tyrannus of Sophocles*, Cambridge 1920, ch. 2

36.2   E. R. Dodds, 'On Misunderstanding the *Oedipus Rex*', *Greece and Rome* 13, 1966, 37–49, repr. in his *The Ancient Concept of Progress*, Oxford 1973.
       There is a comprehensive survey of the controversies surrounding Aristotle's treatment of tragic error in

36.3   J. M. Bremer, *Hamartia*, Amsterdam 1969.
       Discussion has continued since Bremer, and a good article for bringing oneself up to date is

36.4   T. C. W. Stinton, '*Hamartia* in Aristotle and Greek tragedy', *Classical Quarterly* n.s. xxv, 1975, 221–54.

37. *Aristotle's treatment of temptation*

37.1   Richard Robinson, 'Aristotle on acrasia', translated in *Essays on Greek Philosophy*, Oxford 1969, from the French of 1955, and repr. in *Articles on Aristotle*, vol. 2, edd. J. Barnes, M. Schofield, R. Sorabji, London 1977.

37.2   J. J. Walsh, *Aristotle's Conception of Moral Weakness*, New York 1963.

37.3   G. Santas, 'Aristotle on practical inference, the explanation of action, and akrasia', *Phronesis*, 14, 1969, 162–89.
       For an unorthodox view, see

37.4   A. J. P. Kenny, 'The practical syllogism and incontinence', *Phronesis* 11, 1966, 163–84.

38. *Plato's reformative theory of punishment*

38.1   A. D. Woozley, 'Plato on killing in anger', *Philosophical Quarterly*, 22, 1972, 303–17.

38.2   T. J. Saunders, 'Plato on Killing in Anger: A Reply to Professor Woozley', *Philosophical Quarterly*, 23, 1973, 350–6.
       Modern counterparts of Plato's reformative theory are criticised by

38.3   H. L. A. Hart, *Punishment and Responsibility*, Oxford 1968, chs 7 and 8.

Index

Abelard, 186–7

accident, accidental conjunction, see *Kata sumbebēkos*

accidental cause; two kinds of case, one is and one is not a cause, because one does and one does not point towards an explanation, 5–6, 11; coincidences have only an accidental cause, 5–7; post-Aristotelian appeals to accidental or fortuitous cause, 66, 67, 85

accidental knowledge, 258, 283

Ackrill, J. L., 24, 91, 95–6, 197–8, 301, 306

Adkins, A. W. H., 243, 309, 310

Aeschines, 291

Aeschylus, 18, 87, 244, 296

Aëtius, 17, 176–7, 179

akousion, akōn, involuntary *akōn, see* Voluntariness

akrasia, see Temptation

Albritton, R., 91, 191

Alexander of Aphrodisias, x, 19, 22, 27, 64, 65, 66, 67, 70–3, 78–80, 82, 83–8, 93, 104–5, 111–12, 119, 120, 122, 124, 244–6, 252, 308

Al Farabi, 93

Allan, D. J., x, 139, 243, 268–9, 282–3, 309

Amand, D. (now called De Mendieta), 245, 308

Ammonius, 22, 93–4, 122–5, 127

amplification of micro-indeterminacies, 28, 36–7

analyticity, see Necessity and possibility

Anaxagoras, 192

Anaximander, 62, 63

anger, Ar: 263, 278, 294–5, 298; Plato: 264, 291, 294; see also Temptation; Voluntariness

Annas, J., vii, 15, 42

Anscombe, G. E. M., 14, 15, 27, 38, 39, 52, 91, 94–5, 191, 205, 253, 300, 301, 308

Anselm, 126–7

Antiphon, 279, 291–2, 294

a posteriori, see A priori versus *a posteriori*

a priori versus *a posteriori*, 185–6, 210

Aquinas, 112, 122–5

Arcesilaus, 257

archē, origin; not necessarily the first member of a chain, 144, 228; of our actions, 227–32; within a person: defined 234–7; incompatible with determinism, according to Ar, 234–5; *see also* Internal versus external origin

aretē, see Virtue

Aristophanes, 265

art, 167–8, 172–3; *see also* Nature

Ashby, R., vii

Aspasius, 282

assent (*sunkatathesis*) in the Stoics, xiii, 80–1, 257; *see also* Hormē

astrology, *see* Divination

Audi, M., 27

Augustine, 67, 80–3, 122

Aurelius, M., 70

Austin, J. L., xiii, 249, 253, 257, 307, 308

Ayer, A. J., 17, 27, 39, 98, 301

Ayers, M., 79, 130, 253

Balme, D. M., x, 143–4, 147, 149–50, 152–3, 193, 221, 227, 242, 299, 304

Barker, E., 268

Barnes, J., vii, 20, 24, 48, 51, 152, 163, 190, 194, 196–8, 301, 306, 307

Becker, A., 94–5, 106, 202, 205, 307

Becker, O., 91, 105–6, 302

Bennett, J., 160, 221, 305

Berofsky, B., 307

Berti, E., 218, 307

bia, overwhelming force; various definitions and illustrations, 224, 235, 257, 259–61, 275, 283, in definition of voluntariness, 224, 235, 257–60, 275; *see also* Necessity and possibility

bivalence, law of, *see* Truth

blame, *see* Voluntariness; Compatibility

Blanche, R., 104, 302

Bochenski, I. M., 78